How to Be a Superhero

Mark Edlitz

Published in the USA by:
BearManor Media
P O Box 71426
Albany, Georgia 31708
www.bearmanormedia.com

ISBN: 978-1-59393-789-8
Printed in the United States of America
Book design by Robbie Adkins, www.adkinsconsult.com

Table of Contents

Foreword vii
Author's Note xi

Preface. 1
Introduction: Continuity and Change 7
Part One: Caped Crusaders **35**
The actors interviewed in this section have all donned a mask or put on a cape to play these timeless heroes.
Adam West ~ Batman 37
Bob Holiday ~ Superman 49
Jackson Bostwick ~ Captain Marvel 58
Nicholas Hammond ~ Spider-Man 65
John Newton ~ Superboy 80
Matt Salinger ~ Captain America 95
John Wesley Shipp ~ The Flash 113
Kevin Conroy ~ Batman 128
Dean Cain ~ Superman 141
Tim Daly ~ Superman 155
James Marsden ~ Cyclops 165

Part Two: Heroic Women **179**
The actresses interviewed in this section brought the post-Feminist Revolution woman into the superhero world.
Yvonne Craig ~ Batgirl 180
Helen Slater ~ Supergirl 200
Laura Vandervoort ~ Supergirl 211
Malin Akerman ~ Silk Spectre 216

Part Three: Antiheroes. **229**
The actors interviewed in this section have played superheroes that can't seem to get along with anyone – not even the good-guys.
Lou Ferrigno ~ the Hulk 230
Rex Smith ~ Daredevil. 242
Chip Zien ~ Howard the Duck. 246
Alan Cumming ~ Nightcrawler 255

Part Four: Sidekicks. **261**
Scrutizing the work of actors who have played second fiddle to the superhero.
Noel Neill ~ Lois Lane 262
Jack Larson ~ Jimmy Olsen 272
Marc McClure ~ Jimmy Olsen 289
Stacy Haiduk ~ Lois Lane 297

Part Five: Supervillains **301**
This section provides an inside look at evil geniuses who plot to dominate the world and sociopaths who are eager to kill the good guy.
Julie Newmar ~ Catwoman 302
Michael Rosenbaum ~ Lex Luthor .312
Tom Hiddleston ~ Loki. 325

Part Six: Heroes in Hiding 335
This chapter looks at two unreleased superhero projects.
Alex Hyde-White ~ Mister Fantastic 339
Carl Ciarfalio ~ The Thing 344
Joseph Culp ~ Doctor Doom. 349
Rebecca Staab ~ Sue Storm. 355
Adrianne Palicki ~ Wonder Woman. 359

Part Seven: Not All Heroes Are Super. 369
While the actors interviewed in this section aren't technically superheroes, they do share similar qualities.
Leonard Nimoy ~ Mr. Spock. 370
George Lazenby ~ James Bond 380
Roger Moore ~ James Bond. 387
Clark Gregg ~ Agent Coulson 401

Part Eight: Conversations about Superheroes **415**
Comic book, film and TV series creators discuss their work and share their thoughts about the qualities that define superheroes.
Jim Simon ~ comic book writer and son of Joe Simon, ... 416
co-creator of Captain America
Stan Lee ~ creator of Spider-Man, the Hulk, and X-Men 421
Kenneth Johnson ~ creator of *The Incredible Hulk* TV series 426
Tom Mankiewicz ~ screenwriter of *Superman* and *Superman II*. . . .438

Joe Quesada ~ Marvel's Chief Creative Officer. 455
Jon Favreau ~ director of *Iron Man* 465

Appendix 479
World's Greatest Heroes: Additional insights and sourced quotes
from a wide range of actors who have played superheroes including
Robert Downey Jr., Hugh Jackman, George Clooney, Christian Bale
and Michael Keaton.
Part One: The Formative Years. 480
Part Two: In the Shadow of the Bat 492
Part Three: The Superhero Boom 503
Acknowledgments 539
Footnotes. 541
Index 559
About the Author. 570

This book is dedicated to my wife Suzie and to my children
Ben and Sophie.
You make me believe that I can fly.

Foreword by David Mamet
THE PERSISTENCE OF FORM

The great William Bolitho wrote that pulp fiction is just fairy tales in modern dress. The detective is, of course, the Knight; the Abducted Heiress, the Fairy Princess; and the number one Hood, our friend of old, The Dragon. *It's a Wonderful Life*, the best-beloved film of my generation, was, of course, simply *A Christmas Carol* told from the point of view of Bob Cratchit; and superhero stories, to make an end, are fairy tales told from the point of view of the monster.

Give Superman and Lex Luthor each other's lines – the form remains the same, and my assertion is demonstrated: a supernatural being (hero/villain), remote, inaccessible, hidden in a dark cave, or indeed, in plain sight, emerges at night to go among the villagers and exercise its strength.

This, of course, more closely resembles, the behavior of Evil than of Good. It may be then that we, the Villagers, recognizing this in the form, rush to adore, which is to say propitiate, the being with powers far beyond those of mortal men. Why, otherwise, those works both adorative and closely reasoned, cataloguing, comparing, and speculating about these imaginary beings? There is a veritable Talmud elaborating this worship both vertically, through time, and horizontally, through the contemporary spectrum.

This engagement, like any theology, has, at the least, the social benefit of keeping one off the street; and if it is, in fact, in its quality of the Latent Dream, the propitiation of Supernatural Forces, it does no harm, and contrary to Fredric Wertham's *The Seduction of Innocence* (1954), a treatise on the irreparable harm of Comics, it may teach one (which begins in adolescence) a habit of devotion.

The adolescent addiction to worship of minutia (baseball cards, stamps, superheroes, collecting in general) is a protective mechanism for a mind unfit quite yet for self-direction living in a body raging out of control with desire.

I speak only from experience, as a teenager and as a father.

One of the hallmarks of organized religion is its insistence upon occupation with the Ritual (and the senescence of Religion can be charted as, one by one, the rituals are abandoned as "irrational," cf. The Vulgate Mass, and Reform Judaism). For ritual in Religion, speaking to the unformed adolescent, antinomial in us all, may, even absent faith, through mere repetition, train one to avoid evil - whether the Dragon be called Fate or One's Own Mind. (An old Jewish teaching: put on a prayer shawl, wrap tefillin on your arm, pick up a prayer book, now sin.)

(See also Alfred Bester's *The Demolished Man* (1953). Here, in a world full of mind readers, adepts are taught a magic phrase which, repeated, prohibits the unworthy form reading ones thoughts.)

But we are all, in our most private thoughts, found by ourselves to be unworthy. Most of our fantasies are denial and protest, and it is easier to accept the unacceptable truth if it is given palatable form.

Both Superman and the story of Christ are myths of the Superhero. The creators of the modern myths were, like Christ, Jews, and the writers of the Gospels, like Bob Kane, Shuster and Siegel, and Stan Lee, were creating a myth of Longing. Longing, that is, for a Savior whose very existence would mitigate our knowledge of our own worthlessness.

We Jews are debarred by our own Law, from worship of a Human, or indeed, of an apprehensible form: e.g., a God who also was a man. The rejection of that longing (not its denial, but the refusal to act upon it) is the motive force of Jewish thought.

But what is more delicious than the adolescent science of deniable lawlessness?

Our otherwise illegal urges of dominance and self-domination express themselves in Political Worship (Fantasy occupation of the mature), and in that Search for the Untainted, the path toward which is suggested also by Advertising.

American movies have become comic strips. They are multibillion dollar flipbooks (the Phenishkisthescope of the Victorian era, come again).

We note that Spider-Man, whoever is paid to play him, is a cartoon, a figure in a mask. This is at it should be, for as Bruno Bettelheim taught, in *The Uses of Enchantment*, the fairy tale hero must remain *undescribed*: if he is described as tall and we are not, our ability to identify with him suffers.

A person portraying a superhero puts the viewer at a disadvantage. And the blockbuster Summer film is less effective, as a story of Evil, than the tale around the Campfire.

But the form persists, and the audience is invited to worship not the omnipotence of the Actor, nor of the "character," but of the moviemaker, free to create and distort at will.

To regain some perspective: Mike Nichols told a story of an illustrious gathering of wits and philosophers. One had invited a young friend, and she listened to a discussion of *The Wizard of Oz*.

"So, " said one of the guests, "We see that it partakes, in all particulars, of the hero-journey: A young person is lifted from a drab world, and transported to a Magic Kingdom. Here she encounters foes and friends, and, among the lowly, finds those whose simplicity will lead her to her goal."

"Yes," said the young thing," And don't those flying monkeys freak you *out*...?"

David Mamet

AUTHOR'S NOTE

I knew Superman.

Okay, that's not completely true. I never met Superman, but I did have the pleasure of getting to know Christopher Reeve a little. The first time I met him I was working as Gary Sinise's assistant. Gary was starring on Broadway in *One Flew Over the Cuckoo's Nest* and Reeve came to see the show. Word quickly spread backstage that Reeve was in the audience. As a huge superhero fan since I was a kid, I desperately wanted to meet the person who (as the ads for the 1978 *Superman* movie promised) made me believe that a man could fly; and I knew that this might be my only opportunity. I'm not ashamed to admit that years later I cried when I read that Reeve suffered the accident that left him a quadriplegic.

So, when I learned that Reeve was in the theater I did what any reasonable person would do – I hatched a scheme. I asked Gary if *he* wanted to meet Reeve. Happily, Gary was game. With my cover story in place, I nervously introduced myself to Reeve. As we were talking, a fan approached Reeve and said, "Did I just meet Superman?" Reeve thanked the fan, and then very graciously he corrected her, "No. You just met Chris Reeve."

If Reeve was annoyed by the way the fan confused the actor with the character, implying that he was actually Superman rather than a talented actor playing a role, he didn't let on. But the fan's slightly awestruck question does reveal something that is timeless and important: at a deep level people want to *believe* in superheroes.

This ostensibly benign anecdote about Christopher Reeve hints at the involved relationships that fans develop with superhero actors. But there is an equally complicated relationship that often exists between an actor and the larger-than-life character he has agreed to play. Many of the actors I have interviewed for this book acknowledge that they have been ambivalent, and sometimes deeply conflicted, about playing superheroes: the prospect of enormous popularity and a huge payday is frequently offset by the twin fears of being typecast and trivialized as an actor. Reeve, who was a serious and well-trained actor, even went so far as to vow to "escape the cape."

Through my interviews with actors, writers, and directors, as well as my own commentary and pop culture criticism, *How to Be a Superhero* explores the processes and ramifications of creating superheroes. One of the inspirations behind *How to Be a Superhero* was *Hitchcock*, Francois Truffaut's seminal interview book with Alfred Hitchcock. I've always admired how Truffaut seemed almost to disappear so that Hitchock's own words would illuminate his craftsmanship and artistry. I have tried to take a similar approach.

David Mamet wrote, "I admire anyone who can make a living in his underwear."[1] Mamet was referring specifically to Superman and other costumed heroes but I believe the same can be said of the actors who play them. Very few movies and TV shows achieve the artistic success or audience approval of Richard Donner's *Superman*, Tim Burton's *Batman*, Christopher Nolan's *Dark Knight* trilogy, Jon Favreau's *Iron Man,* or Joss Whedon's *The Avengers,* and not all the actors I have interviewed are as universally embraced as Christopher Reeve as Superman and Robert Downey Jr. as Iron Man, but I believed that it would be valuable to ask a wide range of actors to share their varied experiences and perspectives, and I am very grateful to all of the actors who made this undertaking as enjoyable and rewarding for me as I hope it is for the reader.

This book is intended for everyone who ever donned a towel and pretended that it was a cape. Those children, like Michael Chabon, the acclaimed novelists understood that: "All we needed to do was accept the standing invitation that superhero comics extended to us by means of a towel. It was an invitation to enter into the world of story, to join in the ongoing business of comic books, and, with the knotting of a magical beach towel, to begin to wear what we knew to be hidden inside us."[2]

For a moment, while wearing a makeshift cape, the child may feel something like the power and freedom of what it's like to be a superhero. When we mature most of us inevitably stop dressing

up as heroes – a little sadly perhaps since it means we've surren-
dered a portion of our capacity to pretend; fortunately, though,
the movies, TV, and comic books, endure for many of us as a
means of transportation into the world of superheroes. When
adults become engrossed in superhero movies, they can continue to live vicariously through the movie stars who have temporarily assumed the mantle of their favorite heroes.

This book is meant to tap into our fantasies and look behind
the scenes in order to help enrich our eternal fascination with
superheroes.

I hope you enjoy it.

Mark Edlitz
New York, New York 2015

PREFACE

"I believe there's a hero in all of us, that keeps us honest, gives us strength, makes us noble." —Aunt May to Peter Parker in *Spider-Man 2*

Want to know a secret?

Nerds aren't the only ones who revere superheroes, and it's not just the geeks and fanboys who idolize heroes in tights. Nor is it the Internet junkies who post rants on message boards, or the eternal virgins, the pimple-faced teens or the thirty-year-old social misfits who still live in their moms' basements. Forget the stereotypes. They're way off the mark. Superheroes are cherished by virtually everyone.

A big-budget superhero movie couldn't achieve great financial success if only comic book fans and daydreaming teens purchased tickets. In order to make a profit, superhero movies, which can cost over $200 million to produce, have to appeal to a diverse audience. They need to be seen by people we might not ordinarily think of – and who probably do not think of themselves – as fans of superhero movies.

The third highest-grossing film of all time is a film about superheroes. That puts the movie, *The Avengers* ahead of all but two other massive hits – ahead of wildly popular movies about Jedi knights who use the Force, Pirates who swashbuckle in the Caribbean, fedora-wearing archeologists, and boy wizards who study at Hogwarts.

The Avengers has made around $1.5 billion just at the box office. The success of Marvel's super team isn't an anomaly. *Spider-Man* grossed more than $800 million worldwide in its theatrical run. That enormous box office take is supplemented by the very substantial income that it and movies like it derive from DVD sales, cable and network fees, or the many other forms of merchandising. Its sequel, *Spider-Man 2*, was also a box office powerhouse, grossing nearly $800 million. Even the critically maligned *Spider-Man 3* took in almost $900 million. The Spidey reboot, *The Amaz-*

ing Spider-Man has made just over $750 million. The sixth Batman film, *The Dark Knight*, grossed about $1 *billion*, which at the time made it the second most successful film of all time. Its sequel, *The Dark Knight Rises*, has also passed into the rarefied realm of billion dollar earners. The earnings for the six Superman films (all but the last of them made when ticket prices were considerably lower than they now are) exceed $1.5 billion. The first six X-Men movies have made more than $2.3 billion. *Iron Man 3* alone made over $1.2 billion. The collective worldwide earnings of all Marvel and DC superhero movies are over $22 billion (and counting).

Robert Downey, Jr. as genius, billionaire, playboy, philanthropist Tony Stark in a scene from Iron Man *(2008). © Marvel Studios.*

The impact of superheroes is manifest throughout our culture. Toy stores often devote aisles to shelves buckling under the weight of superhero action figures. *Entertainment Weekly*, perennially one of the leading pop culture magazines, routinely features cover stories about superhero movies and TV shows, and it regularly includes columns about topics that might erroneously be thought to be of interest exclusively to die-hard comic book fans; for instance, the magazine featured a story about the Man of Steel's redesigned costume for *Superman Returns*, in which it explained how each component of the overall design – the unitard, the cape, the boots, the insignia – was based on previous incarnations of the outfit. Similarly, the magazine devoted a full page just to the new gadgets that were used in the Daniel Craig Bond movie *Casino Royale*. During the 2008 Presidential campaign, *Entertainment Weekly* pressed Barack Obama and John McCain to reveal the name of their favorite superheroes. Obama endorsed Spider-Man and Batman while McCain chose Batman. However, after six years in office it seems that President Obama's preference might have changed. During a 2014 press conference to announce two Department of Defense Manufacturing Institutes , President Obama joked, "Basically, I'm here to announce that we're building Iron Man." Coverage of superhero movies, actors and directors, and events such as Comic-Con conventions are now a staple not only of niche publications but also of the mainstream print media, television, and the internet, including high-end webzines and countless blogs.

Mainstream publications have also acknowledged the importance of these kinds of details to the vast superhero audience. *Time* magazine, for instance, has over the years run a series stories concerning such matters as the attire and accessories of superheroes, including an analysis of the components of the caped crusader's utility belt and a the history of the Batmobile. Many would assume that only obsessive fans would be interested in such minutiae, but since *Time*, a magazine which aims to appeal to the broadest possible audience, continually runs these sidebars when covering superhero movies, we can infer that even minor details are important to a sizable number of fans.

In fact, comic book heroes are so popular that even the normally un-cool United States Post Office issued a sheet of twenty stamps, each depicting a different superhero.

Comic book heroes have also inspired serious novelists such as Michael Chabon, whose Pulitzer Prize-winning and best-selling novel *The Amazing Adventures of Kavalier and Clay* is about two cousins, a comic book writer and an illustrator, who achieve prominence during the Golden Age of Comics, a period that spanned from the 1930s until the late 1940s or early 1950s. Whereas Chabon's novel is targeted to a more sophisticated audience, *Charlie's Superhero Underpants* is a children's book that instructs the tikes about the importance of taking proper care of their superhero costumes.[3] (And since children are not likely to be taught about the subject in school, shouldn't we be thankful for that?)

Superheroes also turn up regularly on the small screen. NBC's *Heroes* is a show about ordinary people who discover that they have super-powers. With its silly-funny catchphrase "Save the Cheerleader, Save the World," *Heroes* became a breakout hit when it debuted in 2006. Moreover, in addition to countless superhero cartoons, viewers could watch the reality series *Who Wants To Be A Superhero?* During the show's two seasons, twenty-two contestants competed to be the last superhero standing. The winner of the show was depicted in a new comic book, which was written by Stan Lee, the creator of such superheroes as Spider-Man, the Hulk, Daredevil, The X-Men, and The Fantastic Four. Even toddlers can get their hero fix by watching the lovable but not very brave Super Grover on *Sesame Street*. Once heard, who can ever forget the rallying cry of everyone's favorite little blue Muppet, "My cute little ears hear a cry for help!" Other superhero-themed series have appeared on the small screen, among them, *Smallville*, a series about Clark Kent in his pre-Superman days, *Arrow*, inspired by the Green Arrow comic book, *Gotham*, a show set in pre-Batman Gotham City, and *Marvel's Agents of S.H.I.E.L.D.*, which is set in Marvel's Cinematic Universe.

Many of Hollywood's most popular actors are no longer shying away from putting on the cape. Academy Award winners and nominees including George Clooney, Tobey Maguire, Jack Nicholson, Christian Bale, Anne Hathaway, Jamie Foxx, Michelle Pfeiffer, Halle Berry, Jim Carrey, Gene Hackman, Jennifer Lawrence, Anna Paquin, Nicolas Cage, Edward Norton, and Kevin Spacey have played superheroes or supervillains. Academy Award nominee Robert Downey Jr. has now starred in three *Iron Man* blockbusters, and Heath Ledger gave an Oscar-winning performance as the Joker in *The Dark Night*, a film that was for a while the second all-time domestic earner, after *Titanic*.

Batman, Superman, and Spider-Man have always been popular, but the marketplace demand for superheroes is now so great that even second-tier heroes are enjoying their day in the sun. The once maligned Aquaman, for example, is experiencing a popularity surge. In *The Forty Year Old Virgin*, Steve Carell's favorite do-gooder is none other than the yellow and green, spandex-clad King of the Seven Seas who talks to fish.[4] *Entourage*, HBO's series about Hollywood, featured a story line that centered on the lead character's decision to accept a part in James Cameron's feature film version of *Aquaman*. The 42-minute unaired pilot for *Aquaman*, starring Justin Hartley, has become one of the most downloaded television shows of all time.

Most of the major theme parks have superhero rides. Fast food restaurants frequently offer toy tie-ins with the latest superhero movies. Birthday cards, balloons, T-shirts, posters, buttons, school notebooks, pencils, video games, wallets, stickers, pop-up books, costumes, and other paraphernalia – including underwear bearing the images of superheroes – are widely marketed. For Halloween, uninhibited moms and dads can dress up as Superman and Wonder Woman – for a whopping $75 each. Junior can Trick or Treat as the Hulk and his sister can go as Supergirl. There's even a Bat-hound costume for the family dog. The vodka manufacturer Smirnoff launched an ad campaign tied to the release of the James Bond movie *Casino Royale*. To promote *Skyfall*, Daniel Craig appeared in a Heineken commercial as James Bond and traded his signature martini for a beer. Few other forms of pop culture entertainment can be mass-marketed so ubiquitously or profitably. To drum up business for *The Amazing Spider-Man* 2 (2014), Spidey break-dances, moonwalks and jump ropes in an ad for Evian water. When was the last time you saw a Meryl Streep action figure or stood in line on a hot summer's day to ride the *Forrest Gump* roller coaster?

Superheroes are big business due to the massive audience that can't get enough of them!

INTRODUCTION
Passing the Torch: Continuity and Change

"Who are bigger sticklers for accuracy – scholars of Eighteenth Century French History or Spider-Man fans?"
—John Stewart on *The Daily Show*

It is commonly held that people are creatures of habit and that we are generally averse to change. Few groups are as passionate about the importance of consistency as fans of comic books. Comic book fans do not want their superheroes to change – to age, to have the look of their costumes altered, to marry and have children, or to be significantly altered in any other way.

When transferring superhero stories from the page to movie or TV screens, filmmakers tend to base their stories on the established backstory of the characters. For example, *Superman* (1978) depicted the classic story of the young child from the dying planet Krypton who is sent to earth, where he has superhuman powers that he uses (when he's not disguised as Clark Kent) to fight for "truth, justice, and the American way." That story was taken from *Action Comics #1 (1938)*, the very first Superman comic book, and then expanded into a nearly two and a half hour movie.

Batman's origin tale was dramatized in the critically and commercially successful film *Batman Begins* (2005), which earned nearly $375 million worldwide. Writer David Goyer and co-writer and director Christopher Nolan were able to revive the nearly dead Batman franchise by imaginatively replicating the basic plot from *Detective Comics #27* (1939), "The Man Who Falls." That comic presented billionaire Bruce Wayne's agonizing psychological journey and his arduous physical training in order to become the crime-fighting Dark Knight. When *Batman Begins* was released on DVD, a copy of the original comic book was pointedly included in the packaging so that the filmmakers could acknowledge the comic book's decisive influence on the film.

The feature film *Spider-Man* (2002) was, like *Batman Begins*, a big critical success and an even greater commercial blockbuster, grossing over $800 million internationally. That film faithfully followed creator Stan Lee's Marvel Comics story of gentle and studious Peter Parker's transformation into the confident, crime-fighting, wisecracking web-slinger. *Spider-Man* was enthusiastically embraced by fans of the comic book and by the movie-going public.

In making *Sin City* (2005), which stars Bruce Willis and Clive Owen, filmmaker Robert Rodriguez took such great pains to follow Frank Miller's graphic novel that he attempted a shot-for-shot translation of the book – that is, a one-for-one representation of each comic book panel in a film frame. Rodriguez even enlisted Miller (who had never helmed a film) to serve as his co-director. The success of that fidelity to the comic was rewarded by success at the box office and with a sequel *Sin City: A Dame to Kill For* (2014).

Comic book films that stray too far from their origins are not as widely accepted. When the filmmakers of *Superman IV: The Quest for Peace* (1987) gave the eponymous hero strange new abilities – such as the power to rebuild the Great Wall of China simply by looking at it – they alienated the Man of Steel's core fans.

Domestically, that film made less than $16 million – a feeble take even allowing for the much lower ticket prices – which was a significant drop from the nearly $60 million that *Superman III* (1983) grossed and a massive drop from the more than $100 million domestic gross of *Superman II* (1980). The result of the filmmakers' lack of respect for the origins and defining nature of the character did what Kryptonite could not – it virtually killed Superman as a box office draw. It took nearly two decades before Superman was resurrected as the star of his own movie.

To more fully satisfy dedicated comic book fans, it is important for filmmakers to demonstrate their respect for the roots and the history of the characters. For example, in the 1978 *Superman* – the first modern comic book-inspired movie – serious fans greatly enjoyed the scene in which for the first time Clark Kent must shed his business suit in order to reappear in costume as Superman so that he can rescue Lois Lane. Kent searches in vein for a phone booth in which to change, but traditional phone booths have been replaced by freestanding pay phones, which of course are useless for his immediate needs. When Kent gives the pay phone a disparaging glare, it is as if he is experiencing a genetic memory of his decades-old comic book origins; it is as if the comic book world had left its imprint on the consciousness of the Superman of 1978. At that moment, the filmmakers were tipping their hats to the comics and giving a conspiratorial wink to a savvy audience that chortled in appreciation of the in-joke.

When Bryan Singer was hired to direct the big screen version of Marvel's X-Men, he was criticized by the fan community for changing the heroes' outfits from spandex to leather. Before fans saw the finished film, Singer was derided for giving the classic yellow outfits a kinky S&M-inspired look. When in the finished X-Men movie the costumes were revealed to Hugh Jackman's character Wolverine, a new member of the team, he too was shocked. It was as if he expected to see the classic comic book look. To acknowledge the controversy, Wolverine complains, "You actually go outside in these things?" Cyclops retorts, "What would you prefer? Yellow spandex?"

In that moment when James Marsden's Cyclops alludes to the costumes worn by their characters in the comic books, the characters and the filmmakers are acknowledging their debt to the source material.

Singer made another significant change in the look of a popular X-Men villain, one that he anticipated would be warmly embraced even by the most ardent purist. In the comics, Mystique is a blue, shape-shifting alien. She's usually drawn as a slinky woman who wears revealing tight pants and very skimpy tops. Mystique is obviously a character that is intended to titillate male fans, and Singer decided to push her sexy look even further. In the film, except for blue body paint and strategically placed scales, Mystique is completely nude. Supermodel Rebecca Romijn who played the character, was originally surprised that fans objected to her being essentially naked. She and Singer mistakenly thought that the site of a nearly nude beautiful woman would trump fans' interest in fidelity to the comics. They were wrong. She told *Playboy* magazine that, "There's a tremendous amount of pressure when you do a movie like *X-Men*, because you've got characters that people have been waiting their entire lives to see come to life. And, yes, there are those guys. But they're the people we're thinking about when we're making choices and taking liberties with these characters. You have to be extremely careful because you don't want to disappoint the fans."[5]

Will Brooker, the author of *Batman Unmasked*, has written about the tightrope filmmakers must walk between being slavish to the source material and making the character accessible and interesting to a larger audience, and his conclusion differs from those of Christopher Nolan, Bryan Singer and others: "This paradox is central to any major Batman film, and probably to any big-screen adaptation of a 'cult' text. The movie will be tailored for those who care least about the character, while those with the greatest emotional investment became a powerless elite, a vocal minority whose voice is rarely loud enough, and who are fated to watch helplessly as 'their' treasured possession is given over to the whims of the majority."[6]

Once a superhero comic book is successfully adapted into a movie that has been embraced by its audience, fans strongly resist any changes in the franchise. In *License To Thrill*, James Chapman's book on the James Bond phenomenon, he refers to the process of alluding to the past and leaving room for new interpretations of a character as "continuity and change."[7] Which is to say, "continuity" with previous incarnations and a gentle "change" of direction in order to keep the character and the series fresh and current.

Arguably, no hero has had to struggle more with "continuity and change" than the seemingly indestructible secret agent James Bond. In over fifty years of Bond movies, audiences have had to accept six different incarnations of 007 in the twenty-three "official" films. (The Bond films that are considered "official" are those made by EON productions – a film company set up by Albert R. Broccoli and Harry Saltzman.) Here's the score card so far, Sean Connery played Bond six times, Roger Moore played him seven times, Pierce Brosnan donned the tux four times, Timothy Dalton did it twice and George Lazenby played Bond only once. Daniel Craig became the sixth new James Bond in *Casino Royale* (2006). He reprised the role in *Quantum of Solace* (2008) and

Daniel Craig as James Bond. © Eon Productions.

a third time in *Skyfall* (2012), which became the highest-grossing film in the series' long history.

On the surface, James Bond is not an obvious fit with a superhero theme. However, Bond's exploits in the twenty movies before the Daniel Craig era brought a more gritty realism to the series were frequently larger-than-life, in fact, superheroic. Bond's enemies were often monsters who were set on world domination, and Bond was often pitted almost single-handedly against these evil masterminds and their formidable armies. His tux was his recurring costume. These action-filled stories in no way resembled the darker and more realistic tales of espionage in such movies as Michael Caine as Harry Palmer in *The Ipcress File* (1965), or Richard Burton as John le Carré's somber spook Alec Leamas in the grim 1965 film *The Spy Who Came In From The Cold*, or Alec Guinness as George Smiley in the superb 1979 TV miniseries adaptation of le Carré's gripping but cerebral novel "Tinker Tailor Soldier Spy" and its 1982 miniseries successor, again with Alec Guinness, "Smiley's People", and in the 2011 film adaptation of *Tinker Tailor Soldier Spy*. In contrast with the adventures of James Bond, these movies are concerned with the dark, sinister, rarely dramatic, and often lonely world of agents versus agents and double agents. For instance, *Tinker Tailor Soldier Spy* centers on the search for a high-level mole who has penetrated the British secret service. The drama, though utterly absorbing, unfolds at a comparatively glacial pace.

The Daniel Craig version of *Casino Royale* marked the third time this particular story has been translated to film. In 1967, there was a slapstick, everything-but-the-kitchen-sink rendering of the story. In that film, the British government decides to confuse its enemies by renaming all of its agents after the famed spy. David Niven is the British Secret Intelligence Service's actual James Bond, but many actors assume the name or a variation on it. Thus, Peter Sellers is also called James Bond, Woody Allen plays Jimmy Bond, and onetime Bond-girl Ursula Andress is referred to as 007.

The earliest on-screen version of *Casino Royale* was a 1954 live television show in which Barry Nelson played "Jimmy" Bond as an American spy and not a British secret service agent. Despite being the first James Bond (sorry Sir Sean), Nelson is perhaps best remembered for his character's lack of good judgment in hiring Jack Torrance (played with demonic glee by Jack Nicholson) to manage the Overlook hotel in Stanley Kubrick's *The Shining* (1980).

However, if you want to keep an audit-proof account of your stocks and Bonds, you'd have to include Sean Connery's seventh outing as Agent 007 in the unofficial (non-Eon production of)

Never Say Never Again (1983). (The title was a sly wink at Connery's broken promise never to play Bond again.) The film, written by Lorenzo Semple Jr., who helped create the 1960s *Batman* TV show, is deliciously self-consciously aware that it is Connery's return to the role that made him and the franchise famous. The plot is a fairly straightforward remake of Connery's earlier Bond flick *Thunderball* (1965).

It's easy to forget that unlike more recent audiences, who accept that different actors will play Bond, for moviegoers of the 1960s there could be only one Bond: Sean Connery. For many fans of that generation, the names Connery and Bond were interchangeable. Even the movie posters perpetuated that idea: "Sean Connery IS James Bond." The credits implied that Connery was not merely an actor playing a part but that by an extraordinary feat of alchemy he actually became the character. Judging by the reception Connery got when he recreated the part, audiences apparently bought into the hype. While the films probably benefited commercially from the identification of character and actor, Connery privately suffered for it. In speaking of his association with the character Connery said, "It's a cross, a privilege, a joke, a challenge. And as bloody intrusive as a nightmare."[8] In the 1970s and most of the 1980s, audiences often had difficulty accepting the actor in other roles. Subsequent actors learned from Connery's experience and they have opted for different tag lines. Pierce Brosnan was credited "as" James Bond, not "is" James Bond.

When Connery turned in his license to kill, the producers of the Bond movies were faced with a challenge they had unwittingly created for themselves when they were exuberantly marketing Connery: the daunting task of replacing the actor whose name they had helped to make synonymous with Bond.

When George Lazenby took over the role in *On Her Majesty's Secret Service* (1969) the filmmakers needed to show that the new performer could fill the shoes of the famous Scot, had to convince a potentially skeptical audience that change was possible. The filmmakers devised a pre-title sequence in which Lazenby assumes the mantle. In it, Bond sees Teresa "Tracy" Draco (Diana

Rigg) attempting to drown herself in the ocean. Bond saves her but before he can introduce himself to her a thug attacks him from behind and she disappears. After Bond beats the baddie to a bloody pulp, he picks up a shoe that Tracy left behind and dead-pans, "This never happened to the other guy." Though Bond is ostensibly speaking to himself, he's really addressing the audience. Within the context of the movie there is no "other guy." Therefore, Lazenby is referring to the "other" actor who used to play Bond. He is actually saying, "This never happened to Sean Connery. No woman would run away from him." Lazenby is announcing that he was going to be a different, more vulnerable Bond. He is respect-fully acknowledging Connery's irreplaceability and simultaneously asking the audiences to accept him in the part.

Later in the film, Lazenby's Bond is in his office rummaging through his desk, where he finds memorabilia from previous Bond films that starred Sean Connery. Among other effects, he looks nostalgically at the knife Honey (Ursula Andress) used in *Dr. No* (1962) and the garret used by Red Grant (Robert Shaw) in *From Russia With Love* (1963). When viewing these items that he keeps in his desk, Lazenby is in effect saying, "Connery's Bond is in my Bond's DNA. I'm his heir and it is my responsibility to carry his legacy forward." Continuity.

Near the end of *On Her Majesty's Secret Service*, Bond mar-ries Tracy, the women from the pre-title sequence but on the way to their honeymoon, Bond baddies Blofeld and Irma Bunt gun her down. The film ends with uncharacteristic glumness – we see Bond embracing his wife's lifeless body. Lazenby told me that in order to help him portray Bond's grief-stricken state convincingly, he reread the final passages of Fleming's novel immediately be-fore shooting the scene.

Most moviegoers were shocked to see the world's most fa-mous perennial bachelor prepared to settle into marriage and due probably to the combination of Connery's absence and that dour ending the film's box office take suffered. The movie earned about half as much as the previous Connery-Bond film, *You Only Live Twice* (1967). Even so, the producers were willing to make another film with Lazenby. However, the new 007 was neither completely comfortable with the world-wide attention the role garnered to him nor, in the wake of the popularity of such counter-culture films as *Easy Rider* (1969), did he see much of a future for the series. So Lazenby, much like his character in the film, tendered his resignation from Her Majesty's Secret Service.

Wary of the process of looking for another actor to play Bond, and at great expense, the producers brought back Connery for one "final" outing as Bond in *Diamonds are Forever* (1971). The film begins with Bond seeking revenge on Blofeld for killing his – that is, Lazenby's Bond's – wife. Bond's personal vendetta against Blofeld reestablishes series continuity. The new film acknowledges both that Connery is back as Bond and that the events in the Lazenby Bond film were experienced by the character rather than the actor.

However, there are limits to how faithfully and when to respect continuity. After killing Blofeld, Bond never seems to have second thoughts about his deceased wife. After the pre-title sequence, she is never again mentioned – her existence is effectively erased – and once again Bond is a philandering playboy. In an interview conducted for this book, screenwriter Tom Mankiewicz, who worked on the first two Superman movies and several James Bond films, offers an unsentimental, coldly practical explanation to account for Connery's exceedingly brief period of mourning. "I think it's because it was George Lazenby who endured the loss. And nobody was going to confuse George Lazenby's loss with Sean Connery's return. It happened to a different guy. He might have been called James Bond as well, but it was a different guy."

After the release of *Diamonds are Forever*, it was time to find yet another actor to play Bond in *Live and Let Die* (1973). Due perhaps to the trouble audiences had with Lazenby, the producers decided to downplay the fact that they had selected Roger Moore to play Bond. Unlike *On Her Majesty's Secret Service*, the filmmakers did not create a pre-title sequence designed to introduce the new Bond. Instead, they went in the opposite direction. In this film, Bond doesn't even appear until after the opening credits. The filmmakers seem to be saying that it doesn't matter who is portraying Bond, that Bond is bigger than the actor playing him.

In *Live and Let Die*, Tom Mankiewicz wittily confounds the audience's expectations: 007 never identifies himself as "Bond, James Bond." In a scene where Bond is about to introduce himself to the villain, Bond begins to say "My name is—," but before he can complete his famous catchphrase, he's interrupted with the caustic retort, "Names is for tombstones, baby." Mankiewicz also played with the formula by *not* having the agent order a "shaken, not stirred" martini.

Though Connery's period of mourning the death of his (and Lazenby's) wife Tracy seemed callously brief – or perhaps for the purposes of reestablishing Bond's womanizing image, conveniently brief. But Tracy was not completely forgotten. Her memory survived through three different Bond actors in several 007 movies. In *The Spy Who Loved Me* (1977), *For Your Eyes Only*, (1981), *License to Kill* (1989), and *The World is Not Enough* (1999). Roger Moore's, Timothy Dalton's, and Pierce Brosnan's Bonds all experience uncharacteristic moments of vulnerability when people mention Tracy.

After *Moonraker* (1979), it was time to renegotiate Roger Moore's contract. When negotiations with the actor temporarily stalled, the filmmakers thought it might be necessary to find a new Bond. They even got as far as altering the script for the next movie that would have begun with a scene that introduces the replacement. John Glen (the five-time Bond director) came up with the notion that *For Your Eyes Only* (1981) would start with Bond visiting Tracey's grave. He thought that connecting the new Bond to the old Bond's past would maintain continuity and introduce change. Glen said the allusion to *On Her Majesty's Secret Service* was "my way of maintaining continuity with some of the Bond adventures of the past." A "familiar-looking wheelchair-bound villain with a neck brace and a white cat" extends this continuity.[9] Although he is never identified, Bond fans can safely assume that the villain is none other than 007's archenemy Blofeld. Bond had battled the hairless heavy in five previous adventures (four with Connery and one with Lazenby). Moore is the last "official" Bond who apparently kills Blofeld. (However, two years later Connery would again battle Blofeld in the unofficial *Never Say Never Again*.)

The movie with the most overt references to past Bond films is *Die Another Day* (2002). (*Skyfall,* which was released on the cinematic Bond's fiftieth anniversary is a close second.) In it, Pierce Brosnan's Bond visits Q's old equipment supply room. The room is bursting with gadgets from previous movies – including Rosa Klebb's poison-tipped dagger shoe from *From Russia with Love* (1963), the jetpack from *Thunderball,* the fake alligator from *Octopussy* (1983) and the one-man helicopter from *You Only Live Twice.*

In the film, John Cleese, who plays the new Q, gives Bond his twentieth gadget-equipped watch. The reference to the twentieth watch wasn't arbitrary – *Die Another Day* was the 20th Bond film. That allusion was apparently so veiled that Brosnan didn't understand it during filming. It wasn't until he was recording the audio commentary for the DVD that Brosnan made the connection. You can actually hear him figure it out. Embarrassed, he says, "Twenty watches. Twenty movies. Oh, *now* I get it."

Still, there are times when an actor's concerns about a part can trump continuity. Roger Moore told me that for him Connery's Scottish burr was so identified with the line "My name is Bond . . . James Bond" that he refused to say it in any of his Bond movies.

Passing the torch from one Bond actor to another is rarely a smooth transition. Witness the fans' reactions to the announcement that Daniel Craig would be the new James Bond. *Entertainment Weekly* wrote: "Not since Michael Keaton put on a cowl for the first Batman movie has the hiring of an actor for an action film unleashed such a loopy storm of fan fury."[10] London's *Daily Mirror* spoke for many when it characterized the casting of Daniel Craig: "'The Name's Bland . . . James Bland." Fans complained about Craig's hair color (blond) and eyes (blue).[11] The website CraigNotBond.com was dedicated to criticizing the actor. At the website, visitors were encouraged to sign a petition to boycott the film.[12]

Pierce Brosnan did his part to mitigate the anger that some fans felt about Craig. The fifth 007 gave the sixth 007 his blessing: "I know the guy. We've gone out and we talked about it before the whole world knew about it. We had many beers over it and laughed and I wished him well. I just told him to have a good time with it, embrace it, enjoy it and travel through with his head high." Moore stated that he didn't understand why the press was attacking Craig before they had even seen the film. Before seeing the film, Moore, perhaps feeling overprotective and relating to his colleague's predicament, declared that he thought Craig would be the best Bond yet.

Craig keenly felt the immense pressure that surrounds assuming the role of the world's most famous secret agent. He said that after he received the call officially offering him the part he got drunk on vodka martinis. Craig's responses to questions about getting the part have been very diplomatic. He has consistently shown respect for the outsized importance of the role while also displaying an appealing and often self-deprecating sense of humor. More importantly to diehard Bondians, his comments suggest that he understands what has made the character so incredibly popular and he seems eager to grace the tux with the appropriate blend of glamour and danger. What fan wouldn't be at least a little sympathetic to the idea of the new Bond getting a bit tipsy on 007's drink of choice?

All fears of Craig killing the Bond franchise were quickly dispelled. Audiences embraced the "blond Bond." On its opening day in the United Kingdom, over 50 percent of all movie tickets sold were for *Casino Royale*, and most of the reviewers in the United States and England were very enthusiastic about the film. Remarkably, the front page of *The Daily News* featured a splashy color photo of Craig embracing his sexy costar. The caption read: "Best Bond Since Connery," which is the greatest endorsement that an actor playing Bond can reasonably hope to receive. Of the movie, horrormeister and pop culture expert Stephen King wrote, "I came out of the theater thinking it was the best Bond since *Goldfinger*. A subsequent viewing of *Goldfinger* . . . has convinced me [*Casino Royale* is] the best Bond ever."[13]

The box office for *Casino Royale* was as impressive as the reviews. In grossing nearly $600 million, the film became the most successful Bond film to date. *Quantum of Solace*, Craig's second outing as Bond, made about $586 million, just a hair less than its predecessor. *Skyfall* (2012) became the 8th highest grossing film of all time with box office receipts north of $1.2 billion. Not too shabby for a fifty-year-old film franchise.

Continuity and change also encompasses the usually unspoken, but discernible dialogue between the first Connery Bond movie and all of the pre-Craig Bond films. The different films' approach to Bond's character eventually formed a continuum with Connery on one end and Brosnan on the other. The films themselves slide up and down the line as each new film modifies our perception of that dialogue – moving back towards Connery's Bond or further away from him. On the rare occasions when Roger Moore kills a bad guy in cold blood or Timothy Dalton takes the quip quotient down a few notches, the filmmakers were harking back to the Connery era. Occasionally, the filmmakers strike a false note that can briefly sever the thread – usually in sequences that are too outlandish to be excused for their nutty exuberance or as being acceptably tongue-in-cheek: such as when Moore swings and yells like Tarzan in *Octopussy*, and when Brosnan drives an invisible car in *Die Another Day*.

Casino Royale, the twenty-first Bond movie, took that straight line and bent it into a circle. No longer are the films' relationships with one another simply a linear A to B(ond) to C. Instead, Craig's new embryonic Bond manages to embrace his roots and pay homage to the interpretations of the five other actors who preceded him as Bond. Seen through this new lens, Lazenby's, Moore's, Dalton's and Bronsan's Bonds seem to form an organic reinterpretation of the character. Now, it is possible to view Brosnan's lightweight Bond not merely as the road not taken, but as providing counterpoint to Craig's grittily muscular interpretation. By rebooting the franchise and making a "Baby Bond" or "Bond Begins" (as the film was sometimes derisively called before its release), the filmmakers depicted Bond in his formative years. We get to see the younger, inexperienced and unpolished government agent who would mature to become Sean Connery's Bond, a Bond who is as suave as he is cold-blooded. Now that Bond isn't a fixed, immutable character, different interpretations of the part seem both appropriate and welcome. For as long as filmmakers understand and remain faithful to Bond's DNA, Bond films will be able to accommodate new actors and the franchise will remain unified rather than just a series of often giddily entertaining, stand-alone movies. In this way, the films will continue to satisfy (the literary critic) Hugh Kenner's definition of metamorphosis as identity persisting through change.

At the beginning of *Casino Royale*, Craig's Bond is a blank slate waiting to take on the attributes that audiences will, to the surprise of many of them, love about his Bond. Paradoxically, it is the absence of the typical, the iconic, and the expected Bond moments that made the film so enjoyable and refreshing. *Casino Royale* very cleverly defies expectations by withholding from moviegoers what they think they want in a Bond movie. After disposing of a villain, the inexperienced Bond does not punctuate the act with a witty one-liner. Getting dressed for night on the town, Bond does not put on a perfectly tailored tux. He does not order Bond's signature beverage. Instead, when a bartender asks a despondent and defeated Bond if he'd like his vodka martini shaken or stirred, Bond tersely replies, "Do I look like I give a damn?" When introducing himself, he doesn't initially say, "The name's Bond, James Bond" - he utters the classic phrase only in the closing moments of the film. Even then the line is re-contextualized. Unlike his predecessors Craig's Bond is not suavely introducing himself; instead he's threatening a villain who bares some responsibility for the death of Vesper Lynd, a woman he's come to love.

By giving us the still unformed James Bond, a raw young agent who breaks a protocol he hasn't yet learned (he sneaks into M's residence and unwisely kills adversaries from whom valuable information might be extracted), who hasn't yet acquired what are to become his trademark characteristics, we are rewarded with the character-enriching fragments of Bond's backstory. We learn, for instance, how Bond earned his "Double-O" status and witness the first time he identifies himself as "Bond, James Bond," the man who will become in equal parts lady-killer and pitiless assassin. While Craig doesn't mind his Bond films making judicious references to 007's prior adventures, he's wary of overkill. He wants to ensure that his series "doesn't become pastiche."[14] Moore may have been onto something when he said that Craig might be the best Bond yet.

With their effusive comments about Craig, Roger Moore and Pierce Brosnan did their best to shield the newcomer from the anticipated disapproval by the press and the ire of Bond fans. Thirty years ago, the creative team behind *Superman* also knew that when a new actor takes over a classic role, it can be helpful to get the actor an endorsement from an actor who previously was associated with the part. In order to mollify the fans and pay respect to the past, the makers of the 1978 Superman movie utilized actors who had worked in earlier interpretations of the story. So Kirk Alyn, who played Superman in the serials of the 1950s, and Noel Neill, who played Lois Lane on TV in *Adventures of Superman* (1952-58), make appearances as the parents of the adolescent Lois Lane.

In the 1980s, the producers of the first three Superman films created *Superboy* (1988-92), the television series that followed Clark Kent through his freshman year of college. The series underwent a radical change of direction for its second, third, and fourth seasons: Clark now works at The Office of Paranormal Activities where he investigates *X-Files* type cases. In the series' four-year run, two different actors played Superboy (John Newton during the first season and Gerard Christopher for the next three). *Superboy* introduced many ideas and themes that would later be explored in the popular television series *Smallville* (2001-11).

Superboy (retitled *The Adventures of Superboy* after the second season) also featured guest appearances by actors from *Adventures of Superman*. Noel Neill and Jack Larson, who played Jimmy Olsen, reunited for a one-shot appearance on the show. Incidentally, George Lazenby played an alien disguised as Jor-El, Superman's biological father, in the series. A fan might briefly experience cognitive dissonance that James Bond was the father of Superman. In the 1990s, Larson made a guest appearance in the critically and commercially successful television series *Lois & Clark: The New Adventures of Superman* (1993-1997).

In 2006, not only did Superman return, so did Noel Neill and Jack Larson. Both actors have cameos in *Superman Returns*. In

Christopher Reeve as Superman. © Warner Bros.

the movie, Lex Luthor swindles the character played by Neill out of her vast wealth and Larson plays a bartender who, in a nice touch, bonds with the new Jimmy Olsen (played by Sam Huntington).

Of his association with Superman, Christopher Reeve said, "For the Seventies and Eighties, I was the temporary custodian of an important American myth." Reeve, it seemed, understood that his claim on the character would be intense and memorable but inevitably temporary. It was also a felicitous touch to have Reeve appear in *Smallville* as a mysterious professor who would give a young and confused Clark Kent a clue about his past. The inter-contextual references on that show don't end with the appearance of Christopher Reeve. Annette O'Toole plays Martha Kent, Clark's adoptive mother. O'Toole had previously played Clark's childhood friend Lana Lang in *Superman III*.

In *Smallville*, Terrence Stamp provides the voice of Jor-El, Superman's biological father. In the first two Superman films Stamp played General Zod, the Kryptonian outcast and supervillain. In *Smallville*, Jor-El tells his son that he has been sent to Earth to rule it. Jor-El's warning frightens Clark who had hoped that he was sent to make a positive difference. So the casting of Stamp takes on greater significance, as it raises doubts about this Jor-El's trustworthiness. In another episode, the audience sees a ghostlike vision of Zod – and it looks remarkably like Stamp.

After a nearly twenty-year absence of Superman from the big screen, Superman fans anxiously awaited the release of *Superman Returns*, helmed by *X-Men* director Bryan Singer. Arguably more than any other director, Singer has gone out of his way to be faithful to the superhero's past incarnations. Singer's film is a continuation of the myths and themes established by the first two Superman feature films, which were directed by Richard Donner and Richard Lester respectively. Singer was so enthralled by the first two movies that he sought Donner's permission and blessing before he accepted the project.

Singer deemed his film to be the unofficial sequel to the first two Superman films. The plot itself begins five years after the events of *Superman II*. To maintain continuity with Reeve's films, Singer reused parts of composer John Williams' unforgettable score for the 1978 movie. Additionally, Singer was able to use footage of Marlon Brando as Jor-El that was cut from *Superman* and *Superman II*. A more subtle homage to the past occurs in the film when Superman hoists a car over his head, an image that nearly duplicates the cover of the first Superman comic.

Even the casting of Brandon Routh as the Man of Steel is a tip of the hat to the original film – Routh looks and sounds remarkably like Reeve.

When he was promoting the film, Routh always went out of his way to pay tribute to Reeve. Routh revealed how touched he was when he received a note from Christopher Reeve's widow, Dana, who gave Routh her blessing and encouraged him to "Go forward."

The filmmakers behind *Superman Returns* were criticized by some for being too faithful to Donner's interpretation. Although the film earned nearly $400 million dollars worldwide and was the most successful Superman film to date, it failed to revive the franchise. It would take another seven years before fans would see the Last Son of Krypton take flight in *Man of Steel* (2013). Producer Christopher Nolan and writer David Goyer, the principal creative team behind the Dark Night trilogy, along with director Zak Snyder deliberately avoided adhering to both Siegel and Shuster's origin story and Donner's interpretations.

In a comprehensive interview with Jeremy Smith (whose pen name is Mr. Beaks) on the website *Ain't It Cool News* Goyer says, "The only real public conception of Superman beyond the comic books is the Donner films - because the Singer film is basically Donner redux. I'm not saying that's good or bad, that's just what he intended to do. But it feels like Superman has been preserved in amber since 1978, so it was a really daunting task . . . We knew it would be a complicated and daunting task, and we didn't realize how daunting until we were in it. All of the decisions going into updating the "S" or whether to use the underwear or whether to use the spit curl, every little thing became this subject of controversy - even more so than Batman. And yet we all felt that if Superman couldn't be sort of reinvented, then he might never be reinvented."[15]

Man of Steel eschewed most Superman tropes and, for better or for worse, completely reinvented the character. Not only was Superman's classic costume and the spit curl abandoned but Superman's "S" is no longer a part of Jor-El's coat of arms - instead it's a Kryptonian symbol for "hope." For me, the most jarring departure from continuity was not Superman's decision to kill General Zod, (which arguably made sense given's Zod's plan to destroy the human race), but the filmmakers' decision to allow

Lois Lane to learn that Clark Kent is actually Superman very early on in their relationship. After saving her life in civilian clothes in what will become his Fortress of Solitude, Lois tracks Clark down to his hometown of Smallville. Superman/Clark makes little effort to conceal his Kryptonian lineage. By letting Lois Lane in on his secret, the filmmakers have eliminated the important dynamic of both the early comics and the Donner films – the love triangle between Superman, Lois and Clark. In fact, prior to the final moments of the film, the notion of using the bumbling Clark Kent persona as a disguise for Superman doesn't factor into the story.

While some of these departures from established lore have been explored in Superman comics – including *Superman: Birthright* (2005) by Mark Waid and Leinil Franic Yu and *Superman: Secret Origin* (2011) by Geoff Johns and Gary Frank – those concepts have not made any significant penetration into the mainstream. However, the public didn't seem to mind the liberties the filmmakers took or it's tepid critical reception: *Man of Steel* went on to earn $668 million, making it the highest-grossing Superman movie.

When taking over the part of a superhero, actors are invariably asked if they were fans of the source material when they were growing up. This question is one way that the press tests the actor's "worthiness" for the role. It would be an unthinkable faux pas for an actor to say that he didn't like or was indifferent to the original comics, movies, or TV series. Another question reporters invariably ask is, "Who was your favorite actor to do the role before you?" Bond actors always choose Connery.

As previously noted, the inclusion of a cameo by a previous hero or a key supporting player in the newest telling of a mythic story is intended to signal to the fans that because the film respects its roots they can safely embrace the latest incarnation. *Star Trek* fans rejoiced when DeForrest Kelley had a cameo as Dr. "Bones" McCoy in the first episode of *Star Trek: The Next Generation*. Moviegoers cheered when they saw former Hulk Lou Ferrigno's cameo in Ang Lee's feature film *Hulk* (2003) and again in *The Incredible Hulk* (2008). The filmmakers courted the fans in trailers and commercials by featuring the line "Don't make me angry . . . you wouldn't like me when I'm angry." Variations of that signature line were used twice – the second time as the last line of Lee's movie, when Dr. David Banner speaks those words in Spanish.

There are times when it is advantageous to distance oneself from a previous incarnation. When Tim Burton took on the feature film version of *Batman*, he made it clear that he didn't want his movie to be anything like the campy 1960s TV series. Tom Mankiewicz, who wrote an early draft of the film, agreed with Burton's decision. As Mankiewicz amplified in our interview, "It is too easy to stand back and show the audience that you're smarter than the material. That's camp. The old *Batman* series on television was camp. It can work for twenty-two minutes on television. It has never worked for a two-hour dramatic movie: you can't make fun of your characters. You've got to treat them seriously."

The Adam West *Batman* TV series was wildly poplar during its three-year run (1966-1968), but it appeared at a time when "camp" mirrored a significant vogue aesthetic sensibility – one that was celebrated in Susan Sontag's provocative essay, "Notes On 'Camp'."

Before Tim Burton's film was released, Batman purists were so upset by the indelibly negative impression the TV series made, they became outraged when it was announced that Michael Keaton, who had a background in comedy, was cast in the title role. In fact, they protested the casting of Keaton to the studio and threatened to boycott the film if it wasn't recast. They incorrectly assumed the feature film would be similarly jokey. Fans didn't want "Mr. Mom" to portray the new Dark Knight. The controversy reached such a fever pitch that even the staid *Wall Street Journal* gave the story front-page coverage. Michael Keaton wryly remembers the backlash. "It wasn't all that severe . . . Except for the hundreds of thousands of people protesting in the streets, I guess. You know, when they hung me in effigy. That was a little – for me – *harsh*."

Tim Burton rejected many elements of the established Batman legacy when he decided to direct *Batman* in 1989. He brazenly said, "There might be something that's sacrilege in the movie -- but I don't care about it -- this is too big a budget to worry about what a fan of a comic would say."

The biggest such break with tradition occurs at the end of the film when Batman deliberately kills the Joker. In the world of the comics, it is widely believed that an important quality that separates Batman from the villains he opposes is his refusal to kill. That's a line that he doesn't cross, but filmmakers will sometimes argue that what is important on the page isn't always best for the screen.

The most overt intertextual reference in Burton's film is when the Batplane temporarily lines up with the moon and the moon frames the silhouetted aircraft. It is a lovely image, but the most ardent fans cheered the visual reference to the Bat-signal.

After the monstrous success of the first two Batman films and the creation of a new Bat-aesthetic, it became safer to refer to the caped crusader's past. The newer Batman feature films liberally quote from other films and other Batman sources. In the awful *Batman and Robin*, Robin shouts, "Holy rusted metal, Batman!" The line was a reference to the 1960s TV series in which Burt Ward's Robin exclaimed "Holy *something*" phrases over 350 times.[16] In the feature, however, the corny joke was that Robin was referring to an actual metal structure with real holes.

In the 1990s, Batman was once again turned into a daily thirty-minute cartoon. Kevin Conroy provided the deft voice-over for the new Dark Knight in *Batman: The Animated Series*. This Emmy-winning cartoon is filled with nods to previous interpretations of the character. Adam West appears in an episode playing a retired actor who is best known for playing a superhero called The Gray Ghost. The Gray Ghost's fictional story seems to mimic Adam West's long real-life association with Batman. Another episode features three different stories with three different actors playing Batman, each look representing a different interpretation from different eras.

The filmmakers behind the disastrous feature film version of *Catwoman* (2004) completely ignored that character's rich history. Not only did they fail in any way to acknowledge the many previous incarnations of Catwoman, they even created a new origin story.

They brushed off Julie Newmar's minx-like reading of Catwoman in the 1960s *Batman* TV series. They also disregarded Eartha Kitt's powerful and sultry interpretation of Catwoman from the same series. Astonishingly, they completely neglected the entire backstory of Catwoman that was so memorably created for *Batman Returns* (1992). In that film, Michelle Pfeiffer played Selina Kyle, a timid woman. After her boss kills Selina, she's brought back to life by a clowder of stray cats. In her new life, Selina is a fully empowered woman who won't let any man (or woman) tell her what to do. Pfeiffer's Catwoman was a clever offspring of the feminist movement, though pushed to an extreme. Though Pfeiffer's Catwoman may be guilty of overkill, she's never so strident that she alienates the audience. Instead, much of the audience is rooting her on, pleased to observe her transformation from an oppressed woman to an empowered one. Catwoman's costume reflects the change: it is represented by an outfit that she had kept in her closet but never before had the courage to wear.

Halle Berry's Catwoman in the 2004 film is an exploited graphics designer whose company is selling an anti-aging cream even though the company executives know that the product will deform its users. Alas, the script and direction of the movie are clunky and uninspired. Unlike the attractive and sexy costume worn by Michelle Pfeiffer's Catwoman, Berry's suit looks silly and it is utterly unappealing – a failure of taste and judgment that's especially inexcusable when Berry is wearing the duds. Needless to say, the film won more than a few Golden Raspberry Awards (Razzies), which are given to worst movies of the year.

Inexplicably in *The Dark Knight Rises*, Anne Hathaway's Selina Kyle is never once referred to as Catwoman. With a running time of 165 minutes, you'd think Christopher Nolan would have found time to slip the name in.

Putting aside the debacle of Berry's *Catwoman*, there are instances when ignoring a character's backstory has led to a successful adaptation. Kenneth Johnson, creator of the popular *The Incredible Hulk* TV series (1978-1982), tossed out the creature's origins and created a new, more sophisticated myth.

While mulling over a concept for the show, Johnson recalled reading Victor Hugo's *Les Miserables*, a novel that his wife had recently given him. He thought he could transfer the idea of the relentless Inspector Javert chasing Jean Valjean to the Hulk series. The relationship between Javert and Valjean was successfully paralleled by the reporter Jack McGee's determined quest to track down the Hulk.

Johnson completely reworked the origin myth. For starters, the title character's name was changed from Bruce Banner to David Banner because Johnson didn't like comic book alliterations – and *not* because the name Bruce sounded "too gay," as is frequently reported. In the comics, Bruce Banner becomes the Hulk after he is exposed to gamma radiation while saving his friend. In the series, Dr. David Banner fails to save his wife from a car wreck. Plagued with guilt, Banner, as the opening narration intones, is "searching for a way to tap into the hidden strengths that all humans have." His experiments go awry, and from that day on whenever Banner becomes sufficiently angry, he turns into the Hulk.

Johnson also wanted to change the color of the Hulk from green to red because "the color of rage is red, not green."[17] However, after changing the tale of Banner's origin, he didn't feel that he could get away with another significant change without completely alienating the comic's core fans.

In both the comic book and the 2003 feature film, Banner turns into the Hulk after being infected by a gamma ray overdose. However, Johnson didn't think fidelity to the comic book worked in Ang Lee's *Hulk*. Johnson observed, "It worked okay in the comic book, but that took it into the realm of Big Government mobilizing and chasing him. I sought a far more simple and personal story. I believe I was right. Particularly after seeing the feature version."

Even for most serious fans, absolute fidelity to a comic book's origins isn't always necessary. Departures from the origin story are acceptable if they are consistent with the original and, if wisely conceived, they can enrich the myth. Many iconic characters have been changed from their beginnings in comics. When Superman was introduced in 1939, he couldn't fly; he could only leap tall buildings in single bound. When the Hulk debuted, he was gray, not green. More astonishingly, nighttime – not anger – was the catalyst for Banner's transformation into the creature. Until recently, the explanation behind Spider-Man's web slinging ability was that Peter Parker, a science whiz, invented a sophisticated technology that mirrored the unique ability of spiders. However, the makers of the feature film did not believe it to be plausible that a teenager (even a gifted one) could invent such a device. Instead, they decided that Parker's ability to produce his own web fluid derived from the bite of a radioactive spider. In *Spider-Man 2* (2004), the filmmakers added a further twist, and even got a bit cheeky, when they used Peter Parker's temporary inability to shoot his web fluid as a metaphor for his feelings of impotence. Fans didn't mind this important alteration to the Spidey myth because it helped expand the complexity of the beloved character, who felt that his gift was also his curse. However, when the series was rebooted a scant five years after *Spider-Man 3* (2007), the filmmakers went back to Stan Lee's original concept: in *The Amazing Spider-Man* (2012) Andrew Garfield's Peter Parker invents a homemade web shooter to help him battle Rhys Ifan's Lizard.

Comic book writer Dennis O'Neil explains why purists tolerate some of these sometimes significant changes. He writes that if "you have been faithful to the character who's transformed and the changes have happened gradually, you might not be terribly offended by them; they might seem natural and organic."

"Natural" and "organic" changes occur with some frequency in the myths of superheroes. Batman started out as a loner before partnering with Robin. Other accepted changes included Robin growing up and developing another identity called "Nightwing." Batman trained another "Robin" to take his place. The second Robin was killed because of a misguided publicity stunt in the 1980s, when DC Comics allowed the fate of the character to be decided by a poll. Fans voiced their opinions by calling a 900-number at a cost of 50 cents per call. Eventually a third Robin joined in Batman's quest to fight crime. More recently, Robin the Boy Wonder became Robin, the Girl Wonder in a series of comics written by Frank Miller. (Tim Burton credits Miller's seminal work *The Dark Knight Returns* as a major source of inspiration for his two Batman films.)

O'Neil contends that the process of change can be accelerated if a character jumps from one medium to another. When Superman first moved from the comic pages to the radio waves in the early 1940s, he acquired a young pal, Jimmy Olsen; and we were introduced to Kryptonite, against which Superman was powerless.

It took over fifty years for the comic book Lois Lane to discover Superman's secret. (Lois would later fall in love with Superman and marry him.) However, it took only two feature films before Clark let that particular cat out of that the bag. Although it is still an issue that can set off fireworks, it is now more common for the hero's love-interest to find out that the man they're seeing has a second life. For example, Kim Bassinger, Michelle Pfeiffer, Nicole Kidman, and Katie Holmes learn that Michael Keaton, Val Kilmer, and Christian Bale are Batman. In *Spider-Man*, Kirsten Dunst learns that the superhero is Peter Parker. In *Spider-Man 2*, all the passengers on a subway car learn Parker's secret. In *The Amazing Spider-Man*, Peter Parker (Andrew Garfield) reveals his alias to the Gwen Stacy (Emma Stone) character. These films compromise the inviolability and importance of the hero's "secret identity," antagonizing many serious fans for whom the concept is central to the superhero myth. Yet all these films were phenomenally successful.

The most complex and financially successful example of continuity and change in the superhero cinema universe is manifested in *The Avengers* (2012). The film is a mash-up of characters, relationships, and story points originally established in five other feature films, including, *Iron Man* (2008), *The Incredible Hulk* (2008), *Iron Man 2* (2010), *Thor* (2011), and *Captain America: The First Avenger* (the subtitle of the 2011 film seems to have been chosen for its marketing value).

The seeds of anticipation for the film were planted in the post-credits scene in *Iron Man*, in which Nick Fury (played by Samuel L. Jackson) informs Tony Stark that he is in the early stages of forming a team called "the Avengers Initiative." Fury challenges and teases Stark with the question, "Do you think you are the only superhero in the world?" He continues, "Mr. Stark, you've become part of a bigger universe. You just don't know it yet." Fury's goad was probably intended primarily for audience members who are not comic book-savvy and who tend to learn about their superheroes mostly from movies and TV shows rather than from the comic books and graphic novels that spawn them. The scene serves as a bald teaser for a series of not yet written or even fully conceived films featuring Marvel characters.

At the time, only comic book devotees understood the reference to the "Initiative." A mere four years later, this insider's reference would develop into a formidable franchise when *The Avengers* grossed nearly $1.5 billion. Following *Iron Man* and building towards *The Avengers*, the post-credits sequences of each successive Marvel film would hint at their next, seemingly, unrelated film. Tony Stark pops up at the end of *The Incredible Hulk*, Thor's Hammer is unearthed after *Iron Man 2*, the MacGuffin for *The Avengers* is revealed in the post-credits scene of Thor, and a sneak peek at *The Avengers* would appear after the credits of *Captain America*.

Although the executive talent overseeing Marvel Studios carefully cultivates continuity in new films with their established heroes, an equally important aspect of their phenomenal success should be attributed to their nimble ability to create new franchises that are very different in nature. Studio head Kevin Feige, who seems to have comic book ink coursing through his veins, pushes the studio to experiment and grow and to avoid repeating the same tried and true formula. (As one small example, most of their films boldly eschew the notion that superheroes need a secret identity.) Instead, each film has its own style and tone and is tailor-made to fit the eccentricities and personalities of its costumed hero or heroes. Feige, the assured and inventive architect of the Marvel Cinematic Universe, explained, "We love all of our movies to stand apart . . . We don't believe the 'superhero film' is a genre unto itself. We love taking subgenres and putting them together and then adding superhero elements... "[18] *Captain*

America: The First Avenger is a World War II movie and its follow up, *Captain America: The Winter Soldier* (2014), set in modern times, is a political thriller in the vein of the paranoid films of the 1970s. Whereas *Iron Man* is a jaunty action adventure franchise that echoes the sophisticated panache of the early James Bond films, *The Incredible Hulk* is a man-on-the-run movie, *The Avengers* is an alien invasion flick and *Guardians of the Galaxy* is a sci-fi space romp. Remarkably, despite the diversity of Marvel's films, when their characters' storylines intersect, they mesh together seamlessly.

To win the enthusiasm and the respect of large audiences, filmmakers must navigate fine lines between fidelity to their heroes' origins, to their storylines and their natural-seeming evolution over time, and the carefully calculated changes that seem appropriate in order to keep the characters vital and interesting. Filmmakers will have to maintain this delicate blend of continuity and change in order to continue making successful and enduring superhero movies that extend our pre-existing myths and even create new ones.

PART ONE: CAPED CRUSADERS

Adam West is Batman

If it weren't for Adam West, this book might not have been written, and it's possible that you wouldn't be able to go to your local comic book shop to purchase a new Batman graphic novel.

West, of course, brought Bob Kane and Bill Finger's creation to life for three years and 120 episodes in *Batman* (1966-1968), the hugely popular and sometimes misunderstood TV series.

Before the show aired and Batmania swept the nation in a manner that nearly rivaled Beatlemania, the Batman comics were exhibiting sluggish sales. The popularity of Batman ebbed so substantially that the title, which was originally published in 1939, was at risk of being cancelled. In his book *Batman: The Complete History*, noted comic book historian Les Daniels writes: "Although it seems inconceivable in retrospect, Bob Kane has said, "They were planning to kill Batman off altogether."[19] Shortly after *Batman* began to air twice-weekly, fortunes changed for the Caped Crusader. As Robert Greenberger reports in his essay *Gotham City 14 Miles*, a year before the show hit the airwaves it sold "an average of 453,745 copies per month," but a "year later, it took the top slot with average sales of 898,470 copies per issue, a peak which the title has never matched."[20]

Not only did Batman comics survive due to Adam West's *Batman* series, it sometimes seemed that the Batman character actually lived in the actor who portrayed him. In his autobiography *Back to the Batcave*, Adam West recalls the time when the character and he became one. "When the [Batcave] set came to life and I looked down and saw Batman's gloved hands, not mine, I came close to believing in the existence of Batman myself. In the years that followed this would happen the moment I pulled on the cowl . . . I reveled in the power and isolation and beauty of the character. It's the kind of experience that never leaves you, and creates a very special bond with a character."[21]

With matinee idol looks and a flair for both light comedy and drama, West and his collaborators made the show entertaining to audiences on two levels: as a straightforward and thrilling comic book adaptation for the children and as a zany farce for older viewers.

The show was groundbreaking on several fronts including what Les Daniels, in his book *DC Comics: A Celebration of the World's Favorite Comic Book Heroes*, calls "the unprecedented decision to run the half hour show on two consecutive nights, allowed for a cliff-hanger on Wednesday that would be resolved on Thursday."[22] It's difficult to think of any other dramas or comedies that have taken a comparably unconventional path to success.

The show was also daring in its liberal use of "dutch angles" (tilted cameras), brilliant colors, titles superimposed over fight scenes to underscore the action, and head writer's Lorenzo Semple, Jr.'s tongue-in-cheek dialogue. But one cannot underestimate the mnemonic impact of the animated opening credit sequence, featuring Neil Hefti's jazzy opening theme song, which announces the name of the show no fewer than eleven times in roughly forty-one seconds!

Despite all the creative flourishes, the show was painted with the reductive and somewhat dismissive label "camp." Les Daniels argues that the show really wasn't camp: "*Batman* on television created the kind of sensation that sends pundits scurrying to the thesaurus in search of adjectives . . . Critics seized on the word *camp*, previously used to describe entertainments so inept that they become inadvertently humorous. The *Batman* show, however, was spoofing itself."[23]

For any fan who wondered what *Batman* might have been like if the actors played it straight, they need only look at *The Green Hornet* (1966-1967), a TV series produced by *Batman* producer William Dozier and starring Van Williams as the title character and Bruce Lee as Kato. The show, which lasted twenty-six episodes in its only season, took a more solemn approach to depicting its heroic duo's crime-fighting adventures. Despite earnest performances by Williams and Lee, the show lacked the spark, the creative wit, and the wild energy that made *Batman* and Adam West so bewitching.[24]

Adam West's interpretation of Batman was not limited to the TV show. West also played the Caped Crusader in the feature film *Batman* (1966), which was shot between the first and second season of the series, as well as in many animated shows including *The New Adventures of Batman* (1977), two silly TV specials *Legends of the Superheroes: The Challenge* (1979) and *Legends of the Superheroes: The Roast* (1979); the cartoons *Superfriends: The Legendary Super Powers Show* (1984) and *The Super Powers Team: Galactic Guardians* (1985); as well as in the short film *Batman: New Times* (2005), which used Lego figures to depict Batman's battle with the Joker.[25]

West has voiced a number of other characters in a variety of Batman cartoons including The Gray Ghost in *Batman: The Animated Series* (1992), Mayor Grange in *The Batman* (2005), Batman's robot ally, Proto Bat-Bot, and Bruce Wayne's father, Thomas Wayne, in *Batman: The Brave and the Bold* (2010). West also provided the voice of Batman in *The Story of Batman*, a song recorded in the 1970s.[26]

He has parodied his Batman persona in a number of projects including his role as Batmantis in *Space Ghost Coast to Coast* (1994); Mantaman in *Street Sharks* (1995); Jerry Retchen in *Lois & Clark: The New Adventures of Superman* (1995); the Caped Crusader/Spruce Wayne in *Animaniacs* (1997), in an episode titled *Boo Wonder*; as Batman in *The Simpsons* (2002); as a reoccurring character named Adam West in over seventy-five episodes of *Family Guy* (2002); as Catman in *The Fairly Odd Parents* (2003); as himself in a TV-movie depicting the making of West's show called *Return to the Batcave: The Misadventures of Adam and Burt* (2003); as Alfred the Butler in *Angels with Angles* (2005), in which Frank Gorshin, who memorably played the Riddler on *Batman*, also appeared; Manbat in *Super Capers: The Origins of Ed and the Missing Bullion* (2009); as Young Mermaid Man in *SpongeBob SquarePants* (2010); and as Nighthawk in *The Super Hero Squad* (2010). He hysterically lampooned his image in *Lookwell* (1991) – an *Airplane*-style comedy pilot that never begat a full-fledge series – in which he played a has-been actor who foolishly believes that he can actually solve crimes.

In the 2-DVD documentary *Adam West Naked* (2009) filmed in the comfort of his home, the actor recounts personal memories of every episode of his audacious TV show.

Adam West as Batman. © Twentieth Century Fox Television.

The success of *Batman* revived comic book sales, extended the life of the Dark Knight, and led the way towards the success of the modern superhero phenomenon. Any actor who puts on a superhero costume owes a great debt to Adam West.

THE INTERVIEW

My ten-year-old self would not believe that my adult self was talking with you. On a personal note, I wanted to thank you for playing Batman.

It's been my pleasure. [He pauses and adds playfully] Most of the time.

From what I've read, I have the impression that your initial thoughts about playing Batman were a combination of reluctance and hope.

I'd say that's a pretty accurate statement of the mix. But I felt that I might be able to do something fresh with the character. Something a little different. I refused to do what was normally expected [in playing a superhero].

Did you think of Bruce Wayne and Batman as two separate characters?

Yes.

Can you talk a little bit about developing those two distinct personalities?

I'll be frank, it's difficult for me to talk about acting. But let me relate back to your first question. When I decide I want to do a part and I get curious and I start cooking with it, I just go in and do it. I don't even think about it. Seriously. I developed the character as best as I could and I tried to bring something unique and fun to the part, and then I didn't think about it.

In the beginning I got a lot of criticism from people associated with the show. "Oh, he's not as serious as he should be. He's not as wooden as we thought he should be. We don't want to see the twinkle behind the mask."

In other words, they thought it would be better if my interpretation was more mundane. It occurred to me, creatively, that if something is mundane and ordinary that it might not be as interesting. It might not have a lasting impact.

Batman has to be a little bit bigger than life to instill fear in the villains.

Batman was bigger than life. No one runs around like that 24/7. He'd be locked up somewhere. In my case, I reasoned that if I played Batman with utter sincerity — in that *he* doesn't think he is funny — and occasionally with a little wink to the audience, then I could be absurdly big with the character. Those characters became almost Shakespearian.

Did you have to justify why a man would put on the cape to fight crime?

You know, not really so much. I think much of my interpretation came from my sense memory of playing Batman as a kid, and also what happens instantaneously when you put on the cape and cowl. Because I was able to conjure that up with a little bit of thinking and cooking with it, it became an easy way for me to get into that absurd characterization. I'd put on the cowl and say to Burt or myself "Come on, let's go play Batman and Robin in my yard. Come on, it's neat." I knew that if I had the enthusiasm and a kind of the uninhibited quirkiness that you had as a kid playing him, then it might work.

You're saying that the costume does a lot of the work for you.

Oh my God, yes. Good observation. It certainly does. Especially if you use the cape and the cowl and move in a certain way, you can appear dynamic. Batman hardly ever stops moving. Bruce Wayne does. But not Batman. Batman is always moving in some manner, even if he is merely gesturing with his hand or swinging his cape around.

When kids play Batman, they are pretending to be you. But what's interesting is that you were actually pretending to be them playing you. Did you allow yourself to feel powerful (as a kid would) in the costume?

You are very perceptive about this stuff. That first day walking out of my dressing room and walking on the stage was tough. I thought, "Are they going to accept me in this silly costume as the real Batman?" I had to take a deep breath. I walked across the stage towards the crew and everyone turned towards me and there's wasn't a sound. They just accepted me totally.

John Wesley Shipp who played The Flash on CBS told me that he felt powerful in the costume and somewhat diminished out of it. Do you relate to that?

That was not my feeling. My feeling in character was probably more that I felt somewhat diminished when I wore the costume

Adam West as Bruce Wayne. © Twentieth Century Fox Television.

– at least from Bruce Wayne's point of view. Because as Bruce Wayne, I was faking something . . . it's hard to explain . . .

No, I understand. It speaks to the question of who is the true identity: Batman or Bruce Wayne?

It became Batman. And not Bruce Wayne. Batman was part of all the true activity that counted and propelled the story – that is, unless you include the [1966 feature-length] movie. In our movie, I had more of a chance to play Bruce Wayne.

What did you learn about playing Bruce Wayne that you didn't realize before?

That he was a great lover. [Clearly having fun] Especially if he had a brandy snifter of milk to brace himself.

Your Bruce Wayne didn't seem tortured by being a superhero. He seemed to enjoy it.

Yes. Good. If that came across, then good.

Did you try to develop different registers for the voices of Batman and Bruce Wayne?

I don't think so. But I did develop different rhythms. But that came easily. Because Batman was desperately involved in what he was doing, he would have a different rhythm to his speech. It was easier for me to play absurd lines of dialogue when I said them with [a distinct] rhythm. Do you know what I mean?

I do.

[He chuckles] Good. Because I don't.

Your approach is different from Yvonne Craig, who told me that she used the same voice for Batgirl and Barbara Gordon.

That brings up something else too. Someone else playing Batman might have [rationalized that] Batman should turn his head away to avoid being recognized. That was not my Batman at all. My Batman thought that regardless of how his voice sounded he would never be recognized as Bruce Wayne. He thought that the costume was too clever. But of course [if this weren't a fictional conceit,] everyone would recognize him. That was part of the absurdity of the script that I loved.

Are you like Batman in anyway?

Well, at the moment, I'm trying to get these handcuffs on this guy. I don't think I am at all. Well, maybe in one way: we both think funny.

Some actors have told me that playing these heroes has rubbed off on them in some way. Did Batman make his way into your life and vice versa?

I think so a bit. But it evolved so slowly. And it took me years to "sober up." I feel that is it unavoidable. At least in my case I've sensed and seen it. *Batman* was a show that was geared to entire families to enjoy on different levels. But you do develop a sense of responsibility that evolves over a few years when everyone you meet thanks you, and when the kids are really starry-eyed

Batman (Adam West) is ready to vanquish all evildoers in Gotham City. ©
Twentieth Century Fox Television.

and grateful as you said you were. It's certainly gotten to me. And I'd hate to disappoint families.

You are expected to hold the mantle and be a spokesman for this character in some way. Is that exhausting?

Yes it is. But it paid well. And it continues. Of course, I'm joking. But it is a bit of a responsibility. But there is something selfish about it too. I was being turned down for more adult-fare in more interesting work. I felt that I better embrace the thing that I created. Otherwise, I would have never have become an icon.

It's an overused word but you actually are an icon.

I did a little piece for [the now defunct] *Lopez [Tonight]* with Jamie Foxx. I hadn't met him before but this constantly happens. People jump out of their skin. They embrace me and start yelling. I guess that's because what I did was entertaining, evolving, affecting.

Would you have had the same impact if you played a different superhero or was something about Batman and you that made it gel?

Yes, because if I played another character like Zorro or Green Lantern I don't think I'd have been that intrigued by the role or wanted to do it. But Batman has such a rich history. He's an ordinary guy who has crazily embraced a cause and I found it fascinating. I found it very funny, as well. He is so obsessed and crazy that, to me, it was hilarious. That was the tight wire. To make the kids believe it. To love the splash and adventure. And the risk. And for the adults to see the tongue-in-cheek, knowing that it was a satire.

In your autobiography you said that you were "married to the cape." In every marriage, in every relationship there are ups and downs. How did you make peace with the idea that your relationship with this character was going to be a long one?

I think it was a very simple deduction. I think any intelligent person would come to the same conclusion. And that is if I am being turned down for other roles because of my association with Batman, then maybe what I should do is really embrace Batman. Pursue it and keep it alive. Which is what I've been trying to do for well over thirty years.

When you step into the Batshoes for each new incarnation, such as for the two 1979 live-action specials, *Legends of the Superheroes*, does it immediately come back to you?

Yes, but in that case almost reluctantly. Because that show was terrible. When people don't "get it," it makes it very difficult. You want to work with peers. You want to work with other performers, directors, and writers – especially writers, I love writers – you want to work with people who *get it*.

We had some very good writers for the original show. They saw the craziness, the comedy. You know, just as he's about to put her in the joint, Batman says to Catwoman, "You give me curious stirrings in my utility belt." That's funny stuff.

Speaking of Catwoman, Julie Newmar told me that she thought Catwoman had feelings for Batman and that she's not just toying with him. What was your sense about their relationship?

Same thing. Same thing. We had to find a way to create a sexual tension. In the way that I tried to do it, Batman felt sorry for her – even though he was also mightily attracted to her.

At that time you also did appearances in the costume. What's it like to do that without the structure and safety of a script?

It was okay. It was a lot of work. But it was okay. Because once you get into that costume you become that character again. You can speak with those rhythms and with the intent and be kind of funny.

Even today, because of the way that I did it people absolutely believe me and trust me. Whatever I do, wherever I go, whatever I say, I can get away with almost anything. Just between us. [Laughs]. Not that I do. [Mocks whispering] Wife just walked by.

When was the last time you put on the cape?

I think it was for a still shot in the centerpiece of a magazine.

Roughly how long ago was that?

Ten years ago. Maybe fifteen. Then, of course, I still have my Bat-jamies that I wear almost every evening.

How has playing the part changed you?

It's made me an extremely rich man. [Laughs] Personally, the rewards have come from the fans. Wherever I go I am met with such warmth and humor.

What would you have liked to do with the character that you didn't get an opportunity to do?

My own series of movies.

What direction would you have taken with the character?

Multi-directional – in that I think Batman can be expressed in transitional form on so many levels. In time. In space. He can pop up in any time, in any place in any universe.

That would have been fun to see.

Let's do it. But you see, they don't think in those terms. They don't think out of the box enough. They are too concerned with violence, with explosions and trying to uncover layers of the human psyche.

Would you be interested in playing Batman (or a superhero with Batman's qualities) now, at your present age, and in exploring what that means?

There is a character called The Gray Ghost, which I voiced [for *Batman: The Animated Series*] for one or two episodes. What Warners should do is pick that up for an animated series. I would be the Gray Ghost and I could do that in movies. I think the Gray Ghost would make a hell of a film.

Favorite Bat-merchandise.

The condoms.

[Laughing] Are there really Batman condoms?

No. [Laughing]

But there should be. Who would win in a fight: Your Batman or George Clooney's?

I think it depends on the circumstances. It probably depends on the kind of battle. If it were to be a battle of charm, of course, Clooney would win.

I'd like to reiterate how grateful I am that you took the time to talk with me. I grew up on your show so this is a thrill for me.

Oh, no problem. You're a man of quality. I can tell. You've been great.

Bob Holiday is Superman

Pop quiz: Name the Broadway musical based on a comic book where an actor playing a superhero fell from his safety-harness while flying through the air. If you answered: *Spider-Man: Turn Off the Dark* you'd be wrong. Spider-Man doesn't *fly*; he *swings*. The correct response is *It's a Bird . . . It's a Plane . . . It's Superman*, the 1966 musical about the Man of Steel.

Bob Holiday as Superman. Photo courtesy of Toni Collins.

It's a Bird . . . It's a Plane . . . It's Superman boasted an impressive pedigree: the show was directed by Hal Prince (who made a name for himself with *West Side Story* and *Cabaret*); Charles Strouse and Lee Adams (the team behind *Bye Bye Birdie*) wrote the music and lyrics; and the book was written by David Newman and Robert Benton (who, along with Mario Puzo, Leslie Newman and Tom Mankiewicz, would co-write *Superman: The Movie*).[27]

For the dual roles of Superman and Clark Kent, Prince shrewdly cast Bob Holiday, the handsome and square-jawed baritone from the musical *Fiorello!* At the time when *Batman* aired twice weekly on television and superheroes were often synonymous with camp, Holiday bucked the trend by *not* approaching the part with his tongue in his cheek. Instead, he did his best to honor the spirit and dignity of the character.

While *Spider-Man: Turn Off the Dark* broke records for the number of tickets sold in a single week ($2.9 million) and ran for three years, *Superman* did not fair quite as well[28]. The show closed after only 129 performances.[29] Since you can't keep a good superhero down, Holiday suited up again for his signature role the following year for revivals of the musical in St. Louis and Kansas City.

Although it's been years since Holiday performed in the role, he still has fond memories playing the Last Son of Krypton.

THE INTERVIEW

Were you a Superman fan when you were cast?

Yes. I used to read the comics when I was a kid. As early as around seven years old. They were a huge part of my life. I loved Superman. That's why I went in for the casting. Comic books were an important part of children's lives, and I was honored to become a live action version of Superman. I read comic books all the time as a kid. Reading comics let a kid change from one self into another self.

Years later, you auditioned for the part of Superman and Clark Kent. What was casting process like?

It was quick. I heard about the play from director Hal Prince's secretary and went to Hal's office. As I was walking in, the elevator doors opened and Hal walked out with Charles Strouse and

Lee Adams [the composer and lyricist]. Hal said, "Bob Holiday! Bob Holiday! I've got something to talk to you about." Hal knew me from *Fiorello!*, which he had produced. They auditioned about fifty others, but I got the part. But it was my mother who gave me the confidence to be Superman. She told me, "You are going to get the role because you've always been a Superman fan."

How did you prepare for the part?

I'm Superman! I knew him from the time I was a kid; loved the comics since I was a kid. I was a big fan. Understanding the role was rather simple. It was a part of my childhood. I loved it, I loved it. To get the show was wonderful. The producers did very little with me; they knew that I could do the part because I'd been doing these things all my life. When I was sitting on stage as Clark Kent, I'd do schtick with Jack Cassidy and he couldn't beat it. And the producers encouraged that. Whenever I was onstage with Jack Cassidy, who played Max Mencken, my job was to upstage him constantly. So even when Max was alone onstage, Superman was never out of the audience's mind.

What makes Superman tick? What motivates him?

Several things. Lois Lane is number one. The people around him are important to him. Like the song said, his job is "Doing Good!" And then there's the whole love triangle with Clark loving Lois, Lois loving Superman, and all the mix-ups that come from that.

Who is the "real" character? Superman or Clark Kent?

I thought that Superman was the real character and Clark Kent was just a part he played. There's a line from one of the songs called "Doing Good" where I say, "Back into the old Clark Kent disguise." That gave me a big clue.

Given that, did you think of Clark and Superman as two different characters as Christopher Reeve did?

Definitely. You've got to play Superman one way and then Clark the other way. You have to separate the two. But here's the secret: There was always a bond between the audience and me; both of us knew that underneath Clark was Superman, but we couldn't let anyone else on the stage know.

What was your approach to Superman? To Clark Kent?

One was Jewish. Seriously, if you look at pictures of me as Superman and as Clark Kent, my face looks different. I tried to capture the difference in my whole body.

That makes sense Bob. Because Jerry Siegel and Joe Shuster, who created Superman, were Jewish. They saw themselves as Clark Kent but wished they were Superman. You met Joe Shuster. What are your memories of him?

He seemed happy with what we were doing with the show.

Did Shuster give you any insights into the character?

We met when I was prepping for the show. It was so long ago that it's tough to recall his exact words. He gave me little tips and insights into Superman's strength and character.

[Toni Collins's, Mr. Holiday's friend, webmaster and arguably his biggest fan interjects to say, "In Bob's autobiography there is a nice New Years card, from Joe Shuster to Bob. So, Shuster must have appreciated Bob's performance."][30]

How did you feel when you first put on the cape?

Bob Holiday as Superman with Patricia Marand as Lois Lane. Photo courtesy of Toni Collins.

To actually put on the cape just felt right. I enjoyed it. As I've said, I knew and identified strongly with the character from the time I was seven years old. Playing the part was great fun, and I loved it.

Did you ever feel powerful in the suit?

Not at first, because becoming Superman was a matter of acting, not of clothes. We rehearsed for a long time in street clothes, so I got used to being Superman without the suit. It was natural to put it on. [Laughs]. But you're right. Because once I started to get into the part I felt, "I am Superman."

You just said, "I am Superman." How so? Can you elaborate on that?

It's a feeling. You just get into the role, and it's all summed up in that statement, "I am Superman." You can't say any more, because words just reduce the feeling. But that's just my approach as an actor. As an actor who had to create both parts, I had to capture the spirit of both characters. But it doesn't mean that I'm actually like either of these characters. But in everyday life, Bob Holiday and what he's like has nothing to do with either one.

I understand you would appear in the suit as personal appearances. What was that like?

After the show, I would stay in costume and greet the audience until every fan left the theater. That's the way it should be done. It has to be that way. Make it real for them.

[Toni says, "I've been a fan for over forty years. Because I remember going to the theater and I still remember how wonderful Bob was to all those little kids back then. I can tell you as an eleven year old, I felt like I had met Superman."]

It must be both somewhat surprising and gratifying that a decision you made, to stay in character and meet fans, would be something that would be remembered for forty years.

You've got Toni right there as an example of that.

[Toni adds: "I hasten to add that it's not just me. Running Bob's website, I come across fans all the time who remember him and can't wait to get in touch with him. All of us remember what a great Superman Bob Holiday was. We all remember what an impact Bob Holidays on us as Superman."]

Bob Holiday's headshot from the playbill of Starlight Theatre's revival of the musical in Kansas City, Missouri. Photo courtesy of Toni Collins.

When was the last time you put on the cape and how did it feel?

The last time was for the 1967 St. Louis and Kansas City revivals of the show. The crowds were huge; upwards of 20,000 people saw those shows. They cheered Superman and it felt great. I did a lot of publicity appearances to promote the show. The most meaningful was when I visited a children's hospital, in costume, and got to interact with the children there. It was marvelous.

When the show's villain turns the people of Metropolis against him Superman faces a crisis of confidence

That's right. That was beautifully explored in a song called "The Strongest Man In The World." There were some marvelous lyrics: "Why can't the strongest man in the world be the happiest man in the world? Why does the strongest man in the world have the heaviest heart in the world? Why must I, the Man of Steel, feel as helpless as a man of straw . . . don't they know the strongest man can cry?"

Finding the right tone for a musical version of Superman must have been tricky.

While it was a show that we hoped would appeal to children, it wasn't a kid's show. Unlike the television version that they did years later with David Wilson, our show was not campy at all. The television version was very much in the style of the *Batman* TV show. Very campy. Mocking the character to some extent. That was not the case with the Broadway show at all. We took the character very seriously. Hal Prince told me very directly, 'You will play this character seriously. You will not make fun of him. We are going to treat this character as a real person.'

There seem to be some parallels between your show and the Spider-Man musical. Both shows were highly scrutinized. Both went through a similar process of trying to find the correct tone of the show. And like them, you also had a mishap during a flying sequence.

Absolutely. A single wire was suspending me and I was dropped. I was about six feet off the ground. Although at times, I probably "flew" as high as twenty feet. I was in pretty good shape at the time. So after I hit the ground, I immediately jumped right up. I turned to the audience and said, "That would have hurt any mortal man." The audience roared.

Because no one taped the show much of your performance hasn't been properly documented. So new Superman fans can't watch your show (although they can listen to the cast recording.) Is that somewhat disappointing? How do you think you'd be remembered if your show were properly recorded and documented?

The show made it into the book, *The Best Plays of 1965-1966*, so it will be remembered. A lot of the show got captured by that book. And then, on my web site, you can watch a couple of clips of me as Superman. One's an Aqua Velva commercial, so it has little bit of an edge to it, but the other is a part of a "documentary" that was actually shown on stage. That one shows exactly the way I played the character. So, there's a little bit of a legacy there. There it is. Somewhere along the way, someone will say, "Bob Holiday did this." And that's nice.

How has the part changed your life?

Bob Holiday will always have the honor of being Superman. I still answer, "Up, up and away" when anyone calls me. Seriously though, I used a Superman-like character for the logo of my home building business. I'm proud to have been a part of the Superman legacy. Christopher Reeve once wrote that in every decade, a new man carries the legacy of Superman, and I'm proud to have done so in the 1960's. I got to build a live action Superman on Broadway, calling out, "Up, up and away," with people actually looking up at me. That was an important and unique aspect to my Superman. They actually saw me fly; it wasn't movie magic.

Do friends and family ever refer to you as Superman?

Are you kidding? All the time!

What's the best part of the association?

The best is the pride of being Superman and "Doing Good," to have the interaction and effect on the audience. I'm very proud of what that was. There was no playing and no fooling around in the whole of the show. I took Superman seriously.

The worst?

The worst was when the shackle broke and I dropped six feet. But it was a case of making lemons into lemonade. I was in good shape, my knees went down, and when I bounced back up the audience roared. Other than that, there's no downside to having played Superman, no downside at all.

I take it you don't believe in the so-called "Superman Curse?"

No, I don't. In fact, I think the idea of a "Superman Curse" is silly. Look at me, I'm still here. I love life. I'm seventy-nine-years old - and my hair is still brown! I have had nothing but good come from me playing Superman. Life is good, and I'm having a ball.

How has playing the part affected you personally – not publicly or professionally, but personally?

I love it. It's me. Superman has got a certain feel, and it was good to play the part. I still hear from fans today, and it's wonderful. Over and over, someone will find me, get in touch, and let me know how much they loved the show (and even me personally). You can't imagine how much that means to me forty years later!

Jackson Bostwick is Captain Marvel

Captain Marvel, created by C.C. Beck and Bill Parker, first appeared in print in 1940 – a mere two years after Superman first leapt his first tall building in a single bound. On the surface, Captain Marvel might appear to bear more than a passing resemblance to the Man of Steel. Captain Marvel, like Superman, is impervious to bullets, flies, wears a cape, battles a bald, evil scientist, and lives a double life as a mild-mannered reporter.

However, there are substantial differences between the two supermen. Most significantly, Captain Marvel's alter ego is a young boy, not an adult. Billy was an ordinary kid before the benevolent wizard, Shazam, granted him his special abilities. When trouble arises, as it often does, all Billy needs to do is speak the wizard's name and he is transformed into the powerful Captain Marvel. When Captain Marvel incants the magic word "Shazam," he turns back into his true self, Billy Batson.

Shazam is both the sorcerer's name and an acronym for Captain Marvel's powers: the wisdom of *Solomon*, the strength of *Hercules*, the stamina of *Atlas*, the power of *Zeus*, the courage of *Achilles* and the speed of *Mercury*.

One of Captain Marvel's nicknames, "the Big Red Cheese," suggests that the character's adventures will be lighter fare than those of his contemporaries. While Batman is referred to as the World's Greatest Detective and Superman is hailed as the Last Son of Krypton, Captain Marvel is tagged with the belittling label The Big Red Cheese. Even though Doctor Sivana, a supervillain, first disparagingly ascribed the name to his arch-nemesis, fans of the superhero have appropriated the moniker and use it as a sign of affection.

Jackson Bostwick played Captain Marvel from 1974-1975 in the live-action television show *Shazam!*. With only a handful of credits to his name, Jackson was a relative newcomer when he was cast in the lead role. "I walked in and met the producer, Bob Chenault. Bob told me later that he knew when he heard my voice and saw my smile that I would be their Captain Marvel. I didn't realize that they had been looking for more than four months! They had narrowed it down to four people, and had gone from actors who were athletes to athletes who were actors. Now they were back to actors who were athletes."[31]

Shazam! was not a sophisticated meditation about a conflicted superhero; and since the show was aimed squarely at children it wasn't dark. In the series, Billy Batson drove around in an RV (because nothing says high-adventure like a recreational vehicle) with his guardian (played by Les Tremayne), is aptly named the Mentor. As the opening narration informs us, Captain Marvel's "never ending mission: to right wrongs, to develop understanding, and to seek justice for all in the time of dire need."

In each episode, Billy (played by Michael Gray) encounters someone, often an adolescent, who is going through a hard time. When it's time for Billy to seek counsel from Solomon, Hercules, Atlas, Zeus, Achilles, and Zeus, he calls on them by passing his hand over a glowing orange orb and says, "Oh, Elders, fleet and strong and wise, appear before my seeking eyes." The elders, who appear in animated form, impart bits of wisdom and advice that will invariably prove useful later in the show. In the first episode of the series, *The Joy Riders*, Achilles quotes Shakespeare to Billy: *"This above all: to thine own self be true."*

The bad guys in the show are not supervillains intent on dominating the world. Instead, they are often young, misguided and misunderstood teenagers whose biggest scheme might involve something as relatively benign as stealing a bike or taking a car for a joyride. Although Captain Marvel does sometimes rescue people from certain death during the course of an episode, his real victories more typically concern protecting children from hurt feelings and bolstering their self-esteem. In an episode called "The Delinquent," the World's Mightiest Mortal helps a boy adjust to summer camp by teaching him that "before we like others, we must first like ourselves."

Bostwick played the superhero as a comforting, paternal figure. Each episode ends with Bostwick, in character, talking directly into the camera and imparting "a valuable lesson that we can all share." Bostwick spoke to his impressionable audience about gender equality, sportsmanship, the importance of staying in school, non-violent conflict resolution, teamwork, resisting peer pressure, respecting other cultures, and concern for the environment.

After playing Captain Marvel in fifteen episodes during the first season, Jackson filmed only the first two episodes of season two before the show's producers recast his part with John Davey. The change in actors was apparently the result of miscommunication between the actor and the executives. When

Jackson Bostwick as Captain Marvel. © Warner Bros.

Bostwick was unavailable for filming, the producers thought he was refusing to work as a ploy to get an unscheduled raise. However, Bostwick has always maintained that he had a work-related eye injury for which he was seeking medical care.

Irrespective of the reasons behind the casting change, the show suffered when Davey took over the part. Davey, who played Captain Marvel for the rest of second season and for the third and final season, was simply miscast and didn't have the same affable touch that Bostwick brought to the part.

Children who grew up watching Bostwick on Saturday mornings fondly remember his gentle portrayal of the Big Red Cheese.

THE INTERVIEW

Where you a fan of Captain Marvel when you were a kid?

As a youngster, I liked that the little boy could say a magic word and lightning would strike him and he would be strong and could beat up the bullies and the bad guys – [he became] an instant Charles Atlas.

He also had a great costume with a big lightning bolt on the front, and he fought imaginative villains like Mr. Mind and the Worm, and he had weird friends like Mr. Tawny, the tiger.

Were you at all reluctant to play a superhero?

Never crossed my mind. First of all, this was a Saturday morning show aimed towards the kids, not a prime time show meant for adult fare. And secondly, the Good Captain was one of my childhood heroes along with the Lone Ranger and Tarzan.

What was your approach to the character?

I tried to offer the audience the same type of hero I grew up with in Clayton Moore's rendition of the Lone Ranger. I even talked about this with Clay – who was a good acquaintance of mine – and told him how his character was my role model growing up and that I wanted to give the present generation of kids a character that they could follow and look up to as a good guy, too.

Whereas, I can say I played the part as a professional actor, anybody who puts on a costume – whether it's just a towel as a cape, or a full-blown getup – if they have a good enough imagination, they can say "*Shazam!*" and have almost as much fun, if not more, pretending to be The Big Red Cheese as I did.

Billy Batson is a boy who turns into Captain Marvel by saying: "Shazam!" So even though Captain Marvel in an adult, he's also part kid. Did that affect how you played him?

Billy and Captain Marvel to me were two different characters with a lot of the same traits. I tried to capture a childlike innocence in order to convey Captain Marvel's uneasiness around a pretty girl. This was taken from one of C.C. Beck's Golden Age traits that he gave to Marvel. I think Solomon's wisdom (Solomon represents the first 'S' in the acronym Shazam) about the guiles of the fairer sex served Captain Marvel well in this respect.

How did it feel to wear the costume and to put on the cape for the first time?

When I wore the costume, I never felt that it was me actually being the character, but that it was some totally different being that I could somehow imagine secretly watching through a peep hole. I think the reason for this was that I was constantly concentrating on the appearance that I would be projecting to a bunch of five-year-old kids and, further, that I was presenting the costume properly for their oh-so-critical eyes (no wrinkling of the Danskin tights, etc.). As for the cape, it was made of pure silk and was somewhat heavy, but all and all, it presented no problems.

And as for my delivery of the dialogue, I always made sure that I was never talking down, or preaching, to the kids – which I felt would be an immediate turnoff for anyone, much less a super-judgmental, younger audience. So, you see, there was very little time remaining for me, Jackson Bostwick, to think I was actually the Good Captain who could fly and stop bullets.

Did wearing the costume make you feel heroic?

Not in the least. My feeling was that Captain Marvel has the power; he doesn't need to flaunt it. And I followed that approach.

Did that feeling of power impact you in your everyday life? Did the character's confidence spill over to you?

Maybe a little of Jackson Bostwick spilled over into Captain Marvel, but Captain Marvel never inhabited Jackson Bostwick.

For better or for worse, did people treat you differently when you wore the outfit?

On the set the crew treated me with the same aloofness that crews would treat any other actor: "Don't touch that cable, pal!" Sometimes better, sometimes worse. Not really, they all were great. On a different note, though, I did notice, initially, when going out in the evenings on a first date that normal girls – as opposed to the kinky ones – would usually be taken aback if I arrived in full costume, so eventually I opted to being a little more discreet and would wear it under my street clothes and use the cape more as an accessory. However, toward the end of the evening I assure you, kinky or not, they all would be howling, "*Shazam!*" Just kidding!

What were your family and friends' reactions to your "being" Captain Marvel?

My family and most of my friends took *Shazam!* for what it was – a Saturday morning show that was enjoyable to watch and thought it a hoot to see me in tights. As for me "being" The Big Red Cheese, they all would get a kick out of seeing the reactions on people's faces when we were together and total strangers (adults, as well as kids) would stop me in restaurants, or walking down the street, or visiting noted hotspots like Disneyland, Magic Mountain, etc., and would ask me for an autograph. My dad, a brilliant neurosurgeon, once told me that he knew things must be going all right with me when back home he and mom were no longer introduced as Dr. and Mrs. Bostwick, but as Captain Marvel's mom and dad.

In people's minds, did the magic of being Captain Marvel transfer over to you. Unconsciously, do you think people thought of you as Captain Marvel?

Unconsciously, maybe not. More like consciously. When the show was on, I imagine the kids sitting in front of their television sets pretty much got into the spirit of things and would go along with me being the Good Captain. But as far as an adult watching the show, I would certainly hope they could smile and reflect back to their childhood fantasies and the heroes they grew up with and maybe suspend their disbelief for a half hour or so of pure escapism, but when it was all over, be able to have a reasonable enough grasp on reality that they could step out of the illusion and get on with their lives – the same as I and millions of other young folks eventually did growing up with The Lone Ranger and Tarzan.

However, at the time, I discovered in some of the fan mail I received that there was a certain amount of overly zealous hero worship (both male and female) which could have been seen as a bit disturbing to say the least, especially, knowing that it was a mere fictional comic book character that had evoked these enormously powerful emotions and beamed these individuals out of some galaxy far, far away. So, consciously, yes, I think that some fans can be excessively adoring, sometimes even a little spooky.

For fun, have you ever dressed up as Captain Marvel for Halloween?

Twice, once in Newport Beach, California, and again, in Las Vegas, Nevada, and both were private get-togethers with friends.

How important has playing Captain Marvel been to your life?

As a person, I'm still, Jackson Bostwick, and it hasn't had any affect on my outlook, or my basic philosophies, on life; and as far as the scheme of things go, I'm only the second guy in history to play the character and I have no control over that.

Who would in a fight: Superman vs. Captain Marvel? And why?

Captain Marvel would triumph. Why? Magic – *Shazam!*

Nicholas Hammond is Spider-Man

More than twenty years before Tobey Maguire and Andrew Garfield brought the web-slinger to life in a billion-dollar-plus franchise, Nicholas Hammond played Spider-Man on television in *The Amazing Spider-Man* (1977-1979). Unlike Maguire's hundred million-dollar budgeted films, Hammond's show was made with pocket change (or so you'd think after watching a few episodes).

Hammond, who achieved some fame for playing one of the Von Trapp kids in *The Sound of Music* and for kissing Marsha Brady on a memorable episode of *The Brady Bunch*, is still very proud to be recognized as Spider-Man, and it's not easy to be recognized when your superhero costume covers your face.

Many heroes like Superman, Wonder Woman and Aquaman, don't bother to wear a mask. The vast majority of those who do – among them, Batman, Batgirl, Captain America, the Green Lantern, the Green Hornet, and the Green Arrow – wear a cowl or a mask that reveals their jaw line. When Stan Lee's creative partner, Steve Ditko, designed the outfit in 1962, he had a practical (as well as aesthetic reasons) for completely concealing Peter Parkers face: Spider-Man is not a man, after all, but a boy. If any of Spidey's baby face were exposed, his enemies would know he was just a teenager, and a Spider-Boy is likely to seem a lot less intimidating to evildoers than a Spider-Man.

The probably unintended effect of this artistic choice is that Spider-Man fans of all races and ethnicities could see themselves as the person under the mask. Spider-Man didn't have to be another white hero; he could be a person of color. Thus many of his followers identified with him in a way that they didn't with the obviously white Superman.

Novelist Walter Mosley called Spidey "the quintessential black male hero." He wrote that: "Spider-Man's problems were much like the issues that faced most young black men in America. He was shunned and feared despite his abilities and contributions to society. He was misrepresented in the media to such a degree that no one knew or understood or even cared about him . . . He

Nicholas Hammond as Peter Parker in The Amazing Spider-Man. © CBS.

perseveres in a world that demonizes and fears him; he contributes to the survival of a nation that would rather forget he ever showed up on these shores. He is the unconscious engine that runs American's culture, as America, and in turn, it runs from the implications of his existence."[32]

In our interview, Hammond spoke passionately about how Spider-Man's appeal rises above ethnicity and how playing the superhero made him more moral. He relayed a story (echoed in his interview with me by John Newton, who played Superboy) about a time when he had the impulse to thwart a robbery in his real life but stopped when he remembered that he really wasn't a superhero.

THE INTERVIEW

[Hammond begins talking before I ask the first question.]

From the Batman and Robin days (of the 1960s *Batman*) to the days of Tobey Maguire, that's quite an arc.

And you're somewhere in between.

I'd like to think that we were one of the first who were at least trying to do it in a legitimate, serious way. And we were. They wouldn't have hired me otherwise. I was doing theater at the time I was hired. I was doing two plays in repertory at the Center Theatre in Los Angeles. We were doing Tom Stoppard's *Travesties* and Oscar Wilde's *The Importance of Being Earnest,* and I was doing the leads in both of them. Somebody from CBS saw me in the show. Playing a superhero was the last thing on my mind.

I had been very impressed with what Christopher Reeve had done. You have to give him credit because he was an actor who maintained a certain degree of gravitas in the *Superman* movies. Reeve's standards and work ethic were undeniably high. He somehow gave everyone else permission to go into that world and not feel like you were going to be doing something that would put you in cartoonland. I was about twenty-eight at the time, and I had been working as an actor since I was little. I started working here in New York when I was about eleven. Spider-Man was the first chance I had to carry my own prime time television series. I had played the lead on Broadway. I had been in a couple of movies that were very well known and I had done lots and lots of guest starring roles. I had always recognized the fact that when you walk onto the set of a television series that there's one person upon whose shoulders that show rests. Everyone's job on that entire show is dependent on that one person. I remember thinking, "What an extraordinary responsibility that would be knowing that it ain't just me who I'm responsible for. If I make an idiot of myself and the ratings don't stay high enough for the show to be renewed then there are 150 people who will be out of work. When the opportunity came for me to do it I thought, "This is another box for me to check off as an actor." Where you can say, "I climbed that mountain. I did that."

What did you like about playing Peter Parker?

The thing that any actor would love about playing Peter Parker is his vulnerability. The fact that he's vulnerable and not a muscle-bound, rock-jawed superhero. He has asthma, he lives with his Aunt May, and he's the nerd of all nerds. Then to go from that to having this thing thrust upon you. How do you deal with the moral responsibility of having this power? I thought that was an interesting question.

I used to say, "I would really like that if someone tuned in late and they didn't know they were watching a show based on a comic book." I would want them to just get involved in the story as they watched a young man dealing with his problems. I would want it to come as a surprise that he's also a superhero. I didn't want the human part to be irrelevant.

I wanted to investigate the idea that if he has to keep his identity secret what happens with girls? Any woman that he allows in his life becomes a target. If he entrusts her with his secret, then it's going to be hugely dangerous to her. I was always intrigued by that idea. He's a young guy who is very interested in girls but he can't have a relationship. That's his moral dilemma. We touched on it a little bit in a couple of episodes. I always thought it would be great to do an entire show on that. Where he's fallen head over heals for some girl and really wants to pursue her but can't.

Were you ever worried that the Spider-Man suit would upstage the rest of the show?

No, I wasn't. I probably would have been if they told me, "In this episode you're only going to be in it 20% and the stuntman will be in it 80%." Then I would think, "Where's the story there?" I understood that there was a responsibility to all those Stan Lee fans, to the millions of people around the world who loved the comic book – there was absolutely a responsibility to honor that. But at the same time I was trying to do something with it that I thought would make it better. And I never thought that I didn't get that chance because the stories are Peter's stories. They're not Spider-Man's stories.

Peter was a very complex, funny, sweet and shrewd character.

Thank you. That is very nice to hear because that was the intention. One of the things that I was very happy about – and I know that this didn't please the orthodox comic book fans – but I was very happy that the nemeses that my Peter Parker faced were real people. They weren't cartoon monsters. I know that in the films and because of the miracle of what they can do – that they can now have larger than life and fantastic evil forces that Peter goes against. Because of our budget limitations it would have been stupid for us to have attempted that.

I was happy that Peter went up against drug syndicates, corrupt scientists, and criminals. It kept it more rooted in a world that I could relate to. If I were standing there with a sword in my hand and attacking a giant bumblebee I would have thought, "Why am I here? This isn't what I do." If you convey three different emotions conflicting with one another – on one hand, I want to save the woman who is about to die, but on the other hand, I don't want her to find out my secret and at the same time I want to get my pictures back to the newspaper because I don't want to lose my job. That to me is fun. That to me is acting.

When you put the suit on for the first time how did that feel?

I really liked it. I was completely anonymous. I found it quite freeing. Truth be told, the only times that I can remember actually wearing the suit was when it was a scene with another actor. I did always say that [stuntman] Freddy [Waugh] – bless his heart – was really great at climbing up and down the building, but he was no more an actor than I was a circus performer. I said, "It's not fair to the other actors to play these scenes and do dialogue with Freddy. I will always come in and do whatever action is involved when there is going to be dialogue. I wore it quite a lot in the pilot. The suits were always evolving. The suits were a never-ending issue because the glass would fog up and you could never see while wearing them. They would be incredibly hot and they would tear. The wardrobe department kept experimenting with different kinds of material. The suit was almost completely

While Nicholas Hammond played Peter Parker, it was Fred Waugh who per-
formed the dangerous stunts as Spider-Man. © CBS.

airtight. To have it on more than half an hour was not much fun. Especially in the middle of summer in Los Angeles.

How did you approach the physical nature of the show?

I just tried to stay as physically fit as I possibly could. I went to the gym a lot. I didn't try to get enormously huge. I just tried to look like someone who was in good shape but not overly muscular. I used to say that he should look like a guy who can play a couple of sets of tennis two or three times a week. And that's about it. Not a guy who is in the weight room. I think we sort of achieved that.

How did you approach how Spider-Man moved?

This was something that I wasn't completely happy about. Freddy had this idea that he should move with these spider-like moves, which was something I wasn't totally comfortable with. We sort of have a bit of a compromise. I think even to this day, in my eye there's a difference to the way Freddy moves and the way I do. In my mind, the only time that it's justified for him to move like a spider is when he's trying to intimidate his enemies into thinking that he's a creature. In some of the fight scenes, it sort of works to make it look like Spider-Man is going to fool his adversary into thinking that I've got some skills that I don't actually have. But in the scenes where Spider-Man is just standing and talking to someone, I would just stand there and talk. He's an absolutely average guy who is no different from you or anyone else but when he wants to call upon it he can be ten times stronger than any other person on the street.

How did the suit help you in your approach to the character?

It does. It's liberating. It's a mask that you're behind. You are no longer thinking that the audience is going to be looking at you and thinking, "That's Nicholas Hammond, the actor." They are going to be thinking, "That's a powerful presence in the room." I always thought there was something anonymous about putting the suit on. When you're wearing it, you've got no features. Okay, it's a male. But other than being male there's really nothing you know about him. When the fan mail started coming in what surprised me and is than an enormous amount of fan mail was coming in from African-American kids. When I was asked to speak at schools, the reactions I would get at African-American schools were mind-blowing. Stan Lee said that was true for kids who read the comic as well.

For me – a nice little middle class white boy who had grown up in the suburbs – this was perplexing because this had never been part of my audience base. I think that show was very, very popular with kids of color because Spider-Man has no ethnicity. As soon as the suit was on, that could be them. Whereas with Superman, and a lot of other superheroes, there's always a white face there. It's a weird thing because they look at me as Peter Parker. I would walk down the streets of New York City, and if ten people called out "Hey Spidey," then eight of them would be black. Here I am this white guy, and yet they would all feel a connection, and it can't possibly be because of my face. It's got to be because when the suit is on, they can relate. That's my own sociology theory that I've developed. But I'm not kidding you, I would say to this day on the odd occasion that I still get recognized as Peter Parker it's almost always by African-Americans. They seemed to have a real love of the show.

When I went out on these readership drives to encourage inner city elementary school kids to start reading, afterwards the teachers and the principles would always come up and say, "To have you stand there and say that Peter Parker loves to read books means more than you can imagine. We can talk to them for a year and we wouldn't have as much luck at getting them to go to a library and get a book out as you saying that. Again, I can't take any of the credit myself. If I had been on some other series they wouldn't have listened to me. I just attribute it all to the suit. It has to be.

Did you ever allow yourself to feel heroic in the suit?

Of course, of course. That's part of being in character. When I say "heroic," I mean that I used to allow myself to feel capable of doing everything he had to do. I don't think there's any part of Peter that feels that he's better than anyone else or heroic in that sense of the word. But putting on the suit was part of the preparation to convince an audience that this one guy can frighten ten bad guys.

Did you feel any responsibility that you were the embodiment in people's minds of Spider-Man?

Yeah, of course. You can't help it. But it's a no win situation because you're never going to conform to everybody's mental picture [of who Spider-Man is].

Why do you think superheroes are so popular in the first place?

It's vicarious. There's a fantasy aspect to it. Superheroes do things that people would like to be able to do but can't. Seeing a mugging on the subway, they wish they could step in there and stop it. Make the bad guy go to prison. Save the innocent. But nobody does because we are too afraid. We always get pleasure when we see justice rewarded.

Superheroes are fun. They do the sort of things that children imagine they can do. They can fly. They can sail from one building to another. I remember countless times mothers coming up to me in the street saying, "My little boy broke his arm because he jumped off the top of the garage because of your show." It's that wonderful thing where kids don't say to themselves, "You can't really fly. You can't climb down the Empire State building." They say, "Oh I see. I guess if you're heroic enough, you can.

And specific to Spider-Man?

His humanity. He didn't come from the planet Zircon. He wasn't born from extraterrestrials. He's an average guy. He's just had this thing thrust upon him. Again that's part of the popularity. Part of the popularity of buying a lottery ticket. You think, "If a spider can bite him then maybe it can happen to me too." You think, "What would I do if I had his gifts?"

Spider-Man is ready to swing into action in this promotional still for The Amazing Spider-Man. © *CBS.*

What insights did Stan Lee have into the show?

Stan Lee wasn't entirely happy with the show for a lot of reasons; some of them were probably very legitimate. As far as I was concerned, he was always tremendously supportive. Very kind. Between you and me, Stan is Peter. I'm absolutely sure. I would just look at Stan and think, "Forty-five years ago this is what he would have been like." It's not so much the advice he gave me. It was more about talking with him, having lunch, and I would just try to pick off things from this guy and think, "I'll bet when you were in high school and you were in college you were the skinny guy with glasses who was really good at drawing pictures in the back of your notebook of pretty girls without many clothes on. And you parlayed that into a career. This is a little bit of Walter Mitty in Stan that I find completely endearing. It's what gives him this wonderful kind of imagination and understanding of these characters. I learned a bit just from observing him. When I would ask him about the character he would say, "He's just a guy. He's just a guy." And I would think, "Yeah, he is. He's just a guy." He was good to look at and listen to.

How are you similar to Peter Parker?

I think any actor lives something of a double life. Particularly if you've been a child actor because you do have two personas. You have a persona when you're at school and you just want to fit in and be anonymous. You want to be a teenager like every other teenager. And then you have a persona when you're on a film set or on a stage on Broadway. They are radically different. They have to be radically different because you have to draw upon things different aspects of yourself.

You asked me if I felt heroic putting on the suit. In a sense when you walk onto a film set you better damn well feel pretty good about yourself or else your not going to deliver the goods. If you walk out in front of a thousand people eight times a week in Times Square at the Barrymore Theatre, it's the same thing. But you don't want to carry that same energy into algebra class because everybody is going to think you're a snob or whatever. It's the last think you want to do. So, you get used to playing two different roles. I think in that regard I'm a lot like Peter. So, it wasn't too difficult for me to understand what it would be like for Peter to run into the classroom or the newspaper office and pretend that's all he was when he's just come from being the other persona where he's had to be so much bigger than life.

Was it frustrating for you at school, where you probably just wanted to blend in, knowing metaphorically speaking than you can jump six feet but you will only jump three so that you don't stand out – knowing that you're not showing the full you?

That's a very interesting question. No one has asked me that question before. I think there is some truth to that. I think it is a little frustrating. It's weird because you're only half a person in school and you're only whole when you're doing the thing you love to do. Which is your place of power. As you said, that's where you jump the full six feet. But at school you kind of have to make yourself only jump three feet. I was the type of person who always wanted to fit in. Look normal. Not have any money. Don't treat me as though I am different. Probably in more ways than I seriously thought about there have been similarities between him and me. Frankly, including on how to deal with girls as a teenager. Suddenly you're in the most famous movie in the history of movies and every girl wants to meet you. But two months before none of them would look at you when you asked them to the dance. Well, I suppose if you're a different kind of personality you can say, "This is great!" But there was a part of me that was always thinking, "I'm exactly the same person I was two months ago. I'm sorry but I can't suddenly believe it's me who they are dying to walk down the hall with. They just want to show off in front of their friends." Maybe that was being a little tough. It puts you in a strange world. In her own inimitable way, Carrie Fischer saying after she had done *Star Wars*, "I never knew if the guy wanted to fuck Princess Leia or me." Well that's being a bit blunt about it but that's frankly in the back of your mind. It's the flip side of what Peter had where nobody wanted to be with him. They probably all wanted to be with Spider-Man but nobody wanted to be with Peter. It's the same disconnect where you're never sure if they are seeing you for who you really are or for what they want to see.

That's one of the central ideas behind this book. How much of the way people perceive you as a superhero affects the way they relate to you in your daily life?

I think that the analogy between child star and superhero is probably a fairly valid one. As we know, some child stars can't handle it at all. Stardom can have really damaging effects. I thank god that I had a lot of good stuff going on in my life – great parents, great friends, girlfriends, and all that. But it doesn't mean it's easy. You go home at night at when it's four in the morning and you're staring at the ceiling, there's a little bit of you wondering, "Which one am I? And in their mind, which one is he?"

Along those same lines Carrie Fisher said, "I'm not famous. Princess Leia is."

Yeah and I think that's a very healthy way to look at it. In my case, I had already been made well-known from something else – far more so than I ever would have been from playing Peter Parker. But it's a different sub-set. The Spider-Man fans are different from the Brady Bunch fans, who are different from *The Sound of Music* fans, who are different from the Ray Bradbury fans. [Hammond starred in the TV miniseries adaptation of Bradbury's *The Martian Chronicles* (1980) with a cast that included Rock Hudson and Roddy McDowall, who had appeared in three different Batman TV series: he played the Bookworm in *Batman* (1966) and the Mad Hatter (Dr. Jervis Tetch) in *Batman: The Animated Series* (1992) and in its spin-off *The New Batman Adventures* (1997).]

Have you ever tried to distance yourself from this association?

No. I haven't. I don't see the point in it frankly. That's where other actors make lives hard for themselves. You have to embrace roles you play. When they are over, they are over. If they're not over in the minds of the public, well there's nothing you can do about that. It's sort of like a relationship. You say there were very good things about it, but its come to an end for a reason. I should look back at it with fondness and say, "What's next?" Otherwise, you are going to get yourself into the painful spin that people do when they don't let go of a past girlfriend or boyfriend.

I ask each superhero/actor I interview to come up with a question for my next subject. John Shipp, the actor who played The

Flash, asked the question: How did playing the part affect you personally?

In a weird way it increased my sense of morality. I started to feel and act how I imagined a cop would. You think you have a greater awareness of right and wrong. A heightened morality. A heightened sense of social conscience. And also a sense of personal responsibility. Particularly towards the kids. If you have a dozen kids a day running up to you looking at you in a way where you know they totally admire you, any normal person is going think, "You know what, maybe I shouldn't get drunk and risk crashing the car. And that has stuck with me some time after the show. Because I don't want that kid picking up the paper tomorrow and reading that his hero has done that. So, you alter your behavior accordingly.

The second part of Shipp's questions is did you feel powerful playing the character and slightly impotent when you were not.

That's quite true. Once I saw a purse snatching. My instinct was to go after the guy. I was in Rome and a guy on a Vespa grabbed a woman's purse and sped off. I was on foot and started to run after the Vespa. I ran like a block and said, "What the hell are you doing? He's going fifty miles an hour through Rome traffic." I just stopped and felt like a complete fool. So yeah.

John Newton who played Superboy asks if you kept the costume?

To my bitter regret I didn't. It's that stupid thing you do at the end: I just thought, "I never want to see that thing again." It had been hot and I had sweated in it, and I was blinded by my memories of sweating in it. I wish to God I had kept it.

John Shipp grew to hate his costume. He said he called it the creature.

I can't say I felt that. I felt like it was putting on really uncomfortable ballet tights. That was full body. Covering your head. Like you were going to rob a liquor store. It was really disorienting. I was blind in that thing. It was really uncomfortable. You get pointed in the direction where the other actors were. You're in this fog. It just irritated me. I never felt like I had my wits about me.

Did you write a letter to fellow Spider-Man Tobey Maguire?

I did. [Hopefully] Did he get it?

I'm sorry, I don't know.

I wrote a long letter and sent it to his agent. I don't think he received it because he would have answered or someone would have answered. I feel very badly because it was when I first heard he got the job. The letter said, "I think it's great that you got it. I'm a big fan of your work. I'm thrilled to pass the torch to you. I know you'll do a terrific job. It's a great idea. You're just the right age. You're just the right type. Have a good time. I'm sure your movie will go miles and miles beyond what we were able to do." It was just as simple as that. I was sad when I realized that he never got. It probably went into a big stack of fan mail and he probably never got it. It was a little stupid of me. I probably should have invested a little more time in actually finding out specifically how to get it to him. I should have done it better. I hope somebody someday tells him that I did write it to him because I'd like him to know.

If I speak to him, I'll ask.

That would be great. I'm constantly being asked what I thought of the movie and about him playing it. Whether I'm sorry that I wasn't asked to be in the movies – which I'm not. My god, it's an entirely different thing. There's no reason to put me into one of the films. It would just be a stunt. It wouldn't have any kind of bearing on the story. I wish them all the best. I think it's fantastic what they've done.

It seems that your answer will be yes to this one, but knowing then what you know now would you have taken the part?

Of course. Definitely. It was an extremely positive experience. I was given a challenge, and I feel that I rose to that challenge. And to play a superhero. It opened up a world to me that I really didn't know that much about. All these people. These huge fans. To have fifteen thousand black kids in an inner city Los Angeles school look up at me adoringly and hang on every word I said, that wouldn't have happened. I have had some really rich and rewarding experiences thanks to that show.

When's the last time you've seen the show?

Oh god, years and years ago.

Do you have a copy?

Is it on DVD now?

Not officially. It's on bootleg DVD. You can have mine.

Really? Have you got the pilot?

Yes, all the episodes. [I get up to look for my *Spider-Man* DVDs.] Let me do this now before I forget.

My wife has never seen it. We have a DVD player in the hotel. That would be fun to watch them.

[I hand over the Spider-Man DVDs to the man who once was Spider-Man]. My gift to you.

Oh great. That's very kind of you. My mom will also want to watch them. I'll give them to her as a late Christmas present.

My last question is going to be a silly one.

Silly is okay.

Who would win in a fight? Spider-Man vs. The Hulk?

Spider-Man for sure. The Hulk is brute strength but Spider-Man is agility and cunning. With all due respect to the Hulk. The Hulk is a rhinoceros. A very good one and a very frightening one. If it were only a contest of brute strength than Spider-Man would lose, but he's got these other things going for him.

John Newton is Superboy

I own Superboy's cape.

That's not completely true; I own the cape that John Newton wore when he played Superboy on TV in the late 1980s. That's not completely accurate either. I own a very small swatch of fabric that purportedly was cut from the actor's cape. I know the swatch is authentic because I bought it on eBay for the whopping price of $16.50 plus shipping and handling. There's no way an item this rare or valuable could be a fake. Plus it comes with a "certificate of authenticity" – a document that's impossible to fabricate.

Truth is I'd like to meet the butcher who thought it would be a good idea to cut up the unique piece of memorabilia into hundreds of tiny little pieces. As Indiana Jones would say, "That belongs in a museum!"

I would like to own Superboy's entire costume. If only I had an extra $6,000, then I could have purchased one at an auction in 2007, but apparently, my shortsighted wife thought that the money would be better spent on our children's college education. Or rent. Or food. Personally, I think the suit would be a good investment for the little ones. And even if it weren't, I probably would have looked very heroic in it. But alas I read the fine print and discovered that the seller didn't even possess Superboy's red boots. So what would be the point in getting a costume if it wasn't complete? Any hero will tell you, you're never fully dressed without the boots.

After *Superman III* was released, Alexander and Ilya Salkind, (the producers of the first three Superman movies) were looking for other ways to exploit their franchise. So they shaved about ten years off Superman's age and shrunk him down from the big screen to the small screen for their new show, *Superboy* (1988-1992).

The Salkinds cast John Newton in the dual role of Clark Kent/ Superboy. At the time, Newton, who later went on to star in the reboots of the TV shows *The Untouchables* (1993-1994) and *Melrose Place* (1998-1999), didn't have a lot of on-camera acting experience. If you watch the episodes in order, you can actually see the actor improve as he got more comfortable in the role. While reading this interview, note how critical Newton is of his *own* performance.

Newton played Superboy in 1988, in the first season of *Superboy*, which explored Clark Kent's college years and his love for Lana Lang, who was played by the fetching Stacy Haiduk. Newton didn't return to the show the following year due to a salary dispute. *Superboy*, which was renamed *The Adventures of Superboy*, continued for three more seasons with Gerard Christopher in the title role.

Superman is one of my favorite superheroes. I've always been attracted to his powers – his ability to leap tall buildings in a single bound, to look through walls, and to fly. But I was never able to relate to Superboy's personality. To me he seemed too much like an overgrown boy scout – too good, too uncomplicatedly decent – I couldn't empathize with him.

Moreover, I always found the mere existence of Superboy problematic. If Clark Kent lived in Smallville, where Superboy routinely and publicly saved the day, when he grows up, moves to Metropolis, and fights crime as Superman, wouldn't someone make the connection that Clark and Superman were one in the same? Like most people, I wasn't at all alienated by the fact that he was a virtually indestructible alien who wore red and blue tights and cape. I fantasized about Superman's powers and I ignored the rest.

David Goyer, one of the writers of *Man of Steel* (2013), seemed to have had similar reservations. In an in-depth interview with Jeremy Smith at the Ain't It Cool News website, Goyer said, "That was another thing that had always bothered me, is this idea that no one would ever, especially if they were aliens, be able to figure out that Superman might've been from Smallville."[33]

Even as a kid and at a wish-fulfillment level, I found Superboy to be utterly unsatisfying. He seemed like a diluted version of Superman. Why would a child want to be the younger and less powerful Superboy when he could imagine himself to be the older and a great deal stronger Superman?

Unlike me, Newton was able to relate to Superboy. He thinks of Superboy as an example of living up to one's potential and as being a role model who puts others before himself. In his book *Reading Comics*, Douglas Wolk wrote, "Oddly enough, the 'what does this character metaphorically stand for' schema" is difficult to 'apply' to Superman." Wolk concludes that the character is a metaphor for "human perfectibility . . . Superman is effectively capable of doing anything, humble and compassionate . . . the catch is that he's not actually human except for the extent to which he's made himself human; Kryptonite – the remnants of his home planet – is the thing that reminds him that he's not a real Earthling."[34]

More than twenty-years after he hung up his cape, Newton was given an opportunity to realize his dream of playing an adult Clark Kent and Superman in two charming animated shorts, *Superman Classic* (2011) *and Superman Classic: Bizarro (2012),* in which Newton also voiced Superman's imperfect doppelgänger Bizarro.

During our conversation, I was struck by how much Newton identifies with and looks up to Superboy.

John Newton as Superboy. © Warner Bros.

THE INTERVIEW

Did you read Superboy comic books growing up?

As a kid, I didn't collect comics. We'd go visit my grandmother on the weekends and she had this big basket of comic books and all these Superboy comics. I don't know whose they were or where they came from. Some of them were *Action Comics* and some of them were *Superboy* comics from the 1960s. I now suppose she bought them because she thought us grandkids would like them. But I remember being fascinated. There was one issue with Superboy in the boxing ring. He was saying, "I've got to get that bad man" or something. And he's punching the dirty boxer out of the boxing ring. I remember as a kid thinking they were so cool, and I used to love those comics. So when I got the job I thought, "That's interesting."

How did you approach playing the characters of Clark Kent and Superboy?

You know it was such an unusual type of role – obviously. I was very young and other than commercials and theater it was my first real, meaty, actual role. So I didn't have a lot of experience. I had just finished a two-year acting program. I was kind of intimated by it. There was one part of me that was disappointed that the show was about Superboy and not Superman. I wanted to play a more manly superhero. Superboy is kind of a teasing thing. My brothers would always tease me. I am the youngest of five and so they used to always call me the "boy." I was the "baby." So, when the show was called *Superboy,* they used to always tease me that way about it.

I took playing the part seriously. In hindsight, I probably took it too seriously. I would have done a lot of things differently if I had the chance to go back. Like a lot of things in life, you can look back at them and think that.

For me, my approach was to think, "What would it really be like to have these qualities? To be someone who has risen above the kind of limitations of humanity and embraced all the qualities we would have if we were using 100% percent of our brain? If we were in touch with all the esoteric qualities that religion promises, that Nietzsche wrote about.

In mythology, it says we can fly. A lot of mythology says we can have these kind of superhuman strengths. I study it very seriously because I have had a very disciplined spiritual practice in my life of meditation and marital arts. I felt this was one more avenue to explore that.

How would you have approached the characters differently if you went back?

Oh my God. I would have done *everything* differently. It was what it was. It's like getting upset at a dog for barking. I was young. Creatively, I would have done things very differently. I was so afraid of being compared to Chris Reeve that I went the other way. I didn't want to play him bumbling and stuff like that. I would have played Clark more insecure but not nerdy or bumbling. I would have played him not sure of himself. Like someone coming of age. I think *Smallville* probably touched on a lot of that. Although I haven't seen the show, I would have guessed that they touched on a lot of things that would be interesting about an adolescent Superman. You know the obvious stuff. Stuff that we didn't touch on during the twenty-six episodes that I did. I never saw the show after I left.

Creatively, you want to do things differently if you did them over again. But we can't change the past. There's a certain maturity that comes being present in your life, realizing that you did your best and deciding to move on. It's hard to look back and think that I wish I acted differently.

It seems to me that the biggest traps in playing the parts is making Superboy too much of a boy scout and making Clark so klutzy that he ceases to feel real and multi-dimensional.

Yes. To me what makes any superhero interesting is his weakness and his humanity. Nobody relates to a king on a throne. That's why Jesus, Abraham, Siddhartha , Buddha were seemingly normal people. At least they climbed the ranks. So people can relate to them. If you're just super, and you can do everything and you can kick everybody's ass, then it gets boring. To make a story interesting is for the character to have an Achilles' heal and see how the hero deals with that. Adolescence, in and of itself, can be an Achilles' heal.

You're right, there are a lot of pitfalls in playing superheroes. From a storytelling perspective, it's been almost exhausted. I can only imagine going back and watching every episode of *Smallville* and the seventy or so episodes of *Superboy* they did after me - and they've probably exhausted all those scenarios.

How did it feel to wear the costume for the first time in a heroic situation?

The first time I wore the costume was for a screen test and it was Chris Reeve's actual costume. It actually fit me, which was odd. We have the same shoe size. He's taller than I am. But the torso had shrunk; it had been in a storage facility over in England. They had gotten it out and they were fabricating new costumes for the series. But they had the original one for the screen test.

It was very intimating putting on Chris Reeve's costume. The whole thing felt surreal. It's like walking on the moon. Yeah it was great. But looking back the whole thing seemed like a surreal chapter in my life.

The first time I felt the superhero-ness was the first time I was on the crane. Which was without the costume. They were doing tests with the wire effects guys. I took to it naturally. They said they'd never seen someone take to the wires like they did. I wish they had said that about the acting.

There were times when the wires wouldn't work properly and I was disappointed. Because I felt that I got so into character that I felt like I was actually flying. I didn't delude myself. But I was so in the moment that I would put my arms up to fly, which was the cue and I wouldn't go up. I'd be like, "What happened? What went wrong?"

I think that the crew and cast must try to create a situation where you feel heroic and powerful, that feeling can transfer over to you - even just a little bit.

What happens with any actor on any show - unless you're a guest star - is that you're invisible and the lead gets treated like royalty. It's a form of modern royalty. All the star's jokes are funny. So they actually think they are funnier than they are because the whole crew is laughing. But a lot of times they don't realize that they are not funny. People have to treat them that way. They want to kiss butt. They don't want to lose their job. It can only behoove them to schmooze with the powers that be. That happens with any kind of character on a movie set or a TV series.

With Superman I think that would fall right into it. I think that an actor would use that treatment to support the character and to straighten their presence.

We missed this big time and I made the point so many times with the writers and the director that it finally set in. I would say, "Superman doesn't get his powers so much from who he is but how people react to him." I'd fly into a scene and the extras wouldn't even look at me. The extras would be walking around like they were on campus and wouldn't react when I arrived. I was like, "I just flew in. I've come in here to save the day and you guys are just walking by. Come on."

Did you feel that Superboy costumes did a lot of the work for you in seeming heroic?

The Superboy costume is a thinly veiled skin. You almost feel more vulnerable, more exposed. Obviously, I wore a cup. I don't know about Chris Reeve. I think he wore a cup too. When you're wearing the suit, you're more vulnerable. If you get a little heavy or if you perspire there's nowhere to hide, man.

Does that feeling affect how you play the part? You're feeling more vulnerable when you're meant to appear invulnerable.

No, you can't think about that. I would will myself not to sweat. We were in Florida, 100% humidity, 95 degrees, wool cape with a spandex outfit in the direct sunlight, and I'm being physically active. One wet spot completely darkens the suit. I would literally get to the point where I would will myself not to sweat. It felt to me to be a superhuman quality to do that. I'm not saying I never sweat. We would take the costume off and cool down. But when you're in a scene, and some of those locations weren't air-conditioned. - one set was a freezer, which wasn't plugged in and it was probably 120 degrees in there at times -you can't sweat or your day becomes very long and it costs them a lot of money.

Who do you think is the real identity: Superboy or Clark Kent?

It would have to be Superboy. It would be Superboy in Clark Kent's clothes. You know, Superboy's costume is all marketing. It has to be. Superboy has to market himself somehow. But in real life a real superhero would never put on a costume. A real superhero would be behind the scenes. A real superhero wouldn't need the glory. He wouldn't need all that. He would just do what he does because it's who he is.

Do you think of Superboy primarily as a metaphor or as source of entertainment?

No, it's all metaphor. Any great story is metaphor. The Bible is all metaphor. The Old Testament, The New Testament. The problem is when people take stuff literally and they miss the message. Back in Shakespearean days, in order to get your message out you had to go underground with it. To me that is symbolic of the unconscious. If a girl is a certain weight and she doesn't feel beautiful then you can't just go up to her and make her feel beautiful. She's not going to hear you. But if you tell her a story about a sheep, and the sheep did this and that, then you're totally communicating.

You're doing two things - you're communicating to her unconscious so that so that she can actually hear you; and you're not taking credit for giving her the compliment. Because you threaded it into a story and you don't have to take personal responsibility for the information.

And so specifically what is the metaphor behind Superboy?

Aspiring to who are you really. Who are you really? Are you writing paperback novels or do you aspire to write a piece of literature that they'll teach in school? You as a writer, Mark. Who are you? Who are you really that you're not being. And everyone has that. Everyone has that quality. They know they're supposed to be doing this and yet they're showing up this other way.

Being the authentic you.

Then there is a deeper question, which is: Why aren't we doing that? Why do I get up in the morning and have a Twinkie instead of a piece of fruit when I know that the piece of fruit will further me in my life and the Twinkie will not. That's a stupid analogy for something much bigger. We do that constantly in our lives. We are afraid of success, we are afraid of greatness. We are afraid of standing up on a podium and screaming the truth or singing our song – the Mark song. And we all do this in our lives and the question is why?

So if a great mythology piece can communicate to our psyche or to give us permission on some level or to show us the way – which I think all the Christian myths speak to. Jesus wasn't saying follow me, meaning "Worship me." He was saying, "Do as I do." He didn't want people going to church to worship him. That's the stupidest thing ever. He wanted people doing good. Treating their neighbors as themselves and so on and so forth. That to me is so obvious. And we all miss that. We're all trying to eat the menu when we should be eating the meal. You can't eat the menu. It's not the meal. It describes the meal.

In terms of your metaphor, do you think the authentic self is Superboy and the boundaries and hurdles that we create for ourselves are as Clark Kent? [Long pause] Or did I go too far 'round the bend there?

[Warmly] Yeah, I think you went around the bend. I don't know if it's that complicated. I really think it's simpler than that. I really think we need to simplify a lot. Simplify it as much as we can and then simplify it some more. What's really important in your life? Figure out what that is and do it. And if you're not, take responsibility for that. But don't stick your head in the sand. Don't turn the TV on. Don't take a swig of something that's going to make you not feel. Because the truth is painful. Through that pain is alchemy, and alchemy is transformation and out of the fire rises the Phoenix. And that's what we need to do. All of us. Everybody. The whole world. Because otherwise we're not going to make it. These mythologies give us the clues. And it's our turn to pick up the pace, do it, live it.

In mythology what function does a character like Superboy serve?

There is an element of this is who you can be if you lived up to your full potential that's deep in our psyches. I read a great quote recently, which said: "On the last day of your life, Hell is meeting who you are and not who you could have been." I think a lot of us live mundane lives. We function day to day, hand to mouth. We get home and we look for escapism. We don't deal with our feelings or with our emotions. We're looking to try to escape to anywhere but the moment we are in. I think what these characters do is to allow us to look at what we could be. To being super. To being more.

On the other hand, we can also relate to the secret identities, to being underdogs in our lives. Even Bill Gates. Everybody looks at him and thinks he's some type of superhero. Maybe financially he is. But maybe his marriage sucks. Or maybe he feels like a nerd. Or maybe he doesn't feel that he's any good at sports. Or whatever. We relate to these superheroes because we all have that within us. We have this potential being that is way more than what we are. And it's a form of escape to watch these other people doing it.

I was trying to figure out beside his powers, what made Superman so popular. Then I came across a quote from a deleted scene from *Superman*. In it, Jor-El asks Superman, "When does a man's obligations to those around him exceed his obligations to himself?"

That's the root of Judaism right there. If you go to the core mystical route of Judaism, that one phrase sums it right up. At least from my studies. For Jewish kids growing up in Cleveland, the question that Superman's father asks is the root of Judaism. It's all about service. We've come so far from that in society. It's all about self-service. A lot of traditional religions put stock in family. It's for the family, but can you go even beyond that? Can you do it for the community?

And do it not because you want to be famous, not because you want the recognition, not because you want people to approve of you, not because you want to look good in God's eyes but to do it because it's who you are. Because it's the core of our being. It's what makes humanity work. That's why it's not working right now. We're all about secular, tribal stuff and commercialism and capitalism and it's not working.

I wasn't intending to ask you the following question, but you just said something that suggested it. Is Clark Kent a nice Jewish Boy who turns into a gentile?

A goy? That's funny. I never thought about it that way. That's funny. Wow. That's a great take on it. That's interesting. Let's take the Jewishness out of it. I could see these kids – just because they wrote comic books – probably aspired to posses all the physical qualities that they probably didn't have. Let's be honest. They were these traditional comic book nerdy guys. The people who write the comics traditionally see themselves as non-athletic and they want to get the girl. And in the sheep's clothing would be the Clark persona and the girls don't get Clark. But when he turns into Superman, woman love him. Then he does well. Then he's strong. That's a great take on it.

I think Siegel and Shuster were trying to assimilate into society and were attempting to figure out how to do that without losing their identity.

That's great. That's brilliant. That'll be a great chapter in your book. I haven't read a lot of books about superheroes since the show. Probably none because I've tried to distance myself a little bit. But that's great. I don't know if anybody has written about that.

When you first got the part were you thrilled or did you have any reluctance to playing a superhero?

I had a huge reluctance. Two reasons. One I didn't want to go into syndication history and never work again. And two, is that the show was about Superboy and not about Superman! I wanted them to call it *The Adventures of Young Superman*. If they had done it, it would have been an entirely different series. I really feel that way. I think a lot of people don't know who Superboy was and they didn't take it seriously.

Unfortunately, [series producers] the Salkinds had licensed out the name Superman. They couldn't use it. They licensed it to the Cannon/Golan Globus Company for those guys to do *Superman IV*. They weren't able to use anything to do with Superman. But because Superboy was his own entity they got away with it. I think there was a lawsuit but Superboy was its own entity with its own comic book.

What did your family and friends think about your being Superboy?

If I had come from Los Angeles, more of a hip community, I think it would have been different. But I came from North Carolina and humble beings. No one in my family had ever been in show business. No one we knew had ever been in show business. So I think it was cool to them. It actually turned into a little bit of a hassle. For years, my nephews and nieces called me "Superboy." They didn't call me by name. It was so annoying. Especially after the show was done. They'd see me twice a year at holidays in person, but they would see me hundreds of other times on TV and that was as Superboy. They'd watch the show; it was cool for them.

Did you feel a responsibility to carry on the tradition of the character? Or was it just a cool job?

I definitely felt that. I totally felt that responsibility. If someone wanted me to smoke pot I'd say, "No, I can't do that." If I ever got into trouble with the law, I thought it would be a horrible image for kids. I took it seriously for years after the show was first aired because of reruns and things like that. My driving habits are another story.

What do you think the biggest perk of having played a superhero?

I don't think there is one to be honest with you. Other than having had the experience. Anything that you do in life – good or bad – makes you a stronger. It makes you a better person if you integrate it and learn from it. Other than that I can't say there is one. I think it has a lot of pitfalls and traps in it. But I don't know if there are that many benefits from it.

What do you think are the pitfalls and traps?

The obvious one is ego and getting caught up in it. A lot of the holier-than-thou stuff that comes with celebrity. Take the story "The Emperor's New Clothes." The way that you're treated has an affect on you. I'm sure, to an extent, it affected Christopher Reeve his entire life. I'm sure he would have loved to have walked away from it and have people forget that he ever played that role. I think that it haunted him in some ways. I think that's also the case with George Reeves.

Does having played Superboy feel like a big weight to carry?

No. No. If I had done all 100 episodes and never worked again it would have been a huge weight. I luckily went on to do other projects and to improve creatively and artistically. In my own mind at least. It's not something that I carry around. It's definitely a notch in my belt. I'm grateful for the experience and it was a great first job. So, it's not a burden for me.

Have you ever felt a need to distance yourself from this association?

All the time. I didn't have it on my resume for two years. I didn't ever put *Superboy* on my resume. I was so wanting to distance myself from it. I think it was a combination of false humility and also not being proud of my work. There's been other work that I've been more proud of. But I'm not proud of my work on that show. I think I had my moments. To be honest with you, I just don't know if I was ready for it.

Since you feel that, why are you kind enough to participate in this book?

Because I did the work so I can't pretend that I didn't. I think those who teach are those who most need to learn. The fact that I'm able to speak about it means to me that I've made my peace. Maybe someone can learn from something I have to share about something. Who knows? Lord knows I've learned from other people sharing what they've been through. Whether it be good or bad. There are all kinds of stories out there and we take what we need to hear. So why not share my experience? I think it's interesting for someone to be honest. Instead of saying, "Yeah, I'm so great." But that's bullshit. I can't say that.

What would an actor know about playing a superhero that a civilian wouldn't know or understand?

I think all of it. Until you've done it, I don't know if you can really relate to any of it. William Shatner probably spilled more of the beans than he should have when he said how sick he was of having all the people come up to him and telling him about *Star Trek* episodes. [In a skit on *Saturday Night Life*, while playing a version of himself at a sci-fi convention] Shatner said, "Get a life."

I'm *not* saying that though. I'm saying that he went a bit overboard. But I think there's a certain amount of that that a lot of people playing these familiar characters feel. A lot of people want to be famous. And when they are famous they don't want to be famous anymore. I think there's a lot of that that goes on.

I'm asking each superhero to ask their fellow superheroes a question. John Shipp, who played The Flash, asks: Was there ever a boomerang effect on them personally? Personally. Not professionally. Not publicly. But privately. Was there ever a boomerang effect in situations where they deeply regretted not having an extraordinary ability to do good? When you got out of the suit did you ever feel a particular sense of inadequacy?

Definitely not. In fact, if anything else, I probably assumed some of those heroic attributes and roles when I didn't have the suit. I think there's a part of my personality that probably has those qualities anyway. I swear on my life this is a true story. I actually saw a mugging. This guy actually took this other guy's wallet, and when he started screaming, I started chasing the mugger down. I don't know how many blocks. I'm running through New York City. It was like out of the frickin' movies. I thought, "This is fucking ridiculous. And no one's going to believe me." I was late for the shoot and I had to tell them why. I said, "You're never going to believe this." But yeah, I chased this mugger down. Eventually there were four or five of us because I was yelling a head saying, "Grab that guy." And he went into a building. Luckily the elevator wasn't there or he could have gotten away. We all pinned him down and called the cops. Some guy from Atlanta got his wallet back. That kind of thing. To answer your question I would say, "No, it's the opposite." I would say if anything, part of the character bled into my personal life.

Do you identify with Superboy?

I think we all do on some level. We all aspire to be more. But there's no part of me that feels like a superhero. If anything I feel the opposite. I think anybody who actually needs to be a superhero actually feels less than adequate. If you study the hero's personality, the hero is someone who is usually plagued with guilt, who doesn't think they are enough, and that's how they are able to commit these superhuman acts of running into a building or things like that. They feel there is something lacking there.

For fun, for Halloween, have you ever dressed up as Superboy?

Hell no. I would refuse to appear in costume in public.

The producers asked you to?

Oh, all the time. I would refuse to. I would go as Clark Kent. I wouldn't appear in public at a store opening or at a mall. Although we did have a reveal at the top of the Empire State Building and I had the costume under my shirt. That was before we actually started shooting the series. They were just announcing the series. And I popped my shirt open for photos. But to answer your question about dressing up for Halloween no, I wouldn't do it.

Would it feel silly?

It's not that it feels silly. It's like, would you sleep with your ex-wife from ten years ago? You know what I mean. Maybe someone else would like to. But not with your ex-wife.

I get the sense that some of the actors felt they were treated as objects when they were dressed in the superhero costumes.

That's exactly how people treat you like. As an object. In fact, as a joke the Assistant Director on the show would say, "Bring in the Superboy." When they were ready for me on set they would say, "Bring in the Superboy." It was perfect. I loved it. That sums it up perfectly. You know it wasn't about me. It had nothing to do with me personally. . "Bring in the Superboy." It could have been anybody playing the part.

Any Superboy will do.

[Laughing] "Bring in the Superboy." I love that.

Who would win in a fight: Superboy or Batman?

Superboy would kick Batman's ass. Because Batman relies on a lot of trinkets and weaponry and little things like that. But based on pure strength and the ability to fly I think Superboy would pretty much kick his ass.

Matt Salinger is Captain America

It's always been difficult for me to comprehend the appeal of Captain America. I've perceived him not as an independent-thinking and altruistic individual but rather as a blunt instrument of the state – an unquestioning automaton designed to serve at the will and whim the United States government, irrespective of whether the government's policies were wise or reckless. Apparently I wasn't the only one.

In an essay for the *New York Times* called "Star-Spangled Schlemiel," Austin Grossman, the game designer turned novelist, wrote: "The Captain was a propaganda stunt from the get-go: a former art student, Steve Rogers, finds himself pumped up with a super-soldier formula, dressed up in stars and stripes, and sent out to the front lines of World War II to boost morale . . . Captain America was more like the guy on a street corner dressed as a hot dog. Trapped in a branding exercise, he literally wrapped himself in the flag, red, white, and blue painted onto chain mail, like a super-patriotic Renaissance Fair attendee."[35]

I believe that Austin Grossman and I can be excused for coming to similar conclusions. The character's very name binds him to the America's military; he is a Captain in the United States Army. He is obligated as a soldier to follow orders: he is not permitted to question authority.

Captain America was created by Joe Simon and Jack Kirby in the 1940s to bolster the nation's morale, to win patriotic support the war effort, and by doing so they hoped to help bring the war to a victorious conclusion. Captain America seemed to be doing a good job of thwarting Germany's expansion. In the very first issue of *Captain America*, published in March of 1941, the super soldier socks Adolph Hitler square across the kisser. His mission was undisputedly a noble one. Hitler's forces were advancing and on the precipice of exterminating millions of Jews, homosexuals, and others whom the Führer capriciously deemed undesirable.

In eight pages, the first issue depicts Steve Rogers' journey from being a patriotic American who wants to enlist in the army, but who for health reasons cannot, to being a super-powerful soldier, transformed by a serum that alters his "body and brain tissues, until his stature and intelligence increase to an amazing degree!"[36] At the end of the story, readers were invited to send 10¢ to the publisher in exchange for a Captain America Badge (in the colors of red, white, and blue naturally) and a membership card, which enlists them to "solemnly pledge to . . . assist Captain America in his war against the spies in the U.S.A."

Given the exaggerated nationalistic trappings of the character, it's easy to understand how readers like Austin Grossman and I, who were introduced to the character in more cynical times, formed our unsympathetic views of Captain America. But I must confess that at that time I had read very few of the original Captain America comics. I was forming my conclusions based on a congeries of vague impressions that I culled from the zeitgeist, from scattered bits of (often distorted) information, and a mash-up of the prevailing attitudes of pop culture during 1970s and 1980s. As I delved more deeply into the comics and thought more about the historical context in which they appeared, I discovered that I didn't really know Steve Rogers.

As early as 1954, with America prospering and as the importance and painful impact of the war were becoming fading memories, Captain America's relevance also receded. This led to diminishing sales and to the cancellation of the comic. No new Captain America stories appeared for a decade.

In 1963, a trial balloon designed to gauge reader interest in the character was floated. Marvel published a story in Strange Tales #114, in which a villain named the Acrobat tries to outsmart the Human Torch by pretending to be Captain America. After the Acrobat is exposed and his nefarious plot is thwarted the issue ends with the Human Torch, now back in the non-flammable form of Johnny Storm, asking himself, "[I] wonder whatever did become of [Captain America]? Is he still alive? Will he ever return? I'd sure like to know!" On the heels of Storm's question a note from the editor reads: "You guessed it! This story was really a test! To see if you too would like Captain America to return! As usual, your letters will give us the answer!"[37]

Fans sprung into action and wrote in favor of Captain America's homecoming. Marvel responded to the outpouring of support in *The Avengers #4* (1964). In the issue, the real Captain America is found in the Artic in a block of ice. We learn that his body was frozen in ice after the plane he was flying for a mission was shot down. His body is recovered and, miraculously, he is still alive.

Captain America would eventually become disillusioned with contemporary America's domestic and foreign policies. In *Captain America #122* (1970) Captain America says to himself, "I've spent a lifetime defending the flag – and the law! Perhaps – I should have battled less and questioned more!"[38] In 1974, in the wake of the Vietnam War and President Richard Nixon's abuse of power, Steve Rogers retired his Captain America persona, and in an effort to continue protecting his fellow man without the trappings of the American flag, he resumed fighting for what's good under the name Nomad. Apparently neither Steve Rogers nor his fans could live for long without the Star-Spangled Avenger, and four issues later Rogers assumes his old identity as Captain America.

Captain America's personal politics were progressive for the time. He supported the ongoing civil-rights movement and joined forces with the first African-American superhero called The Falcon. From 1971 to 1978, they were the eponymous heroes of the comic book *Captain America and the Falcon*.

When Marvel "killed" Captain America in 2007, in a story named *The Death of Captain America*, I entertained the idea that this time the character would remain dead. But Captain America is nothing if not resilient: after Steve Roger's friend Bucky assumed the persona for a while, Steve Rogers returned in 2009. Captain America is still with us; he's still ready to fight all enemies, foreign or domestic, ordinary mortals or superhumans, who threaten our inalienable rights.

It's not really Captain America's name or costume that defines the man: it's the quality of his character. I didn't initially realize that what made, and makes, Joe Simon and Jack Kirby's creation so appealing is that Steve Rogers is a man who always seeks to do the right thing. He is noble, brave, honest, heroic, and absolutely selfless. Simon and Kirby's character would always put the needs of others above his own interests.

Most interestingly, unlike Peter Parker or Bruce Wayne, Steve Rogers demonstrated his heroic qualities even before he assumed his secret identity. Before he acquired his super powers, Rogers wanted to serve his country by joining the army. As we're told in the first issue, he "volunteered for Army Service, and was refused because of his unfit condition!" But the "frail young man" stepped into the laboratory and "calmly the young man allows him-self [sic] to be inoculated with the strange seething liquid." Although Rogers couldn't imagine the effects the serum would have, he was determined to do his part for the war efforts. Becoming Captain America didn't essentially change Steve Rogers; rather, it provided him with the means to fulfill his patriotic aspirations.

Despite his complicated feelings about the character, Grossman concludes his piece for *The New York Times* with the sentiment: "So, sure, Superman has plenty of fans, but I prefer my superheroes like Cap: earthbound, struggling, and all too human."

In 1990, Matt Salinger played the "all too human" Steve Rogers/ Captain American in the critically eviscerated feature film *Captain America*. The movie was made for $6 million, which is pocket change when compared to $35-48 million, the reported budget of Tim Burton's *Batman* (1989). Putting aside the disparity of the talents behind the camera, with those financial constraints, how could *Captain America* hope to compete with Tim Burton's spectacular gothic vision?

Captain America, which was never released theatrically, was directed by Albert Pyun, a director who has since earned a reputation for making low-budget B-movies that often go directly to video. Pyun's previous release was *Cyborg* (1989), an action movie set in a post-apocalyptic world that starred Jean-Claude Van Damme.

Pyun and Salinger had hoped that Menahem Golan, *Captain America*'s producer and the head of 21st Century Film Corporation, would use his clout to treat their project as one of his more important films. In addition to the many B-movies that Golan produced with Yoram Globus as the co-heads of Cannon Films — including the sequels in the Charles Bronson *Death Wish* series and several Chuck Norris action pictures — Golan also backed adult-minded fare, such as John Cassavetes' *Love Streams* (1984), Neil Jordan's *The Company of Wolves* (1985), Andrei Konchalovsky's *Runaway Train* (1985), Franco Zeffrelli's *Othello* (1986), Norman Mailer's *Tough Guys Don't Dance* (1987), and Barbet Schroeder's *Barfly* (1987).

Instead, Golan insisted that *Captain America* was to be made on the cheap. Such ruinous decision-making was evidently in Golan's DNA. His former company Cannon had cut the legs out of Christopher Reeve's *Superman IV: The Quest for Peace* by halving the budget shortly before production commenced.

Despite the fatal lack of support, Pyun did assemble an enjoyable supporting cast, including Ned Beatty and Ronny Cox, who worked together for the first time since John Boorman's *Deliverance* (1972). Beatty had prior superhero experience: he played Lex Luthor's dim henchman Otis in *Superman* (1978) and again in *Superman II* (1980).

Pyun demonstrated his grasp of the essential nature of the character when he observed that the "super-soldier experiment didn't make him a hero . . . he was already one and just had to find his way to it . . . The first time he puts on the costume because he's told to, the second time because he wants to and he accepts all the responsibilities that go with the symbolism."[39]

Even after the film was made, the studio cut a significant amount of vital material from Pyun's cut. The deleted footage includes character-defining and -deepening moments that, according to Pyun, explore: "Steve Rogers' confusion about his place in the modern world and whether the concept of America, right or wrong, was proper in the world today. Scenes that show his idea of heroism [are] sort of outdated. That the real heroes were individuals like Martin Luther King and Robert Kennedy. He struggles with the idea he's just a symbol with no real weight. He understands that the idea of superheroes is outdated and the whole rah-rah aspect to heroism is misguided. He better understands the values that [make] one an American and it's not defeating super villains or ridiculous evil plots."[40]

Captain America ambitiously, perhaps unwisely, attempted to encompass the entire Captain America mythos in just one ninety-seven-minute film. The first and more satisfying part of the film takes place in the 1940s, and the rest takes place in the present, where Steve Rogers is an anachronism. When Marvel Studios made their own version of Captain America in 2011, they considered but abandoned the idea of setting the film in contemporary America. Instead, with the exception of the framing device set in the present that bookends the story, the film takes place during the 1940s.

Although Pyun's movie has its faults, I'm an unabashed fan of Salinger's interpretation of Steve Rogers. Salinger captures the essential spirit and the earnestness of the character. Pyun said he cast Salinger "because he was tall and he had this sort of All-American face and plus I had really liked his audition reading because he did a great job at showing the sensitive side of Steve Rogers. He was great and could convey the hurt and pain of having to live up to someone else's idea of who he was supposed to be."[41]

In the movies, Captain America has also been portrayed by Dick Purcell in the fifteen-chapter serial *Captain America* (1944); by Chris Evans in *Captain America: The First Avenger* (2011); *The Avengers*; in a cameo in *Thor: The Dark World* (2013)), *Captain America: The Winter Solider* (2014) and *Avengers: Age of Ultron* (2015). There were also two TV movies that starred Reb Brown as the son of the original Captain America/Steve Rogers: *Captain America* (1977) and *Captain America II: Death Too Soon* (1979).

The various Captain America movies provided me with a cinematic re-introduction to the character. They also served another function; they made me want to "read the book."

I have now read or reread many Captain America comics – including the original ones written by Joe Simon and Jack Kirby. I've come to admire Simon and Kirby for the way they used their most potent weapon – their art – to try to effect social change. An old boss of mine used to say that all art is political; it's just that sometimes art reinforces the status quo and sometimes it challenges it. Through their craft Simon and Kirby proudly dared their readers to do their part to fight and to expunge a very real menace.

A final thought: one day when my young daughter Sophie was doing her math homework, she was stuck on a particularly thorny question. Ever resourceful, she took out her trusty Captain America action figure and declared, "Captain America can help me with my math." What more can one ask of a great American?

Matt Salinger as Captain America.

THE INTERVIEW

Did you read comics as a kid?

Yes, I did. At one point, I graduated from *Richie Rich, Little Lotta,* and *Little Dot* to *Captain America.* I read his comics when he was teamed up with the Falcon. It was called *Captain America and the Falcon.* I also like the Sub-Mariner. Those were the two action adventure comics that I loved. I still think they should have made a film version Captain America with the Falcon. [The two heroes team up on the big screen in 2014's *Captain America: The Winter Soldier.*] It would have brought an interesting multi-racial, multi-ethnic dynamic. Those were the two that I read.

What did you like about Captain America when you were a kid?

It was a cool costume. [Laughs] Like a lot of them, he had a good moral compass. I remember in second grade I was being beat up by one of the bullies. A guy by the name of Richard Slack, I think. The schoolyard was set up so that first, second, and third grades were together on one playground and fourth, fifth and sixth grades were on another. This guy named Chris Klink came down from the upper playground, took Richard off of me and started pounding on him. Chris Klink was the policeman of the lower playground. I remember looking up and the sun was behind him. This was the late 1960s. He had long blonde hair that came down to his shoulders. I thought this God had come down. That made quite an impression on me. When I became an upper classman I took on that role as well. I hope I lived up to his image.

Captain America had a moral compass like that, and I really liked that he was more *extra* human than *super* human. He didn't fly. He could win pretty much every event in the Olympics but he wasn't an alien. It's a similar explanation to Peter Parker being bitten by a spider. He wasn't from another planet. Captain America's powers were a chemical thing. He was just a *little* bit faster than the rest of us.

How did the movie come your way?

It was just another audition initially. I had done a couple of things already. I did a few starring roles for movies of the week but I hadn't been the starring role in a feature. I only did supporting roles in features. I had auditioned for Albert Pyun, the director, before and he sent me a couple of projects that I passed on. I think that really registered with him. Creative Artist Agency had recently signed me and they were a big powerhouse company. I think that got his attention, too. Albert said he wanted someone really human and a good actor. I became friendly with Howie Long [the football player] and apparently he offered it to Howie Long so it was kind of a line he was feeding me.

I had to go to England to get measured for a muscle suit. I mean I'm a big guy and I'm athletic. I did crew in college. But, you know, I was never a weight-lifter or bodybuilder. Jesus, it was quite a process to get fit for a suit. It was really cool but they took an entire mold of your body. Then they made a foam muscle suit first and then they put the latex on top of that.

So, you had to stay in this goo for a long time and have it dry on you. I had two straws in my nostrils so that I could breath. I remember thinking, "Wow, this is like the super serum that Steve Rogers took. They are applying it externally, they way they might have applied it internally to make Steve Rogers Captain America."

I turned the film down a couple of times because the company making it was not the most reputable company. Menahem Golan has a huge heart and loves films. [In 2014, Golan died at the age of eighty-five.] He gave a lot of people their first chance and deserves credit for those things. But he also made a lot of bad movies. He was one of those people who was attracted to the movie business because it was the Wild West. He said the future of his company was at stake based on the success or failure of *Captain America*. He talked a good game but he really let me down. He was victimized by a situation of his own creation. He was depending on revenues from other films to come in to fund *Captain America*. But the revenues never came in.

After we shot the bulk of the movie oversees, we were supposed to come back to the States to do a couple of weeks of filming here. We were supposed to go up to Alaska for a few weeks. None of that happened. When we were shooting in Yugoslavia and Italy, when we didn't get certain shots, someone would always say, "Oh, we'll get that in the States." I was just young enough and naïve enough to be trusting.

I think Albert probably really thought that we would have that chance. They basically pulled the plug and handed the footage over to their editors and told them to make the best of it. Which they did.

What did you and Albert talk about in terms of your approach to the film and what you were trying to accomplish?

It was really the humanity of Steve Rogers. We both wanted to bring out Steve Rogers and have Captain America be the uniform that he put on. To be the role that he was honored to play. But Steve Rogers lost everything. He gained this amazing ability and gained these incredible powers but lost everything else in his life. He missed out on what would have been his life as a youth had he not been frozen in ice. [Laughs]. It was the humanity of it.

What was your take on Steve Rogers and Captain America? What was your approach to handing the role?

He was a kid with a limp, with a bum leg who was very patriotic who couldn't serve his country. I asked myself what was it like growing up, what was it like on the playground being somewhat handicapped? What affect did that have on him? And then coming back to life thirty, forty years later. How aware was he about what he lost? How aware was he of what he gained. What moral questions would come to him with these powers? Would he be tempted to use them irresponsibly?

It's a situation that most humans don't find themselves in. And that comes with a charge; it comes with an expense. I wanted to play Steve Rogers. I thought if I made Steve Rogers work, made him believable, then Albert, the stunt director and the technical guys could make Captain America work. That was the division.

You refer to his costumes as a uniform, which is interesting.

Costume even seems weird to hear you say it. This was his military service. This was his way of being a patriot. It was his uniform. It was designed by the military and that's exactly the way I thought of it. I still have one uniform left. And I still have the jumpsuit. One of the uniforms was starting to get moldy in a box ...

[Interrupting] You tossed that out?

Yeah. When I put on the uniform for the first time my first thought was, "Oh my God, am I really going to wear this for eight weeks?" It was very constricting. It was hot as hell. We shot the film in the middle of the summer on the Adriatic. I lost twenty-five pounds. I couldn't do the flips and certain stunts but there were a lot of the stunts that I could do. I was running all over the place with a thick layer of heavy thick foam and latex over that. It was brutal. Just brutal.

They'd pour talcum powder and water over me, but by the end of the day I had a pool of sweat in my pants. Then when I put on the headpiece, my reaction was two-fold. I didn't like those goofy wings that they put on the helmet. I thought they never got that right. I thought *I'm going to look like a dork with these wing things*. And it also pulled my face. I already have sort of a flat nose. It really pulls at you. Instead of pulling it up, it pulls it to the sides. And that was painful.

Beyond that I also realized that I have to get used to it. I was very aware as an actor of every feeling I had because I thought that most of those feelings were also things Steve Rogers felt as well. To the degree that it was cool, I also wanted to enjoy it. It was an interesting time in America. I don't want to get into a political discussion. There have been times when I've been really proud of this country and times when I haven't, so to have an opportunity to present some of the better things of what is American. That was gratifying. I remember when I was in school in France when I was sixteen. I really felt that as an America abroad you have to really be a diplomat. You have to represent your country. I felt that immediately putting on the uniform.

I would feel that a lot more today. It would be a lot riskier to make a Captain America today when America's place in the world is much more questioned. [Author's Note: This interview took place during the height of the Iraq war when President George W. Bush was in office and the nation was greatly divided about his leadership.]

How did people react to you when you were dressed up as Captain America?

It wasn't that dissimilar than the way they react to a movie star. To the way *I* react to a movie star. "It's that . . . oh my God, that's so and so!" And I was very aware that I was not the object of that. They weren't reacting to Matt Salinger. They were reacting to Captain America and to the uniform. They were reacting to that iconic figure.

People walking by would stop and say, "Oh, my god it's Captain America. [Laughs]. So, that was fun. I love kids and wearing the costume was like being a magnet for kids. That was fun, but it was so grueling that between takes I just wanted to find somewhere cool to lie down. We did have trailers but they also seemed to be so far away that I'd just grab a chair or find a tree in the shade, slump down, and want to pass out. Then people would start coming up. I felt the pressure of representing America. We were filming in what is now Croatia. So I felt a huge responsibility.

You couldn't be rude and grumpy while wearing the Captain America uniform.

I really couldn't. I really couldn't.

I assume that the kids thought you really were Captain America.

The younger ones did. It was fun having my picture taken with the tourists. A lot of European vacationers came back from the coast with their picture taken with Captain America.

Michael Keaton has said that he found that the suit did most of the work for him.

The suit does a lot of work. It's the division of labor thing again. My work went into making Steve Rogers a believable character. It was everybody else's job – with Albert, the DP [Director of Photography], the stunt coordinator, the special effects supervisor, and the costume designer, it was their job to make everything else work. But then again a lot of their work was done by Stan Lee who was around for a while and by the way, very cool. Nice guy. A supportive guy. He really understood and liked what I was trying to do with the character. I think he had similar worries about what lay in store with us for the film. I think that's why

Marvel became a film company as a result of seeing Stan Lee's babies not treated the way they should have been. I remember his advice was meaningful. I remember he helped me as much as anyone on the film.

What do you think about the film in retrospect?

It was a missed opportunity. The script was really nice. It was a good story that was strong, wistful and heartfelt. It had a good villain. I think Albert could have probably made a fun, entertaining film given more support. But they concentrated on the big set pieces without having the budget to pull it off. So beyond having a good stunt double there really wasn't much they could do with what they had. I still have posters that say: "Coming to Theaters Everywhere!" It might have been shown in a few cities to qualify for overseas film deals. But I think it was deservedly a straight-to-video film. If you're under ten, you can like the film.

Were you at all reluctant to play a superhero?

I was and I did turn it down initially. When you're dealing with pop culture, it runs a risk of being seen as cheesy by a certain population. I took my acting and my craft fairly seriously. Not *very* seriously but *fairly* seriously. I'd been on Broadway, I had done a lot of theater, and I studied with the people you study with. I certainly had ambitions for my acting career. I realized that doing something highly recognizable and potentially cheesy would potentially endanger my goals. But ultimately I kicked myself in the ass and said, "Don't be ridiculous. You loved this guy as a kid." Part of acting is playing. I chose to embrace that and rejoice in that. I got to be a kid and run around – not with a cape – but with a shield. How cool is that? I remember Jimmy Spader [the actor James Spader, who would later voice the titular cybernetic supervillain in *Avengers: Age of Ultron*] was over for dinner right around the time that I got the part. He jumped over the couch and started chasing me around the room. [Laughs] I went into it with my eyes open and decided to take a leap of faith.

What did your family and friends think when you were offered the part?

I think they saw the opportunities that it would potentially present more than the problems.

Have your thoughts about the association changed over the years?

I was angry for a while because I thought that I was misled and let down by 21st Century [Film Corporation], the company, and Menahem. But that passed. People's careers are long. I still act but now it's merely more for fun. I don't think of it as my career. Really more for the health insurance. Like a hobby. It's something amusing and unusual. Most people haven't really seen the film. When my friends hear that I was Captain America they usually ask, "Was that a TV series?" But just the fact that I played him is cool to most people. It's interesting. And you don't meet that many people who have played a superhero, as you're finding.

Do you think Captain America had a negative impact on your acting career?

I do. Sure. It was playing a superhero that was a proven draw in comics. And the movie didn't work. And it never got into the theaters. With *Captain America*, the people making the film made the choice that they didn't really need a big name to play Captain America – and I think that was right, but when something doesn't work, people wonder why.

What reviews there were were pretty favorable for me. It wasn't as if the movie was great and I was slammed. The movie wasn't great. Certainly if it had been a big success, it would have been hugely beneficial for me. Going around on auditions later, producers and directors would say, "Oh, I see you were Captain America. What happened with that?" It would just put a cloud of doubt in casting people's minds, in producers' minds, in directors' minds, without them having known the full story.

Have you met other actors who have played superheroes?

I met Christopher Reeve. Dean Cain. I did get a chance to talk to Chris Reeve about it at a Yankees game. We talked about a shared sense of responsibility that came with the role. But *Superman* was a good, very successful movie that played on hundreds and thousands of screens. And there were sequels.

What does a fellow actor who has also played a superhero know that an outsider wouldn't?

I understand what Chris Reeve said about being a "custodian." Because the character is the character and it exists differently to different people at different times, depending on the contextual relevance of what's happening in the world. Different people see different facets of the character and seize on those and disregard others.

It's not really yours. What you're doing by portraying any iconic character, all you're really searching for is where their spirit and character and intellect intersect with yours. And depending on what aspects an audience picks up on, it works or it doesn't work. It's interesting or it's not. It's hackneyed or it's not. But that's something we would all share, I'm sure. We'd all share a sense of responsibility.

I still have a photo of me with one of my body doubles. He had these enormous bodybuilder legs. Sometimes the second unit would use him from behind. Anyway, I have a photo of him and I holding hands and skipping down a field. It was done because we were bored. But it was also done because there's a tendency to want to debunk and deflate the cliché idea of a superhero.

But that sense of responsibility would also be there. And just dealing with the pros and cons of being in the world of pop culture.

Can you separate Captain America from the politics of America?

I did. And I think anyone playing him has to. But can an audience? No. I mean there's a big fucking star right on his chest, and he's wearing right, white, and blue, and he's not Captain Courage. He's Captain America. So, no, I don't think the general public can.

There was an op-ed piece in *The New York Times* that said that Captain America was simply a "propaganda stunt."

It's hard to find anybody who could argue with our entering World War II and the fight we fought then. Obviously it's very different the reasons for that, the justifications for that, the moral imperative for that rather than for the political choice we're seeing now. It was a different time; it wasn't a simpler time though. Humans are always complicated. There are a lot of different levels. That war was as close as we can imagine today to a black and white choice. In a black and white world, a red, white, and blue uniform with a big star on a chest doesn't seem to much of a stretch or obnoxious or overreaching. With today's largely borderless, capitalist driven economies, and nuanced relationships, it's very different.

Why do you think Captain America isn't as popular as Superman or Batman?

Superman was a superhero. I don't look at Captain America as being a superhero because he wasn't super-human. He was extra-human. Superman could fly. He looks through walls. All those things that as kids we'd dream about. Batman is a different story. Batman was dark, brooding. His house was gothic. Through all this strife and angst he was able to do some good. Captain America might be seen through the simplistic broad stroke of: "Here's your country."

Is that the essential element of Captain America: "Here's your country?"

I don't know if there's one essential element. Certainly, it's *an* essential element of who he is. He represented our country. He was Captain America. He wore the red white and blue. You know that [David] Halberstam book about the 1960s, *The Best and the Brightest*? Captain America was "the best and the brightest." We were sending him overseas in World War II as an example of our best and brightest and to "show the Krauts what for." Or whatever the jargon of the day would have been. And we were certain it was a fight of good against evil. In that context, it was like carrying the torch of the Statue of Liberty -- which was made in France.

Were you aware that in the comics Captain America was shot and apparently killed?[42]

Yeah.

Did you have a reaction to that?

It was complicated. Because in some ways he died for me a while ago. He died for me when 21st Century didn't support the movie. They allowed him to die in my experience and in my psyche. I came to terms with that. I put him to rest. I was able to watch my kids and their friends enjoy the movie. Then it was,

"Oh that was kind of cool. I did get to do this. It might not have been as good or as successful as I wanted but it's still a cool thing to have done." And I'm proud of having the opportunity and having done it. So, one aspect was his death is right because he had already died for me.

Another one was, "How can he exist in this world?" I would think that if Captain America were alive today he'd want to take on some of the companies and some of the people who got us involved in Iraq. Because of what it means to his beloved America, I think he'd be more horrified about that then he would be some of the easier choices. Would he want to go after Bin Laden? You bet. But the beauty of comics is that there are superheroes and there are arch-villains. And it's almost always really clear. I think that's what's so compelling about that. Going back to grade school, I think it's much more nuanced. And that's what you're trying to learn as a kid. How to live in the gray areas. How to make sense of them. How to find your moral compass. So when they're bigger than life it's compelling.

I also thought, *How long is he going to be dead for?*, and he follow up question to that is: *How does the world have to change, how does our perception of ourselves as a country, as a people and our place in the world, and how does that have to change to welcome him back?*

I think it would be a very good sign for America if our collective consciousness feels that we deserve him again. To me it will imply rightly or wrongly that we feel we are on the right path again. Look at the polls. Look at everything. Nobody feels we're on the right path as a country, and that sucks.

[At this point in the interview, I take out my VHS copy of Captain America.] When you look at this, what do you think?

I think it's cool. Those aren't my legs. [Laughs] Those are the other guys. I don't know. [Pauses] I didn't get to keep the shield though. I wish I had that. That was fun. I was always a good Frisbee player and I could throw that thing really well. On *The Colbert Report* they have Captain America's shield in the background. It looks a lot like the ones we had. I think it's cool. It was a past life. It's funny. It's amusing. With a little tinge of disappointment.

Final question: Who would win in a fight, Captain America or Superman?

Superman would kick the shit out of Captain America. It would be horrendous, but that's what I really like about Captain America. Were it not for his uniform, he was much more accessible, much more human, much closer to us. He could be killed any number of different ways, as we now know.

John Wesley Shipp is The Flash

In 1989, Tim Burton's *Batman* brought back the Batmania of the 1960s and renewed the public's interest in caped crusaders. The movie set box office records when it opened and grossed an impressive $400 million worldwide. The movie became an inescapable cultural phenomenon; teens everywhere wore Batman t-shirts, Joker sneakers and many of them even shaved the Bat-emblem into their hair.

Hoping to reproduce the phenomenal success of *Batman*, CBS looked for other superhero tales to tell. The Eye Network pinned their hopes on The Flash, another champion of justice, whose name was familiar (if only vaguely) to the general public. His backstory was less known. When forensic scientist Barry Allen is caught in a freak lab accident he acquires super speed. After becoming the fastest man alive, Barry dons a bright red suit and fights crime as The Flash.

[Note to the scientific community: Please be more careful when working in your laboratories. Lab mishaps are one of the leading causes of infecting people with superpowers. Just ask David Banner, Peter Parker, Dr. Manhattan (from Watchmen), and Spider-Man's nemeses Doctor Octopus, and Dr. Curt (the Lizard) Connors. The hair follicle-challenged Lex Luthor lost his mane in a lab mishap that he mistakenly blames on Superboy. Lab accidents are prevalent in superhero origin stories because they are straightforward and somewhat magical explanations for the existence of superpowers. What these backstories lack in elegance they make up for in simplicity. How many times can heroes arrive from far away galaxies to live on Earth, where the planet's yellow sun is the source of their powers? In a variation on the lab explosion cliché, the origin story that Stan Lee created for the X-Men is that this more recent group of heroes are "mutants" who were born with special abilities.]

Created in 1940, The Flash was one of the earliest superheroes with only one superpower. Many others who are also known by self-explanatory names such as The Invisible Girl, Plastic Man, and The Human Torch would follow.

Whereas superheroes invariably have one alter ego, four different people have fought crime as The Flash of the comics. The original Flash, Jay Garrick, retired and was replaced by Barry Allen. When Allen was killed saving the world, his nephew Wally West took over. Eventually, Wally retired and Barry's grandson Bart Allen became the fourth scarlet speedster. Proving that unfavorable fan feedback can be just as lethal as a supervillain, Bart was killed off. Barry Allen was eventually brought back to life and (for now) he is Flash. All four versions of The Flash meet in a 5-part story collectively titled "The Flash: Rebirth." David Goyer, co-writer of *Batman Begins, The Dark Knight, The Dark Knight Rises, Man of Steel,* and would-be writer/director of a cancelled Flash feature film says that the "legacy aspect of the hero" makes the character unique.[43]

The Flash's original outfit, with its winged helmet and boots, recalled the imagery of the Roman god Mercury. Less impressively, the early Flash's costume is comprised, in part, by blue slacks. Sixteen years later, he got a much needed makeover, when his costume became a more contemporary, and sexier, full-body, form-fitting suit. The Flash uses his super speed in a variety of ways including time traveling, creating the illusion of invisibility, generating multiple copies of himself and accelerating to speeds that approach flying.

With the exception of two campy one-hour TV specials made in the 1970s, *The Flash* would effectively be the first live-action incarnation of the hero. Without being limited by previous popular and indelible interpretations, producers Danny Bilson and Paul De Meo could have put their own creative stamp on the show. However, it is clear that Bilson and De Meo were unduly influenced by Tim Burton's inimitable vision of Batman. They hired Danny Elfman, who scored Burton's film, to create the theme music. Alas, it isn't always a good idea to follow in other people's creative footsteps. Taking a page from the Bat-book, the Flash's new costume was muscular and intimidating, rather than the sleek streamlined, aero-dynamic design of the comic which, not insignificantly, is more conducive to super speed.

With a budget of $1.4 million per episode, *The Flash* (1990-1991) was one of the most expensive programs on air at the time. The series was a well-intentioned effort to treat superheroes with a seriousness that had been lacking in many [or most] of its previous incarnations. The producers seemed to have made an earnest attempt to pay homage to the comic book on which the series was

John Welsey Shipp feels the need for speed as The Flash. ©
CBS/Warner Bros.

based. John Wesley Shipp, a two-time Daytime Emmy winner, delivers a well-grounded and heartfelt performance as Barry Allen/ The Flash. However, the series lived in the shadow of Burton's film and the dark sensibilities of Batman didn't always translate to The Flash's relatively jovial and humorous persona. Ultimately, despite initially strong ratings and reviews, the show was not renewed for a second season.

In my interview with Shipp, he speaks candidly about playing The Flash.

THE INTERVIEW
When you were offered the part of The Flash, what did you think?

I thought, "No.". Up to that point, television treatments of superheroes were not taking the material very seriously. You know, I have pretensions to being an actor who wanted to play real gritty parts. So, I thought "No" to a tongue-in-cheek, half-mocking characterization of a comic book character that was so far removed from reality. They said that the suit would be a high-tech production and that they'd be spending $100,000 just to build four costumes for The Flash. That, I found out later, was a curse as well as a blessing.

[Series creators] Danny Bilson and Paul De Meo told me that it would be dark. They told me it would be a dark motivation. When he first gets the powers, he's freaked out. He decides to use the powers only to get revenge. It's a dark, human motivation. And there was contrast in playing both identities. Superman has the same thing; this sort of dweeb alter ego: namely working in a crime lab – something that in that time wasn't as cool as it is today. This was before *CSI* and all that stuff. We were ahead of our time there.

They should have called it *The Flash: CSI*

CSI: Flash, yeah. Also in the drama of the Allen family, Barry was not his father's favorite son. Barry defaulted by going into the crime lab so that he wouldn't be a street cop like his dad. His father was always looking down on Barry's profession because to him real cops work the streets. He was suspicious of all the techniques employed in the crime lab and considered them [highfalutin and] suspect. So the fact is that Allen through an accident acquired these powers that his father would think were awesome and yet he couldn't tell his father about it – I thought that the human dynamic in all of that would be very interesting.

The producers also said that they planned to treat the material with respect. The show wouldn't be a send-up. There would be humorous elements but it would be rooted in character and the human reality of the situation. For example, what would you really do if one day you found out that your cells were rearranging and combining in ways so that if for instance you reached for a cup of coffee, you lost control and knocked the cup across the room? Or ran to catch a bus and you ended up 35 miles past it and in the water? How would you react to that?

I thought the script was really interesting. There were things that as an actor I could wrap my mind around. As long as I knew that they would want to be playing the situations seriously and for a sense of truth within a larger-than-life sense of reality, then I thought, "Yeah, I would certainly be on board for that."

We were hoping in the second season to investigate what happens once you have that new power. So you've gotten revenge against your brother's killer, then as a nice guy you're sucked into crime fighting generally, and when supervillains appear, then you *have* to combat them because you have the *ability* to combat them. But what happens when you have the ability to vibrate through walls? What happens to a person who is an ordinary guy who suddenly has extraordinary abilities and he starts abusing them? What would happen if you crossed that line? What would happen to this ordinary guy who suddenly realized he could do all these things. Wouldn't there be temptations? Would it affect your personality? Would you get cocky? Would you go a little bit too far? Would you have to be reigned back in? And what about the issue of vigilantism?

There were a lot of interesting topics and subjects to explore within the framework. We came out right around the time when the Batman movies first started to use a darker, more threatening, and sexier sensibility. It wasn't just goofy. It wasn't going to be like [the inexpensively produced TV show] *Spider-Man* where you go, "Let's stand off camera and throw ropes at the actor for the spider-webbing." It was going to be a big budget. When you're doing a superhero movie, unless there's some darkness and complexity and threat, it's insufferable. It's uninteresting.

The TV show *The Flash* continued on with the popular comic book notion that the death or absence of a family member is a factor that often helps to shape a superhero. Many comics seem to be about unresolved father or surrogate father issues. In Batman, Bruce Wayne watches the death of his parents. In Spider-Man, Peter Parker selfishly lets the small-time crook who will eventually kill his uncle and surrogate father get away. Clark Kent never got to know his biological father and his adoptive father Jonathan Kent dies when he's a vulnerable adolescent. Father and son relationships seem central to so many superhero stories.

I think it is the drama of the unblessed child. Sensing that you were not the blessed son. Then having powers, which would enable you to do so much more. One of the defining moments in the relationship between Barry and his father is the scene at his brother Jay's gravesite. The father says, "You don't fire a gun without a bullet in the chamber." Barry says, "I have the bullet." But he can't tell his father what that bullet is even though his abilities so far exceed what would have been his father's wildest fantasies, and would get him the kind of admiration and acknowledgement that he longed for from his father. The [said with pride] "Yeah, Barry's my son" reaction that he never got and that his brother Jay did. But he can never tell his dad that he's The Flash. It was bittersweet. It was an interesting ironic twist.

If you're a child watching that episode, are you that person who isn't yet powerful enough to impress your father?

Yeah, you wish you could have more of an effect on things. Because you feel to a certain extent victimized. I remember thinking when I was a kid, "I can't wait till I'm older." But adults say, "Okay, but try to enjoy where you are right now because once you pass through childhood, it's irretrievable. And you'll look back on it." But that doesn't mean very much when you're nine, eleven, or thirteen. Because you just want to get out and exert some con-

trol over your environment. But the dream of a wonderful secret
– that without anyone knowing it you are at a super-human level
controlling and fixing everything. That's the underlying fantasy.
[Author's Note: In the CW's *The Flash* (2014), Shipp plays Barry
Allen's father. Grant Gustin plays Barry Allen/The Flash.]

**Can you talk about the voice you used while playing The Flash
and how it differs from Barry Allen's?**

We never really settled on it. I always felt that dialogue in the
suit was kind of ridiculous. At the beginning, with the darker motivation, I played around with a voice that fit the body of the suit.
A bigger, deeper voice than Barry would have normally used. Because he's filling out this outsized ability with his rage over the
death of his brother.

We tried little quips. In the middle all of this superhuman
daring-do he would throw a sideways glance and say something
smart-ass. Which I thought was effective too. But [in the two-
hour series premiere] when he's confronting his brother's killer,
Pike, I thought there were too many lines that didn't quite work.

I was always uncomfortable – as I think Barry would have been
– hearing himself talk in that context. His suit came out for a
specific purpose, a specific task. It was physical in nature, it was
active, it was to get the thing done and then to come off.

If we could have begun to see the effect of this on his ego, that
would have been interesting. Maybe down the road, he could have
have enjoyed being The Flash a little more. He might have become a little cocky, and he might even have abused his powers
a little, thrown his weight around a bit. That would have been
interesting to explore.

I always thought the dialogue in the suit should be minimal. It
should be monosyllabic. There shouldn't be any Shakespearean
monologues in the suit.

**When you put on the suit for the first time, what was your
reaction?**

[He laughs] In Los Angeles, shooting in 100 degree heat, I
thought, "How am I ever going to survive this thing?" My feeling
always was once the suit came out and we cued the orchestra
and the streets were wet and the lighting was very dramatic and

the special effects began, my job was essentially over. My job was to bring the audience emotionally onboard with the guy. If they liked who the guy was outside of the suit and if they could identify with his humanity, then when it was funneled into a superhero context it would be more fun for them. In other words, if you can't identify with Barry, if your weaknesses, insecurities, foibles, hopes, and dreams do not correlate in any way with Barry's, then why would you care what The Flash does? I think the reason that they hired me was for my ability to play Barry in such a way that people could understand the human element and the human motivations of the man – we always talk about the man behind the mask.

I was very gratified that the reviews – in *The Washing Post* and in the major newspapers – did talk about the acting – which is unusual in an action series. I thank Danny and Paul for that as well because I think they also understood that you have to like, understand and empathize with this guy so that you're really rooting for him when he finally has the ability to do all of these extraordinary things.

Besides the physical discomfort you felt in the suit, did wearing the suit ever make you feel heroic or, at the other end of the spectrum, self-conscious and silly?

It had the potential to make me feel self-conscious and silly. However, I thought it looked great. But practical problems arose once I started sweating through the suit and the foam latex started crumbling. And then there was an artistic concern because the network started petitioning to see more and more of it. At the beginning, you were never supposed to see the whole thing. Maybe just one reveal, but mostly it was supposed to be a blur of red. One side of the body darkly lit. Everything in shadows. The audience and the network were saying, "We want to see the suit. We want to see the suit." Sure, but once you've seen it, then what? It's kind of like Gypsy Rose Lee. Keep them wanting more. Don't ever show them the whole thing. That was another struggle.

The suit played itself. What I would go to was not trying to play a superhero – but I would go to what I thought was the central question of what was Barry feeling? What intensified emotions or intensified situation or feelings of obligation or desire for revenge would motivate him to do something that he didn't initially want to do? Originally he felt, "I want to get rid of this. I don't want to know anything about this power." He said to Tina [a fellow scientist and Allen's love-interest], "I want to get rid of it." I think he was a little bit in denial.

What would motivate him to put on the suit? It's easy in the pilot – revenge for the death of his brother. But what about after that? He gets a taste of blood in his mouth, then his willingness to get in it again and to do it again and use it again. But it was always for me, "What is Barry feeling at this moment? Why is he doing it?"

I had to find ways to make it real regardless of what I thought other people might be thinking of it. I couldn't step outside the character and judge it or I would have been commenting on it as an actor. I had to stay within the truth and the reality of the given circumstances and invest it with as much humanity as I possibly could.

Did you find that when you were wearing the suit people on the set or the crew treated you differently from when you weren't wearing it?

They saw how really difficult it was to work in it. Mostly what I got was sympathy. I'd wear it for fifteen minutes, take the gloves off, and the gloves up to the wrists would be full of water. They finally had to come up with a vest like race car drivers wear that I would have on at all times and they would plug me into an ice chest and circulate ice water to jolt me back awake. To keep my body temperature down, to keep me from overheating. I couldn't sit down. I had to lean on a slant board.

Did you find that people were deferential to you as if you were The Flash?

What I noticed at the beginning was if we were standing around – lets say a group of guys on the crew – I would say something that might be funny on an off Thursday afternoon in the rain – and they would laugh like it was the funniest thing in the world.

For a while, I began to think, "I am the funniest person in Los Angeles." Then you realize and catch on to the manipulations and then you understand it. Unless you go off completely into dementia you have to bring it back and say, "Don't do that. Don't insult my intelligence by being dishonest with me." I made it clear that when I get to the set we're all working very hard and I, as a professional, don't have to be coddled in order to have my ego boosted so that I will show up and do my job. I do my job because it's my job.

Another example, once, at the end of a very late day, they started this, "Hip-hip-hooray" business when I got to the set. I appreciated where they were coming from but I stopped them and said, "Don't ever do that to me again. We're all working here to get as good a product as we can under extreme conditions. That embarrasses me. Don't single me out like that again. Let's just all work together to make this as easy as we possibly can." I mean everybody loved the suit. They were very impressed with it. Everybody wanted to see it, but then it becomes like anything else - we were working eighteen, nineteen, sometimes twenty-hour days. I think the transportation department would log in twenty-five, twenty-six-hour days. We were working until eight or nine o'clock on a Saturday morning back in at seven a.m. on Mondays. We did that from the third week of August until the second week in May with four days off for Christmas. And that was it. We were all just working as hard as we possibly could. And it does become a bit like a factory job. You just have to show up and do it. [Laughs] Because of the number of hours and the kinds of hours you don't have much time to talk about anything except about what you're trying to get, what you're trying to do. That's especially true with a character like The Flash, where I was in practically every scene either as The Creature, (which is what I called him), or as Barry. And being shuttled between two units. In the suit, out of the suit.

You called the character The Creature? Did you feel like a creature in some ways?

A creature when I put the suit on - I certainly did. I felt like a creature. Yes. And not in a bad way. There was something definitely superhuman. There was something altered. There was an alternation in - I don't know - the only thing I can liken it to is

John Wesley Shipp as The Flash. © CBS/Warner Bros.

anger. I know that sounds weird, but it's anger, aggression, hostility; the feeling of power in that way. Maybe it's an absolute knowledge that you could absolutely bring about whatever effect you wanted to have in a way that other human beings can't. Maybe it's an absolute certainty of the ability to achieve intention. I don't know what it is, but it was an aggressive feeling.

Was that because of everything you had to do to get into the suit? That's a very interesting thought. Can you expand on that?

It was more about – maybe you're right. I hadn't thought of that. Maybe part of my anger was fuelled by the suits, which were always wet when I put them on. There were four of them, and the foam latex was always crumbling. They were hung up in the trailer overnight, and they were still wet at six in the morning when I put them back on. Because you couldn't clean them they were sprayed with Lysol. So I was always breaking out under the suit. I had a rash on my face – bridge of my nose and under my chin – where they were glued and taken off with Acetone. So there was a certain amount of, "[Exasperated] Oh God" just involved with that, and that probably fed into those feelings, but it was more of a feeling of, *I am outsized. I am oversized. I am more than human.* Which in a way had a strange boomerang affect on me. You simultaneously felt more than human and not quite human at the same time. It's weird. I can't quite explain it.

John Newton said that when he was dressed as Superboy sometimes people related to him as an object.

When I was in the suit, people didn't talk to me, and I think they knew that it was fucking difficult. I was sweating through the suit within ten minutes and they had to spray it with sealant. If you walked up and grabbed my arm then water would pour out. It was like a sponge. They knew it was uncomfortable, and I was tired, but the irritability, the discomfort, the not being spoken to – maybe that's what I always took it for. Maybe there is a certain intimidation factor, or maybe they just thought I looked like a jerk. I'm not sure what they were thinking. All I know that I didn't have much spare time when I was in the suit. When I was in the suit, I was in it to get the work done so that I could take the damn thing off again. It all contributed to the final performance. There is a certain rigidity or intensity of purpose – of course, everything is heightened in the suit – but then again everything is heightened in the storyline when the suit comes out – so it's hard to separate them.

Why do you think superhero stories are so popular?

I think it comes from a sense of powerlessness that we feel. With all the injustices in the world, who wouldn't want to escape to a place where ultimate justice could be achieved?

Why do you think The Flash is a popular character?

Speed baby, speed. Look at it - if you want to take it across culture lines, what is this huge epidemic that is sweeping this country? The possibility that you can at least feel like you are going 90 miles an hour, you can do fifty things at once and that you can vibrate yourself through a wall, doesn't that sound like crystal methamphetamine to you? It's all of a piece. Taller, bigger stronger, louder, more intense. It seems like we are searching for more - bigger, faster, stronger. Of course, with The Flash, it's faster.

If you knew then what you know now, would you have taken the part?

Yes, in a heartbeat. I would be more convinced to do it now than I was at the time.

Why is that?

Because I now have the confirmation that the result, which I could not have predicted, was going to be something that I could be proud of . . . and that other people, fifteen years later, would come and express what seems to me to be heartfelt appreciation

John Wesley Shipp as forensic scientist Barry Allen in The Flash *(1990).*
© CBS/Warner Bros.

that it has touched and entertained them. The most gratifying thing is when people talk to me about the *Twin Streaks* episode or when they talk to me about characteristics in Barry's life that they could identify with, and this wish fulfillment that he achieved with superhero powers and how they get a kick out of that. I'm very gratified by that.

When the series ended, did you get to keep anything from the set?

You know I didn't. I didn't think about it at the time. I should have taken an outfit and hung it on a cross and put in on a hill.

What question would you ask the next superhero that I interview?

I guess I would ask, "Was there ever a boomerang affect on them personally? Personally, not professionally, not publicly. But privately. Was there ever a boomerang affect on them from playing situations where they had an extraordinary ability to do good? Was there ever a boomerang? Did you got out of the suit and ever feel a particular sense of inadequacy?"

How would you answer that question?

Yes. Absolutely. Absolutely. Because you're playing something that is so heightened and you try to make yourself believe it. But then you come out of it, and the lights are turned off and the orchestra is silent. The very dramatic lighting isn't there, and the suit, after all, is just a lump of foam latex dripping in the corner of your trailer, and you're sitting there in your jockey shorts looking like a drowned rat, thinking, *Oh Boy, now it's back to just being me.*

It's interesting that you say that. One of the original ideas behind this book is just that thought, that filmmakers create a situation where the audience instilled the character – and by extension the actor playing the superhero – with all these extraordinary traits and characteristics. Then, when it's over, how does it make them feel?

Inadequate. Drained. I look at it now and I go to conventions and people say, "Are they going to do another Flash?" And I say, "Come on guys. It's fifteen years later. When they do, it won't be me." I'm really glad I was able to do it and chances are I'll never be a superhero ever again. [Laughs]

Who's faster, The Flash or Superman?

Oh, The Flash, come on. [Laughs] Can Superman vibrate his cells through a wall?

In the George Reeve's *Superman* TV show, he did once.

Ahhhhh. You're kidding. I'm crushed. I wished you hadn't told me.

[Feeling inordinately guilty] I'm sorry.

[Laughs] Let me just say this, if The Flash's main power is speed and if Superman is faster than he is, then the Flash is not much of a superhero, is he? So I would say The Flash is faster.

Given that, would The Flash win in a fight?

I don't know. Personally, I'd say, "Sure." But Superman can fly. Although The Flash can go so fast he breaks the sound barrier. I'd say that the fight would go on for a very long time and would end up with the universe splitting.

Kevin Conroy is Batman

Time for another pop quiz. Who played Batman the most? Christian Bale wore the cape three times. Michael Keaton, twice. Val Kilmer, once. George Clooney, just once. [44] In the 1960s, Adam West played the Caped Crusader for three glorious seasons in 120 episodes and in one feature film. In 1979, he played Batman in *Legends of the Superheroes: The Challenge* and *The Roast*, a pair of forgettable and silly TV specials. Additionally, West provided the voice of Batman for several animated shows including *The New Adventures of Batman*, *The Super Friends: The Legendary Super Powers Show*, *The Super Powers Team: Galactic Guardians* and *Batman: New Times*, a short film depicting the superhero as a Lego toy. Despite his striking list of Bat-credits, West finishes in second place on the list of performers who have appeared most often as the Dark Knight.

It's possible that (unless you are a superhero fanboy) you haven't even heard of the actor who has played Batman most often. And despite his record number of performances, I can guarantee that you have never *seen* him in the part. The actor is Kevin Conroy.

Conroy is known primarily as a "voice actor," which is to say, that he performs Batman's dialogue in animated films, television shows, video games and even the occasional theme park ride, and he has played Batman more times than West, Bale, Keaton, Kilmer, and Clooney combined.

Here is a sampling of Conroy's performances:

Animated Movies

Batman: Assault on Arkham 2014
Justice League: The Flashpoint Paradox 2013
Justice League: Doom 2012
Superman/Batman: Apocalypse 2010
Superman/Batman: Public Enemies 2009
Batman: Gotham Knight 2008
Batman: Mystery of the Batwoman 2003
Batman Beyond: Return of the Joker 2000

Batman Beyond: The Movie 1999
The Batman Superman Movie: World's Finest 1998
Batman & Mr. Freeze: SubZero 1998
Batman: Mask of the Phantasm 1993

Animated Series

Batman Beyond (short) 2014
Batman: Strange Days (short) 2014
Tales of Metropolis (short) 2013
Justice League Unlimited 2004-2006
Justice League 2001-2004
Batman Beyond 1999-2001
Superman: The Animated Series 1997-1999
The New Batman Adventures 1997-1999
Batman: The Animated Series 1992-1995

Video Games

Batman: Arkham Knight 2015
Injustice: Gods Among Us 2013
Harley Quinn's Revenge 2012
DC Universe Online 2011
Batman: Arkham City 2011
Batman: Arkham Asylum 2009
Batman: Rise of Sin Tzu 2003
Batman: Vengeance 2001
The Adventures of Batman and Robin 1994

Quite an extensive list. And even though Conroy has a very impressive resume as a serious actor with formidable training, with his expressive, gravely voice, Conroy makes his living primarily by being Warner Bros. Animation's "go-to guy" to play Batman. He approaches the role with dedication and he is grateful for the opportunity to play the beloved character. But he also recognizes that being Batman is just his day job, something he does to pay the rent. Some actors work as waiters to cover their expenses, Conroy moonlights as Batman.

Playing Batman sometimes has unexpected rewards. In 2010, I attended the New York premiere of *Superman/Batman: Apocalypse,* an animated direct-to-video feature film, at the Museum of TV & Radio in New York. After the screening Conroy spoke to the audience and shared a personal memory. Conroy recalled that shortly after the 9/11 attacks, he was doing some volunteer work as a cook in the World Trade Center area. One of the other volunteers learned that Conroy played Batman and urged him to say something as Batman. Conroy reluctantly obliged. Much to his surprise and delight, he was met with thunderous applause by the weary firefighters and police officers. It seems that they too were fans of Conroy's Caped Crusader.

Kevin Conroy, the man behind the microphone. (Photo courtesy of Kevin Conroy.)

THE INTERVIEW

How'd you get the part? What were your initial thoughts about playing Batman?

To be honest, I came into it as a blank slate. A lot of fans get disappointed when they find out that I didn't have any knowledge of Bob Kane's early Batman comics or [Frank Miller's revolutionary graphic novels] The Dark Knight series. I was pretty ignorant. The only exposure I had was the TV series in the 1960s, and that's a real tangential interpretation of the character. That show was not what the Dark Knight was at all about.

When I went into the audition, they asked me what I knew about Batman. I said the TV series. They said, "No, no. no. Wipe that out. That is not what we're going for. This show is very dark, very noir. A young man loses his parents tragically, he is avenging their death. He spends all his time in a cave. He's tortured." I said, "Oh, you're telling the Hamlet story." They laughed and said, "Well no one has actually said that before." The fact that I had no background at all was a blessing because I had no preconceptions. I came at the part fresh. So I said, "Let me use my imagination and see what sound I can come up with for the voice."

How close was that audition voice to the one you ultimately decided to use?

The sound for Batman was exactly the same, and that's what we ended up using. They loved it. The sound for Bruce changed. Actors always love to challenge themselves; sometimes to the point of making more out of something than there needs to be. In the initial episodes, I did Bruce with a very "urbane" accent – similar to my own voice. There was a much bigger distinction between Bruce and Batman in the early episodes. The early voice for Bruce Wayne was very sophisticated and overly humorous. With a lot of sarcasm. It was fun to play.

Once we established the character – about four or five episodes in – they had me go back to re-record the voice of Bruce Wayne to bring him closer to the voice of Batman. They didn't want so dramatic a difference, especially as they darkened the pallet of the show. Early on, I enjoyed playing some of the humor of Bruce Wayne. As the show evolved they decided to play down the comedy.

Would you call your original idea WASPy?

Yes, a WASPy, stereotypical lock-jawed Scarsdale playboy, which is the way he's described. It's the way he conceals himself. He hides behind that persona.

Who is the real character, Bruce Wayne or Batman?

I've approached it from the very beginning that Bruce Wayne is the alter ego and Batman is who that character really is. Everyone has a public face and a private face. For that character, the private face is Batman. The public face is Bruce Wayne. Bruce Wayne is the performance. He's most comfortable as Batman and the only time he can be himself is with Alfred.

Is a third voice necessary when he's talking to a trusted ally like Alfred who knows his true identify, when he doesn't need to be Batman or Bruce Wayne?

There are basically only two voices. The only time I had to go into multiple voices was in the classic episode "Perchance to Dream," which is my favorite episode. In it, Batman is drugged and he goes into a fantasy world where he loses track of reality. In his fantasy life, I had to be young Bruce Wayne, older Bruce Wayne, Bruce's father, and Batman. Each voice had to be distinct from one other and yet believably related. It was a fun recording session. It was largely just me and they had me do it in real time [without stopping] to go back and forth between the two characters.

Did they show you the artwork for the character when you were developing the voice of Batman?

It's interesting. They explained to us what the show was going to look like and they did show us some sketches to get our imaginations going before we went into production. But we originally didn't have a clue to how extraordinary it was going to be until we saw it. The artwork was initially (and I think still is) done in Korea. The masterwork is done in Los Angeles, but the actual cells were drawn in Korea. So we didn't see any of the finished work until we went into do ADR [Automatic Dialogue Replacement. It's also known as looping]. That happened a good five or six months after laying down the initial tracks. We were well into production to

A scene from Batman: The Animated Series. © *DC Comics/Warner Bros.*

do ADR. Mark Hamill and I went in at the same time to do ADR, and when they screened the show for us on a large screen and as the score swelled and we saw the beautiful artwork, we were both speechless. Finally I turned to Mark and said, "Did you have a clue that this is what we were doing?" He said, "No. I had no idea it would be of this quality." It was so overwhelming and so beautiful.

Your take on Bruce's father is a benevolent character.

Right. Everyone's idealized father. Not the real father that we all had. [Laughs].

Unlike other animated projects, you all stood around and recorded the voices together.

Yes, that's what's unique about Warner Bros. and the Bruce Timm and Paul Dini productions. It was like doing a radio play. Most studios record the voices separately. It's the way they get to book what is called "stunt casting" where they cast stars for each role. The only way they can book all those people is to record them separately. Warner Bros. didn't go in for stunt casting – especially when we started the show in 1993. Though they did get high-profile actors, they had everyone record their lines together. They got some wonderful actors. The booking sessions were phenomenal. It was a great experience to work with those actors. The advantage of recording the voices separately is that you get a completely clean recording and you can control every aspect of it, whereas if you are recording a group, all of the mics are live, and that makes it more complicated. But there's no comparison between the quality of the two approaches, because when you're recording as a group, the actors are able to feed off one other.

Do you change physically when you're Bruce or Batman?

I do tend to transform somewhat physically when I'm doing Batman. But not as much as Mark Hamill who plays the Joker. He has a rubber face like Jim Carrey. His face really goes wild when he's doing the Joker. It's fun to watch him. Mark goes through an entire physical transformation.

Do you feel the power of the character?

I think the fact that I use so much of my body voice - my lower register - that I do feel it. I have a theater background. I trained at Julliard and did a lot of the classics with Joe Papp at the Public. I have a big voice and I'm comfortable filling a space. It can be exciting. It's an exciting sound to produce.

How is it exciting?

There is a lot of low timbre to the sound and you can really feel it fill a space. When I give talks at conventions, it's fun to blast them with the voice just before I appear on stage. You get this huge response - 500 people go "Woo-hoo." I know when they see me they'll be disappointed. The fans imagine that, like Batman, I must be larger than life or imposing in some way. But I'm just Joe Schmo, a regular-looking guy. To create a little excitement I love to have the voice precede me. I say, [in his Batman voice] "I am vengeance. I am the night. I am Batman," and then fans cheer.

You can slip into it fairly easily.

Yeah. I've been doing it for over fifteen years; it's bizarre. It's been a wonderful job.

Do people ask you to do voicemail messages as Batman?

They have. Yeah. I think my natural voice is different from Batman's but sometimes when I'm in line at a movie theater and I say,

"Two adult tickets please" and if it's a little kid, I'll get a look of horror. The father will say, "What's the matter?" [In a child's voice. Near tears.] "Daddy I think that's Batman." Then I'll explain to the parent, "Your kid is not freaking out. I do the voice of Batman." I'm always amazed when that happens. I think it's a totally different voice from mine but they must hear something.

Have you ever worn the Batman outfit to help inform your performance?

I did it once but not to inform the character. I used to do a lot of volunteer work with kids at a foster care facility outside of Los Angeles. They found out what my day job was. Suddenly, I was a hero and my stock went through the roof with the kids. For a Halloween event they begged me to bring my "work clothes," as they put it. I tried to explain that I only did the voice but that didn't translate to them. So I purchased a costume and wore it to the place so that I could appear as Batman. I didn't want them to see me change into the costume. When I was driving on the freeway in my Batman outfit, I'd have a lot of truckers blasting their horns at me. "Go Batman!" It was very embarrassing. The arrival was perfect. When I got out the kids yelled, "Yo! Batman!" So it was worth it. That was the only time I've worn the costume.

What motivates Batman?

He's the most popular animated character and why the character has remained popular so long is that he speaks to everyone's inner angel. He's the voice inside of us that wants to heal the world and do heroic deeds. Every one of us has a voice inside of us that wants to be a hero and Bruce Wayne has it because he's avenging his parents' death, so he has that inner calling which will follow him for the rest of his life in all of our names. He's doing it for all of us.

You think Batman is listening to his inner angel and not inner devil?

Absolutely. It comes out of his darkness and through his dark angel. Lucifer is a fallen angel, you know. Sometimes there can be a fine line between an inner angel and inner devil. He supposedly had a cathartic experience in the cave under Wayne Manor.

There's an episode that deals with his cathartic moment with that force of darkness.

I read an article that was written by a psychiatrist who suggests that when Batman is helping people it is a side effect that masks his underlying aggression towards others and the pleasure he derives through intimidation.

There has to be a certain pleasure in what he's doing it, but if it's about pure aggression, why is it that Batman has never killed anyone? [45]

Why do you think he decided to put on a costume and fight crime as a superhero?

He felt that society was sick and the system was corrupt; and because he couldn't trust the system, he had to work outside it; he became his own system. People generally don't trust the government and other institutions. Which is a sad fact, but they don't. People can relate to his being a vigilante. That's the downside to Batman. He *is* a vigilante and there are a lot of negative associations with that. He handles that responsibility quite well.

What if his judgment were less than perfect?

We see what would happen in an episode when he gets drugged by villains. If you give that power in someone whose judgment is off, the consequences can be terrifying. In our own lifetimes, we've seen what happens when governments in power lose their moral compass. It's a very dangerous line that he's walking. I think he knows that. Alfred knows it and tries to keep him from straying.

Does he view being Batman as a burden or does it give him pleasure?

Both. It's his burden to carry, but it's a curse that he also obviously loves. He would probably have preferred a normal family life but circumstances intervened to prevent that from happening. There are those episodes where he fell in love with the character played by Dana Delaney. We see brief glimmers of what his life might have been, but it didn't happen, and given his other life, it couldn't happen.

If Batman is a loner, why would he work with (and endanger the life of) a young sidekick like Robin?

That's why they didn't do a lot of stories with Robin. His character didn't fit our series, which was a return to the original Dark Knight concept when Batman was much more of a loner. For a while, though, it gave him someone to interact with, another relationship to explore. When you have a solitary character, it's more difficult to sustain dialogue and that makes it harder to create tension. In that sense, working Robin into the script helps the writers tell stories. It also shows Batman's paternal side and helps to fill out his character by having him interact with a surrogate child, which is what Robin is; but it plays against the isolated hero that Batman is.

Earlier you were talking about the idea that fans might be disappointed when learning you weren't a big Batman fan prior to playing the character.

I might be reading that into the situation.

No, I think you're right. I think fans want the actors who play the superhero to feel an intimate and personal connection with the character. That playing the hero was somehow fulfilling their life's dream.

That's true. They expect me to be much more aware of the Batman legacy that I am. I always have to explain to them that I'm an actor and that it's an acting job. If, as I hope, I'm doing my job well, then I'm fulfilling their fantasies. But it's *their* fantasies. For me, it's an acting job.

That's really interesting. I think that fans often want superhero actors to embody their fantasies.

Yes, they do anticipate that. I can sense their disappointment that it's not the case. But I respect and honor their take on it when I'm doing the job. Still, for me it's just a job.

You're the first person I spoke to who actually admitted that, which is great. You're a working actor and this is simply another professional opportunity. It's an opportunity for exposure and financial stability, and those are legitimate considerations.

Absolutely. When I first went into the audition I wasn't even trying to get the part of Batman. I wanted to be [police officer] Bullock or one of the other supporting characters. Because it's so much more fun to do character voices. But they explained to me who Batman was and how the leading man was a "character." That made it more fun to create a voice for Batman. But yeah, it's an acting job. I don't say that to diminish what the audience is experiencing or anticipating. I respect the audience. It's just not part of my work as an actor.

Do you relate to the character?

I think everyone does, which is what makes him so appealing and so universal. I don't have a cave under my house but I think everyone relates to the darkness of the character.

Before taking the part were you concerned about the negative impact it could have on your career. Or did you think, "It's voice work I'm safe?"

It's funny you ask that, because now it's hip thing to do voice work in animation. You almost can't get the work unless you are a star. The business has changed so dramatically in the past ten years, but you're right. Fifteen years ago that was a consideration. It was natural to ask yourself if you wanted to risk becoming associated with a cartoon voice. I discussed it with my agents who felt it was anonymous enough. I was just lucky enough to be in that business at a time when it became mainstream. Now people are competing hard to get work doing animation voices.

You worked with fellow Batman Adam West in an episode where he played an actor who once played a Batman-like hero.

He is such a gentleman. I wasn't sure what to expect from him when he came in to do voice work on the episode "The Gray Ghost." He couldn't have been any happier for me. He said [impersonating Adam West perfectly], "Boy have you got a great job. And you're doing a wonderful job with it."

You knew Christopher Reeve, too.

Chris was at Julliard when I was there. I was seventeen, and he was a few years ahead of me in school. We considered sharing an apartment at the time. Chris wanted to rent this wonderful loft in SoHo, but I just didn't have the money. We were friends. I did end up rooming with Robin Williams because we were in the same financial shape. Chris was such a class act. He came from a strong theater background. It was so tragic what happened to him and to Dana. He was such a classy guy. He had a square jaw and he was about six foot four. He really did seem larger than life, and that, apart from his exceptional talent, helps to explain why audiences so readily accepted him as Superman. But he was a great, sweet, sweet man.

How has this part affected you personally?

To be honest, for me it's been an example of how life is what happens when you're making other plans. I moved to New York at seventeen and was a full scholarship student at Julliard. I had this clear vision that I was going to be a classically trained stage actor and that was what I was going to do, and I did that. I fulfilled that goal, but the nature of the business changed while I was doing it. You couldn't make a living in the theater any more. That lifestyle has changed. You have to do television or film to supplement your theater work. Theater is almost an indulgence for some actors now. Doing theater is what they love to do but they can't make any money doing it.

In terms of Batman, I made all these other plans and then I found myself doing the voice of this animated character to pay the bills, and it became a way for me escape having to worry about paying the bills. The job went on for over fifteen years, and the residuals went on for years after that. Without my planning it, it became a way for me to live and to do the theater I wanted to do.

It's about being open to what life brings your way and being prepared to go with it, and then working to make it into something. Doing Batman freed me from having to worry much about finances, and it offered an opportunity to find ways to express my creativity just using my voice. Acting is a very youth oriented business, especially on camera. To be getting older to be able to rely on my voice is an incredible blessing. It was a very lucky break for me.

That's very interesting. Someone said, "One's happiness is in inverse proportion to one's expectations."

Right. That's what they say in AA. Yeah.

Having said that, do you harbor even a touch of lament or regret about not experiencing what your life as an actor might have been if Batman hadn't come along, what else you might have achieved in film or on stage?

Oh, God no. I don't think there would have been any other road. If it hadn't been for Batman I would have been one of those sad characters you see sitting by the pool in Los Angeles waiting for the next job to come along. Groucho Marx has this wonderful line describing Los Angeles. He said, "It's the one place where you fall asleep at the pool and you wake up and you're eighty-seven." It's so true. These people wait by the pool – waiting for their phones to ring. Suddenly they're eighty-seven and their lives are gone. You think, "What did you do?" It's a very easy trap to fall into, and sadly it happens all the time.

Before Batman I was a busy actor. I always had a pilot or a Movie of the Week. I always had a twelve-episode pick up of a series that didn't get into the second year. I was always working but I never had a long running series. Everything I worked on led to something else. It's really a crapshoot out there. If it hadn't been for Batman, I have a terrible feeling that I would have been one of those guys sitting by the pool and waiting for the phone to ring.

What question should I ask the next hero I speak to?

How would you like to be remembered?

Who would win in a fight: Superman vs. Batman?

I'd like to believe Batman because he works with his wits. Superman has those superpowers, and that's hard to overcome, but finally Batman is so quick-witted that he would outwit Superman.

Dean Cain is Superman

If you think of Clark Kent only as a bumbling, stumbling, mild-mannered man who repels woman, then you probably aren't reading enough comics. That all changed back in 1986, when writer and artist John Byrne was handpicked by DC to overhaul their Superman comics, whose plotlines had become increasingly Byzantine.

Byrne rejiggered Superman's origin story, eliminated Superboy and the ostensibly endless number of Kryptonians who survived the destruction of his home planet, scaled back on Superman's seemingly limitless powers, and changed Clark Kent's personality from klutzy reporter into a capable, confident man of his time.

It is from the Byrne's interpretation that Dean Cain's Clark Kent is born. Dean Cain played Clark Kent/Superman in *Lois & Clark: The New Adventures of Superman* (1993-1997), the TV series created by Deborah Joy LeVine. While the title was a tip of the hat to George Reeves' *Adventures of Superman* the show was anything but a throwback. Gone were the days when Lois Lane was perpetually tied to a chair, waiting impatiently for Superman to burst through the door/wall/cave-entrance/warehouse/bank vault to save her. This Lois Lane, as played with excellent comic timing by Teri Hatcher, was capable of saving herself.

The best episodes of *Lois & Clark* were less concerned with Superman battling a supervillain than they were when they focused on the budding romantic relationship between the two bickering reporters. In many ways, the show owes more to *Moonlighting* (1985-1989) and the banter between Bruce Willis' David Addison and Cybill Shepherd's Maddie Hayes than to any superhero comic, movie, or television show.

Over the course of four seasons and eighty-seven episodes, Lois and Clark would feud, date, fall in love, and eventually marry. When the couple tied the knot on television, their comic book counterparts were also married in *The Wedding Album*, the cover of a more than ninety-page issue that depicts Superman carrying his new bride in her wedding gown over the tranquil skies of

Metropolis. As a nice touch the first printing of the comic came with an actual wedding invitation that read: "The Family of DC Comics invites you to share its joy at the wedding of Lois Lane to Clark Kent."

Cain played Clark Kent as a capable and confident man. His Clark wasn't an act he put on; his Clark Kent was the real character. In the series, Cain shines more brightly as Clark Kent than as Superman.

Dean Cain as Superman. © Warner Bros. Television

THE INTERVIEW

When you were cast in *Lois & Clark*, the character of Superman was already more than fifty years old and there was a lot of source material to draw from. How did you create your version?

Well, I certainly didn't feel fifty years old at the time. [Laughs] My version of Superman and Clark Kent was really well spelled out on the page by our show's creator Deborah Joy LeVine. She did a really nice job of reinventing Clark Kent and Superman in a way that had nothing to do with me. It was all on the page. The part just felt very comfortable to me.

The director at the time was a guy by the name of Robert Butler, who had worked on and helped shape a number of successful shows like *Hill Street Blues* [Butler also directed *Batman, The Twilight Zone,* and *Remington Steel,* and he directed the pilots for both *Moonlighting* and the original *Star Trek* (1966-1969).] I walked into the audition and I said, "I think I have a pretty unique take on the read and I don't know what everyone else is doing but I'd like to show you my approach." He said, "Let's see what you got." So I did my reading.

I was the first person the producers had seen and then I went away. Normally you'd hear some feedback like, "You were great. They are going to see other people but maybe they'll bring you back next week." But they didn't give me any feedback. So I assumed, "There goes another audition."

Around two weeks later, I was at a party and there was a casting associate from Warner Bros. who said, "Hey, you're Dean Cain. They really like you for that Superman project." Then lo and behold the call came a couple of days later and they asked me to come back to read again. I did a couple more auditions for them.

There was one scene they had written in which Clark is home alone and Lois had a couple of drinks and she decides, "I want Clark and I want him now." She is a little inebriated and she throws herself at him. She plants a kiss on him and although he wants her he doesn't take advantage of her. When I read that scene I thought, *I understand this character. This is mine.*

That scene was very representative of who I thought Clark was. Although he has needs and desires, he's a gentleman. With his small town values and upbringing he was raised to do the right thing.

For me, Clark Kent was the real character and that's really who he *is*, and Superman is what he *did*. His mother had created the costume for him to allow him to do these wonderful things to save humanity and help people while maintaining his anonymity. Making Clark the real character is how we were different from previous incarnations of Clark Kent and Superman. How is that for a short answer? [Laughs]

You said the part spoke to you. What about it spoke to you?

His morality and his desire to do the right thing stood out. Although he has all this power and all these gifts he always does the right thing. People say men are inherently evil. Maybe. It's possible. Maybe Krytonians are inherently nice. This guy certainly was. That's the part that spoke to me. He's not perfect. But everything he does comes from a place of goodness. Unlike the Dark Knight and some other comic book characters he comes from a place of goodness.

Do you think it was fitting that you played Superman as opposed to another superhero?

There had been jokes about it when I was growing up and people called me Superman. I would leave it for other people to say, but the people who knew me really well were not shocked that I got a role like Superman. They said, "I thought it was apropos that you would wind up playing Superman."

Did you read the comics?

I didn't read the comics, but I watched the *Super Friends* and I saw the animated cartoons. I watched the Christopher Reeve films, which had a tremendous impact on me in how I played Superman, not in how I played Clark Kent, but in how I played Superman. I had also seen the George Reeves' version and I liked his Clark Kent quite a bit. More so than I liked his Superman.

I love George Reeves, but he didn't differentiate between the two characters. He didn't change his voice or his physicality.

[Laughs] No, he didn't, but I liked his Clark Kent very much. I liked how his Clark Kent was a man. I liked how his Clark Kent was almost a throwback to the men of the 1940s. I thought that was cool. His Superman, that's a different story, but I like his Clark Kent very much, and I liked Christopher Reeve's Superman. I sorta married the two into my version of both characters.

What did Christopher Reeve bring to Superman that you responded to?

He was the first man I saw fly. He was my first Superman. He was Superman to me. He had that twinkle in his eye when he played Superman. That little twinkle in his eye suggested that he knows just a bit more than everybody around. He has that little sense of fun with the character. I really, really liked that in the films.

Fans often want actors to be lifelong fans of the heroes they play.

I understand that. Nicolas Cage [who almost played the Man of Steel in Tim Burton's never made Superman film] was a huge comic book fan. I read them casually and enjoyed them but I was never a big comic book fan. But if I had to pick a favorite superhero I would have picked either Superman or Aquaman because he seemed cool. Although I'm not really sure why I liked Aquaman as a kid. I certainly would not want to play Aquaman.

[Laughs] Wait. Let's go back to that. Aquaman. You have to explain it. Why did you like him?

I don't know. It's something that I liked as a kid. Maybe it's because someone else took Superman and I wasn't allowed to be him. Or maybe it was because my brother was two years older than me and I thought, "If my brother likes him and if Aquaman can talk to dolphins then I want to be him." But growing up my two favorites were Superman and Aquaman. As I grew into manhood, I became more Superman and less Aquaman.

What parts of yourself did you bring to both characters?

For me and Clark, I think it was my honesty. I am an honest and direct person, but I'm also very kind. At the heart of it, I'm a very kind person. I certainly don't have all the wonderful characteristics that Clark Kent and Superman have but I do have a number of them. I'm much more apt to react angrily to something than Clark Kent would, but Clark also knows that he has the advantage that he can take care of any situation without having to resort to anger. So he has that added bit of oomph that I as a mortal human being don't have, but the two attributes that I brought to the part were honesty and kindness.

Sounds like you enjoyed playing Clark a little more than you enjoyed playing Superman.

A lot more. I really enjoyed playing Clark Kent. To me Clark Kent was the real character. That's the real guy. Superman was a character that Clark Kent and his mother created. Superman was a man of action. I always wanted Superman to come in, do what he had to and get out. I didn't want him to sit around, talk, dilly-dally or give speeches. Whenever that did happen, I always felt uncomfortable. So, I fought for that approach as much as I could.

I think the better scenes in your series are the ones between Lois and Clark. In fact, in the show's title, Lois & Clark: The New Adventures of Superman, the Man of Steel gets third billing.

Absolutely. There's no question about that. I watch a lot of superhero films today and every one of them are replaying moments that we first did in Lois & Clark. I'll watch a film and think to myself, "Oh we did that. We did that too." Whether it's a Spider-Man or Batman movie, it's really interesting to watch it and think, "Wow, we did that a long time ago." Twenty years ago. Good lord.

Did you ever wear the suit during the audition process?

No. No.

That's seems unusual. I know Brandon Routh and Henry Cavill had to test with the suit on.

Nothing at all. They didn't put us in a suit. They didn't do anything. At the end of the whole process when it went to the network, it was down to me and Kevin Sorbo [who would later go on to play Hercules in the series Hercules: The Legendary Journeys].

Kevin Sorbo? He's a very different type from you.

Extremely. So, I was feeling pretty good about it. He's blond. I was thinking, "I got this!" Although after I did two auditions for them and they wanted to see a third, I thought, "Oh, no. I screwed something up." I think they were concerned about my age. Because at the time, I was twenty-seven years old, and I was the youngest guy to ever played Superman. I could understand their concern.

Tell me about the first time you put on the suit.

The suit was its own whole thing. There was definite trepidation. Because all they gave me was tights. Lycra tights. A little tight suit. As a football player and a guy who was in good shape I didn't worry about that. I thought, *Great!* But when I put it on I thought, *Wow. There's nothing there. It's just me.* So, it was important for me to be in great shape and work out during that very demanding schedule. They weren't very accommodating in that respect. I'll be dead honest. They didn't make any time for me and they could have. I wanted to do it, but they weren't as accommodating as I would have hoped. They didn't have a whole fitness center in there. It would have been nice.

That just seems like one of the tools you need to have if you're going to play the Man of Steel.

You definitely need to. At one point I offered to be the Overweight Superman. To be the Fat Superman. I was only getting six hours of sleep a night. That was very tough on my body and my mental state. We would work for fourteen hours or fifteen hours a day. That was *every single day.* Five days a week. Nine and half months a year. It felt like there was no break. On the other hand I was twenty-seven. I could do a lot more at that age. Being a single father I could never do that now.

Did you ever allow yourself to feel heroic in the suit?

No. You start putting on the airs when doing so. Then a little kid will show up on the set and will stare at your with these wide eyes and they're thinking, "Oh my gosh. There's Superman." Then they watch you shoot a scene where you're supposed to fly away during the scene. We had this thing called a "cape-out" where I would hold my cape, jump up as if to fly away, and I'd just duck behind the camera while the other actor would look up in the sky. But a kid will see that and think, "What is that? I thought he was Superman." As soon as that happens, any power you might have felt is *removed.*

A long time ago, I worked on a Batman movie, and the Batsuit had a kind of hypnotic affect on people.

The Batsuit is different. The Batsuit has muscles built into it, and he has all these gadgets hidden away in it. For Superman, it was just me in a pair of tights with cape and boots. It had a hypnotic effect on children, but adults would look at it and say, "That's it, huh?" [Dismissively] "Those tights, wow. All right."

But hear me out on this. When a guy goes to a store, buys a Superman t-shirt and then puts it on, I think he gets a little goosed, feels a little surge of power.

Sure.

But while you see it in others you didn't allow yourself to feel that?

I was definitely goosed and excited to play the part, but I just didn't feel powerful. I thought it was a thrill and a kick in the tail to play this character and to be forever associated with him is fantastic. What a lucky thing for me to experience that in my life. Especially about this character that I admire and adore. So I was as happy as a clam. I'm an actor first and I never believe the hype. I was on *People's* Fifty Most Beautiful People one year (1994), but I didn't make it on the list the following year. I thought, "What happened? Did I just get unsexy?"

Did you get a little less beautiful?

[Laughs] I come from a very strong family. If you start to believe your own press, then that will inevitably lead to a very bad fall from grace. I'm also an athlete, and as an athlete I know that there will always be someone bigger, stronger, faster. So you just need to do your best and not worry about anything beyond that. Don't believe the hype. Don't believe the good things. Don't believe the bad things. When you stand in front of the mirror you should know who you're looking at and that's all that ever mattered to me, but I never said to myself, "I am Superman." That was never, ever the case.

There have been huge changes in the industry about the perception of acting in a superhero project, and many actors, perhaps most, who have worn a cape have expressed their con-

Teri Hatcher as Lois Lane and Dean Cain as Superman.
© Warner Bros. Television

cern about being typecast, but ultimately the answer is that it's too big of an opportunity to pass up.

Yes, it's changed tremendously. There are a lot more superheroes out there. There's a lot more product out there today. I've witnessed incredible generation changes. Where people of a certain age know me as the guy who did *Ripley's Believe It Or Not!*

(2000-2003), or they see me as Scott Peterson [in the TV-movie *The Perfect Husband: The Laci Peterson Story* (2004).

What audiences see you in first is often how they know you. I've done a hundred different parts since *Lois & Clark* and I've played all kinds of different roles, but you still could be typecast. They'll say Dean Cain is Superman, or Brandon Routh is Superman, or they can now say it with Henry Cavill, but being typecast is not something that I was ever concerned with. I just never was, and I'm not concerned with it now, and I don't think it's something that Henry has to worry about . . . nor Brandon.

You made a funny video about your association with the character. Where you Tim Daly, Brandon Routh all induct Tim Daly's son, Sam, who voiced Superman in an animated film into your secret society of actors who have also played the Man of Steel.

[The club was called] The League of Supermen. That was with Tim Daly and his son Sam [who plays the voice of Superman in the animated film *Justice League: The Flashpoint Paradox* (2013)] and our friend Ben Shelton [who wrote and directed the short]. They recruited Brandon and I. You have to be in on the joke. Back in the day George Clooney said something like if you put on the suit, you have to get the joke. You have to be in on the joke and you can't take yourself too seriously.

I thought there was something fun and special about seeing all the Supermen together. I saw your interview with Katie Couric in which you said the only downside to having played Superman is going to the park these days to play ball, because inevitably someone will razz you about playing Superman.

By the way, that was not a problem in my twenties, even into my thirties, but now in my forties that stuff has begun to hurt more. "Hey Superman!" And I'm like, "Come on." I play in a basketball league with Brandon, Tim Daly, and Sam Daly. Of the four of us, Sam is the best player. I'll say it openly. He's also the youngest. I'm saying there might be a correlation there. There was a long time where I'd be like, "Bring it on." Nowadays I'm like, "Look, I *was* Superman, but now I can almost play Jor-El."

So, the three Supermen play basketball together? You, Tim and Brandon?

The four Supermen. Sam is the voice [in *Justice League: The Flashpoint Paradox*]. Yeah, it's called the E-League. The Entertainment League. There's all kinds of people who have played in it over the years – Will Ferrell, Adam Sandler, Justin Timberlake, to DiCaprio and Tobey Maguire. It's taken pretty seriously. We have former D1 players. It gets pretty serious.

How has playing the part affected you the most?

That's a good question. For me it was a career builder. It was the role that started my career. As an actor, you are known as the work you do. So if that's the big role you played, that's how people know you – until you start doing something else.

What about personally?

I don't know if it's done anything else besides give me a career. It's associated me with a fantastic good character, but like I said, I think I'm a kind person at heart, and I don't think I've said, "I should start being a kind and good person because I played Superman." I've always been a good student and a good athlete. I've been judged by a higher standard because of that. I was a student leader. I've also held myself to a higher standard because of that.

I don't think taking the role of Superman has changed me personally other than giving me a good job that has given me international acclaim, which are pretty big things. But other than that it hasn't made me a different person. But in some respects starring in any TV show will change you because your personal life is out there. But I will say that as I've gotten older I do talk about myself less. There's less I want people to know about me. Although I like people to know that I'm a father.

Does your son think that there are certain aspects of your being Superman that are cool?

He finds every aspect of it cool. My son thinks I am Superman. That's great. I want to keep it that way.

That might be the best benefit of playing Superman.

It very well could be. Without a doubt. Most people think their dads are Superman; my son is sure of it.

[Laughs] How would you like to be remembered for this part?

Hmmm. Every incarnation is a little bit different. I think our version had a wonderful sense of humanity to it. I think he was a

Dean Cain and Teri Hatcher get cozy. © Warner Bros. Television

very human figure even though he is an alien. It's much different than the one Henry Cavill played. Much different than the way Brandon Routh played really. I liked our sense of humor and our not always serious take. I put way more hours in the suit than anyone else. So if for nothing else, remember me as the guy who put the most time in. If you look at the sheer hours spent in the suit: Four years, twenty-two episodes a year – except for one year which had twenty-one.

Do you still have the suit?

I do not have a suit, and there's a reason for that. We were coming back for season five, so I had no reason to pilfer things from the set, but while we were on hiatus it was announced that Terry was pregnant and not able to work. That's the reason we didn't do a season five; she wasn't able to work. I got a call from Tony Jonas, who was the head of Warner Bros. Television, and he said, "That's the end." I would have liked to have had a season five. I would have liked to have finished it out. I would have liked to have an ending to the show. That would have been great.

Do you know how the show would have ended?

That's a question for our exec-producers. I had some ideas of my own. I wrote a couple of episodes of the show titled "Season Greetings" and "Virtually Destroyed." I had ideas but I don't know if they were the same as our exec-producers.

What were your ideas?

Well at the end of the last episode of season four, there was a baby delivered to the house, and we didn't know whose it was. So, my thought process was it that if we had done an additional season, it was a baby that they would grow to care for but they would have to give it back. Maybe it was a Kryptonian baby. Maybe it was from a regular person who just didn't have the ability to care for the child, but they would grow to love the baby and when they would have to give it back it would break Lois' heart. Then she would say, "Ok, let's have a baby of our own." That's what I thought was going to happen, but who knows?

I thought it would be Lois, Clark, and a Kryptonian baby.

I loved that idea. I wanted them to have kids. Think about what could have happened. There are no rules on what could have happened with a Kryptonian and human mating. We worked a lot with DC hand in hand. That to me would have been a whole new life for the show and maybe even a spin-off. So, I want writing credit for creating *Smallville*. [Laughs]. It could have been anything. He could have grown thirteen years in just five days. It could have been anything. There are no rules. Nobody knows. I would have enjoyed that personally. I thought it would be really fun to create for the first time that whole situation. There are a few episodes that speculate what that might be like. There's one scene that Lois imagines they have ten babies and some of them start floating. There were a lot of silly fun ideas that could have been explored and I would have enjoyed that.

Finally. Who would in a fight: your Superman or Henry Cavill's Superman?

I think if we're talking characters, then Henry's would win. His Superman is a little more bad-ass in that sense. His special effects were a lot better. But it's pretty tough to take out my Superman character. Although he did have a weakness and that weakness was Lois Lane. Henry's character didn't have that weakness. His Superman would probably win.

Let's go in the other direction chronologically. What about George Reeves' Superman?

My Superman would win for sure, but if you're talking about who would win with the real guys, I would mop the floor with them all. [Laughs]

Tim Daly is Superman

Bruce Timm, Alan Burnett, and Paul Dini, the creative team behind *Batman: The Animated Series*, were tapped to bring the same sophisticated and nuanced approach to the Superman mythos that they brought to the Dark Knight. The result of their combined effort was *Superman: The Animated Series* starring Tim Daly as Superman/Clark Kent, Dana Delaney as Lois Lane, David Kaufman as Jimmy Olsen, and Clancy Brown as Lex Luthor.

The show, which ran from 1996-2000, boasted an eclectic array of voice talent, including Malcolm McDowell as Metallo, Brad Garrett as Lobo, Lori Petty as Livewire, Ron Perlman as Jax-Ur, Gilbert Gottfried as Mister Mxyzptlk, Bud Cort at Toyman, William H. Macy as the Director of the Paranormals Institute, and Sarah Douglas, who played Kryptonian supervillain Ursa in the first two Superman features films, as Mala.

Daly also played Superman in the direct-to-video animated films *Superman: Brainiac Attacks* (2006), *Superman/Batman: Public Enemies* (2009), *Superman/Batman: Apocalypse* (2010), and in the video games *Superman* (1998), *Superman: Shadow of Apokolips* (2002), *Superman: Brainiac Attacks* (2006), and *Justice League: Doom* (2012).[46]

Daly passed the torch to his son Sam Daly, an actor, who voiced the Man of Steel in the animated film *Justice League: The Flashpoint Paradox* (2013). To celebrate the occasion, the two Dalys made a tongue-in-cheek YouTube video entitled *The Daly Superman*. In the six and half minute short, both Dalys appear alongside Dean Cain and Brandon Routh, who induct Sam into a secret society called The League of Supermen. The three former "Supermen" give the newest member of this "very elite club" pointers on how to fly but wind up squabbling over who is the "true Superman."

THE INTERVIEW

How did you get cast in the part of Superman?

The producers had been struggling to find someone for the voice of Superman and for whatever reason they didn't think the people who came in to read were right. A friend of mine Arleen Sorkin, [who plays Harley Quinn in *Batman: The Animated Series*], who was married to Chris Lloyd, [co-creator of *Modern Family*], who was a writer on [Daly's sitcom] *Wings*, recommended me. I went in, met with them, did a little reading, and they hired me in the room. To this day, I'm not sure if it was my voice or if there was something about me. Because I can't have imagined that there weren't a lot of good voices.

The one direction they gave me was that they didn't want the voice to be in quotation marks. They didn't want the difference between Superman's and Clark's voices to be enormous. They said it could be subtle and the picture would take care of the larger than life aspects of Superman. I tried to honor that.

When you heard that you were being considered for Superman what was your reaction?

My reaction was mild, "Oh, that would be cool." That was it. I didn't think about it until people started to say to me, "I love you as the voice of Superman. It's awesome." That's when I realized that people take Superman and the cartoon very, very, very seriously. Sometimes I think, "Wow. What have I gotten myself into?"

I felt like I was doing something right, but I began to wonder if I had more responsibility then I considered at first. I started to ask myself those types of questions, and I decided that I wasn't going to drive myself crazy and I was going to continue to have fun. Superman can be picked over in a scholarly way, about what he means and the larger literary and social ramifications. But in the end, it's a cartoon and it should be fun. That's my approach to it. That it should be fun. Primarily, the cartoon should entertain.

How did you find the voice for the two characters? Did you try slightly deeper versions of your own voice for Superman and slightly higher for Clark?

I was essentially myself. Superman is really virtuous and earnest. I tried to not apologize for those things. To let those be heroic. We live in such a cynical time that when people are un-ashamedly earnest we make fun of them. We think of them as chumps. The Joker and Lex Luthor think of Superman in that light. But Superman is very comfortable in his own skin. Even as Clark Kent he knows what he has underneath his disguise. He doesn't feel a need to use his powers unless he has to. He's not a bad guy who goes around destroying things because he can. He only displays his might when he has no other choice.

What motivates Superman?

He's an interesting guy. On some level, Superman is sad. He's from another planet. He's away from home. He's the ultimate lonely guy. He's taken on this responsibility to use this incred-ible power that he has for the purpose of doing good that's been given to him by his sweet, Midwestern adoptive parents. As Clark Kent, he can't really share his real vulnerability or his loneliness or his otherness with anybody. He's really taken on a lot.

What makes Clark tick?

I think Clark is a sad guy. He has to make sure that he doesn't become the tall poppy and stand out too much. He knows so much more than he's able to let on. He's got this unrequited love for Lois Lane: the woman he loves who also loves him even though she doesn't know it. Now that I'm talking to you about it, it sounds more interesting and psychologically complex that I had originally considered. [Laughing] It taps into an adolescent idea of loving someone and being misunderstood and being afraid to reveal yourself because you're afraid to get hurt. In that respect, it reflects a common adolescent's experience. Some would say that it's just like high school.

It's not necessary for Clark to be as bumbling as he frequent-ly appears to be, which actually makes him stand out more. It also pushes Lois away even more.

Right. One of the things I always found funny about Superman is that we ask the audience to buy the idea that he becomes unat-tractive when he puts on a pair of glasses and acts as if he's a little clumsy, which is crazy. He's still freakin' Superman. He's still a big, strapping hot guy. You put a pair of glasses on Chris Reeve and he's still a good-looking guy.

We're asked to suspend our disbelief and accept that just because he's a little bit goony that Lois, or other women for that matter, wouldn't be attracted to him. It's the author's conceit to make Clark a little bumbling to help the audience understand why he isn't recognized as Superman and why women aren't all over this guy. When in reality they would be anyway. On his own planet he would be just a regular guy. He would be like everyone else.

Who is the real person: Superman or Clark Kent?

That is a really, really good question. I'm trying to think of what the right answer is. I think that maybe the real character was lost when he was a kid. He's invented Clark *and* he's invented Superman. Both these personalities are aspects of him that have been exaggerated to keep people from really knowing him. I'm sure a psychologist would have a field day with behavior like that.

Superman's story is sometimes thought of as an immigrant's story. Is that still the attraction, or how has it changed?

It might still be part of it. It's a real American story. We live in a culture now where advertising and the modern media have convinced everyone that there's a superstar inside every one of us, that all of us deserve to be stars; we just haven't been discovered yet. That can cause considerable frustration and dissatisfaction and it may sometimes help to explain why people who feel that they've been wronged are so quick to bring litigation for minor mishaps – perhaps someone has spilled coffee on them – to make up for the larger injustices they feel they have suffered.

The American Dream has for many become the notion that you are Superman or Superwoman waiting to happen. We live in a culture where advertising and the media have convinced (or nearly convinced) many of us that there is a superstar inside each one of us – that all of us deserve to be stars, and we just haven't been discovered yet. The immigrant's dream has long been that if you got to America – the land of promise and opportunity – and if you worked hard, you could become anything. The dream, which used to assume hard work is now predicated on serendipity and a kind of magical thinking: you just have to be in the right place at the right time to be discovered and then you get to appear on *American Idol*. There is certainly seems to be something that's become ingrained in us and in the American dream that we all can be Superman.

Did you ever allow yourself to feel heroic while playing Superman?

No. No. That's one of the things that actors talk about all the time that makes me very uncomfortable. To me, an actor's preparation ought to remain private. I understand that some actors – frequently they're method actors – say they seek "to become" the characters they play, and that sometimes they've immersed themselves so deeply into the character they're playing that they have to struggle to reclaim themselves after finishing with a role; and I also understand that some people who study acting are fascinated by actors' accounts of the enormous effort they've put into shaping a performance. I'm not interested in that. So, my answer to your question is No.

Here's a funny question. When doing the voice work, did you ever put on a Superman t-shirt?

[Laughs] That is funny. No, I don't think I ever wore my Superman shirt.

Do you think it would affect you if you wore it? Because when kids and adults wear the shirt, they feel empowered.

When I was doing Superman, my posture and my presence changed. When I was doing those violence scenes, when there was conflict, my body reacted naturally to what my imagination told it was happening to it. Maybe if I put on the cape, as well . . . [Laughs]. Although I don't think the tights would really help me.

What else interests you about Superman?

It's interesting to me, and it is also very American, that at the end of the day Superman solves all of the problems with violence. He's usually not the first person to attack, but Superman is still violent. All of our superheroes are violent. Even Iron Man gives lip service to the idea that this guy has a conscience. "Oh he's built this weapon and it will fall into the wrong hands and people will use it for evil," but then he rationalizes his use of force. "If the weapon is in the hands of good people, then it's okay." He's the guy who ends up kicking people's ass, and given the nature of the stories, the good guys don't seek to reason or negotiate with the bad guys.

There are scenarios where violence seems to be the only choice. On the other hand, and this is political, the people I think of, the people who have made significant changes in the world have done so by absorbing violence and not returning it. Take Jackie Robinson, for instance: he was a guy who wanted to lash out but he didn't. Through perseverance, he silenced and out-lasted his enemies. Superman is a violent guy. I admire him for trying to avoid violence, but he knows he can go there, and he frequently does.

Are superheroes modern day gods?

In many Biblical myths, there is a lot of violence, and the Greek and Roman gods were often violent. These myths hold up a mir-ror to the human violence that their authors witnessed. It's a democratic story in Superman's case. Superman isn't a benevo-lent god who seeks to control us and reshape our cosmos, and I'm not sure that Americans would want him to take that kind of con-trol. It conflicts with our sense of ourselves as Americans, as an independent, can-do people. We seem almost to like for things to be messy and then have to hash it all out, but we're complicated, and I suspect that many Americans hope that when humanity is seriously threatened, a powerful force will intervene to save us.

Do you think you could have played another superhero, or is there something about you and Superman that just fit?

I think I'm better suited for Batman. My sensibilities are a lot darker than Superman's. The interpretation of me as Jack Arm-strong, all-American boy, suits the version of Superman and the snap shot of Tim Daly. But my take on the world is a little darker. A little more cynical. On the inside I'm a little more like Batman. A little more damaged. [Laughs]

Christopher Reeve said he felt like a temporary custodian of the part and felt the weight of the responsibility. Did you feel that way or was it just a job for you?

Chris Reeve had a very different experience from mine. I show up in my sweatpants and do the voice for a couple of hours. Chris had to embody Superman and the image of Superman in a series of enormously successful movies. I did not feel those kinds of responsibilities. However, I've joked that I'm around to keep America safe from democracy.

We've talked about some political and psychological stuff, but at the end of the day, it is a cartoon and should be fun. When Al Roker was interviewing me about what it's like to play Superman, I said, "Honestly Al, the majority of my work in the cartoon is making grunting and screaming noises because Superman is always getting whacked with a girder or a laser beam. Come to think of it, it's a little disconcerting to think that the children of American know what I sound like in bed." Al thought it was funny, but the rep from Warner Bros. nearly had a coronary. Then I got a nice letter from Warner Bros asking to respect the children audience for Superman and to try to watch the off color jokes.

Have you spoken to any other actors who have played Superman?

I knew Chris, but I didn't speak to him about playing Superman. I knew through mutual friends that he had some ambivalence about playing Superman. On one hand, it gave him a huge amount of power and it gave him a career. On the other hand, it was a stigma that followed him around and it was very difficult to shake. That's always an odd trade-off for an actor, when you do something that so identifies you, you can feel trapped.

When people spoke of Christopher Reeve as Superman, I don't believe it was about typecasting. I think it was about the way they felt about him.

We humans seem to need or want to create heroes. We've done it since we crawled out of the ooze. Whether it's in the form of Gods or champions or superheroes, we need to look up to some figure. If you look at the Greeks, the seeds for all these ideas are there. If you look at Ulysses or Achilles, you'll see certain traits from our modern superheroes in them. Look at President Obama: he makes jokes about that. He's trying to explain to people who are so happy about his ascendancy to power that he's a man. He's not a savior. He's a man who is trying to do good. Maybe that's the interesting thing about Superman. Maybe that's why there's Clark. To remind us that he's a man.

Do you have any Superman action figures?

I do. I have a really cool one made of lacquered wood that I love. It's on a shelf in my home in Vermont. I should cop to this: for a long time I wore this gold Superman pin, and I really like it. It was really subtle. It just had the S on it, his emblem. As a matter of fact, I wish I could find it right now. It bothers me that I don't know where it is. I did like wearing that.

Was there some aspect of Superman that you would have liked to see revealed.

I always liked and continue to like it when Superman injects his wry sense of humor into situations. It's tricky because if it happens too often, Superman becomes a comedian. The movie I did - it's called *Superman/Batman: Public Enemies* - is very political. Lex Luthor becomes President of the United States, and he's very much like George W. Bush. Batman and Superman team up to save the country. Superman has a very wry take on Batman. Superman's amused by Batman's bitterness and troubled worldview.

The thing about Superman and Batman is that they were both orphaned and they responded to their tragedy of life in two very different ways. Superman through inspiration and Batman through terror.

I hadn't thought of that, but that's true. That's a good analogy for how people deal with hardships. You can turn it into an opportunity or feel cursed.

Why are superheroes popular?

Because they can do whatever they want to. All of us want to live forever and to be invulnerable. We want to feel omnipotent. People have dreamt and fantasized about it forever. Superheroes have recently been undergoing a transformation, from being like Superman, pure and kind of a Boy Scout, to being much edgier, to being morally and ethically conflicted. A lot of superheroes now are a little sketchy. Superman represents our innocence. Our wanting to do good. Batman and Iron Man reflect our cultural evolution and our more jaded feelings about people in power, our disappointments, our suspicions. They are a little more complicated.

How has playing Superman affected you personally?

It strengthened my belief that the use of violence is almost always futile. That violence almost always begets more violence. I think I say that because there was so much violence and so little dialogue in some episodes that it became a little – I wouldn't say depressing, but it was shocking to me. I would think, "Is that all were doing for this half hour. Showing Superman warring with other people? Does that become the message?"

The third season was particularly violent. I don't show those episodes to my son.

We live in a violent world. For some reason we Americans, we've resigned ourselves to the idea that violence is something that we need to have and to employ. I think that's really sad. I think it's sad for us.

Michael Caine has said that Superman is how America sees itself, but Batman is how the rest of the world sees America. I think he was speaking particularly about the use of power and force.

That's a very interesting thing to say. I don't know if I agree, but I think it would be interesting to ask a number of Europeans if they share that view of America. I don't know if Europe, Africa or China have their own superheroes. All the ones we've spoken about are American. I remember doing a movie in Australia and people were asking me about living in Los Angeles. They'd say, "Do you see a lot of drive by shootings? Does everyone have guns?" They see us as a very wild, lawless, violent place. Perhaps he's right.

What question should I ask the next superhero I speak to?

I'm interested in this subject of violence. My question would be: Do you think that your superhero could be as effective if he or she didn't use violence? In drama, you obviously need conflict. That's the nature of it, but does it have to be violent conflict? Could a superhero use ideas to solve problems? President Clinton said, "Let us be known by the power of our example rather than the example of our power." That's an interesting and beautiful concept. Can it work? I don't know, maybe it can.

If Superman were a real life figure, should he wipe out all our problems, or is it important for us to do that ourselves? If the end is the same, is the means correct?

That's really interesting. That gets into a whole political discussion about the use of power. For instance, people keep talking to me about Iraq and how the violence is down because of the surge. The question is do you want to live in place where it's necessary to have a soldier on every corner to keep things peaceful, knowing that if they leave, people may resume killing one another? Or do you want to arrive at that peace as an understanding between groups of people? That's a big question.

I feel a little uncomfortable asking this question given the thoughtfulness of your answers about violence, but I will anyway. Who would win in a fight between Superman and Batman?

I'd have to say that Superman would kick Batman's ass, unless, of course, Batman got hold of Kryptonite. In a fair fight, Superman wins. He's Superman! When I watch Superman, I always think they are stretching it when Superman is in duress. It's like, "Come on, he's Superman! He'd be fine."

James Marsden is Cyclops

The first three X-Men movies together grossed over $600 million worldwide in box office revenue alone.[47] Each successive X-Men sequel in the original trilogy has earned more than the previous one.

In all three films James Marsden played the mutant hero Cyclops (whose real name is Scott Summers). Cyclops has the ability to shoot a destructive optic blast from his eyes and the only way he can control his power is by wearing a specially designed ruby-quartz visor at all times. So, except for those instances in which Cyclops temporarily loses his powers, he's always looking at the world through a filter. But at a time when antiheroes are so popular — among them, Hugh Jackman's Wolverine, Thomas Jane's Punisher, and Wesley Snipes' Blade — any attempts to view Cyclops as an isolated and tragic figure don't ring quite true. What makes Cyclops unique is that he loves being a traditional, old-fashioned good guy, and he's not particularly haunted by his powers. Quite the opposite: Cyclops is one well-adjusted mutant.

Cyclops is a member of the X-Men, a superhero group comprised of people who are ostracized from the rest of society for being different. On their best days, they are feared by the public; on their worst, they are hunted down.

In *X2* (2003), the mutants are persecuted when the government passes the Mutant Registration Act, a bill that forces all mutants to register with the government. In *X-Men: The Last Stand* (2006), the government has stepped up its war on them by creating an inoculation that "cures" mutants of their power.

Many see the X-Men as a metaphor for any group that is shunned for being different. In his book *Super Heroes: A Modern Mythology*, Richard Reynolds suggests: "The whole theme of the X-Men – the isolation of mutants and their alienation from 'normal' society – can be read as a parable of the alienation of any minority . . . of a minority determined to force its own place within society."[48]

In *Reading Comics*, Douglas Wolk writes that the X-Men are: "unlike ordinary people and [are] despised for it . . . and X-Men stories tend to be, on some level, allegories about difference and identity politics."[49]

Professor X, the wheelchair-bound leader of the X-Men, encourages them to "use their awesome abilities to protect a world that hates and fears them." His peaceful goals and methods are in stark contract to Magneto who as a child escaped a Nazi concentration camp and came to America hoping to find sanctuary. Instead, he was oppressed further. Magneto believes that "it's just a matter of time before mutants are herded off to camps." He is willing to do anything (including murdering his oppressors) to escape further persecution. His rationale is that: "American was going to be the land of tolerance. Peace . . . [But] there is no land of tolerance. There is no peace. Not here, or anywhere else where women, children, whole families are destroyed simply because there were born different from those in power."

It is not difficult to see parallels between the X-Men's plight and America's civil rights movement during the 1960s. The conflicting approaches that Professor X and Magneto take to achieve their goals, nonviolence versus violence, are analogous to those of Dr. Martin Luther King Jr. and Malcolm X, who was a radical Muslim convert.

In the X-Men films, it's the United States government and not Magneto that is the true villain. Despite his actions, the films always maintain some empathy for Magneto. For on a basic level Magneto, like the rest of the X-Men, is a misfit, and thus he has more in common with the X-Men than he does with their persecutors.

At the end of their journey, all the X-Men must come to understand that what others view as "mutations," they must view as their "gifts." What sets the X-Men movies apart from other

James Marsden as Cyclops. © Twentieth Century Fox

superhero movies is their unique message that people who are discriminated against can rise to the challenge as heroes.

THE INTERVIEW

[I phone Marsden.] Did I catch you at a good time?

You caught me at a perfect time. You called right when I thought you'd call.

Your psychic ability is another one of your super powers.

It helps when I get little hints in your emails.

How did you create the character for Cyclops?

One of the great luxuries is that he was already created by Stan Lee. There was forty-something years of history and a mythology that was very rich in detail. All I had to do was research the character and who he was. That said, [director] Bryan Singer's approach to the first two X-Men films was to introduce them to an entire generation who may or may not know who they are. So he took a bit of creative license to make his own version of the X-Men. There were certain things that were in the comics that weren't in the movies and vice versa. The first film was really about setting up who the characters were and what they wanted. Wolverine is supposed to be five foot three and Hugh Jackman is very tall. Those things usually don't matter that much as long as the essence of the spirit of the characters and what they stand for is there.

I knew who the X-Men were. Though I never really read the comics, I had seen the cartoon and played the video game. I was relatively familiar with Cyclops and the other popular characters. I had a friend who was very into them. He helped me learn about them quickly. I was the last person cast in the film. So, I had to cram for an exam in front of the camera.

I'll stop this answer pretty soon. [Laughs] I was mindful that there is a huge, huge following of the X-Men comics. I really wanted to make the fans happy and do it in the right way. You always hear about a book that's been made into a film and people get up in arms about how the transformation from book into screen falls short. You have to keep it under two hours. That was our big challenge. How do you take the forty-odd year of history of these characters and distill it to an hour and fifty minutes? For me personally with Cyclops, I wanted to learn as much about him as possible and get it right for the fans, within the framework of the script and what Bryan Singer wanted to accomplish in his X-Men universe.

What do you think that essence is of his Cyclops?

Here's my X-Men trading card answer for that. To me what is interesting about the character is that he was the first leader of the

X-Men group and the first member of the team. His mentor and father figure was Professor Xavier [played by Patrick Stewart]. Professor X started his school for gifted youngsters and Cyclops was his first pupil. There is a very fertile relationship there between Cyclops and Professor X.

Cyclops has plenty of insecurities. He often views his powers as a curse. He feels damned. He has to wear these glasses to channel his energy. Professor X taught him how to use them in a good way to the benefit of both humankind and mutantkind. Cyclops grew to be a man who became a very strong leader. He is very good at strategy and rational thinking. And he is very dedicated. He's a boy scout — very straight-laced and very by the book. He's the one you'd want to be your general if you're going into battle. This all laid the groundwork for dissonance between Wolverine and Cyclops. Wolverine was obviously very much a rogue and a fly-by-the-seat-of-his-pants guy. He didn't follow the rules. So they butted heads a lot. That's obviously not my trading card answer because that wouldn't all fit on a card.

How powerful are the optic blasts that emanate from his eyes?

They are often described as "concussive beams of force" that are powerful enough to punch holes through mountains.

Talk a little more about how his powers are a curse. In comics, super powers are usually a desirable fantasy.

They are a curse to Cyclops because he has been conditioned, like a lot of mutants, to second-guess himself and his powers because of the reaction that is generated by human beings who feel threatened by them. That really is a metaphor for living life. At some time in our lives, we all tend to feel like the outsider or the freak. We all feel ostracized.

In X-Men 3, they introduced the idea of the cure [which would take away a mutant's powers]. Would you want to be like everybody else if you could? Would that make your life better? That introduces a real interesting element to the third movie. Cyclops struggles with his self-confidence and with the feeling that he's cursed. I don't think it surfaces very often. It's just beneath all that training and teaching that Professor X has given him, but it's still all there because he lives in a world where people fear him because he's different.

Was there an element to the character that you wish you could have explored more deeply?

I was always campaigning to do more with Cyclops, but there are a lot of characters in each movie. Each character had to be introduced and all the actors were really excited to play them. It's a lot of fun, too. It's a childhood fantasy. You're playing an icon. You're playing someone who is superhuman. Selfishly, you say to yourself, "I really want to show off my powers in these movies." But as I said, you have to keep it under two hours. So, you get to do what you get to do.

Bryan has a very clear idea of what he wants. I love Bryan's restraint in the movies that he directed. He could have had the movies be about just having the characters show off their super powers in lieu of plot or characterization, but that would be hollow. Bryan's take was, "Let's make them the reluctant superheroes. What is beneath all these powers? What are they struggling with internally?"

To answer your question there were times I would say, "It would be great if Cyclops were more physical and was able to exhibit his power more often." You are a very important cog in a very special wheel in Bryan's film and in Brett Ratner's film as well*. You are part of a team. Which is the essence of the X-Men. That spirit carried over for the actors in the making of the film as well.

[*When Bryan Singer left the franchise to direct Superman Returns Twentieth Century Fox hired Brett Ratner to direct the third film. Singer would return to direct X-Men: Days of Future Past (2014), the seventh and highest grossing film in the franchise. The film also marked the return of Marsden's Cyclops.]

As did the struggles of being part of a team and sometimes having to take a back seat.

Absolutely. That's fine. I always felt very grateful to be a part of these movies and to be given what I was given to do with my character. I loved - and I'm remembering from the cartoon, as well - I loved the back and forth between Logan and me. I loved the rivalry within the same team between Wolverine and Cyclops. I felt it would have been great to have a bit more of it in the second and third films.

During the making of the second film, I said to Bryan, "To give Cyclops some dimension what if there was a way for Cyclops could get into a physical fight."

Bryan said, "Well why would he? The logic against that is: why would he when he can just use his powers with his eyes?"

I said, "I don't feel like these characters always want to use their powers. They want to use them as a last resort. They are trained in other areas as well. I think it would be cool to exhibit that and to show that he doesn't rely solely on his powers of an optic blast. He's actually gifted in martial arts and in self defense."

Bryan said, "Why don't you work on the something with the stunt guys and show it to me."

And that became the very quick scene where the guard restrains me from using the visor and I have to defend myself physically with my own two hands. Which I thought was pretty cool.

Just as a cop doesn't always go for his gun. That's always a last resort.

Absolutely. Exactly. You don't want to use your gun if you don't have to. You do "everything but" until if you have to. That was the idea. In some ways, it was limiting because there wasn't a lot to do physically when he used his power. It was literally putting a finger to the visor, which is spectacular when they put in the visual effects, but for an actor, there's not a lot for you to do.

That's actually one of my questions. Part of the fun of playing a superhero is pretending to have the powers and abilities. You want to feel it. But that doesn't happen with your set of powers.

Yes. That's true, and that was the case for a lot of the actors. When Famke Janssen acts out Jean Gray's powers she just stares off into the distance. Our costumes are these tight leather suits that don't allow you much room to move. I remember on the first film we were shooting at the Statue of Liberty and we were stumbling around. We couldn't jump over a little wall. We couldn't make it over a two-foot wall. On the set you work in fragments.

It's often very tedious, very slow going, so we rarely felt empowered by our superhero-ness.

Cyclops (James Marsden) sports a newly designed and decidedly more stylish visor in X-Men: The Last Stand. © *Twentieth Century Fox*

Was there ever a point where you felt, "Damn right! I'm a superhero."

Yes there was. When I put on the outfit and the glasses for the very first time. It was very fortifying. It was very satisfying. I felt very strong. It was a very cool, kick-ass feeling. I would say that first time when we were all in costume together. We all felt very cool and felt like it was something special. The most fun time for me was when I saw the completed film. There's only so much you can do on the set. When you see what you've done and your contribution combined with all the visual effects, that was the most exciting part.

Before *X-Men* was made superhero films were not generally well regarded. Did you have any reluctance about acting in one?

No. I had only done two films; they were mild successes but nothing that catapulted me into superstardom. The idea of being a superhero in a film was something I never had the opportunity to do. I grew up with a great respect for science fiction and films in general. Richard Donner's *Superman* was one of my favorite films. The Star Wars movies informed a lot of my youth. I spent a lot of time dressing up as Han Solo and Luke Skywalker. When the opportunity came to be one of these iconic superheroes in a movie, I was super excited. There was no hesitation whatsoever.

Perhaps it was more true in the past, when an actor who played a character like this was branded as that character. On some basic level, we want the actors to be the characters they play.

When I meet X-Men fans they are always so gracious. You can see how much these movies impacted them. It's the best feeling in the world to witness that enthusiasm. Selfishly for a career, you want to have options. You don't want to play the same part over and over again. The fun of being an actor is playing a lot of different characters and if you're lucky you get to do that over the course of your lifetime. But that said, there are only a few people who can claim the iconic status of playing James Bond, or Harrison Ford and Indiana Jones, or Harrison Ford and Han Solo. That's rarified air. There are only a few people in that club. To be in that club playing a character, who is an icon in the comic book world who then becomes an icon is the film world as well, is something I hold very near and dear to my heart. I wouldn't trade that for anything or replace it with anything.

The X-Men films showed that superhero films could be aimed at adults.

There is something very special about being a part of these three films that brought comic book characters back into the public eye. The 1980s and 1990s weren't a great time for comic book films with the exception of the first two Tim Burton Batman movies. *X-Men* put superheroes back on the map in the film world. I think we paved the way for the successes of Spider-Man and of everything that's come out since then. They made the movies as realistic as they could make them. They made the characters more human than were depicted before in other superhero movies. They tackled issues like bigotry and dealt with tolerance and other issues that are timeless and very human. All the superpowers are ornamental and secondary to the core of these films. That's why these films work and why the comic books have been so successful for the decades they've been around. If they were only about someone being able to fly, or crawl on the wall or fire an optic blast from his eyes, there wouldn't be anything underneath that. I thank Stan Lee for creating these characters, for creating this depth – which was a great launching pad for these films to succeed.

What's great about the X-Men is how they champion diversity.

Right. That's one of the reasons that people respond so strongly to them. I know there have been times in my life where I have felt like a freak or different. There are times when everyone else feels uncomfortable in his own skin and feels like the anomaly. That's going to resonate with many people in the audience who feel the same way. I love that Bryan made that the core of his two movies.

You can substitute being gay or part of the Civil Rights Movement . . .

You can insert that thing that makes you a minority or different. It's there. That's what I love about what Professor X teaches. There is a core group of mutants who wonder why they should care about these people who want to kill them. We are Neanderthals. Combative Magneto [played by Ian McKellen] says, "We [mutants] are the future Charles, not them." Professor X believes that we can embrace each other because of what makes us unique. We can co-exist. What makes us different is what makes us special. It's what makes the world wonderful.

Those two different schools of thought are analogous to the opposed teachings of Malcolm X and Martin Luther King.

That's what makes it very interesting and complicated. Malcolm X, like Magento, had a lot of good points. I can see how I'd feel the same way. Magneto is not a villain who is being evil for evil's sake. He's the villain in the movie, yet you can understand where he is coming from. That's what life is like. Life is very complicated and nuanced. I love that and it adds so much dimension to the relationship between Charles and Magneto, their history together, and how complicated their ideas are about how to deal with this issue. How to deal with needing to fit in when you're not welcome. You really understand where Magnet is coming from. You can say to yourself, "On another day I might side with Magneto." Humans are trying to kill mutants while you're trying to protect them. I could see why he'd say, "Screw you" and [impersonating the sound of a gun going off] bam.

My criticism of the third film that there appears to be some sort of delight in mutant-on-mutant violence. Some perverse satisfaction is watching two groups of disenfranchised super-heroes killing each other.

Yeah, yeah. Well, as an actor, I'm just a player. I am not involved in the decisions being made about the fates of the characters. I kind of agree with you. There was very little involvement with me in the third film. I wasn't that excited about the idea of X-Men going to war and wiping each other out. I thought what made the X-Men ring strongly with viewers and myself is that it suggested an alternative route to deal with issues and problems. In the third film, the solution was to battle. I hate the idea that this is the only way. I've always believed that there was another way. I agree with Charles' philosophy that there should be a peaceful way, that it cannot only be either us or them. The business side of it is that fans are thirsty for more action and more characters and they have to amp it up. It has to be more spectacular and push the envelope even further. To me, killing off half the X-Men isn't raising the bar.

John Shipp asks, "How did playing this part affect you personally, not professionally or publicly, but personally?"

Good question. A lot of these characters including Cyclops, teach you patience. I'm not a Christian, but there are a lot of Christian values in the mindset of the X-Men, most powerfully in Charles' teaching us to love our enemies. I was inspired by Scott and the cause that Professor X was championing. I believe in coexistence. That people can be different and that there is a way that we can all coexist. That we don't have to kill each other because of our differences. That's what I've learned from playing the character.

Is there any downside to playing a superhero?

Sure. The downside is that once you have taken the costume off you realize that you don't have extraordinary powers. There are times where you certainly wish you did. [Laughs]

John Shipp indicated that he felt powerful in the suit and diminished out of it. Do you relate to that?

I can see where that comes from. Then again there were plenty of times that I felt less powerful in the suit and more powerful outside the suit, just because of the physical restrictions the suit imposes and not being able to see a damn thing out of those glasses. In the suit I was a blind superhero. I can totally see why he'd say that although, ultimately, I feel the opposite way. After we put on our costumes, shoot the scene, and then watch the finished film and see how powerful we appear on screen, the fantasy of it fortifies me. It helps remind me of just how powerful – and sometimes super-powerful – humans can be. That power can manifest itself in different ways. It doesn't have to require the ability to lift a giant crater and toss it out into space. Superheroes represent our capacity to do amazing things as human beings. The experience of playing that character and seeing the film helped make me feel like a stronger human being. You don't have to have superpowers to make a difference. I think we underestimate what we are capable of as human beings.

What should I ask the next superhero I speak with?

I can tell you what *not* to ask them. Don't ask them if you could be any superhero or have any superpower what would it be. That's the question we have all gotten very good at answering. Is there a superhero that you grew up wanting to be or that you feel more suited than the character you're playing?

That's actually one of my questions for you. Was Cyclops best suited for you?

When I was younger, I always gravitated to Spider-Man. I always had skinny legs and I thought, "Well I have skinny legs and Spider-Man has skinny legs." I thought he was the only one I could be because all the other superheroes are ripped beyond belief.

What is the biggest perk of being a superhero?

You are immortalized in film playing this character. You will always be Cyclops. It's a great honor. It will outlast me and it will probably be on my tombstone. I do believe these films will hold up and stand the test of time. To have contributed to that, to have been an important piece of that is a huge perk. Every time someone comes up to me on the street and calls me Cyclops it's an unmatched feeling. It's something that is unique and special. I don't think I'll ever be able to do that again.

Christopher Reeve called it being a custodian of the character.

You are the go between. You are the ambassador for the people to him.

Who would win in a fight between Cyclops and Wolverine?

We've actually had this discussion many times. It would be a never-ending battle because you just can't kill Wolverine. He keeps regenerating himself. He's been around for 500 years, but he would never be able to get close to me because I would keep him at a good distance with my blast. Every time he got up I'd knock him down again. He'd never get close enough to use his claws. I'd like to think that it would be a long arduous battle.

PART TWO: HEROIC WOMEN

Yvonne Craig is Batgirl

Bat-Girl first appeared in DC Comics in 1961.

Batgirl first appeared in DC Comics in 1967.

Let me explain.

Bat-Girl, aka Betty Kane, is the niece of Batwoman, aka Kitty Kane, and was created by Bill Finger and Sheldon Moldoff. Batgirl, aka Barbara Gordon, is the niece of Commissioner Gordon and was created by Carmine Infantino and Gardner Fox.

Batgirl was introduced into the *Batman* TV series during its final (1967-1968) season to help boost the series' ratings, which by the end of the second season had substantially dropped. The show's producers, William Dozier and Howie Horowitz, asked famed DC Comics editor Julius Schwartz to help them dream up a new female character that they could fold into the show. Schwartz turned to Infantino and Fox, who, in the Silver Age of comics (1956 to circa 1970), redesigned the now familiar look of The Flash, and who also invented The Justice Society of America, the superhero team which predated The Justice League of America.

Encouraged by the early concept work for Batgirl, Dozier, Horowitz, and Schwartz hatched a plan. The new superheroine would first appear in print in a story fittingly titled *The Million Dollar Debut of Batgirl* and then, later that year, on television in an episode of *Batman* called "Enter Batgirl."

Casting the right actress in the dual role of Batgirl and her alter ego, Barbara Gordon, would be critical to the success of the third season. Enter Yvonne Craig. Craig, an experienced film and television actress, was trained in classical ballet and had appeared opposite a lip-curlin', hip-shakin' Elvis Presley in *Kissin' Cousins* (1964). Craig's Batgirl was quickly embraced by fans. With her character's intelligence and independence, Craig helped introduce the values of the feminist movement into the male-dominated superhero world.

Yvonne Craig as Batgirl. © Twentieth Century Fox Television

THE INTERVIEW

Today superheroes are a big business. It was very different in the 1960s.

You know it *was* different. They hadn't realized that they could make a franchise out of all this. Disney bought Marvel Comics. It's a big business now. I think they've really gone overboard. I mean, I don't really care. [She laughs.] There are just so many of them that you can't keep track.

In those days, superheroes were looked down on a little. Why did you want to do it?

I had done tons of pilots that never went anywhere. So, I wanted to do a series. When I did *Batman*, they had decided to introduce a female character to the third season. They didn't do demographic studies then. They just looked at the fan mail and said, "Look who isn't writing us," and then they'd try to get them. [Laughs] They were looking for pre-pubescent females and over forty males; hence the sprayed on costume.

For the most part, I didn't see my fan mail. Periodically they would give me fan mail and usually it was filled with extraordinary stories like a child was dying and they wanted to meet Batgirl. Of course, we accommodated those, but as a general rule, I never really saw fan mail. So, until I started the convention circuit, I never knew that the producers did meet their goals. Now middle age men will come up to say, and me "You were my first crush," and I think, "You were about *ten*, your hormones were raging, you saw someone in a sprayed on costume, and thought, "Hmmm*hmmm*, girls aren't so bad." [Laughs]

How formative are those first crushes in establishing male tastes in the opposite sex?

One time a guy came up to me when I was walking in Hollywood Hills and he said, "I have to tell you this because it's very important to me. I watched *Batman* and because you were an independent female, it changed my outlook on how I viewed women. I married a girl who was very independent and who has her own career. Nothing like my mother." That was really eye-opening to me. To know that that character had influenced him about his wife for goodness' sake. Girls have come up at me at conventions and said, "You were the first woman I saw on TV who could really hold her own with the guys, and it gave me a sense of empowerment." It had to do with the character I was playing very little to do with me personally. The character was written that way.

They deliberately made the character a librarian. At the time, it was a job a single woman could do without raising any eyebrows.

Yes, absolutely. She was independent, although she and her father had a special relationship with each other. That was a nice added layer. She was also spunky.

And given the amount of knowledge she had, it seemed that she read every book in the library.

I think that's why they cast me. That was so close to who I was. That wasn't a stretch at all. I lucked out because the role combined the two parts of me that had not heretofore been seen on film. It was a breeze to do.

What did [series creator] William Dozier tell you was his take on the character?

He didn't actually say. Mr. Dozier and I had a brief encounter years before. My agent thought it was an altercation, although I didn't see it as an altercation and neither did Mr. Dozier. They were doing a show called *My Little Margie,* and they were replacing an actress. They needed the replacement to be blond. I went in and interviewed.

He said, "Would you be willing to dye your hair blond?"

I said, "No, I wouldn't, but I'd be willing to wear a wig."

He said, "The problem with wearing a wig is that when fans see you on the street and see that you're dark haired, then all the times you're working they'll be looking for a wig and looking for wig lace."

I said, "Not if the dialogue is worth anything." I went back and told my agent.

He said, "You said that to him? You will never work for that man."

But I found out that when Mr. Dozier was casting *Batman,* he didn't even remember the exchange.

I met with [producer] Howie Horowitz and Mr. Dozier and they didn't say anything about the character other than, "We are thinking of introducing a female character and the Dynamic Duo will then become the Terrific Trio." Mr. Dozier said, "Are you interested?"

I said, "Absolutely."

He said, "I'm sure you've seen our show."

I said, "To tell the truth, I haven't seen it."

In those days, I thought television should be more uplifting than reenacting a comic book that I never read. I said, "If you are considering me for this part, I will spend my summer watching the reruns so I know how I fit in."

He said, "Fine."

We did a five-minute presentation reel. It wasn't a pilot; it was a slim story designed to present both Barbara Gordon and Batgirl to the Network. It was only to be seen by the executives of ABC so they could consider if they wanted to incorporate the character or not.

Did you approach them as if you were playing two different characters?

Yes. Two different sides of me. Barbara Gordon was so similar to me that it was just silly. It's who I was. To this day, if you ask me what I'd like to do, I'd say, "Read." I would just like to spend days and days being locked in a bookstore reading. I was a loner as a kid and that's what I liked to do. I used to tutor kids on reading because it's so important. That was no problem at all; that was part of me.

As far as Batgirl, in those days I rode a motorcycle. I wasn't a tomboy at all because I was so reclusive. So, I didn't do those sorts of things. However, I was brought up to believe that anything boys can do girls can do. My mother had wonderful advice. She said, "Boys and girls are exactly alike. They may have different equipment, but they all have the same emotions because they're people." And that stuck with me. I always felt that I was equal to boys. I never had to directly complete. During the 1960s, when the feminism movement started and people were burning bras, I never felt like I was ever put in the position to be a second-class citizen, and that was partly because of my career choices. I was with the Ballets Russes when ice covered the earth, and when you're a ballet dancer, you're really only competing with yourself. You want to be better today than you were yesterday. You want to be better tomorrow than you were today, but I never felt like I had to be better than someone else. I was never put in a position to compete with men for any type of job.

In terms of your independence and intelligence, seems like you and Barbara Gordon had a lot in common.

Absolutely. Absolutely. I graduated really, really early because I skipped a couple of grades in school, probably because all I did was go to study hall. I liked to go there because it was solitary. I joined the ballet when I was sixteen, but I finished high school, so it's not like my education was interrupted. It was wonderful. I saw the United States. I've been blessed in that I've had different careers where I could do exactly what I wanted to do.

How were you like Batgirl?

She was really kick-ass. Can I say that?

[Laughs] Yes, you just did.

[Laughs] She was independent and was very curious. She just wanted to get in the mix. I always wanted to keep up with whatever was going on and I felt that I could get into the mix. To this day, when I walk down the street, I feel like I can take care of myself. I've walked through some very bad neighborhoods and never had any fear at all. Then I have to catch myself and say, "You may think of yourself as thirty-seven, but you are not, and you may not be able to take on some of these people any more." [Laughs]

It's interesting that you'd say that. Other "superheroes" I've spoken to have had similar impulses.

Yeah, you just feel like you're in control. I've felt that way since the time I was sixteen and alone in New York. I walked in bad neighborhoods, but I never felt like I was at a disadvantage.

Did that come from playing Batgirl?

No, because I was sixteen at the time when I originally felt that, but it added to the character. There was an authenticity that I could play because that was kind of person who I was anyway.

Did you like the character?

I just loved her. In the presentation she was a lot cheekier than they allowed her to be once we started shooting the actual show. She was a lot cheekier with Batman and Robin. She would say condescending things like, "I can't believe you did not know that." [Heavy sigh] They toned down that aspect of her personality quite a bit.

Why do you think that happened?

I can understand why. It's because Adam and Burt were playing two characters. I was playing two characters. Then you had Barbara's father, Commissioner Gordon (Neil Hamilton), Chief O'Hara (Stafford Repp), Alfred, the butler (Alan Napier), and the guest villains. You can't be very nuanced in a series that's moving so fast. We shot a new episode every three days, so we had to sacrifice something.

It's an incredible pace.

It *was* incredible. We would get purple pages. When you originally get a script, it's white. Then they give you other pages for changes before a scene is shot. Purple pages on the other hand mean, "We wish you had said this but we didn't write it then." [Laughs] The thing I really respected about producer Howie Horowitz is that he didn't allow actors to change one bit of dialogue. He treated the writers as if they were playwrights. It's really important because the writing is everything. Fans go to conventions and they meet all these actors who played the parts, but they never meet the writers who were really responsible for it.

Would you talk about creating the look for Batgirl?

Mr. Dozier said, "You need to know that DC Comics is coming out with the Batgirl character prior to us putting in on television. It'll be a character that is introduced in the comic book. Their only stipulation is that Batgirl has to be a redhead."

I said, "That's okay."

What we did was that Barbara Gordon has the dark short hair, but when you go into my secret room, you see sitting on a wig stand this red fall that she wore when she was disguised at Bargirl.

It was no problem at all except for at one point somebody said to me, "I have a friend who wants to date you."

I said, "Oh, really."

She said, "He just called me and said that while I like the little dark-haired one I just love the one with red-hair in the show."

I said, "I'm not dating him, he's stupid." [Laughs] I said, "He's as bad as my father who didn't recognize me as Batgirl. Didn't he realize that I used the same voice for both parts?

Did you get the sense that the shadow of Batgirl fell on you?

Not with adults, but I once met a little girl who was just excited to see me. I was in the supermarket and she said, "I know who you really are," and keep in mind one of the reasons I wanted to do a series because I had done a lot of episodic TV, and in episodic TV your face gets known but not your name. When you are coming into someone living room at the same time every week you connect the name with the face. I was so excited when she came up and said, "I know who you really are."

I said to myself [in an excited voice], *She's going to say, 'Yvonne Craig.'* I said, "Who?"

She said, "You're really Barbara Gordon."

I said to myself, *"This is horrible. This is not working."* [Laughs]

There was another kid who came up to me and said, "Oh, Miss Craig. I'm so excited to meet you. Every time I see someone getting kicked in the head I think of you."

I thought, *"Where does she live?"* [Laughs] If people on the street recognized me, they rarely approached me. When they sent us out to do promos they said, "We'll send a body guard."

I said, "Why?"

They said, "When Adam and Burt go out people are tearing their capes off them."

I said, "People wouldn't dare do that to me because I wouldn't let them. Secondly, people are well brought up as far as women are concerned. They wouldn't rip my cape off. They wouldn't manhandle a woman." I was right. I never needed a bodyguard. I guess Adam and Burt did.

I had a conversation one time with Paul Newman and he said, "The difference is that I can walk down the street anytime and because I've been on the big screen no one approaches me. I'm bigger than life on film. I think when you do a TV series you are more approachable because you're in their living room, and they're not paying to see you." But now everyone is up for grabs. The paparazzi are everywhere.

It's one thing to wear your Batgirl suit when you're playing the character and there's a context. How did it feel to wear it in public for the appearances?

I spent my early years in leotards, so it didn't feel uncomfortable at all. It was probably the most comfortable costume I've ever worn. I remember Lee Meriwether said that it was just awful when she played Catwoman and she just hated that costume. I don't know if they made mine based on her complaints but mine was very comfortable. It had a zipper all the way up the back. It was a stretch fabric. The only thing you couldn't do was sit around in it a lot because it would make the knees baggy, and you don't want a superheroine with baggy knees. The heels were easy to work in; even the high heels because I wore a lot of them in those days.

I did a lot of my own stunts because the fight scenes were carefully choreographed, but the other reason is that the villains would try to grab her, but they certainly didn't take punches at her. So, I was never in any danger. If anything it was the poor stuntmen who were in danger. Because I'm so near sighted I can hardly see and I have no depth perception, but it all worked out.

How did you feel about it the first time you tried it on.

It was comfortable. I used to go on talk shows dressed as Batgirl. Let me tell you what Howie Horowitz said. Howie Horowitz took one look at the costume, which had a bodice at the time, and the bodice was hooked in the bottom part because it had to stretch in different ways. He took one look at it, turned to the costume designer Pat Barto and said, "Pat. One of the reasons, actually two of the reasons that we've hired Yvonne have been obfuscated by this costume."

She said, "I'll cut it on the bodice."

They redid the top of it because it made it more comfortable and because it made room for the bullet bra that I was wearing.

Did you feel heroic in the final outfit?

Because of the lines you are saying and the attitude you have it's not quite heroic. In life, I don't know anyone who is truly a hero who actually thinks of themselves as a hero, but I was feeling empowered and spunky, and the costume lent itself to putting your hands on your hips and saying, "No, you're wrong. I'm Batgirl!"

Before donning her Bat-tights, Yvonne Craig wore leg warmers as a member of the prestigious ballet company Ballet Russe de Monte Carlo. © Twentieth Century Fox Television

[Excitedly] You sound exactly as it did then! It sounds exactly as if Batgirl is talking to me!

[Laughs]

Going back to the costume – did you feel sexy in it?

No. I feel that sexy is innate and more about how people perceive you; but I've never felt like, "I'm sexy." I just never have. It sounds weird I know.

Were you aware of the impact that the costume had on others?

Yes. It's interesting. You see guys who are interested in boobs because that was a major part of that costume. You really couldn't see legs or butts, so that eliminated those guys whose interest is limited only to those anatomical attributes, not the whole human being, but only certain aspects of it. The cape covered your butt and the costume didn't really feature your legs. If you were male and interested in the Batgirl character, I would guess that the costume had a lot to do with it.

We did have kids on the set everyday, and their eyes are huge because they can't believe they are looking at all this. It must have been really fun for Adam and Burt, who after the show was cancelled, still went out and did appearances until they were told not to. It had to have been fun looking down at the kids who thought they were seeing the real Batman. Girls haven't said anything about it. Even when I go to conventions girls never say anything about it. Now, guys do. They say, "I was ten years old and I loved that character. I would race home from school and if I saw her come in on her little motorcycle during the credits then I'd watch the show because I was really attached to that character." Gay guys will say to me, "I just loved that character and I wanted to be her."

When men express their sexual attraction to you and the character, how does it feel?

Good. Absolutely. We're all sexual beings, so I see nothing wrong with it. I've been to conventions when there will be a horrible guy who will come up to me and say [in a lascivious voice] "You helped me get through my adolescence." I pretend he's politely saying, "I really enjoyed watching the show." When I was going to conventions, I never gave them any reason to go further than that.

Then there's Howard Stern. Howard Stern is a funny guy. He said that he used to lie on his mother's bed and watch *Batman* and Donna Reed. Then he'd graphically tell me what's happening. Then he'd say he'd switch to Donna Reed. I said, "Oh, great, that makes me feel good." We were entirely different because she's there vacuuming with her pearls on.

The nice thing about having done the show is that it had a couple of layers. All the bright colors and the "Bam! Pow!" were very appealing to children. Underneath all of that, the writers wrote inside jokes and references. Now adults will come and say, "I watched it when I was a kid and now I'm watching it with my kids." It's the kind of show that you can watch with your kids. Silly things happened to people – they were pressed until they were flat – but not anything scary. The villains got theirs but it was just viewed as their comeuppance.

I loved doing the show. People look back and say, "That was a such a good time then," but right there and then, I knew it was a good time. I knew I was having fun. I knew I was doing exactly what I wanted to do. I don't have to look back and say, "I wish I enjoyed it more." I couldn't have enjoyed it more.

Batgirl's introduction to the show really shook things up. She wasn't brought in like Lois Lane to be a victim who needed to be saved. More often than not, she saved Batman and Robin.

Yes. I did a public service spot about equal pay for women. Batman and Robin were tied up with dynamite wrapped around them and a big clock was ticking. They were struggling to get free and I swung in on a rope. They say, "Thank goodness it's Batgirl. Please save us."

And I essentially say, "When I get paid what you get paid, you'll get saved."

It was just so fun, but unfortunately, because it was a pubic service spot, they ran it at 3 a.m., when all the ladies who would have valued the information were asleep because they had to get up at five in the morning and get to work.

That PSA was shot a few years after the show ended. How did it feel to go back and revisit the character?

It was fun. I was in the middle of doing something else so I said, "I'm working so you'll have to pull everything together and I'll just come in and shoot it. I don't know where anything is." I thought that they might have even wanted the Batcycle and then I found out later that it was torn apart and converted back into a street bike. They just dumped the [motorcycle] fairings.

Batgirl wasn't brought in just for girl fights, she also fought men. Just like Batman and Robin.

Oh, yes. Oh, yes. It was an equal opportunity occupation and she was an equal partner in crime fighting.

Surprisingly, Batman's attitude towards Batgirl was not progressive. He said things like "Perhaps it's best to leave crime fighting to the men, Batgirl." In those instances, Batman intentionally looks a bit foolish and behind-the-times.

I think it was the 1960s and men were behind the times and were kind of gobsmacked that women weren't going to be passive anymore.

It's interesting that they allowed their hero to exemplify being out of step.

Yes, yes, but that also appealed to a lot of men who were probably thinking, "That's right Batgirl. You go home and cook." I think lines like that were there to appease someone who would be threatened by Batgirl and to get a larger audience. I could be dead wrong. You were a kid then and I was an adult, but you were brought up after the women's revolution happened. My nephews see no difference between male and female roles, but my husband has friends who see differences.

Did you feel that Batgirl was contributing to the dialogue of the movement?

I never felt that I contributed to the movement. I felt it was narrow. At that time I would say, "I'm not interested in Women's Rights, I'm interested in Human Rights. We should all have the same rights." That goes back to my mother saying, "We're all the same. We all have the same anxieties just different equipment."

What impact has this part had on your life?

I honestly don't know. It accomplished what I wanted to accomplished. It gave me a place to go. The show attached a name to a face. It paid me admirably. When I went on that show, I made more money than Adam and Burt, and that was because I had a body of work. Burt not at all, and Adam not so much. When they negotiated my contract they said, "Please do not disclose that you're making more money than the guys."

Yvonne Craig as Barbara Gordon. © Twentieth Century Fox Television

In that respect, it did a lot of things. I started an art collection and was able to travel a lot. It allowed me to play both characters and to do the work that I loved. And who knew that all these years later – almost forty years – people would still be talking about it? I never knew that was going to happen. I only thought, *This is the greatest job. I just love it,* and then it was over and you go on to other things.

What was the biggest perk and what was the biggest drawback of being a superhero?

The biggest perk is that we're still talking about it forty years later. I've never experienced one drawback. I know Adam did, and I have a theory about that. I've told it to him, but he doesn't listen. My theory is that he did three seasons of it and I only did twenty-six episodes. I also had a body of work before that so I don't feel that anybody has singled out Batgirl as who I was. I've done a lot of cult things not of my doing. I was in an Elvis movie, which has a cult following. I was in an episode of *Star Trek*, which has a cult following. I was in one of the worst movies ever made, *Mars Needs Women*, which has a cult following. I've got all these cults following me around. [Laughs]

For the most part, you've never resisted the association. Although I remember reading an article that when you were a real estate agent you tried to keep a low profile.

When I was doing real estate, I was trying to look really professional, and they didn't know I was Batgirl. Although, if asked about it, I never denied it. Adam complained that he was so associated with Batman after the show ended that it was difficult for him to get work. My view of it is that is that Adam has a distinctive cadence: "Alright . . . citizens." There's a pause and it works for that character. Everybody likes that "Batman . . . said . . . things . . . slowly." He had a funny speech cadence, but when he went to read for people after the series they would say, "Oh, he's still playing Batman," because that's just his voice and how he talks. It didn't work out for him because he and that voice were so inseparably associated with the Batman character that it was difficult to get rid of the association. Now of course he's making tons of money playing that character. It's the Adam West character so it seems that he got the last laugh.

Like William Shatner, he outlasted that association and both actors have had a similar resurgence.

Oh, yes, and Adam's a much, much, much nicer man. I don't think he has an evil bone in his body, and it would be hard not to find a whole skeleton full of them in Batman.

Everyone talks about the comedy of the series, but I think the show only works if you actually believe they're heroes too.

The show only works if everybody doing it acts as if it's a straight show. It's like watching kids work. The minute they know it's funny, then it's not funny anymore. We all played it straight when I did it. We didn't play it for laughs.

Is there a special kind of celebrity that comes with playing a superhero?

I think there probably is. I would say so. Christopher Reeve did a lot of work but what comes to mind is Superman. It's because you are playing something larger than life. Most of the characters you embody are not larger than life. I think they have a more multi-layered life if they are not superheroes.

What do you think is the appeal of superheroes?

I think it's that superheroes can do things that we can't do. Wouldn't you like to be able to fly? Would you like to be able to hold up your wrists and stop bullets? I went to a convention and someone asked me, "What are Batgirl's superpowers?"

I said, "She doesn't have any."

She doesn't have any but there's still something that is elevated or bigger than life about her.

She's kick-ass! [Laughs]

What was the appeal of the *Batman* show in particular?

The appeal of *Batman* was that nothing looked like it before. Almost nothing has looked like it since. You were actually seeing a comic book live. No other show had such vibrant color. When the villains entered, the camera was always tilted. Nobody had "Bam! Pow! Splat!" which was taken from comic books [and superimposed across the screen]. The only thing we didn't have were thought balloons above our heads. It was a look that was just stunning.

When you talk about it that way, it seems more significant than "camp," which is now pejorative; it was more like Pop Art.

It was. It was. It was very much of its time. There were comic book fans that hated what we did with Batman. They were the Dark Knight fans who took comic books seriously. They called it camp because they though we were spoofing something dear to them. Then in 1989, when the Tim Burton *Batman* film came out, the fans that grew up on us were disappointed because they felt they were darkening everything. We were of our time just as the 1989 movie was of its time.

What was the intention of the show?

I think it was to put something innovative and fun on television.

I ask other actors I speak with to suggest questions. John Newton who played Superboy asked if you kept the costume?

Do we really want to go there?

Yes, we do.

The costume was stolen by one of the cast members so that he could dress up his girlfriend and do public appearances. I don't know if you want to publish this or not because it pisses him off. Because now everybody has decided they know who it is.

Who?

I'm not saying. He heard I said it and it leaked. So, now he says that he bought it from the studio, but he did not. When we were trying to get everything together for the public service spot, they couldn't find a costume. So someone said, "I know somebody who knows someone who might have that costume."

They said, "Okay go get it."

It came in and it was the one I wore. It had stuff in it that you wouldn't know about if you just made the costume. It was also my fall, which was expensive. I can't believe he walked off with $600 worth of wig, which in those days . . . it would be a couple of thousands. The long and short of it is that it came in, I wore it, and he stood outside my dressing room door so that he could give it back to his girlfriend.

I consider it stealing but people walk off with things from sets all the time. If I wanted something, it wouldn't have been that costume, it would have been the wonderful outfit I wore on *Star Trek*. It was just a stunning costume. It cut way down and it cut way up. You could dance in it and it never moved. Then it was auctioned off about fifteen years ago and fetched $35,000.

Did you keep anything?

No, I'm kind of not really a keeper. I have no children, so I don't have to prove to them that I didn't know Abraham Lincoln, but I knew Batman. [Laughs] I live in the present and look to the future, and very seldom do I look back, except when I'm doing an interview. I honestly don't look back.

Do you have any Batgirl toys?

Some of those look like me and some of them don't. Since [attorney] Bela Lugosi Jr. won the lawsuit for the Three Stooges, if they use my image, they have to license it from me. So, they can't make mouse ears [merchandise] without getting my permission. I had a great agent and this was way before the Bela Lugosi lawsuit. I had a contract which said that if they made anything regarding Batgirl and it looked anything like me, they had to pay me a license fee of 1% of everything that had a Batgirl image for ten years after we shot the show, and nothing came out until after that, which is fine, and which is also why when they made an action figure for *Star Trek* they used Susan Oliver's character as the green lady – she's dead and they don't have to pay her anything.

The actor who plays the Flash asks, "How did playing the part affect you personally?"

It affected me personally because it was a wonderful job. It gave me a place to go, a schedule, and it paid me very well. The side benefit is that it allowed me to go to work everyday and be so happy. It was just great on every level.

Kevin Conroy asks: How would you like to be remembered?

Gee, I don't know. I never even think about that. Boy, this sounds awful, but I don't really have a vested interest if I'm remembered or not. I just had a wonderful time doing it, but if you want something more uplifting . . .

[Laughs]

Then I guess I'd like to be remembered as one of the first people that portrayed a character that allowed girls to be as good or better than guys.

That *is* a more uplifting answer.

Yes that it more uplifting than "Who gives a rat's ass." [Laughs] Okay, we'll go with that one! [We both laugh]

Did being Batgirl ever feel like a side job?

It's never felt like that to me. Take the website I have. It's not really about *Batman*. It has a large portion devoted to *Batman*, but it's an entire career website. Often when I was doing con-

*Playing Barbara Gordon was a day at the beach for Yvonne Craig in the two-part episode "Surf's Up! Joker's Under!" (1968). ©
Twentieth Century Fox Television*

ventions, people were as interested in those other projects as they are in *Batman*, but the *Star Trek* fans are weird. They'll ask, "What is the third lump from the left."

And I have to say, "Okay you have to know. I didn't watch the show. I only watched the one I did because I wanted to see how it looked and how it was cut. I also watched *The Trouble with Tribbles* and that's it. So, I can't answer those questions."

And they get very upset.

Until recently Adam West's website was devoted almost exclusively to Batman, but now it's shifted to other projects, as well. It's a subtle difference but it is a difference.

Yes, it is a difference. He changed that as he started to do the *Family Guy*. For a while he wasn't doing anything other than public appearances. I haven't done them in about three years and I did them for about ten years. I felt everyone has to know when it's time to get off the stage. I thought *Everyone who has wanted to see me, has seen me and if not, it's their fault because I've been out there, but you never want to get in a position where the fans say, "Oh God, is she back again?"*

Who would win in a fight: Batgirl vs. Robin?

Batgirl, because she has a really good kick!

Helen Slater is Supergirl

When comic book readers were introduced to Superman in 1938, they were informed that Kal-El, the infant sent to Earth in a rocket ship, was the *sole* survivor of the doomed planet Krypton. Over the years, devotees would discover that Superman was not, in fact, "the last Son of Krypton," but one of many Kryptonians, who through luck or circumstance – and DC Comics' desire to add variety to its stories and expand its brand – managed to avoid the planet's grim fate.

One notable survivor was Superman's cousin Kara Zor-El. After arriving on Earth, Kara follows in her famous cousin's footsteps and, when she's not fighting crime as Supergirl, lives a secret life as Linda Lee.[50]

Supergirl, created by writer Otto Binder and artist Al Plastino, first appeared in *Action Comics* in 1959. Twenty-five years later, the Maiden of Might would come to life in the movie *Supergirl*. The 1984 film starred Helen Slater in what the movie poster touted as Supergirl's "first great adventure." While Slater was quite appealing as the superhero, the film failed to connect with critics or audiences, and it earned just a little over $14 million.

The film critic Roger Ebert, who was won over by Helen Slater, wrote: "When we look at her we see Supergirl." Yet, he found the movie "unhappy, unfunny, unexciting," adding that it seemed to "laugh condescendingly" at the characters rather than letting the audience "recapture some of the lost innocence of the whole notion of superheroes."

The most telling referendum on the film came about a year after its release, when DC killed off Supergirl in *Crisis on Infinite Earths*. In that eventful twelve-issue comic book series, Supergirl sacrificed her own life to save Superman from the world-destroying supervillain, Anti-Monitor. After Batgirl delivers the eulogy at Supergirl's funeral, Superman shrouds her in his cape and flies her into deep space while solemnly offering his own tribute that is at once sorrowful, reflective, and determined:

"I will miss you. The days will seem shorter now, the nights that much longer. Sometimes I forget how mortal we really are. I don't believe I'll ever forget that again . . . I live on. Hurt, but not disillusioned. Sad but still hopeful that the dreams shared by you and me and all those others – those with special powers, and especially those with none. Those dreams of peace and hope can still come true. We will go on remembering and honoring the past, but always looking to the future. Good-bye Kara. Linda Lee. Supergirl. I will miss you forever."

Happily, neither Superman nor Supergirl fans would have to miss her forever. Over the years, other characters in the DC Universe, including the Matrix and Linda Danvers, would assume Supergirl's name.

It does not appear that Helen Slater's career suffered from the mostly negative reviews of *Supergirl*. With her natural beauty and gift for light comedy, Slater was able to rebound from *Supergirl* with a string of successful roles in such movies as *Ruthless People* with Danny DeVito and Bette Midler, *The Secret to My Success* with Michael J. Fox, *City Slickers* with Billy Crystal, and the cult classic *The Legend of Billie Jean*, a modern retelling of Joan of Arc but with a happier ending.

In the Emmy Award-winning *Batman: The Animated Series*, Slater voiced Talia al Ghul, who is the daughter of Batman's archenemy Ra's al Ghul and, with apologies to Catwoman, arguably the greatest love of Batman's life.

In 2007, Slater returned to her Kryptonian roots by playing Lara-El, Superman's biological mother, in a few guest appearances on *Smallville*, the television series that ran from 2001-2011 and depicted Clark Kent's development from high school into young adulthood and his early years at the *Daily Planet*.

Helen Slater as Supergirl. © Warner Bros.

THE INTERVIEW

When *Supergirl* was released in 1984, superhero films weren't yet a genre. The Superman films were an anomaly that in retrospect we understand as precursors.

I was young when *Superman* came out. That film had a big impact on me. I loved, loved that movie. I'd say that was the first blockbuster movie that I really loved. *Star Wars* was fine. Maybe it was the romantic aspect but *Superman* really did it for me. [She laughs]

More than the wish fulfillment of watching superheroes in action, it was the romance that you really responded to.

It's a romantic comedy at heart. It's in the mold of the Kate Hepburn and Spencer Tracy movies. It had the great sparring of Margot Kidder and Chris Reeve. It had certain elements of chick movies.

When you got the part, you were fresh out of high school.

Yes, I graduated in June and auditioned for it in October. I mocked up a Supergirl costume for the audition. That probably came from a combination of my attending [New York City's] The High School of the Performing Arts and feeling very fearless.

Did you have any reluctance to playing a superhero?

I didn't. I was fairly naïve at that young, young age. [Slater was twenty-years old when the film was released.] I didn't have any thoughts about starting my acting career in *Supergirl* and using it as a big launch off, as opposed to waiting for something more serious or beginning on the stage or in a film or play of greater depth that might be more of an acting challenge. As a youth, I was just so happy to be working. Getting that role just seemed like a chance in a million. That seemed to drive it more than anything.

What did they tell you about what they were trying to do with the film or your character?

I don't recall any specific conversations of that nature. I'm doing a series right now for Nickelodeon called *Gigantic*. We had a big meeting where we sat down with Nickelodeon and they told us what was acceptable and how to deal with press. That was more for the kids on the show, but when I got *Supergirl*, there really was none of that. They wanted to capture her innocence and her sweetness and her soulful nature. I remember Jeannot Szwarc [the director] talking to me a little bit about that, but that was so long ago that I'd be lying if I tried to quote specific conversations.

Why do you think they cast you?

I don't know. Honestly. Maybe it was my audacity to go to the audition dressed up. I wasn't really an extrovert so it wasn't like I was bombastic.

Christopher Reeve said he thought of Clark Kent and Superman as different characters. Did you think of Linda Lee and Supergirl as separate people?

I did. They had different qualities for sure. They were different aspects of the same person. Supergirl is a fearless and unafraid. She's eyes-wide-open on this new planet. Linda Lee is reserved and trying to fit in. She's trying not to stand out.

What about Kara, her Kandorian identity? Is she on this spectrum or is she a third part of a triangle?

That's an interesting question. I'd say Kara is the daughter archetype. She's the student/daughter archetype.

When you first put on the finished costume how did you feel?

I loved it. I felt great. It felt powerful. I had been training for months – doing weight lifting, running, swimming, doing trampoline work, and I felt so good in my body that it was really fun.

Michael Keaton said that the suit did "most of the work" for him in terms of being heroic. Do you relate to that?

I agree with that. I totally agree with that. You put it on and it makes you feel a certain way. Stella Adler, the great acting teacher, was a big proponent of the notion that the costume can give you the character. In this case, playing a superhero, that is true.

How were you similar to Supergirl back then?

I was so young, unlike my male counterparts, who were doing Superman and Batman movies. I think the innocence, the wonder of going to England and working in Pinewood Studios that, to me, was like going to another planet. I had never been out of the country. There were so many things I had to navigate, including loneliness and being by myself, not being in a college dormitory like most of my friends. In that way, there were many similarities that I could identity with.

How were you unlike her?

Well, I don't fly. I don't have X-ray vision. Just in that way.

What did you like most about playing Supergirl?

The apex and the highlight for me was the flying. As a kid, like many of us do, I had dreams of flying, but as I got older, I had fewer and fewer of them. That feeling of flying, being on the wires and being suspended in mid-air by the pole arm, I loved filming

Supergirl (Helen Slater) takes a much need break from saving the day in this promotional still from Supergirl *(1984). © Warner Bros.*

that part of the movie. We did a ballet sequence where on the wires I did somersaults and swan dives [as Supergirl discovers her ability to fly]. I don't think I could do that now. I think I'd be too frightened. At the time I felt very free-spirited.

Was there any way the character rubbed off on you or you rubbed off on the character?

I remember feeling kind of invincible when doing the part. It was the opposite of being high strung or neurotic or dark or shadowy. When I look back on that part, I recall feeling a sense of openness and expansiveness. I felt that I could do pretty much do anything. Maybe part of that was being eighteen or nineteen-years old but it also came from playing that part. It probably went both ways. Who I was affected how I did the part and the part asked me to amplify those qualities inside of me. I think it did carry through forever. I think it's still with me. That feeling of lightness and joy. That is still with me. Spending months and months doing that – and getting paid to do that – stored it in me for good. It's solid. [Laughs] It's different as you get older but in terms of that particular quality, I'm very grateful.

What worked about the film? And what didn't?

I'd say the general opinion is that the movie didn't work. In terms of my experience, the movie worked because I loved doing it and it launched my movie career. One possibility is that the movie didn't work because they were trying to cut it out of the same cloth as the Superman archetype. Perhaps a somewhat different take on *Supergirl* was needed. I'm of the opinion that it kind of needed to step away from the Superman archetype, but I'm not sure.

It's also hard to have a teenage girl be sort of a rescuing figure. I think that doesn't quite land right. In terms of making her more human, if they were to make the film again, maybe they'd make it more realistic and less grounded in fantasy. They need to find the equivalent of what Chris found when he based Clark Kent on Cary Grant. They need to find the equivalent of what a nineteen-year-old girl might be.

I was reading an essay about this and it seems to come down to the question: Does Supergirl work best as an all-American girl or as a figure challenging the status quo?

Which is what I think you do when you're eighteen or nineteen. That's pretty good. I like that in a short sentence: challenging the status quo. In Supergirl comics now, she's very bombastic. She can't lasso her skills. She keeps blowing it. She's not challenging the status quo but she's not in control of her powers. Which is another way to go with it – where you're just figuring out how to harness your inner power.

Where you're highlighting the anger and confusion of being a teenager?

That's one way to go. From a Jungian perspective or Joseph Campbell where you look at the mythology, the rites of passage we must go through, your late teens are a time of individuation, of separating from one's parents or the tribe you were in high school with.

What do you think Supergirl's archetypal struggle is as opposed to the MacGuffin of the film?

Right, she has to recover the Omegahedron to save the planet. That's the tale. Retrieving something.

How did that change her?

What could have been illuminated more, but didn't get adequately mined is the loss of innocence when you're on a mission and how that gives you more "earth" or more "shadow." At the beginning, she has no loss and no darkness. There is nothing to balance, so that you're not exclusively in either an Apollonian or Dionysian paradise, but I don't think those themes were highlighted in the film; they are only touched upon. I'd have to look at the movie again. I haven't seen it in twenty-five years, but it has to do with loss and leaving the family and trying to navigate you own way in the world.

Do you think down the road Super*girl* becomes Superw*oman*?

I think that would be really cool. I think that's really interesting. I'm too old to do it; I'm in my forties, but it would be interesting to explore what the emotional depth of maturity brings to a superheroine. It's interesting. I still don't know if it's being locked down by the male myth of Superman. If it really needs a reinvention that honors the female archetypes, you can't really put her in the same track as a male. I don't think it can work. Although, I don't know what the answer is.

That's the central question: How *not* to make her "Superman in drag," right? But let's go back to what you said about playing Superwoman. Do you really think you can't play Superwoman at forty, which really isn't that old?

Musing on it, I believe there's a lot of literature, from Greek mythology to the Arthur legend to Baba Yaga [a supernatural entity in Russian folklore], in which strong women, often wise women, significantly influence what is happening. But when you add the "all-American" element to it and you want to keep it within the context of American mythology, that's where you can sometimes come up short.

My mom was just telling me about the Hummus Indians. When Benjamin Franklin was considering how the new government should be set up, he considered the Hummus Indians where the women held tribal council. The men might say they wanted to go to war, but it was the woman who would have to approve it. The Hummus system of checks and balances might have influenced Benjamin Franklin's thinking. Who knows how apocryphal these stories are, but they're interesting to consider if we want to create a modern kind of superheroine.

How does this fit in with sexualizing female superheroes?

I would have to say that the deliberate sexualizing of female superheroes goes against the mythological type. I'm not saying you should cut out the sexuality completely – but an emphasis on it would show that it really derives from a man's imagination.

Exactly. How practical is it to fight crime in a miniskirt?

With your midriff showing!

Do you think that it's important for female superheroes to be sexual?

There's sexuality on one hand, and on the other hand there's Eros – where love is – and that has a sensual and sexuality to it, but it's not pure sexuality. Where the breast is ridiculously oversized. Where the thighs are peeking out. Where it's exaggerated.

Don't get me wrong, I think it's great to celebrate female sexuality. I think it's a beautiful instrument. But maybe we put too much emphasis on it. But on the other hand when you say superhero you think of Batman and Superman. These are not realistic figures. So, maybe it's in keeping with the conventions. I'm backtracking a bit.

But you make a good point. Male superheroes also have overdeveloped physique, but I'm not sure I ever considered if Superman was ever "hunky" or not.

And I don't think girls do. I don't think girls want to have sex with Superman. I think it's more about the romantic aspect. There's this battle about him being Clark Kent who loves this woman who also has this higher mission in life and how he comes to terms with the two things he wants. The sexuality should be something that is gradually revealed. It shouldn't be overwhelming – like a balloon on the Macy's Thanksgiving Day parade!

But for female superheroes, sexuality seems like it has to play a part.

Right. It's best when the sexuality is there but not overt. Right now there's uniformity on what it should look like. It's the American version of what a superhero should look like. It's a bombshell. Supergirl is part of the bombshell idea, a blonde in a short skirt.

She's blond as Supergirl but as her alter ego Linda Lee she's a brunette.

That's true. That's an interesting point that's probably being played on.

There's a scene in your film where there are two thugs who try to rape her. That idea is never explored with male superheroes – where they are being threatened in that sort of way.

No, never, but that's because as soon as you make a girl or a woman your lead you have to include all the things that a girl goes through. Including dealing with a scary outside world – where those type of problems are, unfortunately, not uncommon. That's just part of it.

Can you talk a little about Christopher Reeve?

I was in my twenties when I met him and had the occasion to hang out with him a bit. I did think that for him [playing Superman] was a burden. That was my overriding impression.

But was it a burden because of typecasting or was it a burden because people filter their impressions of you through the lens of being a superhero?

I think it's both. He got put in a very specific category that was very hard for him to break out of it. But he was so good in the part.

You were in Central Park with him when fire trucks drove by with their sirens blaring, and he said, "Here's Superman and Supergirl and there's nothing we can do about it."

That's a great example of him being honest about it and expressing himself with humor, but it's kind of poignant because he can't do what's being projected on him all the time.

But that image of you and Reeve in the park gets translated into the idea that Superman and Supergirl are actually in the park. We want to believe it.

Right. [Laughs]

Did you ever want to distance yourself from the part?

I never experienced that because the movie was never really that successful. I worked immediately after that. After that I did *Legend of Billie Jean, Ruthless People, Secret of My Success, City Slickers*, had a daughter and did two records. So, it seemed like playing Supergirl was a phenomenal impetus but not a defining moment in terms of the rest of my life.

John Newton who played Superboy kept it off his resume.

I never felt that way. I loved playing Supergirl. And I'm a big mythology junkie. I wear it proudly!

Are there drawbacks to playing a superhero?

For me there wasn't. I only wish – that in terms of the story – and it's about twenty-five years later, even I can't tell you how you should make a Supergirl story.

What is it like to be perceived as Supergirl?

For me it was heady. I was plucked from obscurity and placed in, for me, what felt like the life of elite. I came from heady intellectual parents who stressed academics, but not making a lot of money. It was a feeling of being whisked away into an enchantment. It was like an enchantment.

Do you ever feel like you have to be the spokesperson for this character?

I don't. Because it didn't land in a massive way. Because of that I feel like I got all the positive aspects of it and none of the burden. None of the shadow part of it. I was originally signed for three movies, but that didn't happen. It's not that none of that shadow is there, but there's not enough to hold me back.

How do you want to be remembered for this part?

Kindly. Fondly. That I did my best.

Laura Vandervoort is Supergirl

When *Supergirl* failed at the box office, comic book fans assumed they'd never see another live action interpretation of The Girl of Steel. They had good reason to be skeptical; despite Helen Slater's winning performance, the film was a misfire.

It would take another twenty-four years before Laura Vandervoort was chosen to resurrect the role of Supergirl. She was reintroduced to mainstream audiences in *Smallville*, a television show focusing on Clark Kent's pre-tights, pre-flight, pre-Superman years. The early episodes centered exclusively on Clark's life in Smallville, Kansas, but by the time the show entered its seventh season, many familiar characters like Lois Lane and Jimmy Olsen were introduced. Alfred Gough and Miles Millar, the series creators and producers, thought that the timing was right for Supergirl to land in Smallville.

Gough and Millar found their Girl of Steel in Laura Vandervoort, a Canadian actress, who was born in 1984, the same year that the movie *Supergirl* was released. Gough told *People* magazine that Vandervoort's Supergirl was a "combination of beauty, intelligence, a certain warmth, and great attitude. We've wanted a character to shake things up. She may be Clark Kent's cousin, but that doesn't mean she's going to be the obedient one!"[51]

Vandervoort, who is a second-degree black belt in karate, is by any reasonable measure a "knockout." After her breakout role as Kara/Supergirl in *Smallville*, she regularly appeared on the "hottest women" lists that appear in lad magazines such as *Maxim*, *Stuff*, and *FHM*.

The blue-eyed beauty, who majored in Psychology and English at York University in Toronto, understandably doesn't want to be defined by her looks. As you'll discover, Vandervoort is very aware of the underlying messages that she's conveying to her impressionable adolescent fans.

Laura Vandervoort strikes a heroic pose as Supergirl. © Warner Bros.

THE INTERVIEW

What parts of Supergirl's character did you take from the comic books, and what did you deliberately want to avoid?

I did take note of the Kara character from the DC comic book. Some examples would be her strength, her sexuality and her way of appearing so wise. In a lot of the comics the character seemed to use her sexuality to get what she wanted. I didn't like that one aspect of Kara, as I wanted her to be a true role model for young girls. I wanted to make sure Kara came across as a likeable character and also as a strong independent teen. Kara is driven by her need to discover more about her family, to impress Clark as a worthy cousin on Earth, to be a part of the human world and to always do good.

How are you and Supergirl similar? How are you different?

I am not remotely similar to a superhero. I'm human. I can't fly. I do not have laser vision. I don't have super-strength or super-speed. However, I am similar to Supergirl in reference to the second part of her name — I am a girl. I am a young woman still trying to figure out life, just like Kara. I make mistakes, just like Kara, and I am just figuring out who I am, just like Kara. Growing up I was always taking part in sports. I earned my second-degree black belt in karate by age seventeen. In that way I feel I'm similar to Kara. She can take care of herself and has the confidence that reflects that, which I feel I do. I also always want nothing but good things for those around me and I try to do only what is right. Kara is wiser beyond her years, but again I cannot fly and have more then just blue and red in my wardrobe.

Does Supergirl's confidence and power spill over to you at all?

I feel as though her confidence does spill over when I'm in certain situations. Kara went through so much coming to Earth and trying to become a part of it, and she has overcome so much of her own uncertainty. She is strong and gets what she wants. Kara reminds me that things that seem impossible are possible — it just takes confidence, strength, and believing in yourself. Kara carried herself proudly, as do I now because of whom I found her to be.

Would you have been more or less likely to take the part if you had to wear a cape and costume?

I think I'd be a little less likely to take the role if I had to wear a cape and costume. I think those things would stand as a distraction and take away from Kara. The creators and I were determined to make Kara's journey as realistic as possible. *Smallville* has made a name for itself and survived by standing its ground and making sure the show is shot as realistically as possible when dealing with superheroes and their daily lives. A cape and costume would distract from this storytelling and the overall show.

Laura Vandervoort as Supergirl. © Warner Bros.

An actor told me that he thought the central metaphor and meaning of Superman is the importance of putting others ahead of yourself. Is there a metaphor or central meaning behind Supergirl's character?

I feel as though the same metaphor behind Superman that you mentioned would stand true for Supergirl as well. They are essentially the same hero. Both stand for the same rights and morals. The people first, self second. Do what is takes to protect the good people of the world. Supergirl being female can also stand for something in itself: women being strong. It makes it clear that superheroism isn't just a man's world. Supergirl is "pretty and blonde," but she also stands for more then just the physical. What is important is that she is female and can do exactly the same as what Superman does, on the same level. Some might say she even does it with more grace, more heart and compassion as she has innate maternal instincts. I feel Supergirl's existence also stands for women's equality to men, both mental and physical. She can stand with the likes of any male superhero.

How has playing the part affected you personally?

Personally, playing Supergirl has given me the ability to say to myself, "I am Supergirl." Just being able to say those words to myself seems to really lift my confidence. Knowing I was able to play such an incredible hero makes me feel good about myself. Growing up I always strived to be the best, as I wanted to prove I was strong and past all of that. I recall my mom once saying to me when I got the role, "Who would have thought that the sick baby we once had would one day be Supergirl?" That really meant a lot for me personally. Also personally, when I get to meet the young girls at comic conventions who are dressed like Supergirl, girls who are just eight years old, I realize I am creating a positive role model. It also makes me very aware of the choices I'll make when doing publicity shoots and what roles I choose to take in the future.

Who would win in a fight: Supergirl or Wonder Woman? And why?

Obviously Supergirl would win in a battle against Wonder Woman. A) Because she's the cousin of the greatest Superhero of all time, and B) Because she can out "super-power" any of Wonder Woman's powers while using her mind and maintaining her grace, power and femininity.

Malin Akerman is Silk Spectre

More than the ability to leap tall buildings in a single bound or spin webs, arguably a superhero's greatest power is fighting crime while looking smokin' hot. Face it, superheroes are sexy.

Wonder Woman is an alluring, ample-breasted Amazon warrior, who dons a skimpy outfit when battling her adversaries. Superman's body is as sculpted as Michelangelo's David. George Clooney's Bat-suit was designed with protruding nipples. Although Robert Downey's Tony Stark isn't particularly buff, his alter ego Iron Man is, well, well-endowed. *Iron Man* director Jon Favreau puts it bluntly, behind "any superhero outfit you see, I guarantee there's been fifty hours discussion on how the crotch looks."[52]

The sex appeal of superheroes is not always discussed. It is more dignified and it avoids the appearance of prurience to posit that Jor-El putting his son into a rocket ship and sending him to earth is reminiscent of Moses being put in a basket to float down the Nile, to save his life and free him to meet his destiny, than to admit that the only defensible reason to sit through *The Fantastic Four* is the pleasure of seeing Jessica Alba in a skin-tight costume.

The motivation for the creation of many superheroines is often transparent. Someone decides (largely for commercial reasons) that it would be a good idea to have a female hero, but inventing a complex personality with a compelling backstory takes a backseat to the look of the character. It's easy: drop the "man" from a brand name and add "girl." Thus, Batman begat Batgirl. Superman begat Supergirl. Spider-Man begat Spider-Girl. (Though there's a legitimate place for stories about young superheroes, the use of the suffix "girl" rather than "woman" often seems unnecessarily to diminish the stature of a heroine.)

Once created, female superheroes are frequently exploited as walking and talking pinups. Yvonne Craig's slinky Batgirl appeared in Adam West's campy TV show only after the show's ratings started to decline. In the film *Supergirl*, the titular heroine uses her superpowers unimpressively to quickly put on make up and meet boys.

Of course, there is nothing innately wrong with female heroes be-ing enticing. Their male counterparts are usually attractive. How-ever, when superheroines serve no greater purpose than to be ob-jects of desire, the characters lose their mythic power and depth.

Witness the diminishment of Halle Berry's character Storm in the first three X-Men movies. In the comics, she's a powerful Af-rican priestess, who controls the weather and has the ability to manipulate the air beneath her in order to fly. Much to Berry's dismay, in the movie she's diminished to being little more than a comely background player, ceding center stage to Hugh Jack-man's white male antihero. . An incredulous Roger Ebert speaks for many when he writes: "I can't help wondering how a guy whose knuckles turn into switchblades gets to be the top-ranking superhero. If Storm can control, say, a tropical storm, she's obvi-ously the most powerful, even if her feats here are limited to local climate control."[53]

In an effort to raise the level of awareness of their characters between big budget blockbusters, Warner Bros. has been making direct to DVD animated films about superheroes. Bryan Crans-ton, Keri Russell, Kyle MacLachlan,, Nathan Fillion, Neil Patrick Harris, Lucy Lawless, Anne Heche, Peter Weller, and Kyra Sedgwick are some of the actors who play iconic characters in these popu-lar and critically acclaimed films. Perhaps learning from the mis-takes of others, the creative team behind *Wonder Woman* strove to be sure their hero was more than just a pretty face. The film's director Lauren Montgomery wanted Wonder Woman to be, "Re-spectable and classy and not just boobs in your face the entire time." The bestselling novelist and guest scribe for the Wonder Woman comics, Jodi Picoult echoed Montgomery's thoughts when she wrote, "[Wonder Woman] has long been upheld as a role model for young girls – the epitome of the strong female icon – but her sheer "bodaciousness" (and that costume) suggests that it's her body, not her mind, that attracts male readers."[54]

What makes the *Watchmen* unique is the filmmaker's knowing commentary on the seductive allure of superheroes. Superhero films until now have generally skirted the issue; this R-rated film is the first in which superheroes are depicted having sex, and the sex is neither chaste nor coyly suggested. The camera doesn't discretely pan away following an embrace. The audience gets to see two (and sometimes three) superheroes copulating.

Silk Spectre, as played by the luminescent Malin Akerman, is the object of affection for both Dr. Manhattan and Nite Owl. Billy Crudup plays Dr. Manhattan, a character who, like Superman, is all-powerful. Unlike the Man of Steel, Dr. Manhattan doesn't wear any clothes. Throughout the film the blue-skinned hero displays the full monty. More outrageously, the filmmakers treat the audience to a supernatural *ménage à trois*: Dr. Manhattan uses his powers to duplicate himself so that he and his doppelganger can make love to Silke Spectre at the same time.

Nite Owl (played by Patrick Wilson with a beer belly) is an aging crime fighter, who loses his mojo when the government outlaws superheroes. Without his costume, Night Owl (aka Dan Dreiberg) loses his self-esteem, as well as his ability to maintain an erection. It is only when he's wearing his leather getup that he is able to make love to Silk Spectre.

Malin Akerman understands that a large part of Silk Spectre's function in the movie is to be sexy. She feels very comfortable embracing both her own, and her character's, sexuality.

Malin Akerman as Silk Spectre in Watchmen (2009). © Warner Bros.

THE INTERVIEW

(I offer Malin a bottle of water.)

Do I look like I need it? [Laughs] We had a bit of a bender last night. Because it was the last day of press for *Watchmen*. We ended it with a bang. It was so much fun.

Thanks for agreeing to one last interview with me.

Absolutely! We traveled all of Europe and Australia.

I don't think you'll ever *really* be done talking about *Watchmen*.

I don't think so either. Which I'm fine with.

Were you worried not so much about typecasting but about being a representative for Watchmen for the rest of your life?

[Laughs] Yes, but it's not a bad thing. I never saw that as a negative. I hope that I can keep going back to Comic-Con when I'm sixty and I'll show people my action figure and say, "This was me!" I think it's a wonderful thing to carry around. In the end, I don't think it hurts. Definitely not.

***Time* magazine listed *Watchmen* as one of the top 100 novels of all time. When you first read the graphic novel what did you think?**

I was amazed. My understanding of comic books was limited to what my cousins used to read when I was young. Comics seemed to be a guy's thing. I looked at some of them like Batman and Robin and they were limited to "pow, punch, bang" types of scenes. That was my entire frame of reference to comics. So when I picked up the graphic novel I was shocked. It fools you a little bit. If you take away the pictures, it still remains one of the best novels you've ever read. The visuals are amazing and great to have but the writing is fantastic and timeless. I was pleasantly surprised.

What did director Zak Snyder tell you about his approach to the film?

He wanted it to be as faithful to the novel as possible. When we first met, I was auditioning for him in the role. He has so much energy and passion that he doesn't really say it all in just one phrase. Even while we were shooting, he was off on tangents. [Imitating Zak] "And this and this and this is really cool." He draws his own storyboards for every scene. It was kind of a jumble of different ideas. We didn't always understand what we were doing until we saw the finished film. All that we knew is that he was trying to be completely faithful to the book.

Did Zak tell you what your character is supposed to represent?

That's a good question. We had lengthy talks about the character and her history. Her importance is what her character and what Patrick Wilson's character Nite Owl represent together in the novel. They are the most relatable for the audience. They are the most normal of all the Watchmen. We were the grounding pair. Laurie is the only woman in the group and she is allowed to be feminine. She's on an emotional roller coaster throughout the film.

Based exclusively on the costume, I thought of her is Catwoman-ish, not based on the character traits but on her look. Silk Spectre is a very fierce woman who can bring it. If you read the Absolute Edition of *Watchmen*, you'll see that all the characters have crazy character descriptions that are pages long. Silk Spectre gets only half a page. It's as if she's an afterthought, kind of "Lets throw in a woman just to give it a feminine touch." All the other characters were loosely based on different comic book characters. Nite Owl was based on Batman.

What did you take from the book and use in your performance?

I used everything from the book. *Everything.* That was the coolest part of it. Usually when you go into a role you have to figure out the character's history and why the character acts a certain way in certain situations. It's part of the work you do prior to arriving on the set. With *Watchmen,* it was all in the novel. You get everything. All you have to do is carefully read the novel a few times. You get the history of her mother and how she grew up. You get her past, her present and her future, and you get the visuals of her look. It was challenging at times *because* it was so set in stone. There's not much room for improv. It was really helpful at the same time.

Does she like fighting crime?

Ultimately, she does. I think that's what she realizes in the end. It lights a fire inside of her. Obviously in more ways that one. [Laughs] She was absolutely meant for crime fighting. Had she started her life with a different mother whose interests were different she might have had a different passion, but because she was forced into it, that's all she knows. She grew up with superheroes. I think that obviously affects her, but crime fighting is ultimately what she is passionate about.

What makes a person who wants to fight crime take the second and more extreme step of dressing up as a superhero?

That's interesting because in everyday life, people put on a mask when they go to work. If you work in an office, men usually put on a suit and tie, and women often wear heels and skirts, and that's their costume. I think we all wear masks in everyday life. We act a certain way when we are at work and a different way when we are out with our friends. For superheroes, costumes are simply the outfits they wear to work. The costumes create a new persona. When a woman wears high heels, she presents herself in a certain way. She feels a certain way. It's different when you put on flats, which are frumpy.

We see throughout the course of the film that wearing a costume means so much to Dan [Nite Owl]. He really needs a costume to feel like a man. It helps him to put on that mask and get into character. He gets to be someone else. Perhaps it helps you to have a vision of what you think you should be. You get to hide behind the costume, the persona, and to live vicariously through that alter ego's experiences.

Do you think she's happiest when wearing the costume?

I think she's most alive when she's in the costume. It's a heightened experience. It's exciting. It's an adrenaline rush. It's when she feels the most passionate about life. When she's out of the costume, she's just a normal woman.

In all your interviews, people ask you, "What is it like to wear the costume?" I'm going to ask you that, too, but I'd also like to know why is there so much interest in the outfit?

My costume is very sexy. It's very revealing. It's made out of latex. There are apparently a lot of latex fetishists. I don't understand it because latex isn't very comfortable. [Laughs] But the visual is just beautiful. I think it's a vicarious thrill to see someone create a persona. In real life we can't create such an extreme per-

Malin Akerman as Silk Spectre in this promotional still for Watchmen. © *War-*
ner Bros.

sona – we're too self-conscious and we'd look silly. I have a bunch of female friends who don't want to put on high heels or wear anything too revealing. It's like, "Why *not*?! You are a woman. Sex it up. Show it off. Be a woman. Don't be scared to be a woman." You can still be equal with men, but we have one up on men. We can look like this. We can use diversion.

It's really interesting to see how scared some women are of their sexuality. I'm not sure but it may be due to Puritanical values that have been imposed on us. You look at Italian women – they are all boobs-out – they celebrate their femininity. When women look at a costume like Silk Spectre's some of them might think, *Wow that is sexy and hot. I wish I could wear that,* but they don't; they live vicariously through her. Maybe some people will go home and have dress up with their partners and put on a show.

Did you feel like a badass when wearing the costume?

Absolutely. As uncomfortable as it was, when Zak called action, I really got into the role. The costume makes a difference. It definitely has an impact on you. When they call cut, it's a different story. Then you wonder, *What are we doing standing around in these outfits?*

Then you feel vulnerable?

I wouldn't say I felt vulnerable, although I definitely put a blanket around my butt. You don't really want to hang out in that outfit, but I didn't hate all the attention I got wearing it. It was cool to see those guys' reactions.

Did you get any extreme reactions?

There's one comment that I didn't appreciate. There's a scene in the movie where Dan can't perform [sexually without wearing his costume] and some guy on set came up to me and said, "I don't know what guy wouldn't get hard around you wearing that." That was vulgar. That was too far.

Is Laurie aware of the impact she has in that outfit?

No, I don't think she is. Her mother pushed her into the business and made the costume for her, which is crazy. I see Laurie as someone who is street smart and can kick ass but who is also somewhat naïve. I don't think she understands the real world very well. She says, "I only know superheroes." She doesn't present herself in a sexual way. She wears a sexy outfit, but she's not aware that she's a sexy object. It's more like, "This is my outfit for work." Even when she says to Dan, "Can you believe we wore this much latex?" I think she means, "Weren't we crazy?" She's not aware of how the guys might react. I think she feels fierce when she wears it. Not sexy. She gets strong while wearing it.

Comic books (like Greek statues) depict idealized versions of the male and female form. Superman is very cut. Wonder Woman is voluptuous. Yet we pretend that their appeal isn't at least partially based on our being attracted to or turned on by superheroes. *Watchmen* **in general and your character in particular seem to be acknowledging their sexual appeal.**

We do. We acknowledge what these costumes mean to us. Dan is the most interesting because he really does have a bit of fetish. That is how they shot the love scene between Dan and Laurie where we finally consummate. The camera starts on my leg and glides up the boot, the heel, and the latex stocking to show the fetish appeal. We absolutely addressed the sexuality of these costumes and the effects they can have, but it doesn't mean that the people who are in them feel like they are consciously presenting themselves with sexuality. They wear them to feel confident rather than sexy.

There's a poster of you ...

My butt?

[Embarrassed] No, no. Not your butt ...

I've seen the butt one.

In the photo, your body is contorted. It suggests that your character is sexy but also mysterious and powerful.

Yeah, yeah, yeah. I know what you mean. I like that because it's not shying away from the sexuality but it's also very strong. I love that combination. When you're a woman, you have strength and power and I think that you should embrace it instead of hiding behind it.

Watchmen **is unique in that in the central relationship is between a daughter (Silk Spectre) and her mother (Sally Jupiter). Did you and the director talk about that?**

Not the comparison to the other superheroes, which is interesting. I didn't even think about that until you said it now, but Carla [Gugino who played Sally Jupiter] and I spent a full month together before we started shooting. We discussed our lives – our personal lives – trying to figure out where we relate.

We actually have very similar lives. Most girls have a difficult time with their mothers during their teenage years. It's inevitable. It's such a common dynamic. I think the novel is so great in that it explores the mother-daughter relationship on a deep level. The other films that you mentioned just don't elaborate on the father-son relationship — it's never seriously explored the way it is in *Watchmen* where you get a feeling of how those relationships actually work. The two characters reconcile in the end. It's really beautiful.

That's an interesting point. In comics, the father-son relationship is always in the past - the fathers are killed, the sons are abandoned, but in *Watchmen*, the mother-daughter relationship is vital. In the film, as it is with many women I know, after the estranged teenage years, many daughters become best friends with their moms.

Exactly. I think the depiction in the film is really true and wonderful.

Do you relate to Silk Spectre in that respect?

Absolutely. Absolutely. I had so many rough patches with my own mother throughout my teenage years. Now, we're reconciled and friends. As far as soul-searching and leaving a loveless relationship and going out and finding a real one, I can relate to that. I related to her in all of the things she goes through [she chuckles] except for crime fighting.

Emotionally I'm similar to her. I was also naïve as an adolescent. Like her I had to go out into the world in order to understand it and to find my place in it. Eventually Laurie is able to say, "So, this is what the world is actually like." All she knew is crime on the streets. That's it. She doesn't communicate with regular people. It's interesting to play with that childish naiveté and reconcile it with the fact that she's also this super strong, powerful woman.

What do you think is the meaning behind *Watchmen*?

Many things, but ultimately the most important questions that the film and the novel ask are: "How far will humans go to maintain world peace? How are we going to avoid war?" All the characters have different ways of responding to those challenges.

The film also helps to demonstrate why we need laws to guide our behavior and police to enforce them. Why we need policemen and not superheroes. You can imagine the chaos that might result if superheroes did exist. The film explores so many issues – politics, conspiracy theories, humans at their worst and at their best, what we're capable of.

What's the appeal of superheroes?

A superhero is perhaps the ultimate expression of what humans wish they could do and be. I believe that humans are good-natured to begin with. If we spent more time acknowledging and rewarding good behavior and less time being critical and judgmental, the world would be a much better place. Instead we focus on criticism and negativity. It drives me crazy.

Have you kept anything from the film as a memento?

I didn't, except for a few socks. That was it. I did not want to keep the costume. Although now I think I'd love to have the costume hanging at home, not to put it on ever. Now that you mention it, I can't believe I didn't go home with anything.

You should call Warner Bros. and ask them to send you something.

Exactly. I should call them up.

You have your action figure?

That I do. I have all the Watchmen paraphernalia. I have the books, the action figures, the soundtrack, everything that has to do with *Watchmen*.

I went to the toy store *for my son* ...

[Not believing the alibi] Uh-huh.

Your action figure is completely sold out.

It is?

It's gone. The other ones are called "peg warmers."

That's awesome. I love it. That is so great. Wow. [Kidding] I feel very flattered right now.

I ask each superhero I speak with to come up with a question for my next interview subject. Alan Cumming asks, "Is there chafing?"

[Laughs] Yes, yes, there was chafing. Absolutely.

John Shipp, who played The Flash, asks, "How did this part affect you personally?"

The film was a very emotional experience for me. It was a roller coaster ride. It was the first time I felt depressed in my life. Not a deep depression, but I would call my husband – and thank God for him – and we had so many talks. The mood was very dark. It was raining all the time, and we put in long hours and a lot of work, but when I came out of it, I felt like Rocky at the top of the steps. It's a great feeling. It was a joy. It was exciting. It gave me more confidence in myself.

What question should I ask the next superhero?

Now that you've been a superhero, would you feel more inclined to do something heroic? For example, if you saw a mugging on the street, would you feel more inclined to help out?

I spoke to two other actors who played superheroes and had that experience and had the impulse to save the day.

I love it. That is so great.

Both times the actors saw a crime, started to react but then caught themselves and thought, "Wait a minute, I'm not a superhero. What am I doing?"

That is so funny.

Can you answer that question for yourself?

I'm now blowing smoke up my own ass, but I am kind of that person to a certain extent. When something unfair is happening or if somebody needs help, I'm usually the first person there to help. For instance, I was at the farmer's market where a guy started to have a seizure. Since I had a friend growing up who had seizures, I had some experience. I told his companions to help the man down to the ground so he wouldn't fall and hit his head. Then I called 911. Those kinds of things that I can actually do something about I automatically do. There's no second thought, but I'm not going to run after someone who's armed with a knife or a gun. I'm not that brave. And yet when I got mugged in Spain, I ran after the guy and got my wallet back. It was stupid but something in me clicked in that said, "That's not right. That's not fair. My life was in that wallet. I'm in Spain what am I going to do. I've got to get it back." So, I guess it would depend.

Who would win in a fight: Watchmen vs. X-Men?

Watchmen. For sure. Have you seen them? [She pauses to reflect.] That would be a tough fight. I can't answer that honestly.

PART THREE: ANTIHEROES

Lou Ferrigno is The Hulk

It might seem unlikely now, but strongman Lou Ferrigno was bullied when he was growing up. Diagnosed at the age of three with a profound hearing loss, Ferrigno was often cruelly targeted by his classmates.[55] As an adolescent, he dreamed that if he were as strong and imposing as the Hulk, no one would dare ridicule him.

When producer, writer, and director Kenneth Johnson turned Stan Lee's creation into *The Incredible Hulk,* a television series for CBS, Ferrigno almost didn't get the opportunity to play his childhood hero. Johnson originally cast Richard Kiel, best known for playing the villainous Jaws in two James Bond films, as the title character.[56] Shortly into filming the pilot, Johnson decided that Kiel did not have the right muscular look that the part demanded. So he recast the role. It was only then that Johnson turned to Ferrigno, who made a name for himself as a world-class bodybuilder and was a stand-out in the 1977 documentary *Pumping Iron.* The weightlifter turned actor played the Hulk to Bill Bixby's David Banner for five seasons from 1978-1982. The series drew not only upon its comic book origins but also on Victor Hugo's *Les Miserables* and the TV series *The Fugitive* (1963-1967). Each week, when Banner's anger-management issues swelled to critical mass, he would be transformed into the Hulk.

Ferrigno reprised his role for three reunion movies: *The Incredible Hulk Returns* (1988), in which the Hulk battles and then joins forces with Thor; *The Trial of the Incredible Hulk* (1989), where the Hulk befriends Daredevil; and in *The Death of the Incredible Hulk* (1990), where, after being propelled out of an exploding airplane, as the title promises, the Hulk dies.[57]

Ferrigno also provided the voice of the antihero in the animated series *The Incredible Hulk* (1996), made a cameo in Ang Lee's feature film *Hulk* (2003), played a security guard who aides Ed Norton's Banner in Louis Leterrier's *The Incredible Hulk* (2008) and recorded some uncredited grunts and growls for the not so jolly green giant in Joss Whedon's *The Avengers.*[58]

We like him when he's angry. Lou Ferrigno flexes his muscles as the Hulk. © CBS

Since CGI has made it unlikely that another actor will play the character using the low-tech method of wearing green make up from head to toe, the combination of ferocity and the unexpected depth of pained humanity that Ferrigno brought to the role will probably never be duplicated.

THE INTERVIEW

Which superheroes did you like as a child?

The Hulk and Spider-Man and Superman.

What did you like about them?

Mostly the fact that they were respected as superheroes. That people looked up to them. I liked the fact that they were able to control situations. They were heroes. They fought crime, and they portrayed a very positive image, and they had superpowers.

How did you stay in shape, build, and maintain the figure? It must have required a lot of discipline and sacrifice.

The physical part was really easy though – to work out and do a TV series. The problem I had was I was in make up and I couldn't move most of the time. Because of the fact that I could not leave and go work out when I had green paint on. I had to force myself to train before and after shooting. I just made that extra sacrifice knowing that the way I looked on the screen. I would make that sacrifice even though I would lose some sleep over it. I didn't want to miss workouts. I always found a way to work around it.

How long did it take to put on the green make up?

Three hours to put on. The problem is that I had to be retouched every half hour because the make up would run. Because sometimes [the temperature] got hot or cold then the makeup gets brittle, so they had to retouch me. Basically it was the process that went on for twelve hours a day.

How did you stay mentally focused and ready during those long periods of immobility?

I kept in mind that it was a good living, that it was televised, and it gave me tremendous publicity and popularity. It's a weird situation in Hollywood to have a hit TV series. So, I just knew that this was something I wanted to maintain. That kept me motivated. The fact that people loved the show. Because a lot of times you do TV work and you're just forgotten. I knew that this was my one chance in a lifetime, and I wanted to maintain it for as long as I could.

The difficulties of wearing the makeup must have been frustrating. Were you able to use that frustration to get into the character?

Well, the beautiful thing about the make up is that when it's completed, I looked in the mirror. I look at myself and I just knew that I became the character. I loved becoming the character, but it was a lot of work involved to look like the character. I mean, I'd rather have a jump suit to put on and I'd be ready to play the character in five minutes, but the fact that the makeup made the Hulk so believable with my sensitivity and I was able to do pantomime. I was acting without speaking through the makeup.

What was your interpretation of the Hulk? How did you see him?

Very angry guy on the inside. Because people always justified and looked at him as the bad guy and the monster, but he really was a sensitive creature. He basically knew right from wrong and the fact is that he was always a positive force against crime.

Did you relate to being misunderstood - like the Hulk?

Yeah, because I was a Hulk my whole life.

How's that?

Because I had a hearing loss, I had to overcome all the obstacles and all the anger. So I worked out. I was a little Hulk inside. I was that character all my life.

In creating the physical movements of the Hulk, you created something that was not quite human, animal-like, yet still retaining some human characteristics. How did you do that physically?

It had to do with my incredible sensitivity and my incredible genetics. Being in great physical shape and because I was very coordinated, I was able to move and run like the Hulk in the comics. I was very symmetrical as far as my body. So I basically had the whole package. I was able to bring that to the table.

Someone else doing it would only have looked like a man in green make up.

Exactly, but I was able to play that character and become the Hulk because I knew what the Hulk was like from the inside. So that's what came out. That had to do with some gift I have inside of me to bring it out. Because that's not something you can just force. It's something that comes from inside of you.

Bill Bixby as David Banner and Lou Ferrigno as the Hulk. © CBS

You and Bill Bixby played two different halves of the same character. Did you watch Bixby's footage so that you knew what he was doing?

All the time. I watched all the scenes he filmed before I became the Hulk because I had to be connected with that. I watched how he handled the situation, how he got angry, how he became the Hulk, and I had to make that connection. I couldn't just walk on the set and do my thing. It was important to be connected with him and the scene before mine.

Did what caused him to become the Hulk on any given episode — what he was going through — alter the way you played the Hulk?

Well, I related to his character and I related to Bill. Basically, it was like playing two characters in one. So I had to make the connection, knowing that when I watched the scene from the script the way it's written, what triggered him off, what motivated him to become the Hulk. Then I would take that and take it from there, and Bill would take it back to where I left off. So it was kind of like a chain reaction.

Do you think you would have played the Hulk differently if some other actor were playing David Banner? Would that have changed the way you played the Hulk?

That's possible, but I think it was just the time, with Bill and I; it was just the right time and the right place. It was the perfect package. I mean we just blended. It was chemistry. I think with another actor it might have been different but I was fortunate to have Bill play the part. Because Bill was a very fine actor and he knew had to play the character. The guy, you know, was an incredible actor.

The TV show played around with different concepts and versions of the Hulk. In one you played a Hulk in pre-historic times, a primitive Hulk. Did you try to differentiate primitive Hulk from present day Hulk and how did you do that?

Well, basically I went by the story line. I just followed [the script] and used the best that I could bring to that character. I didn't want to confuse it and then make any major changes. I wanted to blend in with the character and the story line.

What about the one "evil Hulk" episode where Banner becomes temporarily evil? Your Hulk was even darker than he normally is.

Well, we were going to do that [in a reunion movie], but then Bill passed away. We were going to do *The Revenge of the Hulk* where you see the dark side, and the Hulk basically has David Banner's mind and he thinks like David Banner. We were going to come to that bridge, but unfortunately Bill got sick and passed away.

Would Bill Bixby have been in that?

He was going to direct that after *The Death of the Hulk*.

Would the character of David Banner been in it too?

Yeah.

What advice did Kenneth Johnson [creator of the series] give you about playing the part?

To be very connected with the scene, following through with the character and not doing anything sloppy, but basically to be a professional. And Kenny demanded a hundred and ten percent, and I gave a hundred and ten percent whenever I came on the set.

Did Stan Lee ever give you any insights into the character that you were able to use?

Not really. The character really came from me. They always said to me, "Just do your thing." It was something I created when I started the series. I've never taken a lesson on how to play the character. It was just something I brought to the character, and they just loved it and they embraced it. They never [asked me] to make any changes from the way I wanted to portray it.

I know it was a disappointment of yours that the Hulk never spoke.

I regret that they never gave me a chance to use the voice because it would have been phenomenal. Because my speech patterns back then would have matched the Hulk. That's the only thing I regret. But I ended up doing the voice for the animated cartoon. I even auditioned for it to convince them that I could speak and talk like the Hulk.

What are your thoughts on the Hulk's childlike behavior?

He is like a child. Or like a creature. He's not going to know any table manners, or basically, he just is. It's almost like – you take King Kong. I mean, King Kong doesn't have table manners. King Kong is like the Hulk but much bigger. So it's kind of similar. Because everyone can be childlike, and that being childlike brings a sensitivity to the character.

The Hulk had no memory of past encounters. He never learns.

Well, it's the way Kenny wrote it, and in the script that when the Hulk lost his anger he would just change back into Bixby. That's why the transformation was quite short.

You've said that you think everyone has their own Hulk inside them. Would you expand on that thought?

Everyone of us has some kind of form of anger and frustration and anxiety inside of us. We are not all able to express and show how we really feel about our anger, but the Hulk was able to do that. I was able to do that, for example, like smashing phone booths. We all have thoughts of doing stuff like that when we're angry. Breaking walls. So the little Hulk comes out. We have that little Hulk inside. That's why [I was able to relate to that] as the character I was able to have the fun to express that.

As angry and as violent as the Hulk became, he never really hurt anyone seriously. Do you think that was a function of his character or do you think that was just a desire to keep the show kid friendly?

No, it was the character. He was a very sensitive creature. He meant no harm, and he would only show his anger when he was being tormented. When he was at the stage where Bill Bixby was. And he's smart enough to know that he's not going to let anything hurt him or hurt anyone else that's close to him.

You played a character who was a childhood hero of yours. Was it important to you to make sure he was presented in a positive light?

Oh, yeah. Because I didn't want him to be in a Frankenstein situation. That's why I portrayed him in a positive light. Take Frankenstein, you like him even though he had a murderous mind, But the Hulk is basically one of those creatures like the werewolf that go down in history as regarded as a hero and a creature but not a monster. That's why I love portraying that.

One of the things you did as the Hulk, was to flex your arms to intimidate people. It's a classic body builder's pose but it's completely in character for the Hulk

Yeah, yeah I adapted that. I brought that to the series. And that's why it made the Hulk so famous because of the muscle flare pose in body building shows. My body matches the comic book version. They even changed the comic book to look more like my body than the original Hulk. Because the original Hulk wasn't built as symmetrical or as defined as I was.

How did the cast and crew relate to you when you were dressed as the Hulk?

It was different because they couldn't see Lou. It was the Hulk's makeup so it was hard to make the connection [with other people]. When we're sitting down trying to have lunch, they just see a different character. And then sometimes we removed the makeup because it was more comfortable because some people just felt uncomfortable even looking at me. Because, you know, I forget because I'm in the make up. I'm just trying to socialize and be with the crew because I don't want to sit in the mobile home twelve hours a day by myself.

What about your fans? Do they treat you as if you're really the Hulk? Or do they want you to be the Hulk? Or are they more savvy than that?

I do a lot of comic book conventions, a lot of autograph signings. They come up to me and ask me a lot of questions. And sometimes some fans really think that I am the Hulk. They wonder if I can do superhuman feats of strength. You know, not all people, some people basically like to live the fantasy and believe that I am the Hulk.

Do you think that's positive or do you think that's somewhat negative?

Well, positive. Because when they come to the convention, they see me and it gives them a sense of belief that they could be a superhero, and they can fantasize about that. Instead of going out and doing something that can hurt themselves or hurt others. It gives them a positive well being. It's not a negative. It gives them a connection. If they have nothing else to look up to, it's important for them to have that.

Have you spoken to other actors who have played superheroes about their dealings with their fans?

Not too much because that's something they probably want to keep private. I've always kept to myself as the Hulk, and I'm sure they feel the same way.

Why do you think we need superheroes? Why do you think the public is so hungry for them?

Because they're very positive. It has a lot to do with power and the fact that it's an escape. People like to fantasize. It's like an escape. When I was young, reading the comics gave me a chance to escape. And they helped me to achieve my dreams. People always fantasize about themselves being a superhero, doing certain things. And they dream about being a superhero. Because it's kind of like a fantasy. Like a little secret they can keep inside of them. But knowing that it's not real. But it's a good feeling they can have, knowing that they have the can have luxury to escape. For the fun of it.

When I was growing up, I had a good friend who was partially deaf and he really looked up to you. Are you conscious of being a role model to people with hearing impairments?

I like it because basically growing up I never had a hero like myself. I kind of like led a sheltered, very introverted life because it was harder for me to express [myself]. So later in life [being famous] gave me a chance when I see hard of hearing kids and deaf people to talk to them. Because I know that it means more to them than the average person. Because, you know, they sometimes have a hard time expressing themselves, but they can express it to the superhero character. And it gives them a chance to feel better about themselves.

How were you able to cope with the hearing loss as a child?

It was tough because I was introverted. And I took up bodybuilding. That gave me a chance to go to the gym and work out. Now I've become a world champion. I've changed myself from introverted to extroverted. And I stayed positive, being connected with superheroes like Superman and the Hulk.

Do you think, as I do, that if your life experiences were different and you didn't have the hearing loss that you wouldn't be the person you are today.

Correct.

And all those difficulties were in some ways a gift.

Correct. Because it's true. You hit it right on the nail. If I didn't go through all these things, then I just would never have achievedl what I've achieved today.

In terms of the reunion movies, did you like them? Did you like it when the Hulk battled Thor or worked alongside Daredevil?

It was fun because it gave me a chance to be with another superhero. The idea was that they wanted to have a spin-off of the other superhero. But it didn't work out because the Hulk is a dominant figure and people want to see the Hulk. It was nice to see the camaraderie of the Hulk with Thor and with the Daredevil. Although the Hulk can hold his own. He doesn't need other superheroes to benefit him.

You didn't like the death of the Hulk. You didn't like the idea of killing him, even if momentarily?

That idea was for the ratings. I didn't like the idea. I thought it was too premature to do that.

It was great to see you in Ang Lee's *Hulk*. Although, I don't think they really captured through CGI what you brought to the role. What did you think of the movie?

Well, I wanted to reprise the role – play it myself on the big screen. But with CGI it's very hard – because you can't have CGI Hulk be as sensitive as the way I portrayed the character. But Ang Lee wanted to break boundaries – matching the comic book version on the big screen. But that's why he went in that direction. It's tough to compare CGI with the human Hulk.

You've said that computer Hulks don't give autographs.[59] The fans can't interact with the CGI Hulk like they can with you.

Exactly. I say there's one Hulk and it'll never be the same again. The mold is broken. It's just like with the original Superman series. Or *Star Trek*. It's just the chemistry. I think the Hulk series will last for many, many more years because it's got that connection with the audience.

Now let's get to the important stuff. Who do you think would win in a fight? The Hulk or Superman?

That's a tough one because Superman can fly. The Hulk is just as powerful. I would say . . . it would be even.

Hulk vs. Batman?

No contest. The Hulk.

Hulk vs. Spider-Man?

No contest. Hulk.

Okay . . . Hulk vs. the entire X-Men team?

No contest. Hulk. But it would be even with Superman. Superman is my other favorite character. So I had to make them both equal.

Rex Smith is Daredevil

Daredevil, created by Stan Lee and Bill Everett in 1964, made his first on-screen appearance not in his own big-budget film but as a guest star on a made-for-television movie spotlighting a different superhero.

The TV series *The Incredible Hulk* aired eighty-two episodes during its five-year run (1978-1982). Six years later, Bill Bixby, as the scientist David Banner, and Lou Ferrigno, as his alter ego the Hulk, reprised their roles in *The Incredible Hulk Returns* (1988), a made-for-TV movie that acknowledged the ongoing popularity of the cancelled series and led to two more TV-movie sequels.

In the second of them, *The Trial of the Incredible Hulk* (1989), David Banner is falsely accused of assaulting a woman and Matt Murdock, played by Rex Smith, is assigned to be his defense attorney. Murdock is, of course, the brilliant and blind attorney who at night becomes Daredevil, the righteous vigilante who seeks to mete out justice where he believes the courts have failed to do so.

At first, Murdock's relationship with Banner is antagonistic. However, during the course of the film, not only do the two men learn to respect each other, but they also discover that they share a secret. Exposure to radiation gave them both their special abilities, and both feel cursed by the trade-off. For Murdock, the radiation that robbed him of sight also greatly heightened his senses of smell and touch, and his hearing became so acute that it resulted in both radar-like powers and his ability to detect lying by the change, now audible to him, in a suspect's heart rate.

By the time Banner and Murdock join forces to take down the powerful crime lord Wilson Fisk,[60] the two men have formed a tight bond. At the end of the film, Murdock tells Banner, "You may take my secret with you." Banner says, "And I leave mine with you. I have a brother in the world now." Murdock replies, "Yes, you do."

Rex Smith, a one-time teen idol, starred on Broadway in 1978 as Danny Zuko, the lead in the musical *Grease*. In addition to many other prominent stage appearances, Smith also starred as Fred-eric in the New York Shakespeare Festival's Central Park production of *The Pirates of Penzance*, and in 1983 he was the lead in the film version of the musical. In Smith's understated performance in *The Trial of the Incredible Hulk*, Matt Murdock is a sympathetic, physically capable but emotionally wounded altruist, who is more concerned for the welfare of others than for his own.

Although Daredevil's powers are faithful to his comic book origins, his costume is not. In print, the hero wears a red outfit with an overlapping DD insignia emblazoned across his chest and a hood with devil horns. In the TV movie, however, Murdock wears an outfit that evokes a Ninja's all black *Shinobi shōzoku*.

The producers hoped that they could the use the movie to spin-off Matt Murdock and Daredevil into their own series but those plans never materialized. Another fourteen years would elapse before the martial arts expert and billy club-toting vigilante would get the big screen treatment in the 1993 feature film *Daredevil*, starring Ben Affleck as the eponymous hero. The film, which also starred Jennifer Garner as Elektra, Colin Farrell as Bullseye, Jon Favreau as Murdock's law partner Franklin 'Foggy' Nelson, and the late Michael Clarke Duncan as The Kingpin, earned an impressive $178 million in worldwide receipts.[61]

Fans can view *The Trial of the Incredible Hulk* to catch a glimpse of a Daredevil television series that never came to fruition.

THE INTERVIEW

Talk about how you built your character.

I have played so many larger than life characters on Broadway that I felt quite comfortable as a superhero. I have always felt a real change in my characterization of a part when I get into wardrobe, and when I first put on the Daredevil suit I felt a tremendous rush. I couldn't help but feel "super" when suited up, with a cast and crew waiting for me to arrive on set.

Did you read the comics for research?

I read the first ten Daredevil comics, and I was amazed at the creative minds behind them. Like so many superheroes, Matt was caught between two fully formed personalities, much like young people who read comics are changing from childhood to puberty. I felt empathy for his loneliness, sightlessness, [and the burden of the terrible] secret.

Christopher Reeve thought of Clark Kent and Superman as two separate characters. Did you take a similar approach?

Chris was one of my best friends, and I see his point, but to me, I feel that Matt and Daredevil are extensions of the same being. He is not a Jekyll and Hyde split personality. The Daredevil is an extension of Matt's fight for a just world.

What do you think motivates Matt Murdock?

Matt's life became something more than his own when he was blinded and [he acquired the] resulting super powers. I don't think he ever thought about a choice once his powers became part of his physical life. The daredevil is grounded; he does not fly. I feel he is closer to a Navy Seal, than to Superman.

What other aspects of Matt Murdock's personality would you have liked to explore?

We will never know what could have evolved for Daredevil; the movie was a "backdoor pilot" for a series. It tested well, but CBS did not want competition for *The Flash* that they were airing, so they bought my NBC contract and I was unable to work in television for a year. It was a really tough situation because, at that time, I was being offered a lot of other television opportunities.

The costume in the movie is different from the one most often associated with the Daredevil in the comics. In the comics, he wears red - like a devil, but in the movie, it was black. Do you know the rationale for the change?

I think black was easier to light for camera. But remember, Daredevil was originally yellow. [In the first six issues, Daredevil's outfit was yellow, red and black.]

When you first put on the outfit, how did you feel?

Like a superhero. I was told by the stunt coordinator, "My people are suited up for fight scenes, so hit as hard as you need to make it real." Some of my fights were pretty rough.

What are your memories of Bill Bixby?

Bill was one of the most professional directors I ever worked with. His presence on set made cast and crew want to give their very best for him. I loved his sense of humor, and I would give anything to see the "Gag Reel" we made. After a tough scene, he would say, "OK, let's get one for the gag reel." I would proceed to do my best [bumbling Inspector Clouseau from] The Pink Panther take. Bill and I had a long scene in the movie, where we talked about our characters' lives. I believe it was more than enough backstory for both characters. We spent much of our time off enjoying good food and as much laughter as possible.

What about Lou Ferrigno? He seemed to really relish playing the part.

When I first met Lou, he was wearing a big sweater, and I thought, He doesn't look as big as I thought. Then I saw him on set and his chest was awe-inspiring. He looked as big as, well, The Hulk!

Has playing a superhero changed your life at all?

When my son Gatsby was little, I would say to him, "Don't make me do a Daredevil on you!" I would half close my eyes, and he would believe [that my eyes were fully shut and that] I could see. One day he came home and said, "Dad, I am the son of Daredevil! Today, I closed my eyes and ran past the swing set and not one kid on a swing hit into me!" That is when we had a father/son chat about "movie magic."

In what ways are you like Matt Murdock/Daredevil?

I am vigilant about the safety of others. I have to admit, it is something to be part of the Marvel Universe.

Who would win in a fight: your Daredevil or Ben Affleck's?

Daredevil against Daredevil? Call Stan Lee and ask him to get the script out. I'm suiting up!

Chip Zien is Howard the Duck

If it weren't for *Howard the Duck,* George Lucas might be rich. *Howard the Duck* is, of course, the George Lucas executive-produced film about a wisecracking duck that lives on planet Duck-World, smokes cigars, beams to Earth, romances Lea Thompson's fetching wannabe rock star Beverly Switzler, befriends Tim Robbin's nerdy scientist Phil Blumburtt, and battles the Dark Overlord of the Universe, Dr. Walter Jenning, played by the always game Jeffrey Jones.

Howard the Duck (1986) was not only Lucas' attempt to create another film franchise after the phenomenal success of both the original Star Wars trilogy and the first two Indiana Jones adventures, the movie was also Marvel's first character to get the big screen treatment since the Captain America serials of the 1940s. Gloria Katz and Willard Huyck, who, along with Lucas, wrote the script for *American Graffiti* and were the sole credited writers on *Indiana Jones and the Temple of Doom,* wrote *Howard the Duck.* Katz also served as the film's producer, and Huyck performed directing duties.

Howard the Duck was co-created by the writer Steve Gerber and the artist Val Mayerik and made his debut appearance as a supporting character in *Adventure into Fear #19* in 1973, in an issue called *The Land Between Night and Day,* which featured the swamp creature Man-Thing. Howard would get his own comic book in 1976. In *Howard the Barbarian,* his first adventure as a headliner, the reluctant hero is introduced with the proclamation "Behold a depressed duck" as he "stands on the bank of the Cuyahoga River, contemplating [taking his own life]."[62] Picking up from where the narrator left off, Howard's first words are, "Suicide? Yeah, well. Maybe."[63]

Howard decides not to do himself in by drowning in the river because it's polluted; he decides instead to throw himself off a nearby tower. Along the way, he gets caught up in a Conan the Barbarian-inspired action-packed adventure in the vein of Robert E. Howard's pulp novels. Howard saves the life of a scantily-clad prisoner who is locked in a tower made out of credit cards, battles a "spuming beast" who turns back into human form after Howard dispatches him, is captured by a powerful wizard and, because "I was about to off myself anyway," the cowardly protagonist turned "courageous duck" throws himself and the wizard off a cliff towards "flaming waters" and towards apparent death until, at the last moment, Spider-Man (an established Marvel star) swoops in to save Howard.[64]

In future issues, Howard the Duck battles villains with colorful names like the Deadly Space Turnip, the Cockroach, Mr. Chicken, Doctor Angst, Count Macho, and Revered Yuc in stories that would satirize Kung Fu movies, religious cults, the self-help movement, the singer turned anti-gay crusader Anita Bryant, politics, pop-culture, and even *Star Wars* in two back-to-back issues called *May The Farce Be With You!* and *Star Waaugh*, which featured a diminutive robot in the shape of a trash can who goes by the designation 2-2, 2-2 or "Tutu for short."

Grady Hendrix of Slate magazine describes Howard as "an oversexed, overly intellectual anti-hero who was constantly in the throes of an existential crisis, and who delighted in puncturing pomposity."[65] Hendrix argued that the early Howard comics initially "parodied Marvel's purple prose style" but that ultimately "the book grew into something deeper. Howard raged against the glorification of violence, had a nervous breakdown, lost Beverly to [the villainous] Dr. Bong, was transformed into a man, and, in the end, rejected his friends and bitterly set out on his own, trying to forget a past of pointless superfights. One issue was all text; another took place entirely on a long bus trip. These were surreal flights of fancy with razor-tipped wings, America's answer to *Monty Python's Flying Circus*."[66]

When Gerber died at the age of sixty in 2008, Margalit Fox of *The New York Times* wrote that Howard the Duck is a "dour, dyspeptic, utterly disagreeable and therefore wildly popular comic-book hero . . . If most comic books are subversive, *Howard the Duck* was especially so, because what it subverted was the very idea of the comic-book hero. Howard was not a nice duck. He had no special powers, nor was he brave. But then again, poor Howard was, in the words of the comic's famous tag line, 'TRAPPED IN A WORLD HE NEVER MADE!' That world was Cleveland."[67]

The film itself is a well-meaning but unsuccessful attempt to capture the subversive spirit of the comic. *Howard the Duck*, (which was subtitled *A New Breed of Hero* in its international release), is an uneasy mixture of children's films sensibilities, superhero pastiche, satire, and bawdy humor. However, it is the sexual humor that is the most jarring. In the first few minutes of the film, a female duck appears topless in a bathtub; later on, Beverly finds a duck-sized condom in Howard's wallet and in another scene Howard gets a job dispensing towels at an unspecified club where couples go for illicit encounters.

The critics didn't completely eviscerate the film. In *The New York Times*, Caryn James acknowledged that the first half of the movie is "a pleasant enough spoof for forty-five minutes or so" and praised "the second half for it's truly magnificent visual tricks, created by George Lucas's Industrial Light and Magic company and equal to anything in that director's *Star Wars*."[68] She concludes her review with the suggestion: "Choose the part that suits your taste, but this is a case where half a movie – either half – is apt to be better than the whole."[69]

In *Variety* Jane Galbraith wrote that while she didn't enjoy the film "there are several amusing sequences as Howard tries to fit into human society, notably his encounter with an overpowering, no-nonsense unemployment counselor determined that he remain off the welfare rolls no matter how strange he looks to prospective employers."[70] For Sheila Benson of *The Los Angeles Times*, "The fun of *Howard the Duck* comes from his heavy-lidded view of the follies of our planet – or from our discovering the details of his."[71] She invites her readers to "imagine a full-throttle mix of *The Blues Brothers*' action and *The Exorcist*'s bile-spewing possession, and you'll get a faint idea of Howard's earthly habitat."

Howard the Duck creator Steve Gerber wasn't particularly fond of the film. In an interview with Diamond Comics Gerber said:

"In the film, and in most of his comic book appearances by other writers, Howard has been treated as little more than a visual gag and a mouthpiece for lame one-liners. In the original series, he was a much more complex character. Howard the Duck was never a "humor" comic in the traditional sense. Howard wasn't even a comedic character. He was frequently depressed, congenitally rude, and had a bad tendency to waddle all over other people's feelings. The humor in the series derived from the absurdity of his situation – a sentient duck from another dimension, trapped in a world of what he called "talking hairless apes" – and from Howard's mordant observations on the world around him. In contemporary terms, Howard had much more in common with Spider Jerusalem [a Hunter S. Thompson-esque character], for example, than with Donald Duck.[72]

Gerber once elaborated on the difference between the film and comic, "Krypton isn't an ice world in the comics, and the Joker didn't kill Thomas and Martha Wayne. The movie was an adaptation of the comic book material. It stands -- or, in this case, huddles shamefully in a corner -- on its own, as another, separate interpretation of the character."[73]

Howard the Duck eked out a feeble $16 million at the domestic box office and managed about $38 worldwide, totaling just under $1 million more than its budget. Including the costs of prints, advertising, and shared revenue from the theaters – an informal rule of thumb is in order to earn a profit a movie needs to double it's budget at the domestic box office – the film lost a tremendous amount of money.

As a result of the box office failure of *Howard the Duck*, flagging Star Wars merchandise sales, and the creation of the state-of-the-art Skywalker Ranch, George Lucas' company was in debt. To become solvent Lucas essentially sold off his computer-animation company that eventually became Pixar to Steve Jobs. That sale might not have been the wisest business decision Lucas ever made. Pixar's first fourteen films have earned an incredible $8.5 billion. In 2006, Disney bought Pixar for $7.4 billion. But one needn't feel too bad for George; in 2012 he sold Lucasfilm and

Howard the Duck. © Lucasfilm

the rights to make additional *Star Wars* films to Disney for over $4 billion.

Huyck, the film's director, was apparently placed in movie jail; despite writing some excellent movies, *Howard the Duck* was the last film he helmed, and he has worked only sporadically as a writer since. Huyck did get one more shot at the big brass ring when he teamed again with Katz, and along with Jeff Reno and Ron Osborn, wrote the Lucas executive-produced, Mel Smith-directed, zany, fast-paced, screwball comedy *Radioland Murders* (1994), which assembled an eclectic group of actors including Brian Benben, Mary Stuart Masterson, Ned Beatty, Jeffrey Tambor, Christopher Lloyd, Harvey Korman, Billy Barty, and George Burns. Unfortunately, that film didn't do well either.

Although seven different actors played Howard the Duck on set, Chip Zien alone provided Howard's voice. Zien's mined all the comedy he could from the part and made his Howard a sympathetic creature that you kept rooting for throughout the film.

Zien probably isn't a well-known name in the superhero community, but he has appeared in several TV roles and he is a respected Broadway actor. He originated the role of the Baker in Stephen Sondheim's Tony Award-winning musical *Into the Woods* and he appeared in Andrew Lloyd Webber's Tony Award-winning *Les Misérables*.

This interview is unlike any other in the book. Instead of directly answering my numerous questions, Zien used them as a springboard to share his memories of playing Howard the Duck in a letter he wrote to me.

THE INTERVIEW

I didn't "do" a voice.

My "process" for creating the "character" was as I would do for anything – I placed myself in imaginary circumstances and tried to figure out how I'd behave. I did nothing to alter my voice. I stood in a room and looped a movie watching Howard's image on the screen interacting with the various characters. I don't particularly know what made Howard tick (he's a duck); I only know how I tick. I tried to imagine myself being hurtled through space, being scared or frustrated or whatever – being pushed around or punched – as I would do looping any movie.

This job was particularly difficult because they were locked into a rhythm and pacing for the lines based on the work of an actor who had been on the set ([using] an off-camera microphone) voicing the lines so the actors on-camera would have somebody to talk to. For whatever reason, they chose not to use that actor's recorded voice and embarked on a long process of trying to find the "right" voice. I know that the actors in the film were not particularly happy about the decision to replace [their original voice performances]. In fact, Lea Thompson, whom I only met briefly, went on David Letterman and said so.

I had auditioned for the film over a period of a few months. The casting director (her name escapes me) came backstage to meet me in La Jolla where I was in the first re-working of [Stephen Sondheim's musical] *Merrily We Roll Along*, [which is told in reverse chronological order]. As I remember it, she mentioned she didn't really care for *Merrily* but that my voice reminded her of a duck and that she was casting *Howard the Duck* and did I want to audition. Initially, I was merely annoyed about her lack of enthusiasm for *Merrily* and I had never heard of Howard the Duck – so I didn't take it seriously. Somewhere along the line, however, I mentioned it to my agent who got pretty excited, said it's a huge deal, and that lots of people were trying to get the job. So I kind of reluctantly went to my first audition (by this time, back in New York City) and read a few lines on tape.

Eventually I auditioned again in New York, then at some point I flew to San Francisco, and, of course, the more I auditioned the more I wanted it. I believe I got called out to San Francisco at least twice – so all the back and forth got pretty intense. There were lots of rumors. For example, I heard that Judd Hirsch was the first choice. Eventually I was devastated to learn that they had hired Robin Williams. That was about it – until I got an emergency call from my agent (Memorial Day – 1984?) saying I had to "get on a plane" immediately because Robin Williams (having looped for only a few days) had quit and they were giving me the role. I threw some clothes in an overnight bag and flew to San Francisco later that day.

The only person who ever recognized my voice was a very stoned young man who was about to marry my niece and freaked out. I'm amused by your question: "When was the last time you used the voice?" The answer is: I've never not used it.

I'm not so pretentious as to talk about the filmmakers overall intentions, etc. I can only say that I loved Willard Huyck and Gloria Katz. I loved spending time with them and I was forever saddened that the film became, unfortunately, a legendary flop. I met Lucas one time, briefly, when I was invited to a July 4th party out at "The Ranch," which was the size of North Dakota. I was treated exceptionally well and I credit him and the whole crew at Industrial Light and Magic, which was an awesome place – particularly if you had any interest in the convergence of tech, computers, art, etc., a very cool place with all sorts of very talented people running around.

To be honest, I thought my life was going to change because I had signed on for a bunch of sequels. I was certainly paid well. It was really fun to do it. I thought the movie was going to be a huge success – I now refer to that as the "Howard the Duck syndrome," when actors lose all sense of reality and believe their play/movie is fantastic in the face of contrary empirical evidence. I didn't talk much about it after the movie did poorly. Lots of people ask me about it now. It was a coup to get the part, and, in retrospect, astounding that I did, in fact, get it. It was, to put it mildly, a very heady experience, which, unfortunately, didn't pan out.

Alan Cumming is Nightcrawler

Unlike most superheroes, Nightcrawler doesn't have the luxury of leading a normal life when not saving the world. He cannot blend in by assuming an ordinary identity. He can't, for instance, put on a pair of glasses and work as a newspaper reporter. He can't disguise his daring deeds by living the life of a millionaire

Alan Cumming as Nightcrawler in a scene from X2 (2003). © Warner Bros.

bachelor. Nightcrawler, whose real name is Kurt Wagner, is unable to hide due to his demonic appearance, and sporting a tail probably doesn't help much in the blending in department. Because he's a blue-skinned, pointy-eared hero whose body is adorned with religious iconography, Nightcrawler is the subject of never-ending ridicule and scorn. To achieve respite, he must use his powers of teleportation to disappear from unwanted attention.

Before becoming a superhero, Nightcrawler worked in the circus, where at least in fiction the odd, the grotesque and unwanted can always find a home. Adding to his already profound isolation, Nightcrawler inadvertently kills his foster brother Steffen, a serial killer of children, when he intervenes to save the life of a child who would have been Steffen's latest victim. Because no good deed goes unpunished, the townspeople jump to the erroneous conclusion that Nightcrawler murdered the kids. Before the villagers can kill him, Professor X saves Nightcrawler and invites him to join the X-Men.

Alan Cumming an acclaimed actor and a gay activist, played the blue-hued hero in *X2*. Cumming has been honored with a Tony and an Oliver Award for his work in the theater. The versatile Scottish actor has played roles ranging from Hamlet and Macbeth to a Bond baddie in *GoldenEye* and a hotel clerk with a crush on Tom Cruise in Stanley Kubrick's psychosexual final film *Eyes Wide Shut* (1999).

Cumming identified with both his character's isolation and, somewhat contradictorily, his mischievous nature. (Cumming did after all put out a skin care line with such wicked names as "Cumming Clean" and "Cumming All Over.") Cumming very deftly shaped Nightcrawler into a hero who is both irreverent and funny. Much like the actor himself.

THE INTERVIEW

How did you figure out who Nightcrawler was and what made him tick?

I came to it very ignorantly because I didn't really know anything about the X-Men. So, I went into it thinking I was little behind the rest of the world. After I got the part, I read a lot of the comics. I did a lot of research about where he came from. What his background was. I did it in the normal way when you research for a role. But there was so much information to cull from.

Was there a particular piece of info that you gleaned from the comic book that caused you to think, "That's the key to understanding my character."

In the first story where Nightcrawler is introduced, he is a very frightened and very vulnerable person. There are lots of religious references as well. I thought that he was someone who was so ostracized that religion was his primary comfort. Religion was the one thing that hadn't let him down in his life. I also learned that he was a circus performer. So he had that bravado and the ability to be a showman as well. It was quite a contradictory backstory. I remember clearly the drawings of the townsfolk flinging torches at him. He's hiding on top of the building away from everybody. That was mainly what I took from the comics.

It's quite unusual to see a superhero with faith.

Yes, I hadn't heard of it in any other superhero movie. It was quite fascinating to me how that happened. I think it gives him an extra layer and makes him more screwed-up. What I like about the X-men is that they all are, "Oops, I'm different." Rather than, "I'm a superhero, get out of the way." There is an interesting difference between the X-Men and traditional superheroes.

Nightcrawler is a blue demonic-looking character with scars in the shape of angelic symbols. Unlike other heroes, he can't hide or blend in.

When you're playing someone like that and you've got prosthetics on, it's a funny feeling when you walk onto the set. Everyone gasps and points at you. They all go, "Wow" and walk up and stare at you. It's a very interesting way to experience what is must be like to be that person all the time. I hated that. I didn't like that at all. I remember thinking, *I'm inside here. I can see you. I can hear you.* In life in general, it's a really weird thing to walk down the street and have people point at you and shout things at you as though you can't hear what they're saying, as though you are not really there.

Because of the time it took to be made up, did you grow to disdain getting into costume?

It was awful. I didn't enjoy playing this part. I really didn't. Although, I'm glad I did it and I really love the film. I'm very glad to have been a superhero. [Laughs] But it wasn't a pleasant or fun experience for me – at all. It was physically and emotionally very draining for me.

How was it emotionally draining?

Partially because you're so tired. That begins to affect your psyche. The atmosphere on the set was not particularly fabulous. Big films sets are not for pussies. You have to stand your own ground. Everyone's shouting. It's a big operation. To be so exhausted and sore, and to be hanging about for a long time with contacts in your eyes while the schedule goes on and on. It was awful.

What are the benefits of being a superhero now that the process is behind you? How does it follow you?

Lots of straight boys want to share a joint with you.

[Laughs]

[Affecting an American accent] "I want to share a doobie with the Nightcrawler, man." That's always very nice. Playing a superhero marks you in some way. You've entered the popular culture and conscience in a way that other roles might not. Worldwide you're always going to be not just an actor, but also as a character that people will always remember. And I love the fact that he's blue and sort of weird. When people meet me they are a slightly mesmerized that I am this person and was able to be so different and embody that character. What's really lovely about the whole experience, I feel, is that people have been so kind as to say that I embodied the character they way they imagined him. Especially the geeks. They've all been really nice about that. That I didn't let them down.

Do you feel that you have to pretend to love the character and superheroes in general, that you have been burdened with an obligation that goes beyond acting and that isn't entirely welcome.

A little bit. I'm always fascinated when fans tell me things about Nightcrawler that I didn't already know. I've let it go. I've moved on with my life. Especially because I thought I was going to do the third film and everyone thought I was going to do the third film but I ended up not doing it. It's one of those things where the studio tells you that it's going to happen. Then the budget changes and the schedule changes and you're not doing it. I thought *Fuck that*, and I didn't pay any attention to it after that. In a way, it's a nice little island of something for me.

Did you expect that it would follow you?

When I was doing the film I realized what a big deal it was culturally. Then when we did the big world press tour, I thought, *This is huge*, but the character has already existed in other people's imaginations before this film, and so it's not just photos of you, it's also drawings of the character. You now embody something that has been in people's lives for decades. You are the human version of that.

Do you think that you were most suited for Nightcrawler?

[Laughs] That's funny. I think I did it quite well. What I think they did quite well is that they got very good actors for all the parts. I think it's really important because they are complex characters and they got really good actors to embody them. I like the fact that Nightcrawler was so complex and had so many facets to his personality. While training for the role, I thought, *Why didn't they get someone more acrobatic than me?* But then I realized, "That's what stuntmen are for."

Is there another superhero that you would be equally suited to play, or is there something about Nightcrawler and his psyche that nicely fit with yours?

That's rather interesting. I suppose I feel that because he's a reluctant superhero that suited me. He had superhero-ness thrust upon him; the way I did.

Were you worried that you'd always be associated with this part?

If I was just "the guy who was Nightcrawler" than that would be annoying. It is going to be with me for life, but so are other things. I'm also considered to be a spokesperson for being gay and I can't do anything about it. That's a very positive thing — same as being Nightcrawler - but I have no choice in that. Certainly there are other characters I've played and I will just have to keep talking about them for the rest of my life. I don't think of that in a negative way. You just don't have a choice about it.

Do publications come at you from a very selective viewpoint and exclude other things? Here's the gay-themed interview. Here's the superhero interview. And all the questions are filtered through that one topic.

A little bit. You'd be surprised by how much those two topics merge. The gay theme and the Nightcrawler theme. I don't think I've ever done an interview for a gay magazine that doesn't ask about Nightcrawler.

There's a lot of talk about how the X-Men are an allegory for what it's like to be gay.

It's about people who are different and have to hide their differences because they are not accepted by society. It's like, "Duh." I think the prejudice against gay people is that last acceptable form of prejudice in this country.

What's interesting about the X-Men is that the outsiders are the heroes.

I think that's a really exciting thing to play. It confounds people's expectations on all levels. I was talking to Lynda Carter. I'm actually seeing her next week. She said this really interesting thing about why she has a gay following. She said that she didn't realize until someone pointed it out to her in the 1980s that Wonder Woman had this power and strength that she could only use, let it bloom, in certain situations and the rest of the time she had to hide it. I thought that was a lovely way of talking about not only the character but about gay people.

One view of Superman is that it's a story about conformity, fitting in. Two Jewish men who were trying to assimilate into America culture created Superman. Whereas X-Men are about celebrating our differences.

And why should you conform? We should celebrate that difference. I love that.

Are superheroes modern day gods? Similar to how the Romans and Greeks thought of their gods.

We like the idea that there are people who have greater powers than ourselves. Because we haven't found them, we invented them. I think it's a lovely idea that people could pop on a cloak and save us all. Because of the association, as an actor you are revered in a way for having played one.

What do you think the X-Men films do best? How do they fit into the spectrum?

They are slightly different in that the world is against them. They exist in a place where they are not these all-conquering heroes. They have to deal with conflict all the time. They are more human in a way. They are outsiders. They have ultimate power and their use of that power is sometimes questionable. That makes them interesting and ultimately more complex.

Do you have any Nightcrawler memorabilia?

From my office, which I can see from here, I have my twelve-inch doll that can be posed, and a wind up me as well. I have my teeth in a box up on my shelf. I let people wear it. From *The Flintstones* film, I have my helmet when I played The Great Gazoo. I let people wear that as well.

Here's a question that another superhero suggested I ask: He wants to know how has playing this part affected you personally?

It made me really happy to think that people understand the gay experience. It made me happy to think that there was a dialogue about that through a mainstream superhero film. I'm proud to be a part of that.

What question should I ask the next superhero I speak to?

Did you have chafing of any kind?

[Laughs]

Please let me know the answer.

For you the answer has to be yes.

Big time.

Who would win in a fight: Nightcrawler or Wolverine?

Nightcrawler. He'd smack Wolverine's pretty ass down. Wolverine has more brute strength but Nightcrawler would be able to trick him. Nightcrawler would just be able to kick him in the groin.

PART FOUR: SIDEKICKS

Noel Neill is Lois Lane

Even without any superpowers or a form-fitting costume, Lois Lane has had a long-lasting impact on the comic book industry. Lane, created by Jerry Siegel and Joseph Shuster, the team who conceived Superman, is one of the few characters who is not defined by her looks. Modeled on several people, including journalist Nellie Bly and Siegel's eventual wife, Joanne Carter, she is not a big-busted, tiny-waisted superheroine. We can now see that Lois was a character ahead of her time: she was an independent and tough-minded career woman, a journalist who aggressively and fearlessly pursued her stories without yielding to (or even seeming to notice) the constraints imposed on women at the time in a male-dominated profession.

While those with only a passing familiarity with comics might think that Lois expends most of her energy mooning over Superman and that her *raison d'être* is finding out if Clark Kent and Superman are the same person, her aspirations are much bigger and she is not so readily pigeonholed. One thing that can be said of her is that Ms. Lane is dedicated to her profession and that her professional mission is to uncover the truth behind any mystery and to expose duplicity.

Yet these qualities are obliged to co-exist uneasily with an adventure story convention that also casts her as the eternal "damsel in distress," who is routinely in need of being saved by Superman.

Noel Neill played the intrepid reporter in the two 15-chapter serials: *Superman* (1948) and *Atom Man vs. Superman* (1950), with Kirk Alyn as the Man of Tomorrow. When Superman was turned into a TV show, producers recast both parts and hired George Reeves as Superman and Phyllis Coates as Lois Lane. After the first season of *Adventures of Superman*, the producers suspended production of the series in order to find a national sponsor. When they were ready to resume production, Coates had already made other commitments, so the producers asked Neill to recreate the

Noel Neill as Lois Lane. © Warner Bros.

character.[74] Neill played Lois in seventy-eight episodes of the series and in the short *Stamp Day for Superman* (1954).

THE INTERVIEW

How did you create the character?

The first time I played her was with Kirk Alyn in the serials. Then years later, when they were doing the TV series and called from New York, I thought *Maybe I better go out and get a comic book and see what she's like.* [Laughs] I realized that she was a young working girl who was getting started in what was traditionally a man's field. I get a lot of compliments from gals who have become writers because of Lois Lane! It worked out fine.

Can you talk about the look of the character?

We took it somewhat from the comic books, but we cut her hair short for a little bit and then it got long again. I did whatever they wanted me to do. It was up to them what I looked like.

What did you learn from the comics?

Not much. I wasn't really into comics. Comic books in those days were really a boy's thing, but I was really just interested in seeing her as a normal working girl.

What did you learn about playing her for so many years?

She was a nice gal. [Laughs] Once you get into a character and used to it, and working with the same people like George, Jack Larson, and John Hamilton, you stay pretty consistent in your approach to the part.

Is there anything you would like to have seen Lois do that you didn't get a chance to explore.

Not really. Everything was fine to me. Working so many shows, that was enough to make life interesting. It was kind of wonderful. In the comics, they got her married. But that didn't work out. The public didn't accept it. So they forgot that soon enough. [Laughs]

Why do you think it's best for Lois to have an unrealized crush on Superman?

In so many pictures, couples get together, get married, and have kids. The thing about our show and George is that it was a little different. People looked up to George as a hero and not as a romantic lead. In the new movie I worked on, *Superman Returns* (2006) they had Lois with child. First time I heard about it was when I got to Australia [to start filming], I said, "Ohhhh my gosh. You ruined Lois Lane for everybody." I don't know how they are going to carry on with that story line. Once people see that the child has special qualities it doesn't take them too longer to figure out, "Ah hah! That's probably Superman's son!"

People really need a hero nowadays. There are enough romantic figures. That's why they still look up to George's Superman or

Lois Lane or Jimmy Olsen. They were so wonderful to work with. We were like a family after a while.

What was the schedule like?

We did twenty-six shows and then took a few years off and did another twenty-six and another couple off. You could go out and do other things, like Westerns. Before that, I was under contract with Paramount for four years, and we did a lot of leg-art [pin-up photos].

Do you feel protective of Lois Lane?

I certainly do, after sixty years. We've been having a few celebrations at the conventions to commemorate that. People are so wonderful. The fans that come see me. They always ask me certain questions and say, "Why can't they have shows like that anymore? Shows that the entire family can watch." Sometimes the grandfather or father makes the little child watch Superman and it's nice to hear.

I have a little boy who I've begun introducing to the show.

You've got him trapped!

Yes, I do. He's got the outfit.

Bless his heart. As Jack [Larson] always said, "It's nice to be loved." They enjoy seeing you, meeting you, having pictures taken. Now we're into the sixtieth year of Lois Lane, and it's been fun. We've had the cakes. It's nice to be loved and to be thought of as helping ladies get their careers going. For them to do whatever they wanted. It's a good feeling. A very good feeling.

Jack always had a great story that he used to tell. His agent called and said, "Jack I've got a job for you." Jack said, "No, no I want to go back to New York to be an actor." His agent said, "Jack listen to me. Do the thirteen weeks, take the money, and go back to New York. No one will ever see this show." [Laughs] I always got a kick out of that. It just goes on and on and on. People say they grew up on me and vice versa. It's a very good feeling.

Accepting the part was a pivotal moment in your life. Once you played the part and walked through that door that became a major path for you.

Right. Right. The strange thing is that my father was a newspaperman. I was going to study journalism. I liked the way it turned out. Being a part of a show like *Superman* is really life changing.

Have there been any negative aspects to the long association.

Not to my knowledge. Lois was always portrayed as a good working girl and getting into trouble together with Jack Larson. She would always do something dumb and would have to wait for Superman to rescue her, but it made a good story.

Did Lois rub off on you or did you rub off on her?

At a certain point we became entwined. It goes on and on. For *Superman Returns*, they said, "I know you're a good friend of Jack Larson's. He doesn't like to travel. Do you think you could possibly talk him into coming to Australia to do a cameo?" I said, "Oh sure, I can give it a shot." But he doesn't usually like to do any of these things. He doesn't like to go to the conventions or traveling. He likes to write. Which is fine. It's his shtick and his life. We all respect that.

I said, "Jack, will you go to Australia."

He said, "Australia? I'll have to get someone to stay with the dogs."

I said, "But it's Superman."

He said, "Oh, okay. We'll carry the flag one more time."

He's so funny. A wonderful person. Still looks like Jimmy Olsen. Bless his heart.

What was George's approach to the role?

He was a wonderful, wonderful person. A great person to work with. George was a very good actor, which a lot of people don't talk enough about. They think of him as someone who just flies all the time. He studied at the Pasadena Playhouse. He did a lot of good movies like *The Sainted Sisters* and *The Adventures of Sir Galahad*. He really wanted to be a serious actor. He did have a good part in *From Here to Eternity*. He was very thrilled about that. The trouble happened after the movie was finished and they had a preview of it. The minute George came on screen, everybody in the audience said, "There's Superman. There's Superman." Then a lot of people got to thinking, *The audience can't think he's Superman when he's playing a different character.* So his part was cut down. He was really, really torn up about that. We could tell how much it upset him, naturally, after working with him so much, but he carried it off well and just realized that was his life.

Superman (George Reeves) sweeps Lois Lane (Noel Neill) off her feet. ©Warner Bros.)

As a creative person, he'd naturally want to do other parts, to stretch as an actor. That doesn't necessarily mean he was sick of Superman or didn't like the association.

That's right. Interestingly enough, the year we lost George, I had gotten a call from [series producer] Mr. [Whitney] Ellsworth from New York, "Hi Noel. We have twenty-six more scripts for you. So, we'll be going in September."

I said, "Wonderful, very good."

He said, "We're at the same studio if you want to come by and see if your old suits still fit."

And I did go in and George was there. He was very happy. He was going to do a B movie first, then maybe going to Australia. He was so happy. He was going to direct most of the new episodes that we were going to do. He had directed three of the last season that we did. He said, "Noel, nothing ever changes in these scripts. Except the heavies have a different name." He was very happy. He jokingly said, "I'm getting a little too old to be running around in my underwear." So, that was his attitude. He was really looking forward to directing. He thought it was a move out and a move up. But unfortunately, that was not to be.

Do you have a specific memory that sort of encapsulates your impression of George's personality?

One thing that happened is in a scene with John Hamilton [who played Perry White], Jack and myself. We were tied up in a cave or somewhere. We were facing a wall that we hoped Superman would break through and save us. The director said, "Now, this is just one take." The set is big. The wall has been made overnight and we don't have time to rebuild it. George can come through and rescue you. Everyone has to be on their toes." Then the director yelled, "Camera." Then we waited and we waited and we waited. We saw one little foot coming through the wall and a little hand coming through the wall and nothing else. Then the director said, "Cut, cut, cut." George had gotten stuck in the wall. It had hardened just a little too much. He very nicely pulled his hand back and walked through the wall and, as a nice Southern Beau, he said [hiding the pain], "Nice to see you all. See you tomorrow." And off he went. There was a big scramble to get the day cleared. Bless his heart. I always remember he was so gentlemanly. He was always so with it. He didn't panic or say, "Ouch it hurts." Or "Ouch I can't get out." He got himself out and away he went.

Did everyone look at him as the off-camera leader of the show?

He was the lead. He was why we were all there working. He was Superman. He always knew his lines and he was so helpful with all the heavies that worked with us. He had worked with them so he had tried to get as many friends who were actors as he could on the show. We always said, "George is the people's friend." I think he gave away more money than he made. He was just a wonderful, wonderful person. He and his lady friend did a lot of charity work that no one ever knew about. He went to hospitals and to schools and made appearances as Clark Kent. He did a lot of good work. It wasn't publicized in those days. He was very good with the children and they seemed to respond to him.

What do you think was the main difference between how George Reeves and Kirk Alyn each played Superman?

Kirk was a dancer originally, a ballet dancer, and George was always an actor. Kirk did a good job. With his dance background, he could always leap and jump out of the windows. He could do it nicely. I found out years later, that he was very upset, very unhappy that he wasn't chosen or asked to play Superman on the TV show, which is understandable.

Is there a club of sorts among the women who have played Lois Lane?

No. Every once in a while someone will say, "We should get all the Lois Lanes together." I say [pretending to be upset], "Why are they all so young?" Margot [Kidder who played Lois Lane in four feature films] is such a nice person. She lives up in Montana. Near her daughter and grandchildren. Occasionally she'll come down and do a convention. It's always nice to see her.

What do you remember about *Superman* with Christopher Reeve and Margot Kidder as Lois Lane?

I did a scene with little Lois Lane and Kirk, which was filmed up in Canada. I didn't meet Christopher [Reeve] until I got to London. Some publicist said, "We will pick you up at the hotel and take you to meet him." Yupity, yupity, yup. Publicity people always look for an angle. Then I got to have lunch with Margot and Christopher. Afterwards, the publicist said, "Do you want to come out on the set?" [Makes disapproving noise.] Going to a set is not something you enjoy doing when you're not working.

But I went out on the set anyway. In Pinewood Studios, they have one stage rigged with wires for the flying scenes and I said, "Gosh, we didn't use those things with George." It was quite interesting to see what they were doing. It was kind of strange because they had different wires hanging from the different tracks. They had Christopher in one. We watched the scene where he flied into her balcony and picked Margot up and took her off. It went on and on and on. People always ask me, "Did Margot Kidder ask you for advice on how to play Lois Lane?" I always say, "Everyone does their own *shtick*. You play yourself so to speak. With a character like that, you do some version of yourself."

What questions do most fans tend to ask you? You must get the same ten questions over and over again.

Now people want to know if I saw *Hollywoodland* (2006). I dance around that question. I checked with Warner Bros. and said, "I don·t want to break up our relationship, but I know I'm going to be asked about it." Sometimes they ask about the other Lois Lanes, and I give them the look, and they say [backing off], "Oh, sorry, sorry." [Laughs] They always want to know about George, of course, and I say, "Wonderful, wonderful," and he was. I wouldn't say it otherwise, but he was a wonderful "Southern Gentleman," as I called him.

And there's the persistent question of how come Lois can't tell Clark and Superman are the same person.

People will say, "How come you didn't realize that Clark Kent was Superman? Those darn glasses don't make a bit of a difference." I say, "Well, I didn't want to lose my job." [Laughs] I finally thought of the answer to that question! I was doing a series of shows at colleges in the 1970s. The students were pretty wild. They would scream out whatever their little minds thought and I had to think of some answers quick, and that was one of them.

This book is about the experience of what it's like to have "been" Superman or Lois Lane, or any other iconic character. Is there something that you can say that would help others understand what that experience has been like for you?

It's very foreign to me, to be tied to Lois Lane. Eventually, that was kind of George's feeling. He really wanted to do really good acting, which he certainly was able to do. He wanted to be a good leading man. Bless his heart; he finally just came to the conclusion that he was Superman.

He worked hard and always knew all his lines. The flying stuff was kind of a chore. The run and leaps through the window and the nip and tuck roll on the other side, like they do in gymnasiums. In those days, he wore a heavy wool uniform. They didn't have the more comfortable nylon outfit they have nowadays. He would be perspiring and all of a sudden the nice wardrobe man would be there with a towel and say, [whispering] "George, George, we've got to go and change clothes."

Do you ever wonder what your life would be like if when the producer called you up and offered you the role, you had said, "No, thanks."

Well, I would have probably married the boy I was fond of then. You do wonder how your life would be. [A pause] I don't know. I did so many parts, and a lot of things were better dramatically for me than Lois Lane, but those parts aren't remembered.

[A few people who are doing work on Ms. Neill's house interrupt our interview. In the middle of explaining the work they still need to do, one of the workers, a woman of Hispanic decent, spots an old photo of Ms. Neill posing with George Reeves. The woman says with unbridled glee, "You have a picture with Superman!" Ms. Neill returns to the phone.]

I heard that exchange. The one thing that was very sweet about her comment was the unrestrained affection that people have for the show and for you.

People really grew up with this, and they like to ask me questions. They are so nice. So, very nice.

Jack Larson is Jimmy Olsen

When watching the TV series *Adventures of Superman,* starring George Reeves as the Man of Steel, younger audience members may fantasize about possessing Superman's powers, but it is likely that they identify more with Jimmy Olsen.

Jimmy Olsen, created by Jerry Siegel and Joe Shuster, made his first appearance on radio in *The Adventures of Superman* in 1940, and then in comics in 1941 (although an unnamed character who works at the Daily Planet and wears a bow tie appears in a comic published in 1938). It wasn't until the 1952 TV series, which ran for six seasons and starred Reeves, first Phyllis Coates and then Noel Neill as Lois Lane, and Jack Larson as Olsen, did the character's look and personality crystallize in the public's consciousness.

Due to Jack Larson's wide-eyed, earnest, and energetic performance, the cub photographer's popularity soared. Just two years after the show aired, the character headlined his own series of comic books called *Superman's Pal Jimmy Olsen.* The lighthearted comic aimed squarely at children ran for twenty years (1954-1974), which is particularly impressive considering that, unlike Superman, Olsen possesses no superpowers. (However, in the comic book series Jimmy Olsen would gain and lose an assortment of superpowers with about the same regularity that children catch colds. Over the course of 163 comics, Olsen temporarily gained the capacity for super speed, elasticity, fire breathing, and the ability to breathe underwater. He also underwent temporary transformations into, among other beings, a giant, a genie, a wolfman, and a human porcupine.)

Jack Larson emerges from a Hollywood era that no longer exists. Listening to him talk, it's hard not to be nostalgic for Hollywood's Golden Age, when deals were made over drinks at Chasen's, studios carefully crafted their stars' on-screen and off-screen careers, and a starlet could still be discovered at Schwab's.

George Reeves, Jack Larson, Noel Neill and John Hamilton play Superman,
Jimmy Olsen, Lois Lane and Perry White. © Warner Bros.

THE INTERVIEW
How did the show come together?

Bob Maxwell was a producer of Adventures of Superman, which started shooting in 1951. He was brilliant with the whole Superman subject. He came to California with the backing of DC [Comics]. Jack Liebowitz, who was a lawyer, came in and took over the whole operation. Before our series, he produced the radio show. I didn't listen to Superman on the radio because I was a Jack Armstrong fan. I used to rush home from school and listen to Jack Armstrong: the All-American Boy. Jimmy Olsen first appeared on the radio show. He wasn't in the comic book at first. That was Bob Maxwell's idea. He was 100% versed and in control of Superman as both a theatrical and radio project.

In fact, when I was first cast, I didn't know at the time that it had been on radio. Before our show went on the air, I went to New York. I met Jackie Kelk at a party. He [along with Jack Grimes] had done Jimmy on the radio.[75] That was the first time I found out about the radio show. Before I came on board, George Reeves was cast as Superman and Phyllis Coates was cast as Lois Lane.

What were you doing before you were cast?

I had been in a play in Los Angeles that didn't work. It was called *The Great Man*. It had a huge cast and it received a lot of press. I got the theater bug very badly. We didn't make it to New York because the lead actor didn't work, but all I wanted was to make it to New York. I got great reviews. I didn't want another studio contract. I wanted to get to New York, but I didn't have a lot of money. In those days, you didn't get paid a lot of money when you were under contract. My friend, Debbie Reynolds, got $65 a week, forty weeks a year. I got about $125. Once I started working on the show, I got $250 a week, which is nothing. [When adjusted for inflation that would now be about $2,200.]

How did you create the character?

At first, I didn't know the character. I didn't know what the hell they were talking about. Everyone told me, "You are a mixed up kid. This is twenty-six shows. You'll make enough money to go to New York and no one will ever see it." It was [one of] the first show[s] ever shot with one camera. *I Love Lucy* was shot with three cameras and with a studio audience. These were the pioneer days.

So I did it. I signed on to do it, and right away, I loved doing it. We started shooting almost instantly after I suddenly had this part. Anyway, I didn't really build the character. I can't really claim any pretensions to that. You have a character who says "Golly" and "Jeepers." [Laughs] I started thinking about comedic bits with Jimmy. They'd let me do them as long as I did them in one take. In the first twenty-six episodes, he was essentially a juvenile in peril. Then they began to discover that I had some comic talent.

People were letting us do anything we wanted to do as long as we worked fast. We were pioneers. We had the best actors, best directors, the best crew you could hire. We had the sound crew that Orson Welles used in *Citizen Kane*.

Do you remember your first few days at work?

They had no standing street sets on the back lot. Not like War-ners. They only had standing sets for Gone with The Wind. So the Superman company rented those sets. The first day I worked, they put Jimmy in a safe. The bad guys had Jimmy suspended by a rope from a tall building. Clark Kent sees this and he changes into Superman. The rope breaks and Superman catches him and saves Jimmy. Superman opens the safe and sees Jimmy sweating. Jimmy says, "Golly Superman. Am I glad to see you." That was the first day I worked. It was very unpleasant to be locked in the safe.

Before we worked, I was sitting next to George and I had com-plimented him on a film he had done called So Proudly We Hail! [directed by Mark Sandrich].[76] And he complimented me on a film I did with Raoul Walsh called Fighter Squadron. After that film, Sandrich told George that he wanted to make more films togeth-er. George went into the army. After he came out, the director had died. Then George said the only negative thing I heard him say in the seven years we worked together. George said, "If he hadn't died, I wouldn't be sitting here in this monkey suit today." That was the only thing that he said that was negative; and that was before we started working together.

What is the key to understanding Jimmy Olsen?

He's eager. He's very loving, but something about him was so dim that he couldn't tell that Clark Kent was Superman just be-cause he's wearing glasses.

The other key to Jimmy is his relationship with Perry White, who was played by John Hamilton. He was in my favorite film, The Maltese Falcon. The key relationship for me was between Perry White and Jimmy. Jimmy was terrified of him, and Perry White would always bellow, "Don't call me Chief!" Off-camera, John was very impatient with me. [Laughs] I would call him Mr. Hamilton for at least a year.

I felt wonderful doing the show. I felt like a pioneer. I felt en-amored with the idea of being a pioneer, and I made up my mind to never throw a scene away. I'd always do the best job I could regardless of whether anyone saw it or not. That's how I irritated people: I never quit rehearsing.

In some ways it seems that you were similar to Jimmy Olsen. He was enthusiastic and green and so were you.

That's true. I was very enthusiastic. I was originally doing it just for the money, but once we started working I forgot about that. My dad, who was a truck driver, said, "Hell they aren't paying you anything. You are just getting back the dimes I gave you to buy the Superman books." And that was true! My mom and dad were fun-loving people. They loved to go out and dance and hang out at the local drug store in Indiana. There was a rack of magazines that they told me not to look at. It was the kind of drug store that had a fountain. There was a stack of magazines with frightening and lurid covers. I remember I had the first *Action Comics*. I would sit on the floor and read them. Later, my mother threw them out. I knew Superman very well but not in the form of a serial or a radio show.

Was there a sense that people were condescending towards the show because it was based on a comic book?

Yes, people looked down on it. I had trouble with that once the show was on the air, but I never looked down on it myself. After I shot the first batch of episodes, I moved to New York. It was a very exiting time. In 1953, I had all but forgotten about Superman. Then Kellogg's bought the show. Kellogg's hijacked it. It went on the air and became very successful. It was on ABC, which was a low-class network at the time. It instantly became extraordinarily popular. I had a little basement apartment and I couldn't walk down the street without having cab drivers saying, "Jimmy Olsen, where's your pal?" I just *became* Jimmy Olsen.

How'd that feel?

Awful. [Laughs] I was frightened by it. I grew a beard. I thought, *I'm ruined.*

You didn't like being recognized or you didn't like being so closely associated with one character?

I was a serious actor.

Talk about creating the look of Jimmy Olsen.

The hair was mine. [Laughs] We all had hair dangling over our foreheads – in curls. The most famous person who wore his hair like that at that time was Tony Curtis. That was the look. Jimmy's clothes were designed by Izzy Burn. They had to get doubles and triples of everything because Jimmy was going to go through hell. They took me to Mattson's, a haberdasher on Hollywood Boulevard, who had triples of everything. We got almost everything there, including the bow ties. Everything else we got at Western Costumes.

The bow tie is an important part of the look.

I used to wear bow ties. I knew how to tie a bow tie, which has become a rarity. I think you shouldn't wear one unless you can tie one.

Do you still have the tie that you wore?

I gave the original to the Smithsonian. They had a big bash for it. I was in New York while I was producing *Bright Lights, Big City*. I heard from Warner Bros. that they were going to do a big event. Mark Hamill was going to present me. "And would I please be so considerate as to come to the event." Of course I did. Mark Hamill couldn't have been sweeter or more effusive. After the press event was a luncheon. The dinner *conversation* was about my bow tie. I was next to the rep from Warner Bros. He said, "Warners is going to give us one." I said, "They don't have it. I do." Everyone dropped their forks. He said, "Would you give it to us?" I said, "Of course. I have the bow tie and an off-white shirt." That's all I ever kept. They threw a party in my honor. And all the top press people were there. All for Jimmy Olsen. The press people said that they loved Jimmy Olsen and I personified Jimmy Olsen to them.

I wasn't prepared for just how wonderful I'd feel when they got me in front of the case [which contained Jimmy's bow tie]. I thought I was going to cry, but I didn't. I controlled myself.

Has playing Jimmy Olsen been a double-edged sword?

I was typecast. George and me we both were. I quit acting because of it. I couldn't get hired in this country. I went to Europe to do some work. [When the show originally aired] I never did any interviews in print. I never did one interview when I played Jimmy. I never did any publicity. I thought it was going to be a nail in my coffin. I was bad. [Laughs]. I think that was one of the reasons why I am remembered. I think you keep a little bit of mystery. Although I don't think I any longer have any mystery. [Laughs]

When the show ended, you were offered the opportunity to do a spin-off series called *Superman's Pal Jimmy Olsen*.

I was. I didn't want to do it.

Why not?

First, what do you know about it? Then and I'll tell you.

I heard that they would have shot thirteen episodes.

Exactly. I was in Europe. We had very odd contracts, which wouldn't exist today. I was under contract for seven years, and anytime during those seven years they could send me a Western Union telegram and thirty days after I received the telegram I was obligated to come to work for them.

It was a very difficult thing for me because I could never get into a play. I was cast in a play and they asked the Warner Bros. people permission to hire me and of course they wouldn't do it. Essentially for those seven years, all I had permission for was to work for up to thirty days, but if it was anything beyond thirty days I couldn't do it.

On the other hand, I'm glad that I did *Superman* and not those other jobs. Because everyone remembers Jimmy Olsen and no one remembers that other parts that I lost out on because of the contract. A lot of fans think the first twenty-six episodes were the best shows. I don't know. What do you think?

I agree. I like the early ones, the hard-boiled crime dramas, as opposed to the later ones, which were aimed at much younger viewers.

The early ones are film noirs. In one, they push an old woman in a wheel chair down the stairs. Lois is always in peril. Two years had passed between the first and second season. Phyllis Coates was offered to do a comedy between seasons and she went off to do a comedy. How she got out of her contract I wouldn't know. Then they got Noel. The show was on in the evening. It wasn't on as a children's show. Later, it became a whole family show. But the more comic Jimmy got, the more comic the villains got, the more it was up my alley. I really enjoyed playing Jimmy for comedy.

The early shows were aimed squarely at adults. You can't show them to kids.

No, they are too violent. If they weren't burning Jimmy to death they were drowning him, and I needed those triple sets of clothes. National Comics were raked over the coals for violence in comic books. Now there was violence in TV. There was a congressional committee investigating violence in TV, so they softened everything. Noel Neill's character was softer than Phyllis Coates'. The later episodes were going to be softer and more comedic.

I'm glad I did it. Otherwise, I'd be a forgotten juvenile. Warners always said they had plans for me, and I know they did because I was successful in some early films. There are other films that I might have done but it makes no difference because no one remembers who did them. I don't want to sound like I'm complaining.

Andy Warhol said that everyone will be famous for fifteen minutes, but look at Jimmy. I've had a whole life of fame. I'm always, always there when I'm asked. I'll always do publicity with the new Jimmy. I will always want them to have a big success with the new version. I don't want to say anything negative or compromising, but no one ever "became" Jimmy except for me. I *became* Jimmy Olsen.

You played an older Jimmy Olsen on *Lois & Clark: The New Adventures of Superman.*

I did. That was fun. Dean Cain is a great guy. Teri Hatcher was gorgeous. Now, she's a big star. They wanted me to do the show from the beginning. They were always asking me to do something. It's about publicity. It's about marketing. They sent me scripts and they always wanted me to play an alien. I called them and said, "I don't play aliens. Write something that makes sense and I'll do it." So I played older Jimmy.

What do you think happens to Jimmy later in life?

I've always had a film idea. Since they have such trouble making epic stories about Superman, I thought they could do Jimmy Olsen as a Don Hewitt-type character, the man who created 60 *Minutes*. In my idea, Superman's retired and there's a lot of crime. Jimmy creates a Superman out of a strong man, and then the world thinks Superman is back. It would be a lower-budget film.

I once pitched it to them as me playing Jimmy as an established newsman.

When *Superman Returns* was released, someone asked the head of Warner Bros. publicity, "Why is it that Jack Larson was publicized more than your new Superman Brandon Routh?" The head of publicity said, "We don't know. It just happened." People love Jimmy, not me, but Jimmy, because so many people identify me with Jimmy, I have so much more warmth coming towards me.

I produced a film called *Perfect*. We had a problem because the research on John Travolta was awful. It said that he didn't have an audience anymore. His former fans were describing him as a "dork." The film was previewing very well, but the problem was that John and Jamie Lee Curtis had no chemistry. In spite of good previews, the studio research was miserable. They decided to do round robins [where the actor sits a table with multiple journalists]. They said, "We'd like you to be by his side at every press event. In New York, L. A, and Chicago, just you and John Travolta. Because the press thinks that you're Jimmy Olsen and they will respect you, if you are sitting next to him, they won't ask him unpleasant or embarrassing questions." Indeed, I did it and it went as they expected.

Why did you quit acting?

I quit acting because I was typecast. I was cast in a film at Fox. The producer was Mervyn LeRoy, who produced *The Wizard of Oz*. The director had cast me, but LeRoy said, "But he's Jimmy Olsen. I can't have him in my fine film." He berated this casting man in front of me. I was so embarrassed. I was humiliated.

I was very upset, and I went directly from Fox to the hotel where my friend, Montgomery Clift, was staying. He said, "This is going to keep happening to you. You've played this part and you're typecast. You mustn't let this be crushing in your life. You have other things to do and you should do them." He was perfectly right, but in spite of all that it was a great joy to do that series. It was wonderful to work with George.

What kind of person was George?

He was a very, very fine actor. George always called himself "Honest George, the People's Friend." He was an accomplished actor and an accomplished athlete. I can say about our series that Superman's take offs and landings are better than they've ever been in any film including *Superman Returns*, where they take off [unconvincingly] like Peter Pan on wires.

We were doing an early scene where Lois and Jimmy were in a forest fire. Superman flies in and George flew in on wires and the wires broke. He fell on his butt. He dusted himself off and said, "That's that. Peter Pan flies on wire, not Superman." Then he walked off the set – badly hurt.

They had to find another way to get him in and out. Our special effects guy put a springboard on the floor for takeoffs. They built something over the camera so that George could leap over the camera and do an overhead tuck and land on the mattresses. For landings, he grabbed a bar and he would jump, grab the bar and enter the room or come through the wall. His take off and landings were better than any multi-million dollar approach.

On set did George seem heroic in his costume?

No. The big thing about the costumes is that they would make his skin breakout. He had some artificial muscles, which were made off sponge rubber. He would develop sores. It was very hot. He could only stay in costume for a couple of hours at a time. The only time he seemed heroic to me occurred when we were shooting on a lot where they shot a lot of Westerns. The doors opened onto the driveway and you can see normal houses beyond the driveway. They opened the sound stage door where George was standing, and there was enough breeze to make his cape flow a tiny bit. I saw him in profile, standing there iconically with the world behind him, smoking a cigarette with his Franklin Roosevelt cigarette holder.

He was an athlete. He had been a boxer. Before he died, he was thinking about going on a wrestling tour. That's definitely true. You can find publicity for that. He tried it out at fairs. He sang with a guitar. He was going to be part of a wrestling exhibition – under the name "Mr. Krypton" or something. He couldn't get a job. I couldn't get a job.

Were you like Jimmy Olsen at all? Do you have the same personality?

I am Jimmy Olsen. Jimmy is nothing other than someone in peril. When you act something like that, there is no psychology. There is no character. What you bring to a character like Jimmy is whatever likeability you have, or bring your smile, your laughter, your voice; you bring whatever people like in you that you know works for that character. In the early days of photography, the American Indian didn't like to be photographed because they believed that it stole your soul. With a character like Jimmy, he steals your personality. You use up your whole personality, your whole being.

Given that, how was George like Superman?

I always thought he had a great deal of nobility. George never complained. I told you he called himself "Honest George, the People's Friend." Early on in the show, the studios had closed down and a lot of actors were out of work. A lot of very good actors who were happy to get the week's work working on Superman. I was present when George gave as much money as he earned to out-of-work actors, who were losing their homes. He was a wonderful guy. I couldn't say anything negative about the guy.

We were under contract. So they could keep us at work as a long as they wanted. For day players, if it goes into overtime, they have to pay them a lot of money. Toni Mannix [George's girlfriend] would bring him lunch. Sometimes George would get annoyed [about working overtime] and when that happened he would occasionally have one martini too many and he wouldn't want to work. Everyone drank in those days. It didn't happen often but when it happened, they would shoot around him. They would shoot the scenes for the day players. I would be waiting to do my work, which would always involve George. Around 6:00 p.m., George would come in and say, "Lets get our work done." Then they'd work me and George to nine or ten o'clock. I didn't like that. I would tell George if you go off the set and don't feel like working, stay off the set. Don't come back and say, "Let's get the day's work. Because I have to stay here all that time in order to do it." Then to make up, George would take me to Trader Vic's. "Junior, don't be mad. It won't happen again." But as I said every-

George Reeves as Superman. © Warner Bros.

one drank at that time. You weren't a real guy unless you drank, but I wasn't a real guy. [Laughs]

What impact did playing Superman have on his film career?

One day George said to me, "Your buddy is being taken advantage of by Frank Sinatra [on the set of *From Here to Eternity*], which naturally disappointed me, especially since Monty [Clift] loved Frank's singing and was very thrilled by Frank Sinatra's comeback. Monty in his thoroughness was trying to find a quartz mouthpiece that appears in James Jones' novel *From Here To*

Eternity that his character carries around for his bugle. No one at Columbia [the film's distributor] could find it. Monty asked if I would go off and see if an old music store had a quartz mouthpiece. He was the most wonderful person in the world. He was funny, wonderful, and generous. We never found a quartz mouthpiece, but we became friends.

Monty asked if I could be his sounding board while he was preparing *From Here To Eternity*. Would I listen to him as he talked about the character and read his lines. Of course I would, it was an honor beyond paradise.

After they finished shooting, he went back to New York City where he lived. When it came time for the big screening [in Los Angeles] of *From Here To Eternity*, he said, "Will you go?" He asked because I knew what he was doing in every scene. He was spontaneous but there was always a point to what he was doing. He asked me to go to the screening and report back to him.

Beforehand, I had to find the nearest telephone booth. I found a pool hall bar across the street from the theater that had a telephone in the back. Monty would be waiting in New York for me to call. I then went to see the film and when George came on screen, someone in the balcony said, "Superman!" Of course, I was stunned. I never discussed that with George. Never. I went to across the street afterwards and Monty wanted to know how they cut a scene. He was very suspicious of Donna Reed's acting ability.

George had quite a complicated love life.

George's girlfriend was Toni Mannix. She was the wife of Eddie Mannix, who was third in command at MGM. Eddie was happy to have her with George. It was an arrangement. He and Toni were supposed to get married. They were waiting for Eddie to die. Eddie had a bad heart, and he died less than two years after George died. This was before heart surgery had really developed. It was well-known that he had a weak heart. There were not going to be any divorces because they were Catholic. George and Toni would have married.

What do you think happened with George? Had he become disenchanted with the direction his career and life had taken?

He was typecast and he couldn't get work as an actor. He wanted to direct. He did direct a few episodes of *Superman*. He did very well. He directed three episodes. He wanted to direct a film. I said, why don't you get Eddie Mannix to get you a film at MGM." He looked at me very sourly and said, "That would be pushing it a bit. Don't you think, junior?" [Laughs] I guess it would.

After his death, I got a telegram exercising my option for me to come back and do twenty-six more *Superman* shows. I went to Rome and there were these huge envelopes waiting for me with info about George's death. I went and got my mail and sat on the Spanish Steps - [the poet John] Keats lived in a house next to them – and I read all the stories reporting that George was gone.

What do you think happened?

I think he did it. I've always said what I think, and I believe it holds water.

Do you think he killed himself because he was typecast or is that an oversimplification?

I think it ruined his life. It hurt him that playing Superman cost him a film career. After he became Superman, he couldn't get film work.

Did you see it coming?

I did not see it coming but I believed it. Last I heard was that George and Toni had split up. I went to say goodbye to her. She was beautiful and generous to him. He never earned the money to live the way he did. If he needed a car, she'd buy him a beautiful Italian car. Anything he wanted, "The Boy" got. She called him "The Boy." I asked, "What could it be that broke you up." He always called her "Mom," which was funny because she wasn't that much older. She had a beautiful body, one of the greatest of all time. "He was back east and he met a new woman. I was here [in Los Angeles] living with him and she made him feel like a boy again." Those were Toni's exact words.

When I got to London, I got into contact with the Superman company and they were very anxious that I return to the New York and I should talk to Jack Liebowitz [publisher of DC Comics], but I was not eager to talk to them. I had no idea what they wanted to talk to me about. I did leave Europe after a little bit. They wanted to talk to me with the story editor Kellogg's had hired to shoot twenty-six shows. They were in preproduction when George died. They explained it to me that they couldn't do twenty-six episodes, but that the story editor found a way to make thirteen episodes. At that time, Jimmy Olsen was the most popular character on the show because the kids related to him, and the best-selling comic book was *Superman's Pal Jimmy Olsen*. They gave people little bits of money and when I asked them about it they got very "righteous" that I thought I had any rights to the character of Jimmy Olsen.

They determined that they could salvage episodes of *Adventures of Superman* and turn it into a new show called *Superman's Pal Jimmy Olsen* with the footage they had already. Superman was always saving Jimmy, and I was always wearing the same clothes. They explained it all. And I said that this was something that I was not going to do. Not at all. I asked some question and they said, "We can always get a muscle man in a suit in the Superman outfit [to double for Reeves] to do run bys or to carry you away."

That's in very bad taste.

It was to me. They said that and I said, "Even if I said I would do it, as soon as the muscle man comes in the Superman suit, I'd start crying." They didn't like hearing that. I left.

[One of Jack's associates] came after me and stopped me. He said, "You've upset Jack very much."

I said, "Well I'm upset too."

He said, "You don't understand. Jack could see how upset you are. Jack wants you to know that if you have money troubles that we're good for a couple of thou."

Barely able to contain my disgust, I said, 'Thank him. Thank you.' And then I walked away."

I came back to Los Angeles and was much relieved when Wilt Ellsworth [producer of the show] said that he didn't want to do it. My agent told me that there was a question concerning if I was contractually obligated to do the episodes, and whether they could get an "injunction" against me preventing me from doing any other work. That was the threat. If only they could. If only somebody wanted to hire me. [Laughs] You can sell this to comedy stores. I'm on a roll.

I'm just back and I hear from Toni right away. I was staying at a girlfriend's house and I asked, "What did Toni want?" She said, "She's going to George's house in Benedict Canyon for the first time." It had been sealed by the police and unsealed after his death was declared a suicide. She was going to go in and she wanted me to come with her.

She picked me up in her Cadillac convertible. We went into the house and she made notes about what needed repairing. She hated this woman [Lenore Lemmon] that George threw her over for. She called her a "who-re." Her driver once told me that Toni came down wearing a mink coat and before she got into the limo, she parted the coat and she was nude underneath and flashed everything to him and then got into the car. I heard Toni talk about their sex life. She said how great he was the night before. All that stuff. Although we've all been around the track. I wouldn't shock you. [Laughs]

I think the mystery surrounding George's death tells us more about human nature than it does about the facts and the particular circumstances surrounding his death – that people subconsciously wanted to believe that he really was Superman and that made it difficult for them to accept that he was a person with a complicated life and problems, that he was fallible, just as you and I are.

Yes. I had never thought of that before. That's very possible.

Why are we still so fascinated by Superman?

The world is a mystery to us in so many ways. A great many science fiction writers, including H. G. Welles, have imagined our world under attack by creatures from outer space, creatures that terrorize us, take over our planet, and want to dominate or kill us. Except for Superman. There's this wonderful creature that comes to us from outer space wants to save us from evil on earth. Superman's adversaries in my day were usually everyday villains. He even fought Hitler. We cherish and cling to Superman for the sense of comfort he provides. He also embodies all the attributes of the handsomest greatest athlete. And he also embodies truth, justice and the American way. Like Obama.

President Obama said that he was a big Spider-Man fan.

We'll send him a few cassettes of our show.

That'll turn him around! Last question. Who would win in fight between Jimmy Olsen and Robin?

Hmmm. Who plays Robin?

Burt Ward from the 1960s.

Jimmy would win. I would win, absolutely. But George Clooney also had a Robin.

Chris O'Donnell.

Jimmy couldn't beat up that kid.

Marc McClure is Jimmy Olsen

Protecting Jimmy Olsen could be a full-time job. Superman is continually shielding the cub photographer from harm, both from evildoers and Olsen's own bad judgment. In fact, Olsen needs to be saved with such regularity that Superman gives him a special watch that, when activated, alerts Superman that his young friend is in harm's way.

For moviegoers of the 1970s and 1980s, Marc McClure was their Jimmy Olsen. He played the character in all four Christopher Reeve Superman films and in *Supergirl*.

McClure appears alongside Jack Larson, Sam Huntington and Aaron Ashmore, the actors who played Jimmy Olsen in *Superman Returns* and *Smallville*, in *Jimmy on Jimmy* (2008), a featurette in which the four actors discuss playing Superman's pal.[77]

Following in the footsteps of Christopher Reeve, Helen Slater, Margot Kidder, Annette O'Toole, Terrence Stamp, and Dean Cain, and extending the tradition of casting actors from previous Superman incarnations in different roles in *Smallville*, McClure appeared in an episode as a scientist from Krypton.

THE INTERVIEW

As a kid, did you read Superman?

Not really. I knew who he was. I read *Mad* magazine. I really wasn't a comic book guy.

So when *Mad* spoofed your Superman movies . . .

That meant I made it. It's like being on the Johnny Carson show. If you are in *Mad* magazine, it means you made it.

Did you feel a responsibility playing Jimmy Olsen?

There's a responsibility there because so many people believe in these characters. The trick is making them real for the people. Once you lose or skew that line of believability, that's where the trouble begins. In *Superman I* and *Superman II: The Richard Donner Cut*, Donner really captured the believability of a cartoon comic character.[78] That's what made it special, that it was so believable.

When I spoke to Tom Mankiewicz [screenwriter of the first two Superman films], he said that Richard Donner had the word "verisimilitude" prominently displayed in the production office.

That was the big thing over his desk. He used to always say that, "For this thing to work, we need to believe a man could fly." Donner was brilliant, to say the least.

Superhero films fail when they don't take the material seriously or when they make fun of it.

You can't do that. There are so many people who want to believe. Once you're making fun of it and make that little mistake of patronizing the character and the world that they're supposed to exist in, you are defeating the whole purpose. The idea is to make it real. When you talk about global recognizability, he's there. I knew it when I got the job, and I knew it from *Adventures of Superman* [the TV series starring George Reeves as Superman]. I knew Jack Larson as Jimmy Olsen. Even then, I knew it was a big responsibility.

Did you know the impact that the role would have on you personally?

Not really. I didn't look far ahead but I knew the project was big, I remember being on the set attached to wires with Chris [Reeve] when we were shooting some of the Hoover Dam sequence and I was rambling on. And he stopped me and said, "If you could talk like Jimmy Olsen or stay in character [I would really appreciate it]." We were fifty feet above the stage hanging on wires, and at that moment, I got where he was coming from. That this is important stuff. It was one of those surreal moments. When you saw Chris in person in those outfits, he *was* the man. I had a lot of respect for him. He worked so hard, both in the workout room and on the set. When he said that I realized how important it was to him. From that point on, when I was on the set, I did the best I could to stay in character as Jimmy.

I never heard that. He stayed in character as both Clark Kent and Superman?

He worked very hard at it. It was important to him that he surrounded himself with actors who were trying to create the same

Christopher Reeve's Man of Steel is about to demonstrate that he's more powerful than a locomotive in a scene from Superman. © Warner Bros.

world that he was. Donner was the guy who got that. We would come in and rehearse and find human moments for these characters. We would make them human. He wouldn't roll film until that credibility was achieved.

He really felt a huge responsibility in playing Superman.

Absolutely. There wasn't a moment when he wasn't involved in making it better. My whole career has been about trying to be believable on film. It requires the other actors to have that same goal. Otherwise, everything looks a little off. From Donner to Mankiewicz to Geoffrey Unsworth [the cinematographer of *Superman* and *Superman II*], everyone was a true pro. It made the job easy because we were working with such professionals. Everyone was on top of their game. At that time, you couldn't find a better group of people.

What was your take on playing Jimmy Olsen?

I understood his energy. I understood his naivety. I understood his eagerness. He wanted to be as good as he could be as a young kid in that adult work environment. Understanding that Jimmy represents all of those things – that's what I brought to it.

The wide-eyed, eager, willing to do something before he thinks about it quality. I had that going in. Jack Larson, who I watched, understood it. I got to meet Tommy Bonds [who played Jimmy Olsen in the serials], which was great. But as far as knowing Jimmy Olsen and understanding who he was I got through watching Jack Larson's performance in *Adventures of Superman*.

It must be tricky to play these characters. An actor's impulse is to see where the characters can grow and evolve, but these figures must remain largely unchanged.

Like the comic books, in movies these characters are very consistent. However, in *Superman III* Chris gets exposed to Kryptonite and becomes mean. I don't know if people really understood [the implications] of a bad Superman. When it comes to Jimmy Olsen, if he got angry or more forceful, he would cease being Jimmy Olsen. It would take away from who he is and what he represents. Maybe that's the important thing. Jimmy is wholesome, eager. There are a lot of good qualities about Jimmy. As an actor if you start to change some of those things and make him a little tougher, it would be a big mistake. That's not who Jimmy is.

Jimmy is one of the few character's who looks up to Clark Kent.

I would agree with that. I think he respected Clark. I think he knew Clark was missing a beat, and always running a little late on things, but he was an authority figure to Jimmy. I think Jimmy just respected people. Jimmy is also the kind of character who does things without thinking about it. Then he's suddenly in trouble. He doesn't edit his words. He says what he feels without any real understanding of the consequences. He's not quite sure how he gets into trouble. But that's Jimmy. He leaps into things before thinking about the consequences, which makes him a fun person to watch. Jimmy represents a lot of innocence. It's important for anyone who ever plays Jimmy Olsen to capture that, along with his youthfulness, his zest for life, and his love of his work.

The signature look of Jimmy is his bow tie. How much of that informed how you played the character.

The bow tie immediately puts you into a certain category of appearance. For people who wear bow ties there's something very proud about it. There's something very individual about it. The

wardrobe is so important to me. It helps me become the character. For Jimmy, he's a total original. I love the bow tie.

**Would you ever wear a bow tie in private life or would that
just invite comparisons?**

It would never happen in my life. The bow tie is a character
thing. It defines a person. I'm just not that person. I'm not a bow
tie guy. I'm very far away from Jimmy. Although we do share a
zest for life. And I do like to make other people happy.

How are you unlike Jimmy?

I don't have as much "get up and go" as Jimmy. He seems to want
to get involved in a lot of things. I'm more of a private person.

**There is a small fraternity of people who have played Jimmy
Olsen, and it seems that you are all somehow connected to
each other.**

I believe that. I think everybody who has played Jimmy appreciates the character. I know Jack Larson does. He has great
stories. I know he walked into the job thinking "I'm going to do
this for a couple of months, maybe weeks." And it turned into
seven or eight years. Back in those times, it hurt you more than
it helped you. The Jimmy Olsen character was more known back
in those days. I think Jack had to live with Jimmy his whole life.
Whereas people kind of recognize me and they wonder where
they know me from. Then they get it and say, "Jimmy Olsen." But
I think Jack was really locked into Jimmy.

I met him after we made the movie. I called him up and said, "I
played you." He said, "That's great. Come on down to my house."
He lives in this Frank Lloyd Wright house down in Brentwood. I
went down and we talked. It was a fabulous conversation. We
still stay in contact. He still looks like Jimmy. I believe he still
wears bow ties. He really pulls it off.

He was a player for the studios and the part came along. Tommy Bond was the first actor to play him.[79] Bond was a bit hard.
He was too tough. That's not Jimmy. Jimmy is a guy who is very
approachable. I don't want to say that he's defenseless, but he
certainly doesn't have any guards up.

I think the producers of *Adventures of Superman* realized that
Jimmy had to have that vulnerability. Jack had that. He did it

really well. He would pop in with his eyes wide open and say, "Jeepers." He was really good.

These characters have so many good qualities that are so important to our society today. Jimmy, Lois and Clark can teach people how to interact with one another. How to convey that to an audience today is tricky. Maybe the characters are living in an age of innocence. Maybe it doesn't work. Maybe we have to harden everything up [for them to be seen as relevant today].

Do you think Reeve, while respecting the character's legacy, got a little tired of playing him after a while?

I don't think it took a while. I think it happened right away. He played Superman, and as soon as he finished the film he did *Deathtrap* where he played completely in the opposite direction of the Superman character.[80] Chris was a stage actor and the stage was his home. His work in theatre was really important to him. Yeah, he fought it. He fought it the whole time. It was his theater background that he was trying to hold on to. He had a tough time doing that. In all of his film roles he tried to stay as far away from Superman as he could. My opinion was that he should have continued playing that strong character. Maybe fashion himself after, I don't know, maybe a John Wayne. Somebody who found a comfortable spot where people liked him. They liked him as the big guy in the room. But Chris wanted to play all those other roles.

When people met Christopher Reeve, I think they believed on some level that they'd actually met Superman.

Oh yeah. That's really saying something for Chris. It's really saying something for what he did for Superman. And for what he did for that movie. It says something. In a lifetime, I think it's something of an honor to be associated so strongly with a popular character. I don't think it's a bad thing. I think it's a good thing. I think it's a great thing. Very few people get the opportunity to do that, and to pull it off in such a way that the audience accepts you and that's what you're known for, I think that's pretty good.

In terms of his lasting appeal, Superman is the king of them all.

The king of them all. It's amazing what playing Jimmy Olsen has done for me. In terms of being able to go to fund-raisers, being invited to events, where they introduce you as Jimmy Olsen, then they mention *Back to the Future, Apollo 13* and other projects I've done, but it's my association with Superman that will be with me for as long as I live. Jimmy Olsen is historical. It's a name that resonates. If you did an experiment giving people just the names Lois, Clark and Jimmy, I think most people would know exactly who you're talking about.

Are there any downsides to that association?

No. No. Not these days. For Jack it was tough, but for me, no there is no downside. He's such a likable character that when I do meet people, they feel very comfortable approaching me as that character. Anyone can walk up to Jimmy. With Dennis Hopper and his character from *Blue Velvet*, you kind of have to hesitate before saying hello, but Jimmy is a totally approachable person. So people associate the actor with the character and think of them as one. There's nothing wrong with and there never will be anything wrong with being Jimmy Olsen.

Do you think Jack Larson would have taken the part of Jimmy Olsen if he knew what lied ahead?

I don't think he would have. I think he accepted the role thinking he would be doing maybe seven or twelve shows – something like that – and it ended it up getting picked up. He was doing it for work, and I don't think he would have done it if he knew it would turn into a multi-year commitment.

Kevin Smith asked Mark Hamill if he ever got tired of talking about *Star Wars*. Hamill replied, "To be honest with you, sure. I'm human. I mean, I like ice cream, but I don't eat it three times a day."81 Do you get tired of talking about Superman?

No. No. What's there to get tired of? It's a part of my life that and [getting tired of it would mean] I'd have to admit that I haven't liked what I've done in my lifetime. I'm happy with all of my choices. I'm very grateful to have been given the opportunities I've been given. I have no regrets. I have total appreciation for every character I've played. I'm one of the lucky ones. The quality is there. I'm very lucky there.

Who would win in a fight: Jimmy Olsen or Dick Grayson?

I would say Dick Grayson. Jimmy's got a lot of energy, but I think Dick Grayson's hyperactivity would scratch Jimmy to the death. Dick Grayson looks like he's ready to get in some trouble.

Stacy Haiduk is Lana Lang

It's hard not to like Lana Lang. Unlike Lois Lane, who sometimes barely tolerates Clark Kent, Clark's hometown friend from Small-ville respects and understands him. While others overlook Clark or dismiss him outright, Lana, as depicted in *The Adventures of Superboy* (1988-1992), seeks to protect him. Lana's acceptance of Clark's essential decency probably mirrors, and tacitly validates, the prevalent sympathies of the series' viewers, who are more likely to identify with Clark's beautiful imperfections than they are with the near flawlessness of Superboy and his pious Boy Scout-like persona.

It's also hard not to like Stacy Haiduk's characterization of Lana Lang. Haiduk infused the part with charm and vitality in ninety-nine episodes of *The Adventures of Superboy*, acting opposite two different Boys of Steel – John Newton in the first season and Gerard Christopher in seasons two through four.[82]

The original comic book conception of Lana Lang was quite different from her television namesake. In the comics, Lana is not unlike a younger version of Lois Lane: a foil for Clark. Lana Lang was dreamed up by Bill Finger (who with Bob Kane created Batman) and the artist John Sikela, and she first appeared in *Superboy #10* (September/October 1950), in the story "The Girl in Superboy's Life!" In her first appearance, Lana is bent on exposing Superboy's secret identity.

In "Rites of Passage," the final episode of *The Adventures of Superboy*, it seems that Lana is on the verge of learning the truth about Clark Kent. In the last shot of the last scene of the last episode, when Clark turns his back on Lana, she thrusts a pin towards his derriere. The image freezes just before the pin makes contact, and of course the viewers know that when the needle cannot penetrate the surface of his Kryptonian skin, Clark's secret identity will be revealed.

Haiduk, who has been acting steadily since the series ended, has appeared, among many other parts, in *Heroes*, in the Steve Spielberg-produced *SeaQuest 2032*, in the *X-Files*, in the police

John Newton as Superboy and Stacy Haiduk as Lana Lang. © Warner Bros.

procedurals *CSI: Crime Scene Investigation, CSI: New York,* and *CSI: Miami,* in HBO's vampire show *True Blood,* and she was featured in six episodes of the nighttime soap-opera *Melrose Place,* which also stared Newton, though her character's story arc concluded before Newton's character appeared, thus denying viewers a Superboy/Lana Lang reunion.

Stacy Haiduk's wit is on display in her answers to my questions.

THE INTERVIEW

What did you know about Superman and Lana Lang before you were cast?

When I was a little girl I remember the Saturday morning cartoon *The Super Friends,* which Superman was a part of. Loved that show. I did not come across Lana Lang until the first Superman movie [in which Diane Sherry played her]. Once I saw the first Superman movie I was a big fan!

Did you look at the comics for insight into the character? If so, was there anything in particular that you found useful?

I did not look into comic cooks for guidance. Although I enjoyed some, I did not know there even was a Superboy comic book until after I was on the show. Then I found out they shot a pilot back in 1961 [*The Adventures of Superboy* with Johnny Rockwell as Superboy and Bunny Henning as Lana Lang], which I had the honor of seeing.

How did you create your character?

Well, I was already halfway there by being a nineteen-year-old girl from the Midwest. Then you add the red hair, wardrobe, makeup, a script, and a good director. Put me in the right setting and then add a Superboy.

What is the key to understanding Lana's character?

Her innocence without naivety. Lana is extremely curious and very ambitious. But oh, she has so much heart.

Sometimes Lois Lane comes across as a little cruel or insensitive towards Clark. That's not true of Lana. She seems to be one of the few characters who likes and respects Clark.

Lana and Clark grew up together in Smallville. There is a strong childhood connection. I believe Lana felt she was always there to help Clark and that he needed her. She genuinely loves him. Even though she has a massive crush on Superboy. Lana feels protective of Clark.

In what ways are you like Lana Lang?

I am ambitious and in love with a superhero.

In what ways are you different?

I am not a natural redhead.

Both you and Lana went through two Superboys and a big format change over the course of the four seasons.

Yes, it was a huge change over the years, but it felt very natural. I was happy to change with the show. I grew up on the set of *Superboy*. So when Lana was going through changes, so was I. [Stacy Haiduk was twenty in 1988, when the series began.]

Can you talk about John Newton's take on Clark Kent and Superman? How about Gerard Christopher's?

I always liked John's Superman and Gerard's Clark Kent, but looking at the show after all these years Gerard's Superman was really good, too. I also felt John took it a bit more seriously -- not that Gerard didn't take it seriously, but I feel he had more fun with the parts.

What impact has playing the character had on you personally? How has it changed you?

I am part of a classic American lore and that doesn't come to someone very often. I feel very lucky to have had that opportunity. It came at a time in my life when I really needed the confidence it provided. I am not sure I would be the same actress today if that opportunity had not come along when it did. There is a lot to be said for working on a show for three-and-half-years.

How would you like to be remembered for the part?

The fun and sassy redhead that never gave up!!

This is the last question and the silliest. Who would win in a fight between Lana Lang and Lois Lane and why?

Probably Lois Lane; she would fight dirtier.

PART FIVE: SUPERVILLAINS

Julie Newmar is Catwoman

Created by Bob Kane and Bill Finger in 1940, Catwoman made her first appearance in the comic book *Batman #1*. Over the years a diverse and illustrious group of actresses have played Catwoman, whose relationship with the Batman seesaws between being his love interest and being his archenemy: these include Oscar-winner Anne Hathaway, Oscar-winner Halle Berry, Oscar-nominee Michelle Pfeiffer, Emmy- and Tony Award-winner Earth Kitt, former Miss America Lee Meriwether, and, memorably, Tony-winner Julie Newmar.

Newmar appeared as Catwoman in thirteen episodes of *Batman* opposite Adam West's Batman. In 2003, she played herself in *Return to the Batcave: The Misadventures of Adam and Burt*, a made-for-TV movie about the making of the series and, in 2010 she provided the voice of Bruce Wayne's mother, Martha Wayne, opposite Batman/West's father Thomas Wayne in the animated series *Batman: The Brave and the Bold*. Newmar's book, *The Conscious Catwoman Explains Life On Earth*, was published in 2011.

THE INTERVIEW

After you accepted the part, how did you create the character?

It happened very quickly. I was in New York and I got the call on a Friday. I flew to Los Angeles, had a costume fitting, and I was on the set Tuesday morning. With so little time to prepare, I initially just did the best I could and relied on my instincts. I was a member of the Actors Studio. Normally, the work I like to do is enormously detailed. My scripts end up looking like sheet music with counts and fortissimos and numbers on them, which indicate points or seconds of pauses between words or lines. I hear dialogue like music in my head. I was a serious pianist, so most things to me are music. Out of music came dance. That was my second career, my favorite career. Thankfully I had more time to prepare for the second episode. That's why I'm better in the second episode than in the first.

Julie Newmar as Catwoman. © Twentieth Century Fox Television.

The way you moved was key to your performance. You wouldn't just *sit* on a couch. You'd glide or crawl onto it.

Exactly. That's where this tremendous inner life - my conscious use of expressive physical movement - came into play, but the first step is to find your motivation, and you always ask yourself, *What is my motivation to say these words?* Then your physical movement comes from that.

How catty can you be before it's too much?

You can't be too catty. It's impossible.

Who was Catwoman to you? In your mind what made her tick?

I always take it from the writing, from the dialogue. If the writing isn't any good, then you're up a creek. Somewhere inside my gut the words need to flow like water, or they've got to move up and out and soar into space. Words do that. They have to have their rightful force. Maybe it's a dribble or a mist. Maybe it's the powerful hose from a fire engine. Of course, these were brilliantly written scripts. If the words are good, then fifty percent of your job is done. As any good English actor knows, all you have to do is speak the words.

While growing up did you read the original Batman comics?

As kid, I wasn't allowed to read comics.

How did it feel to wear the costume for the first time?

Gorgeous, wonderful, and fabulous. My heels on the boots could have been a little higher, but I didn't want to tower over Adam West. There are pictures of me in the costume taken twenty-years later that were taken by Harry Langdon. Those photos are far superior to the originals from the set.

I think I saw one on the cover of your book.

That's it. Although in the photos by Harry Landgon I have blond curly hair.

Do you still have the costume?

I gave it to the Smithsonian Museum. They have the gloves, the jewelry, and the belt. I tweaked the costume from their original design. I said, "We're going to put the belt around the hips instead of the waist because it makes the figure curvier this way."

Did wearing the costume help you find the character?

Always. Costumes matter a lot. You can have a concept of your character in your mind but once you put the costume on, your imagination flies.

Did your colleagues treat you differently when you were in costume?

In one of the episodes, James Brolin was playing a part opposite me. It was his very first role. He's now married to Barbra Streisand, but he met his first wife in the production office at the studio. I had a dual part in this episode. I was also playing an eighty-year-old thief. I loved that because I didn't have to look

Julie Newmar is the purr-fect Catwoman. © Twentieth Century Fox Television.

glamorous. Being glamorous is easy. Being eighty-years-old, that took some work.

I would go to the park and watch the elderly people. I also went to a dentist and got some cotton and put in my mouth like Marlon Brando did [when he played Don Vito Corleone in *The Godfather* (1972)]. Then when I came out of my dressing room as an eighty-year-old woman, the men who were working on the set would rush over and give me a chair. They would treat me as my character.

Why do you think she dressed up to be Catwoman?

Power. Power. Oh my God, yes. Are you kidding?

For such a sexy character, there's no "skin" showing.

It was a very simple costume. A zipper down the back. You just peal it off. You don't need a lot of skin. You need shape and facility of movement. Nudity can be uncomfortably distracting. Nakedness is a distraction, but why all these questions about the clothing?

The primary idea behind talking about clothing with a character like Catwoman or with any of these superheroes is to begin to understand the iconographic nature of the clothing. As an actor, you had to understand for yourself why a person would dress up in these outlandish outfits. You had to make sense of all of it.

But from the actor's point of view, that's about seventh or eight on their list of concerns. It starts with the words and it has to key off in your imagination. Then you have to take it to your highest level of inspiration to find the fundamental idea, the essence of who you think the character is. Then it explodes into all these other conditional areas such as the clothing.

Did men and women respond to you differently?

Both love it. It's salacious; it's sumptuous. Any S word you can think of applies. Sensuality. I have found something, which I wrote down about Catwoman – some impressions of who I thought this complicated character was. Let me read you some of these things:

> "She's a fantasy female. With one-upmanship and one-downmanship. She lords it over others but she can get down underneath too. Hatching plots and diabolical webs of deceit. And a conceit. Punishment postponed. Satisfaction ensured. Almost. S&M. Safely manipulated. Better than anyone else. In charge of all that exists. Greed, greed, greed. And then oblivion. The comeback kid. You know, nine lives. Sensuality, pleasure, earthy delights. Having monstrous paybacks. Deeds of decency and debauchery. Schemes, plans, artfulness. Intention and self-annihilation. Attracts fools then tolerates them poorly. Flawless clean.

Cleaned, cleaned and polished. Timidity; only for sissies. Upfront and certain. Rules, regulations; all hers. Suffering but as pleasure. Entrapment without disguises. Perfection. Certainty of purpose. Me, me, me. And then you."

All these things I relate to. I think up to that time women were well-intentioned and accommodating. You don't want to be proper a hundred percent of the time. You want to see the good and the bad because that's what we are as human beings. Of course, as the World War II song goes, we want to "accentuate the positive, eliminate the negative."

Does Catwoman have real feelings for Batman?

Absolutely. Opposites attract. He had all this goodness and she was wanting to improve herself. On the other hand, Batman's entire working life depended on characters such as her. We need each other. Criminal and law abider need each other. Always. Right?

One can't exist without the other.

Sure. More fun that way.

If she had a choice would she love Batman or kill him?

Both.

Depending on her mood?

Yes. When she gets what she needs and wants, then she moves on to something else.

Do you relate to Catwoman?

Absolutely. The character of Catwoman generates a sauciness. A playfulness. That's the best word. Playfulness. You can sit with that one for a long time. You win, I lose. You lose, I win.

Do you see a difference between the fans that were already adults when they watched you versus how fans think of you when they "grew up" watching you?

None whatsoever. It was lovely unrequited desire. Even the youngest fans became a little more aware of human nature – their often preverbal consciousness was raised to some extent – from the subconscious level to a higher level of consciousness. Since it exists in us in an atavistic way. Little children who grew up would later say, "You were my first turn-on." I say, "How old were you?" They say, "Four." That is a visual impression to the mind. Several years later, when they're in, say, their mid-teens, they connect with some of the visual pleasure that they might have had in seeing some moment in the show. That's why the Catwoman was the favorite villain for so many people.

They bring up really personal things and tell me stories, and sometimes if I'm doing a personal appearance tour, a father will walk up dragging his son. Depending on his age, he'll hide behind his father's knee not knowing what this is all about. The father will enthusiastically say, "Oh she was this and that." They'll take a picture and take it home. If he grandfather is there, he'll walk up to me without any embarrassment or apology and say something like, "You were it!" I love the popularity and affection that this character has brought to my life. It's always a blessing when fans tell me about the role I played in their lives and how they feel connected to me.

Did the character awaken something in you?

Not at the time. It was another good part to play. Everything in television happens so fast.

At that time were you as connected . . .

Nope

. . . with your sexuality as you are now?

No. It's far better now. You might have more of it when you're younger, but now it's deeper and it's richer. We have a greater connection, but it's always better. I see young people walking around with natural beauty but they just don't have a clue yet. It's going to take time. I have a website called JulieNewmarWrites. com. I wrote a book called *The Conscious Catwoman Explains Life on Earth*. You can order the book on my regular website JulieNewmar.com. It's filled with teachings and epigrams on how to be a more magnificent person. I've done some fabulous healing. I was a day and a half away from having my spine fused and I healed myself. I think it will be very helpful to people. I like being able to help people, to inspire them.

What I've learned is very interesting. It has to do with receiving information from the higher intelligence. We all have it all within us. You can be your own best friend. You can heal yourself.

How has playing Catwoman changed your life?

Well, for one thing it filled my office with boxes of fan mail, which haven't been answered. I wonder how am I going to handle all that. It's lovely to have a grateful worldwide audience.

Are there any negative associations?

No.

. . . to being so closely tied to a character?

No. No. Couldn't be. Never will be.

What was your take on Adam West's approach to Batman?

Perfect. Perfect. Perfect casting. He's the best Batman that I've ever seen. But keep in mind that an actor's take on Batman is largely influenced within the framework of how the show is interpreted. Each decade has its own angst and faces its own difficulties in the world. When we were making the show, our country was just getting embroiled in Vietnam and it was popular to be against things. The show was entertaining but not in a pontifical way. It wasn't heavy and dark. When you listen to the dialogue there is a light but smart teaching to youngsters. Batman would teach Robin; he would direct him to be a right-minded young man. There was lots of good teaching beneath the fun and games.

What's your fondest memory of the show?

There was quite a delicious vignette in which I danced with Robin. In the scene, I'm in Wayne Manor and he's not supposed to know who I really am. So my character is in disguise. I always like not being me. I like it when I have to stretch as a performer. I put a hump in my back and I put on these granny shoes that were several sizes too big for me. The great thing about comedy is that you can take it to the extreme. These things are fun.

You were funny in the show but never at the expense of the character. Never by robbing the character of her dignity.

Yes. From what I understand, some actors came in and didn't play it for real. They played the superficial effect. You have to play it for real in order to project it as far into the audience's mind as possible. If it doesn't come from a true place of being, then it doesn't have much impact. As I mentioned, I was a member of the Actors Studio, so that was impressed upon us.

Was there a particular key to understanding the character?

It's all about sex, isn't everything? The subtext, anyway.

It's hard not to look at the character and think about her sexuality.

That part's the most fun, and it seems to work.

It does, doesn't it? People seem to like that.

Yes, yes, yes. Let me read you a little more of this poem that explores Catwoman's complexity:

> "Knows the good stuff, as in life. Attracts her opposite. Tension for the love of it. Sexuality as the release of tension. Always on the prowl. Cool. Stamina. Protective. Dedicated. Determined. Calculating. Wise. Playful. Sexual. Thrifty. Sensuous. Organic. Faultlessly clean. Cleaned, cleaned, and polished. Attracts fools and then tolerates them poorly."

There was very provocative line that you said in one of the episodes that I'm sort of surprised got by the censors. You said, "You can brush my pussy willows before you leave. And don't go against the fur."

What's wrong with that?

Nothing, I mean that you were really able to get away with a lot.

The kids wouldn't understand it. It was tame, especially compared to the way they would write it today. When it's not overwritten, when you draw back on your reins somewhat, there's so much further to go. Fans always compliment us and say, "We like the way you did it in your time." You let the audience contribute to the final pleasure. You don't want to take away their pleasure by doing it for them. You have to stir the pot to the right level. Then let it develop in their minds.

It sounds as though you are saying that fans have told you that as Catwoman you awakened their sexuality.

Yes, yes. How fabulous. My god, what a gift to me this was, is and always shall be. It's a gift.

Is there power in sexuality?

Yes. What's more fun in life? Is there anything more fun than sex? No. No. Eating? No. Working? No. We all like to work but it's my intention in life to be in or near ecstasy all the time.

It seemed that Catwoman was always moments away from ecstasy.

Yes, of course. That's the secret. It's the theme of sexuality. It's primal, and it's like a diamond that from different perspectives and in different light can be seen in thousands of different ways. It thrills us. Everything is experiencing or moving towards that thrill. We're told from childhood on to: "Follow your bliss. Do what gives you the greatest joy."

One final question. This is my silliest question.

I love that.

Who would win in a fight between Catwoman and Batgirl?

Forget it. One stomp of my foot and she'd be wiped out. She'd be oblivion. She's a munchkin. Forget it. Downtown.

Michael Rosenbaum is Lex Luthor

The roots of Lex Luthor's antagonism towards Superman trace back to a childhood incident. As depicted in *Adventure Comics* *#271* in the story "How Luthor Met Superboy!", which was written by Superman co-creator Jerry Siegel, Lex and Superboy meet after Lex saves Superboy's life by disposing of a chunk of Kryptonite. To repay Lex, who has "hero-worshipped [Superboy] for years," Superboy builds a lab for the junior scientist.[83] Later, Lex attempts to return the favor by concocting a serum that will render Superboy immune to Kryptonite. However, before Lex can administer the antidote, the lab catches fire.

Superboy comes to the rescue by extinguishing the blaze with "a mighty super-puff of breath!"[84] That heroic gesture eliminates one problem but creates another: not only does Lex's irreplaceable formula get destroyed but the vapors from the beakers of various chemicals, which were inadvertently smashed together by Superboy's breath, cause Lex to become permanently bald. From that moment on. Luthor vows revenge on Superboy. The rationale for the vendetta is as silly as it is unsatisfying.

When the writers and producers Alfred Gough and Milles Millar created the series *Smallville*, which ran for ten seasons (2001-2011) and 217 episodes, in addition to depicting Clark Kent's pre-Superman years, they also wanted to create a more nuanced history of the relationship between Lex and his eventual adversary.

Prior to *Smallville*, the public's perception of Lex Luthor was shaped largely by Gene Hackman's wickedly funny interpretation of the supervillain in three Christopher Reeve Superman films. Hackman, in keeping with the tone of those movies, played the role for laughs. Kevin Spacey, who played Luthor in *Superman Returns*, described Hackman's interpretation as having "a wonderful used-car-salesman quality."[85]

The producers of *Smallville* knew that in order to sustain viewers' interest over the course of a potentially long-running series, they would need a radically different take on the cunning supervillain. Gough and Millar wanted to depict Lex as a sympathetic and misunderstood teenager who was Clark's friend before he evolved into a sociopath. In casting Michael Rosenbaum, who played Lex Luthor in 155 episodes, the producers found a worthy foil to Tom Welling's earnest, wounded, wide-eyed, trusting, and compelling Clark Kent.

In *Smallville*, Lex's ruthless father, Lionel Luthor (played with long, flowing locks of hair as a tacit taunt by John Glover), instigates and goads his son's inevitable path to the dark side. Ultimately, it is Lex's knotty relationship with Clark that is his undoing. Lex is in desperate need of a friend who will accept him and will neither lie to him nor attempt to manipulate him as his father does. Although Clark accepts Lex, and many other characters learn about Clark's powers, he is unable to be completely honest with Lex. In fact, Clark routinely lies to Lex about what he does and, more importantly to Lex, who he really is.[86] Over time, Lex feels so painfully betrayed by what he perceives as Clark's duplicitous nature that he surrenders to his darker impulses and sets out to destroy Clark.

In his vengeful resolve, Lex does help to steer his former friend, now mortal enemy, to his greater purpose. There is a telling scene is the series finale where Clark, who doubts his ability to save the world, still hasn't made the decision to become Superman. It is in this moment, when Clark is at his lowest, that Lex Luthor, after a three-year absence from the series, returns to give Clark a final push towards embracing his higher calling.

Lex:
You know I used to think that it was our families that made us who we are. And then I hoped it was our friends. But if you look at history the great men and women of this world have always been defined by their enemies . . . You and I, we will both be great men. Because of each other. We have a destiny together Clark. Only on different sides.

Clark:
And I'll always be there to stop you. Always.

Lex:

Oh, I'm counting on it. Our story hasn't been written yet Kal-El.[87] Every villain is only as great as his hero. You see, that all relies on you saving us from the coming Apokolips [sic] . . . .They [the Veritas Journals, a text written by a secret society,] foretold of a chosen savior. The light that will inspire this world out of darkness. You are the light Clark. Only you hold the power within you.

Clark:

I'm not so sure that Clark Kent can save the entire world on his own.

Lex:

He can't. We both know who can.

Clark:

I'm sorry I couldn't save you Lex.[88]

That seminal conversation transforms Clark, who sets off to the Fortress of Solitude where for the first time he will don his Superman suit and embrace his destiny as the world's greatest hero. After Clark leaves, the camera lingers on Lex for a few moments, as a faint smile crosses his lips. Each viewer will have his own interpretation of that ambiguous smile. It is possible to believe that Lex has diabolical reasons for giving Clark a pep talk and that he was acting selfishly, knowing that in order for him to become the consummate villain it was necessary for Clark be a great hero and worthy adversary. It is also possible that he was acting selflessly by encouraging his former friend to accept his true purpose in life.[89]

Michael Rosenbaum, who also voiced the superhero The Flash in the animated series *Justice League* (2001-2006) and in the video game *Justice League: Doom* (2012), wrote, directed and starred in the comedy *Back in the Day* (2014).

Michael Rosenbaum as Lex Luthor. © Warner Bros. Television.

THE INTERVIEW

What was your first reaction when you heard about *Smallville*?
To be honest with you, initially I scoffed. I loved the Superman movies and I loved Gene Hackman [who played Lex Luthor] and Christopher Reeve but I thought, *Eh, it's the WB* [a network known for insubstantial shows cast with incredibly good looking actors] and I don't know how good this show is going to be. *It's not going to have enough edge.* I was skeptical. I didn't take it se-

riously. Then a couple of months later my agent called and said, "They're doing this series *Smallville* and it's a really unique take on Superman. It takes place before Lex becomes the villain and before Clark becomes this ultimate superhero. They're friends in this little town of Smallville and it's wonderful."

So, I said, "Ok, let me read the script."

"They're not releasing the script."

"How can I commit to six years of my life without knowing if it's good. I might as well do porn." [Laughs]

They told me that 700 actors auditioned.

I said, "I'm sure these 700 other actors are just as good as me. What are these 700 other guys doing wrong?"

The direction was, "We want to feel a sense of danger but also comedic timing and charisma. All in one." They gave me just three pages and I remember circling areas and thinking, "I'll be dangerous here. I'll be charismatic here. I'll be funny here." That's how I went about it.

I went in and read for it. Then they called my agent to say they wanted me to test for it. There's always this process where actors are going in again and again. They think that somehow it's going to be better each time. I don't get it. I feel if you go in and you nail it and they're recording it, then they can just rewind the tape. Why put an actor through that process? He's either got it or he doesn't.

So, when my agent said, "Now they want to test you."

I said, "I'm not going to do that." I wasn't being an asshole; I just didn't feel like I could do better than I did in that room. It was one of those days when I felt very comfortable and very confident. So ultimately I said, "I'm not going to go in and test. Ultimately I said, "Take it or leave it." They were interested and they wanted to meet with me. So I met with the producers [and series creators Alfred Gough and Miles Millar]. They said, "We want to do it a very classy way. It's going to be dark and the characters are going to have great story arcs and develop over the course of the series. We don't want Lex to be a one-dimensional villain who is twirling his mustache." I felt that Al and Miles were very competent guys and I immediately responded to them and their strategy. So, I said, "Yes." Then they made me an offer and for seven years I was bald and living in Vancouver.

Nothing is a guaranteed hit. Nothing. Unless Spielberg is directing it and DiCaprio is in it. But it was a smaller network and it didn't have a lot of credibility. I think *Smallville* was the first show that gave the network some credibility. After it aired the critics and the other networks took note and said that the WB, which later was renamed the CW, really found something and they have a show, which is unique, fun and interesting. I really applaud the network for allowing us to grow as a show. There were times when the show was just a "freak of the weak" [villain] and we fell into the same routine, but there were all those episodes that went to another level.

But before we aired, I remember shooting it and thinking that it seemed great and that it seemed cool but I really didn't know how it was going to turn out. I remember going in to record some ADR [additional dialogue recording.] I had to record groans for the scene where Lex's Porsche goes off the bridge and Clark has to save him. I remember the director David Nutter [who also directed some standout episodes of *The X-Files*], who I think is phenomenal said, "I want to show you the first ten minutes of the show. It was just David and I and a few technicians. I remember watching it and saying, "This is a hit" and that it might bring some fame my way, that it might make me a little famous.

I remember calling my mother and father. I said, "I think this might be it."

They said, "What do you mean this might be it?"

Then they started naming projects that I was in that weren't so good. I said, "No, this is a slam dunk."

They said, "I've never heard you say that before."

I said, "Well, I've just seen the first ten minutes of the show. I have a feeling that this show has some longevity and will be successful." It's been an incredible ride.

Your Lex is very unlike the Gene Hackman Lex. How did you build the character?

I wasn't a big comic book fan. All I had to go on was *Lois & Clark* and the Christopher Reeve movies. I really loved Gene

Hackman. He's funny and engaging. But if you played it like that for an entire series you would get tired of that because it's not grounded. I'm not comparing myself to Gene Hackman because his was a very different approach from mine.

I thought that the only way that an audience was going to buy into the show and empathize with the characters is if they really believe in the characters. They need to believe that Lex is a tortured soul. That was the main reason I did the show. I wanted Lex to have a vulnerability, a kindness and a sincerity. I felt that if we established his likeability early, then audiences will engage. Once we have them, then we can go in different directions [and make Lex evil]. But if you don't have them in the beginning, then you'll never have them. There are exceptions but it's important to establish Lex's humanity early. I wanted there to be an arc. I wanted to play it real. Even in that original audition with the three pages, I played it real. I played it gentle and with sincerity. Lex was this young guy who didn't have the best upbringing and he had an overbearing father. Lex was always in his father's shadow. If we could show that, and show his torment. It was all in the writing in that pilot. I was trying to be subtle and it paid off.

Originally people were asking, "When does he become evil? When does he become evil?" But I didn't want him to become evil. I would tell the producers, "Don't let him become evil." But the fans wanted him to be evil. As an actor all you could do it sit and wait to read what they're writing you each week. Sometimes when it was too early [for Luther to act evilly] I would call the guys and say, "Hey, it's too early. It's too early to do something like this. Once we go down this path [we can never go back.] So, we had to be really strategic. I think they did a great job.

But to get back to your original question it was important to me to give him a soul. To give him a purpose. This was a guy who didn't want to follow in his father's footsteps. In one of his first lines he said to Clark, "The apple doesn't fall far from the tree." He's speaking of Clark but the same can be said of Lex. Is he going to become his father? He tried everything in his power not to.

Did you relate to Lex? What parts of yourself did you bring to him?

That's a deep question for me. That's a deep thought for me. Yeah. My father was 1420 on his SAT. He's a math and science wizard. He runs a company. I was an actor, I was an extrovert. Although growing up I was all shy and I didn't know where I fit in. I don't think my father got me in a lot of ways. It was hard growing up. I always wanted my father to be impressed. But I wasn't [academically] smart and my grades weren't really there. My dad had great grades and he was a problem solver who could figure out anything. I was more of an entertainer. I used to perfect impersonations that I saw on *Saturday Night Live,* characters like the Church Lady and Hans and Franz. I wanted to make people laugh and be the center of attention. So, my father and I were two different people. The reason I say this is because it wasn't always that easy. Lex isn't like his father either. Lex is trying to do the right thing in a lot of ways. It's hard to impress your father and earn his respect. You're always fighting for acceptance to get his approval. I think that's the similarity.

At the heart of these superhero stories is father and son relationships.

My father was there, but he wasn't an affectionate father. He wasn't the kind of guy who would say, "I love you son." That wasn't him. That wasn't in the cards. Which is not to say that he didn't love me. It's hard. Lex was trying to impress his father but he never got what he was looking for out of him. One of my heroes is Rodney Dangerfield. Rodney could never win with his father. It took years and years and he never got that acceptance. Even after he did stand up and movies and made all that money. If he didn't please his father something was empty. It was a sad story. You hear it a lot with comedians and actors.

For Lex, it's a sad case because he *really* wanted to please his father. He wanted his father to love him, but their entire relationship was based on deceit and lies. You can't change anyone. Or I should say something catastrophic has to happen for someone to change in which case it's too late. In Lex's case he eventually threw his father off a building. We sometimes think we have a God-like persona and you can change someone and help them but ultimately you have to recognize that they have to do it on their own.

You had as many scenes with Lionel Luthor, your on-screen father as you did with Clark. Were you able to say things to your real father vicariously by saying them to your imaginary one? Do you know what I mean?

I understand exactly what you are saying. You're saying did I have any experiences where it was cathartic to express something I might want to say to my own father. That's an interesting question. I love my father, but there are times when I want to tell him to fuck off. Or to say, "You're wrong. How about you're wrong for once in your life." There are those moments. Certainly they were exorcized where John [John Glover played Lionel Luthor] and I were in a scene and I would lash out and channel something that upset me about my own father. Maybe a time when he just wouldn't listen or he's being so stubborn. Absolutely.

The best actors – and I'm not comparing myself to them – but the best actors channel something from their own experiences into the scene. They call in sense memory or method acting. I ultimately just say, "Let's imagine that's my father. Let's imagine I lived through this situation. Let's imagine that I felt that way when I was younger and try to imagine what made me feel that way." Then I bring those things into the scene and I know I can trust them. They are real so they work. I had love in my family, but I also had a lot of volatility. I was able to channel those experiences through all my characters but especially in the Lex character. I used the experiences in those scenes.

After a while of playing a character, you more easily navigate those scenes. You don't get so comfortable that you don't care but it gets easier. But you go, "Oh, this is a scene where Clark walks in. I have a drink. I yell at Clark and he leaves." Or I say, "How the fuck did you get in this room? Where's my fucking security?" If I read that I can say, "Oh, we're shooting that tomorrow. I can have a drink tonight. I'm not that worried about that one." But it's the emotional scenes where Lionel comes in and I want to kill him that I really needed to be rested, and prepared for those scenes to take the life out of me emotionally. I knew I would be exhausted. John and I put 100% into those characters as I'm sure everyone else did on the show.

Did playing Lex give you tools to use for speaking to people in your own life?

Just the way he talks with his father. I really liked the way he stood up to his father. He really didn't let his father walk over him. Yeah, sure. Something would come out and I would say how it would affect the other character and the other actor. I would say, "I really should do more of this." It's not as big but it is in a certain way. "If I could just say these things to my father or to my friend instead of holding things in." There were those moments where I would think that I need to be a strong as Lex is when talking to certain people. Where I would think, *I need to say to certain people, 'I'm not going to compromise my needs or my desires so that's how it is.'* Obviously, Lex took some of these things to an extreme and did certain things that he couldn't take back. That's another tough question.

The other important dynamic on the show was Lex's relationship with Clark. It seems that Clark contributed to Lex's downfall because, understandably, he was never truly honest with his friend about who he was and it was probably that lie that tipped a wavering Lex Luthor to fully embrace the evil side of his nature.

Ultimately I think that's what it comes down to. Seldom do you find a friendship broken or severed because of truth. Seldom. Ultimately it's doing the right thing and if it's tactfully done then the truth is always stronger. Truth is always the way to go.

Maybe I inadvertently learned this from Lex but I always say, "You want to be my friend? I will love you unconditionally. Don't steal from me. Don't lie to me. Don't talk behind my back, but that's it. That's what a friend is. If you're honest, we'll be friends forever, but if you lie to me, it's over. I don't ever deal with people after that."

If you really think about it, Clark is absolutely the reason Lex becomes who he is. There's no doubt about it that if Clark said to Lex, "Listen Lex, you're my friend and we're going to be friends for life and we can do great things together, but I want to confide in you," then Lex would have grown into a very different person, and he didn't. Not only that but Clark lied to Lex for years and years and years. When Lex learned the truth about Clark he realized that their whole relationship was a sham. Lex was embarrassed. There was no turning back at some point. In the beginning there was no reason that Clark shouldn't have trusted Lex. Lex wasn't such a bad guy at the beginning, was he?

Not at all. I found myself rooting for him. He was very sympathetic. Do you think if Clark opened up to Lex early on that Lex would never have betrayed that trust and it would have kept Lex on a better path in his life?

It's hard to definitively say that because obviously the writing is on the wall and we all know the mythology and we know it couldn't, but if you're thinking in a more hypothetical way, then yes. But if he sat down with his friend and said, "I know you're father and I know how deceitful he's been with you. I'm going to tell you something and I hope that we can do good for humanity. I'm going to confide in you." I'd like to think that at that point it would have been ok. I really do. I know if I told my friend Tom, who is my best friend in the entire world, something that I wouldn't want him to tell anyone else, he wouldn't. Obviously it's a huge risk. It would be an amazing thing to hear.

You played Lex Luthor for seven seasons in over 150 episodes, but the series continued on for another three seasons without you – until you returned in the series finale. Did you just need a break from playing that character and living in Vancouver?

Something like that. Most people are pretty respectful but there are people out there who aren't. Someone asked me if I would play Lex Luthor in the next Superman movie and I said, "Of course I would. Why wouldn't I? Zak Snyder is a genius. I'm not an idiot." Some guy out there wrote something about me saying, "This is the same guy who quit the show and now he's dying to come back and play Lex Luthor in the next Superman movie." I didn't quit the show. The contract was for six years and I worked on it for seven years. That always really bothered me. I've never quit anything in my life. I don't quit. Ever. After I did my seven years. I did an *extra* twenty-two episodes. I felt that I was too old now and that they could've wrapped up this story easily. It should have been wrapped up after six years – seven years *tops*. But for purposes of monetary gain, they decided to go year after year. It would have been much tighter and much more compelling storytelling if we stopped then. But they kept bringing in all these other characters and I wasn't sure where the story was going anymore. I felt it's not the same show I signed on for. Then they decided they were going to do an eighth season and they wanted me to sign a two-year deal. I'm a comedian and I wanted to grow my hair back, start writing again, start to produce, start to direct. As a matter of fact I just directed my first movie called *Back in the Day*. I'm really proud of it. We shot it in my hometown for around $1 million. It's a funny, raunchy comedy.

But in the end, when it was in the tenth season and the show was wrapping up and they invited me back for the series finale, I felt like I owed it to the fans. It's not like I really "owed" it because I had done a lot already. But for the rest of my life I didn't want to hear the question, "Why didn't you go back for the final episode?" I did it. I went back for one. It pleased the fans and it ended the show perfectly. That's why I did it. Most people realize I didn't quit the show. But I loved the show. I loved the people. I loved the character. I owed the world to the show. But for a while the impression that I quit the show bothered me.

I think most fans get that.

I agree. It's really just a couple of critics. The fans are really great to me. These people are amazing. These Superman fans are unbelievable. They're better than Star Wars fans. They're better than Star Trek fans. I really believe that. They are so supportive. I'm just living the life. I say that as I stare at a Gene Hackman Lex Luthor doll.

[Laughs] Wait you have a Gene Hackman doll?

Are you kidding me? He's got like six different wigs that he can change into and he's holding Kryptonite. He's wearing a plaid jacket. He looks great.

They made a Lex Luthor doll from *Smallville* didn't they?

They did, but it doesn't look like me. It doesn't have any detail at all. To keep me grounded one of my friends put it [in an unmentionable place]. He was like, "Hey, Rosenbaum. Look at me.

I'm Lex Luthor." I'm like [disapprovingly], "Really." He's like [defiantly], "Yup." My friends make sure I never get a big head. They keep me grounded.

Tom Hiddleston is Loki

50,000 fans can't be wrong. 50,000 Tom Hiddleston fans petitioned Marvel Studios to create a stand-alone film featuring the
critically acclaimed theater, film, and TV actor as the villainous
Loki, the adoptive brother of Thor. The fans were on to something. After all, Hiddleston steals every scene in the blockbusters
Thor, *The Avengers*, and *Thor: The Dark World*.

Created by Stan Lee, Larry Lieber, and Jack Kirby, Loki first
appeared in the Marvel comic *Journey Into Mystery* #85 in 1962.
Remaining faithful to the character's origins in Norse mythology,
the trio shaped Loki as the god of mischief.

In *Thor*, both Loki and Thor want to be king of Asgard when
their father Odin abdicates his throne. However, Thor is too im-
mature, impetuous and arrogant to rule effectively; and Loki (the
biological son of Odin's enemy) is unsuited to power because he
is consumed by malevolent rage, fueled in part by his abandonment in childhood and informed by his erroneous belief that his
adoptive father doesn't think he's "worthy" because Asgardian
blood doesn't run through his veins. After Loki has learned that
Odin has kept the fact of his adoption from him, Loki rejects Odin
and questions his motives, "[Is it because] I am the monster parents tell their children about at night? . . .You know, it all makes
sense now, why you favored Thor all these years, because no matter how much you claim to love me, you could never have a Frost
Giant sitting on the throne of Asgard!"

The palace intrigue, the vicious infighting and the raw lust for
power call to mind Shakespeare's historical plays and tragedies.
Hiddleston's Loki is as "lean and hungry" as Cassius, as manipula-
tive as Lady Macbeth and as power hungry as Julius Caesar. In
describing a scene in *Thor: The Dark World* between Loki and
Thor, the *New York Times* critic Roslyn Sulcas observed, "For a
few memorable moments, a multimillion-dollar, wham-bam com-
ics-based action movie is a study of fraternal love and hate, of
familial rage and thwarted hope, of the strange combination of
nature and nurture that governs an individual's actions. It's not

the only moment in *Thor*, and its sequel, *Thor: The Dark World*... when Mr. Hiddleston achieves this kind of Shakespearean resonance."[90]   In an interview with *The Washington Post*, Kenneth Branagh, director of *Thor*, talked about the connection between Thor and Shakespeare, "Prince Hal in the *Henry IV* plays is as reckless as Thor is in the brutish beginning of our film. There you have Hotspur as a rival; here we have Loki. Also, in 'Hamlet' and 'Henry V,' conflicts may change whole nations, and so it is in *Thor*."[91]

Loki's myriad abilities include superhuman strength, telepathy, and shape-shifting, but his greatest strength is his ability to manipulate others. In *Thor,* when Loki wants Thor banished from Asgard he goads the God of Thunder into picking a fight with King Laufey and his army. Then using reverse psychology Loki pleads with his brother not to do battle, "Thor, stop and think. Look around you, we're outnumbered." Thor bristles at the advice and cautions, "Know your place, brother!" Loki's cunning has the intended effect of edging his short-tempered sibling into battle and it results in Thor's expulsion from Asgard.

Later in the film, Loki seems to make a deal with Laufey to kill Odin (played as a Lear-esque figure by Anthony Hopkins), "I will conceal you and a handful of your soldiers, lead you into Odin's chambers, and you can slay him where he lies." Laufey takes Loki up on his offer, but just before Laufey can murder Odin, Loki turns the tables and strikes Laufey down. In the eyes of the people of Asgard, Loki is now their savior.

The Pulitzer Prize-winning novelist Michael Chabon wrote of the multi-dimensional Loki that he is: "Ally and enemy, genius and failure, delightful and despicable, ridiculous and deadly, beautiful and hideous, hilarious and bitter, clever and foolish . . . Loki was the god of my own mind as a child, with its competing impulses of vandalism and vision, of imagining things and smashing them, and as he cooked up schemes and foiled them, fathered monsters and stymied them, helped forestall the end of things and hastened it, he was god of the endlessly complicating nature of plot, of storytelling itself."[92]

Second only to Robert Downey, Hiddleston, (who before being cast as Loki screen tested to play Thor), is arguably the biggest breakout star of the Marvel Cinematic Universe. He was part of an attractive panel for *The Avengers* panel at the 2011 New York Comic Con that included *Captain America*'s Chris Evans and the *Hulk*'s Mark Ruffalo, where a clear majority of the audience's questions were directed at Tom Hiddleston. And his fan-base has been growing steadily. When he appeared at the 2013 San Diego Comic-Con, his greeting by an estimated 6,500 fans was characterized as "hysterical."[93] Moreover, he bravely appeared dressed as Loki and *in character*. While it's *de rigueur* for fans to come to conventions in costumes it's practically unheard of for an actor to come dressed as a character that he's made famous.[94]

There, as Loki, Hiddleston playfully, imperiously, sneered to those in attendance: "Humanity – look how far you've fallen. Lining up in the sweltering heat for hours. Huddling together in the dark. Like beasts. I am Loki of Asgard and I am burdened with glorious purpose. Stand back, you mewling quim." The actor demanded that the audience, "Say my name." The standing room only crowd in Hall H shouted back, "Loki!" Hiddleston, still in character, replied: "It seems I have an army." The same can be said of Hiddleston and his dedicated fans.

Marvel Studios soon recognized the outsize allure of Hiddleston's Loki. After *Thor: The Dark World* was wrapped and a rough cut was assembled, the filmmakers realized the film was light on Loki. So, they went back to shoot additional scenes with Hiddleston.[95] Alan Taylor, the director of the *Thor* sequel, described the nature of the new scenes, "A lot of it was getting more Loki stuff, because we realized how successful he was in the movie, so we sort of 'Loki-ed it up' a little bit."[96] Their gambit paid off: *Thor: The Dark World* made over $632 million, which bested the box office of the first film by $183 million.

Hiddleston, who has garnered critical acclaim for his supporting roles as F. Scott Fitzgerald in Woody Allen's *Midnight in Paris* [2011] and as a young cavalry officer in Steven Spielberg's *War Horse* [2011], was again singled out by many critics for his performance in the sequel.

Marvel Studio's President of Production Kevin Feige attempted to explain Hiddleston's striking appeal this way:

"I've been surprised and happy that so many cast members and characters have gotten that response. Hiddleston is a case in himself. We discovered that when we were going around the world promoting the movie, in Moscow and in the U.K. and in Rome, and all these people behind the barricades at the premieres were holding "Loki's Armies" signs or wearing homemade helmets with horns on it. We sat around years ago saying we needed a villain in the MCU [Marvel Cinematic Universe], as complex and dynamic as [Ian McKellen's] Magneto is. Magneto is one of the best villains in both the comics and in the movies. The way that Tom brought Loki to life, with all of those different emotions . . . Even if you didn't read comics or weren't versed in mythology and had no idea who Loki was – and he's kind of out there with his big horns – they responded to him, particularly women. Tom is an amazing looking specimen but also because of that darkness, I think they find a sexiness with him as a bad boy.[97]

The British actor is a graduate of England's Eton, a private boarding school (whose graduates include nineteen prime ministers, and such writers as George Orwell, Aldous Huxley (*Brave New World)* and Ian Fleming), Cambridge University (where he was a Classics major and graduated with honors) and London's prestigious Royal Academy of Dramatic Arts. In 2012, he played Prince Hal and Henry V in a series of TV-movies for BBC Two, and his 2013 stage performances in England in the title role of the Bard's "Coriolanus" elicited critical raves. One writer said, "Hiddleston's Coriolanus is a masterclass in layering; a celebrated warrior with matinee-idol looks who is part venomous despot, part isolated soul-searcher. For a full two and a half hours, the 6ft 1in actor commands the stage with a complexity that leaves the audience in silent rapture."[98]

Hiddleston has grasped the impelling force of Loki's wounded psyche and he plays the character as an open sore that won't, and possibly can't, heal. Hiddleston's Loki is a flimflam man working both the short and long cons simultaneously. His motives

Tom Hiddleston as Loki. © Marvel Studios

are always in question. Although his immediate ambition to rule Asgard is clear, his true end game remains cloaked in mystery. Attempt to identify it and you will find you're playing a hustler's shell game: when the shells are turned over, you discover that you've again been deceived. Could Loki ever be satisfied or is true contentment forever out of his reach? It's a question that might stymie Loki himself.

One quickly learns that Hiddleston is a well-read and deeply thoughtful person who can also be engagingly playful about his approach to the part. He gave the following advice for anyone who wanted to play his signature role, "If you're wearing the horns, keep your head down. If your head goes back, you genuinely look like a reindeer."[99]

THE INTERVIEW

I saw you at New York Comic Con on *The Avengers* panel, where you demonstrated tremendous knowledge and understanding of the comics, more in my experience than any actor who has played a superhero or super villain. What did you take from the comics and what did you deliberately avoid?

It's difficult to be specific because once ingredients are mixed together in a cocktail it's impossible to separate them thereafter. Certainly "mischief" became a guiding principle. Look up "mischief" in the dictionary and you find "playful misbehavior, especially on the part of children" and "harm or trouble caused by someone or something." The character created by Stan Lee and Jack Kirby in *Journey Into Mystery* was certainly mischievous: turning cumulonimbus clouds into dragons; shape-shifting whales into sea-serpents; metamorphosing lines of cars parked along New York streets into ice cream. Add to that the stories of his childhood: for example, the occasion Loki cut the golden hair of Sif while she slept, whereupon Thor demanded he restore it, and dwarves Brokk and Eitri (unpaid by Loki) forged new hair for her, rendering it black from the Night itself.

Above all, I suppose, the key to the character for me lay in Loki's resentment of the favor bestowed by Odin upon Thor, whose nobility of spirit and natural excellence marked him out above other Asgardians. Loki was the son of Laufey, king of the Frost Giants of Jotunheim, by whom he was left to die on a frozen rock, abandoned, betrayed, lost. He was adopted by Odin and taken in and raised as Thor's brother, but he would never be his equal. This lethal cocktail of playfulness and resentment in Loki, his inclination to mischief and charm, coupled with his spiritual loneliness, his damage, his rage, is a thread that runs through every single Thor story in the comics. Walt Simonson made Loki very slick and charming. J. Michael Straczynski explored his rage and hatred. Robert Rodi and Esad Ribic gave Loki what he wanted – a throne – which he found wanting and empty. Kieron Gillen made him vulnerable, made him cry. Before I played the part for the first time in Kenneth Branagh's *Thor* I immersed myself in the forty years of comic book storytelling. I took pieces of him from everywhere: his sorcery, his intelligence, his charm, his comic-book-sized megalomania, his grandeur, his vanity, and his all-too-human heartbreak.

Besides being the "forgotten son" what drives Loki? What motivates him?

What motivates any psychopath is as mysterious and opaque as an ancient riddle. At the end of Kenneth Branagh's *Thor*, Loki barks at his 'brother': "I never wanted the throne; I only ever wanted to be your equal." I think perhaps there is some truth in that. I think Loki's resentment of his loneliness – his need for (and lack of) familial love and equanimity – has taken over his entire being, and his rage has become his secret weapon, the engine behind all his intelligence, strategy and sorcery. But perhaps that's too simple. There are many occasions where Loki is offered an olive branch of peace, and every time he rejects it. My point is that I think that even if Loki was given what he wanted – what he thought he wanted – he would not change, he would not accept a peaceful resolution. In the Marvel Universe, as in Norse mythology, Loki is the agent of chaos. Disorder and unrest is his milieu. Loki has found his place: he exists to resist. Loki's raison d'être is to subvert the status quo.

What parts of yourself did you bring to Loki?

I promised myself I must have a good time. Loki is anchored by a very dark, very damaged heart, but he's often having the time of his life. He's the smartest person in the room, and the most refined strategist, much sharper, and smarter than I am. When I play chess you can see me sweat, but Loki doesn't bat an eyelid. What I enjoyed most was allowing my own playfulness to inhabit Loki in these moments. Loki has an easy charm, a caustic wit and effortless grace. The easiest way to access that was simply to try to enjoy myself. As for the vulnerability and the anger, Loki wasn't the first, and won't be the last, character I've played to feel unsettling and disturbing emotions on a large scale. All drama is founded on this kind of catharsis. In those scenes of pain and rage, I just had to summon it from somewhere. I can't explain how. As an actor you just instinctively know that you have to; you know that the scene requires it. Possibly it comes from empathy, in the final analysis; it comes from an understanding that in the end we're all vulnerable; that we're all flawed; that we all feel pain.

What aspects of your personality have rubbed off onto Loki? And what traces of Loki now live within you?

The truth is that I really don't know. I hope it's obvious that I have taken enormous pleasure in playing him. I've had the time of my life. I hope that my enjoyment has rubbed off on him: Loki's having a good time; I'm having a good time, and I hope the audience is having a good time. I have a hunch that whatever connects myself and Loki existed within me before I played him, and no doubt that's probably why I was cast in the role. Most acting is about expanding and diminishing aspects of oneself according to the interior truth and external silhouette of the character. The rest is simply an act of imagination.

You created Loki for Marvel's Cinematic Universe. What do you know and understand about the character that might surprise even the most devoted Loki fan?

I know that we've been making it up as we go along. There was never a long-term "master plan" for Loki's evolution in the Marvel Cinematic Universe. [However,] I know what's coming up next.

Shakespeare heavily influenced Stan Lee when he, Larry Lieber and Jack Kirby created the Thor universe. Can you talk about the Shakespearean connection and what elements of Shakespeare you drew from?

Kenneth Branagh and I discussed Shakespearean archetypes and allusions because those plays and characters were references we both shared and understood. Edmund in *King Lear*, like Loki, is an illegitimate, bastard son, jealous, and resentful of his brother Edgar. Iago in *Othello*, like Loki, is a master manipulator and immaculate strategist with a deep, dark, vengeful, interior life. Macbeth in *Macbeth*, like Loki, is obsessed (to the point of madness) with ambition for the throne; he is the man who would be king. Cassius in *Julius Caesar*, like Loki, is characterized by a "lean and hungry look" It goes without saying that the pictorial medium of a Comic Book cannot afford the same psychological rigor or textual refinement as Shakespeare's writing, but these characters were helpful corner stones for us in constructing the soul of the character within our collective imagination. The precision in the psychology of those characters, and the objects of their obsession, gave us a compass to be guided by.

Michael Chabon called the outfit that superheroes wear their "secret skin," something that reveals the true nature of the character wearing it. In what ways is Loki's outfit his secret skin?

Loki's clothes are fashioned from black leather, green moleskin, and burnished golden metal. Its layers suggest the character's elegance, his vanity, and hint at a magician's inclination to concealment. The costume is also, in its way, martial. Loki's armor is exactly that: armor. His clothes are his defense against the world. The color scheme and design (of which he may or may not be conscious) denotes hostility and danger. His horned helmet, only worn on occasions where regal formality is appropriate or required and for battle, is manifestly an emblem of his villainy. The horns evoke the iconography of the character's roots in Norse mythology, while also clearly demonstrating his 'devilish' spirit.

When you put on Loki's uniform did you feel powerful? Does wearing his costume help transform you at all?

Loki's costume has the effect of making me feel taller, heavier, and harder. The weight of the leather tails on Loki's long coat makes me feel more grounded, and the close-fitting straps of the breastplate behave like an armored corset. It feels as though my back is held straighter and higher and my shoulders broader. It feels powerful, and dangerous.

What is the best part of being a supervillain?

The best part of being a supervillain is without question being able to see the joy it has given to audiences all over the world, across all ages and cultures, to see these characters come to life. When I've attended early screenings of the Marvel films (and have met children and families and groups of friends afterwards), the greatest reward is to see them laugh, gasp, clap, and cheer with delight. All you can hope for as an actor is to make a connection. And if that connection is entertaining, and gives a degree of pleasure, I feel proud to have been a part of it, and to have done my job.

The worst part?

I don't know that there is a worst thing. If there is, I can't think of it now.

The most surprising part?

The most surprising aspect is certainly the extraordinary level of affection in which Loki is held. I might have once hoped to make Loki a villain whom audiences could love to hate, but I never expected him to become a villain they might actually love.

How has playing this character changed you personally? Not professionally, but personally?

It's hard to say. It's probably given me greater courage and confidence to stretch myself in new directions as an actor. Loki was the first opportunity I had to play someone so physically different from myself. Loki is a photonegative of who I am. My hair is fair and curly, my complexion Celtic and plain. His hair is raven-black and his skin is white. It was interesting to wear that 'mask' and see how the character's truth could perhaps be expressed through that filter by something within me. Loki has also introduced me to a huge audience. That changes you.

Can you describe what it's like to "be" a supervillain in the superhero universe and in the eyes of the public?

It's dizzying; the lights are very bright, the scrutiny can be almost impossibly forensic, and sometimes the height and scale of the whole enterprise can feel vertiginous and head spinning, but ultimately, above all else, it is enormous fun. I have the extraordinary privilege of being able to say that I have lived out a childhood dream. As a child, I loved the magnitude of the world inhabited by superheroes and supervillains. The size of the superhero universe with its particular laws and connections seems appropriately scaled to the size and energy of every child's imagination. As a boy, I wanted to fly, fight, and make magic. That I have been allowed to try, even if though it's make-believe, is an opportunity for which I am eternally grateful.

PART SIX: HEROES IN HIDING

The Fantastic Four

Alex Hyde-White is Reed Richards
Carl Ciarfalio is The Thing
Joseph Culp is Doctor Doom
Rebecca Staab is Sue Storm

Stan Lee said it was the film that you weren't supposed to see. Roger Corman, the legendary B-movie producer/writer/director/king-maker, called it an experiment. *Arrested Development*, the subversive comedy series, spoofed it. The "it" in question is the unreleased *The Fantastic Four* (1994), a feature film adaptation of Marvel's quartet of heroes, which has become a superhero urban legend.

Bernd Eichinger, who was one of the key players in the Constantin Film Group, the German production company that had early success with George Miller's *The NeverEnding Story* and Jean-Jacques Annaud's *The Name of the Rose* starring Sean Connery, obtained the rights from Marvel to produce a film version of *The Fantastic Four*. Eichinger was having a hard time raising enough money to make the film on a budget sufficient to deliver the spectacle that audiences demand. Because Marvel wouldn't grant an extension and Eichinger didn't want the rights to lapse, the company decided to go forward with their production by joining forces with Roger Corman, who signed on as an executive producer and through his company Concorde Pictures funded the film for a scant budget of $1 million. They hired Oley Sassone, who directed *Bloodfist III: Forced to Fight* (1992) and many music videos to helm the superhero romp.

Sassone cast a group of game young actors to play Stan Lee and Jack Kirby's famous surrogate family.

Alex Hyde-White, the British actor who had parts in *Battlestar Galactica*, the TV movie *Captain America II: Death Too Soon* (1979), *Buck Rogers in the 25th Century* and *Pretty Woman*, was cast as Reed Richards/Mister Fantastic. Hyde-White has appeared in three films directed by Steven Spielberg – *Catch Me If*

You Can, The Adventures of Tintin and *Indiana Jones and the Last Crusade*, where he played a younger version of Sean Connery's Henry Jones, Sr. (although his face doesn't appear on camera). He has also made guest appearances on *The Unit*, *NCIS*, and *Dexter*.

Rebecca Staab played Sue Storm/the Invisible Girl, Jay Underwood, who starred in *The Boy Who Could Fly*, played Johnny Storm/the Human Torch. Staab went on to have a busy career including appearances on *Desperate Housewives*, *Glee*, *Dexter*, and *Masters of Sex*.

Michael Bailey Smith, played Ben Grimm He also played Super Freddy, a supervillain-esque version of serial killer Freddy Kruger, in the horror film *A Nightmare of Elm Street 5: The Dream Child*.

Stuntman-turned-actor Carl Ciarfalio played the Thing, the creature that Grimm turned into. Ciarfalio has done stunt work on Sam Peckinpah's *The Osterman Weekend*, William Friedkin's *To Live and Die in L.A.*, Tim Burton's *Beetlejuice*, David Fincher's *Fight Club*, and Steven Spielberg's *A.I. Artificial Intelligence*.

Joseph Culp, who went on to appear as Don Draper's abusive father in the critically acclaimed TV series *Mad Men*, played the villainous Doctor Doom.

In order to retain the movie rights before they reverted back to Marvel at the end of the year, production would need to commence quickly. Corman devised his plan of attack, "I said [to Eichinger], 'We need all the time we can. This is a complicated film with special effects. Let's start filming December 31.' He said, 'No, they'll understand what we're doing if we start on December 31st. Let's start on December 26th.' I said, 'Bernd, they'll know what we're doing anyway. It doesn't make any difference. I think we finally compromised on December 28th"

The film was shot, edited, scored, and readied for theatrical release. Corman was pleased with the finished product. In fact, the film stars had started preparing for a publicity tour when they received some unsettling news; the film would not be released. Producer Bernd Eichinger sold the rights of the film to Twentieth Century Fox with the intention of burying this version of *The Fantastic Four* in order to make a new version of the film with an appropriate budget.

In talking with *Los Angeles Magazine* in 2005, Stan Lee said, "The tragic thing is that the people involved with the film were *not aware* that the movie was never supposed to be shown to anybody. Do you see? It was never supposed to be seen by any living human beings [sic]."[100]

For his part, Roger Corman was eager for the film to be shown theatrically. "That to me was very interesting because the distribution methods for independents, the low budget pictures were starting to fade away and the majors were really dominating . . . I thought this might give us an opportunity with a slightly better known property to see if we could revitalize our distribution."[101] In another interview Corman lamented, "I wanted to see how it performed. I never got the chance to try the experiment."[102]

In the end, the undistributed film is uneven and rough in spots but it was clearly made as a labor of love and in many ways the film shows more understanding and respect for Stan Lee and Jack Kirby's characters than Twenty Century Fox's $100 million *Fantastic Four* (2005) and its $130 million *Fantastic Four: Rise of the Silver Surfer* (2007). Both of those listless films starred Ioan Gruffudd as Mister Fantastic, Jessica Alba as the Invisible Girl, Chris Evans (in his pre-Captain America days) as the Human Torch, and Michael Chiklis as the Thing. The films did well at the box office, with a combined gross of nearly $620 million, but neither film is well-regarded.

At least one of the film's stars was not happy with the finished product. Jessica Alba expressed her frustrations when she said, "[Tim Story, the director told me,] 'It looks too real. It looks too painful. Can you be prettier when you cry? Cry pretty, Jessica.' He was like, 'Don't do that thing with your face. Just make it flat. We can CGI the tears in.' I'm like, 'But there's no connection to a human being.'"[103]

In contrast, the actors who worked on the unreleased *The Fantastic Four* are very proud of their work on the film and they hope one day that it will be widely available for fans to see and evaluate.

While Marvel did succeed in scuttling the release, the film didn't completely disappear. Bootlegged copies of the film are widely available for sale online, at conventions, and in comic book shops. In many ways the film's turbulent history has given the film a secure place in the memories of superhero fans.

Alex Hyde-White, Rebecca Staab, Jay Underwood and Carl Ciarfalio as Mister. Fantastic, the Invisible Woman, the Human Torch and the Thing. © Photo courtesy of Carl Ciarfalio.

THE INTERVIEWS
Alex Hyde-White played Reed Richards/Mister Fantastic

Although it's popular in comic book circles, the Fantastic Four doesn't have the same name recognition as Batman, Superman, or Spider-Man. What did you know about them before making the movie?

I remembered the cartoon, as I quite enjoyed it. My favorite was Johnny Quest, which is similar to Fantastic Four. I also really like the Beatles cartoons on Saturday morning. They were the Fab Four, weren't they? So, I guess I was warmed up to the idea of the Fantastic Four being a part of 1960s to 1980s popular culture.

Did you have any reservations about accepting the part?

"We're all in the gutter," Oscar Wilde is quoted as saying, "but some of us are looking at the stars." A fairly well known manager said to me a few years ago that he knew me to be a very good actor, and that playing Reed in that film was not a good career move. At the time, lots of leading men were up for it. You know, I was buying in to the idea that it would be good experience for me to play a hero in an American movie.

Was there anything that particularly appealed to you about playing a superhero?

Yeah, I was going through a divorce at the time and it was fun being referred to as Mister Fantastic. The ex kind of got tired of me not working all the time, and you know Reed, he's always doing something.

What was your approach to playing Reed Richards?

Be like a big brother to Ben, a good Uncle to Johnny, and good friend to Sue. After reading the script and starting to learn the lines, there was a specific energy to the role that appealed to me. This was a thinking part, obviously being Reed, so the actor would naturally want to "use his head." That could mean using facial gestures that someone who is "using his head" would do, sometimes frowning, glancing away, you know *thinking*! Once we get on the set and started filming the movie, then the character comes to life, at least in the actor's imagination.

With Reed, the character came to me and was most welcome. I found myself sometimes speedily rushing to a conclusion with the dialogue and then slowing down after for the explanation, again, which can be quite natural, expected and interesting for a character with a scientific nature. Think Spock: he traditionally weighs information before making a conclusion. Reed is different than that; almost opposite in that he thinks so fast that the answer comes to him before he realizes it. And you know what was cool – I kind of figured that that's what it meant to *stretch yourself thin*. Playing Reed required me to lead the team and the cast and this approach gave me the key to it.

How would you describe your Reed Richards? What motivates him?

He always wants to get to the next thing, and, he doesn't much like procedure and process; he likes results. If it were the real world, he'd want to be President of the United States of America, I think. Because he genuinely believes that he can adjudicate any issue with resolve and natural fairness. He is elastic in that way, and can handle anything. Probably except jealousy, as in if someone wanted to take his girl or his team away. Except Johnny. They could have Johnny. He's probably a little jealous of Johnny.

How did you feel when you first put on the costume?

Thin and goofy. It was full body spandex. The arm rig [a special effect, which allowed the actor to appear to stretch his arm to punch out bad guys] was cool though.

Did wearing it ever make you feel powerful?

Yeah, it did. I kind of liked it and felt it fit well.

I understand that without the support of the studio, you went to conventions to drum up awareness and excitement for the film. Sounds like you were personally invested in the success of the film.

Yeah, a few of us went on the road, which was fun. I like that, getting out and engaging with the audience. I learned more about the Fantastic Four and the comic book world doing that than in making the film. Really glad I did it. We were so well received at some wonderful locations. Jim Hanley's Universe in midtown New York City had a good turnout. We did a few comic conventions, one in Florida and I attended the one in San Diego when it was still small. One time me and the Thing costume made a personal appearance in Charlotte. All of that finding an audience stuff is great.

What do you think the film's shortcomings are?

The music is kind of out of sync with the film. The Ben Grimm/Alicia storyline is over the top. The sound mix, much of Dr. Doom's stuff needed to be better. Simply put, a longer shooting schedule would have helped the overall production value.

When you found out that the film wouldn't get released, you must have been quite disappointed.

Yeah, it sucked. I felt the director, Oley [Sassone], was the one who was gypped. He worked hard and the gangplank was sawed off behind him. It wasn't that bad for me as an actor. Not now, not even then really. You know in all honesty this experience of playing Reed in 1994's Roger Corman infamous unreleased, shelved to be reborn, version of the Fantastic Four occupies a unique, quirky, and quite interesting place in indie film folklore. It's like Yeti, more interesting because no one has seen it.

Also, the quality of the film leaves much to be desired and even though it was a great role to play at the time, if it had come out and critics and audience were anything less than pleased and supportive of the film, then it may not have been anything more than that, a nice part in a bad film. I was in a Captain America TV-movie starring Reb Brown, one of my first jobs around 1978 as a contract player at Universal. Probably ended up being a high point in his career and he may have suffered because of the reception of that film. It's not just then, even though it was harder to produce comic book movies then. Look at the new fine, graphic masterful big comic book films — heck, the newer Fantastic Four films had their problems, too, with so many of the critics and fans. It's a slippery slope.

What are your thoughts about the experience?

I am glad, looking back, that it wasn't released and then forgotten. I am glad now to have it as a milestone in my career, and obviously not because it prevented a possible ascension to that of action/indie star, but because of the place in pop culture this film has achieved. I believe our version has a right to be viewed and judged by the audience, a commercial audience. Perhaps, when Fox finally "rediscovers" it in the vault and releases it and it sells a million copies, I will be very happy.

It looks as if the film was made with a great deal of passion and appreciation for the characters. Can you talk about that?

We were young, naïve, and easily fooled. It takes passion to allow that to happen, but there was no other way. The Fantastic Four are kind of like that anyway.

Did playing the character change you in a way?

Playing Reed helped me hone my leadership characteristics both on-set and off-set.

Who would win in a fight? Your Reed Richards or the one Ioan Gruffudd played in two Fantastic Four films?

Me. Because I kick his ass every time I see him. Except once when he was on that boat! That's all I'm gonna say on that one!

Carl Ciarfalio trying on his new skin during a costume fitting. © Photo courtesy of Carl Ciarfalio.

Carl Ciarfalio played The Thing

What do you think motivates The Thing? What drives him?

Interesting question, especially for this kind of character, because I was hired to be in the Thing suit, but Michael Bailey Smith was hired to play Ben Grimm. So, I actually had to conform my movement and gestures to fit how Michael saw the Thing. Michael was very informed about Ben's persona, and I did my homework as well. Our director, Oley Sassone, was knowledgeable about the story and characters and insistent that we stay as close to the original comic book as possible. Michael and I talked a lot about Ben's motivation. Ben's passionate, but he had masked that passion for life for fear of seeming weak or vulnerable. As the Thing, Ben can release all the pent-up passion, frustration, and power that we would all like to exhibit at times. Therefore, Ben is as human as the rest of us and the rest of us are as human Ben. It's really the through-line for all the characters.

Do you relate to him at all?

I can relate to Ben in a few ways. I think that I'm a passionate man. I'm passionate about my family, my work, paying forward. Sometimes I feel like there are some obstacles and/or people who could use a lesson in humility or kindness or who might need a "nudge" to see just how ignorant their words or actions are. I'm a pretty good-sized guy, was pretty strong in my day, and sometimes I would like to just go whip some ass that I think needs to be whipped. Now I don't do it but I'm thinking that I'm not the only one that thinks that way at times. Admitting this is tough, though I've mellowed with time and try to follow a more Buddhist style of life — but there are times.

Can you talk about The Thing costume?

Working to make the Thing look like he was moving like a big human was tough. I was pretty agile and the suit looked and fit great, but the suit was sculpted from rubber and was a couple of inches thick. It had a Velcro flap in the back and the head snapped onto the shoulders. Under the suit I wore a "thin skin" that you would wear under a wet suit for an extra thin layer. The budget was very tight so the was no cooling suit built into the Thing's rubber.

We shot almost everything on stage, and the only way to get any air into the suit was to open the mouth and hold a fan up to the opening. I would loose several pounds of water every day. They had made a rubber head for me when I was doing the stunts — fights, breaking through walls and such — and a full-on remote control head for the close-ups and dialogue. I did Michael's dia-

When Carl Ciarfalio played The Thing it was always clobberin' time. © Photo courtesy of Carl Ciarfalio.

logue, which helps me as an actor to be true to my movements and keeps the character real. The remote control guys would make the mouth, cheeks and eyebrows move along with the words. All I could hear was bzzzzzzzfffff . . . bzzffff . . . bzffffffbfbffbfbzzzfff.

Did you ever feel power in The Thing costume?

I felt a certain power with the suit on, but let me tell you, everyone wanted a picture with The Thing. I have pics with almost all of the cast and crew including the artists who made the suit. The girls – all the girls that I have photos with while I'm wearing the suit – are saddled up next to me, holding tight to my massive rock-like chest, and their eyes sparkle like they just caught the bouquet. So at the end of the day, when I get out of the suit, jump into my best sweats and throw on a baseball cap to go say goodnight to the crew (the same people who were starry eyed twenty minutes ago) I get a wave and a "See ya." Ouch, my ego. The Thing suit definitely has something special going for it.

What do you think are the film's strengths and weaknesses?

Carl Ciarfalio with director Oley Sassone. © Photo courtesy of Carl Ciarfalio.

I think that the strength of the film is the truth to the original story and the characters. Real fans get that. The weakness is that it had a small budget so some of the special effects and the sets took the hit; but also, it's over twenty years old, and there wasn't any real CGI then. Everything was an expensive process. I think that Oley Sassone did everything he could to bring the film in ready to go.

You've worked with Lou Ferrigno. Can you talk about him?

I worked on the TV show, *The Incredible Hulk* from the late 1970s till the end of the show. I played bikers, thugs n' drunks, all in stunt roles. I doubled him a couple of times after that and I played yet another bad guy in *The Incredible Hulk Returns*. Louie and I have stayed friend ever since. I just spoke to him at Comic Con; he looked as great as ever and is most likely the sweetest guy in the biz. Like me, he was the first to portray that iconic comic book figure, and for as long as the Hulk exists, it will be Lou Ferrigno. Just like Superman and the Lone Ranger, the first ones to play the part win. Louie appreciates the comic world and does his best to keep the Hulk true to form.

You've worked on a number of superhero films as a stuntman, including *The Amazing Spider-Man*, *The Green Hornet*, *Daredevil*, *The Incredible Hulk Returns*, and *Batman & Robin*.

On *Batman & Robin*, Clooney never looked comfortable in the suit, and Arnold was in all his glory. I had been killed by Arnold about nine or ten times on *Commando*, so I went over and said hello, and he always had that blue frozen face and a stogy smashed in his mouth, always with the same smile for everyone and that devilish look in his eyes like he just has to play a joke on someone. This time the way he gets me is in the museum where he throws everyone around and then freezes them. I played a security guard on the stairs when I'm suddenly yanked backwards, off the stairs and onto the floor where I was dragged about eighty feet. After about the fifth take, I was wishing I was back on *Commando* just getting shot and falling down.

Who would win in a fight between The Hulk and The Thing? And why?

They are the same. They both hide behind their passion, their feelings. Each one knows what is morally and ethically right, each one [starts as a smaller character and turns into another one who is] huge and fights for what he believes in. One is green, one orange, and they're brothers from a different mother.

Joseph Culp played Doctor Doom

Were you a fan of The Fantastic Four comic books while growing up?

I think as a little kid I was more fascinated by The Fantastic Four comic than just about any other comic. I thought the four characters were more interesting than the other superheroes like Superman or Batman. I was a fantasy, horror and monster fan from early on, knew all the classic movies, built all the models, and it's possible that I was drawn to The Fantastic Four characters because they didn't just have super powers or great strength, but they had been mutated, even deformed in a sense, and were kind of "monstrous" in their way. I think that appealed to me.

What was your process for creating the character of Doctor Doom?

Once I realized I had the task of creating Doctor Doom on film for the first time, I felt a great sense of responsibility to all the fans out there. I wanted to get to know Doctor Doom as deeply as possible and I took the challenge pretty seriously. I read as many back issues as I could find and started to work on his body, voice, and psychological position. Doom has this epic, grand manner, a real showman in a way, with a profound rage and a devilish sense of irony as well, all due to his brilliant mind coupled with emotional and physical scarring. He really is one of the classic villains, not unlike Richard III or the Phantom of the Opera, and of course he is the absolute precursor to Darth Vader. So I knew that I would have to give myself permission to go very big and be larger than life. That's the way he is in the comic, and I wanted to honor that. I worked on the physicality constantly. I was concerned about the limitations of the suit and mask, so I explored as many ways as I could think of to "physicalize" his inner life and use my voice to convey as many colors as possible so I would not be standing there like a big tin can. I went to a theater and spent many hours doing vocal and physical improvisations, going over the lines one by one. I even spent time in a ski mask to explore Doom's extreme feelings of affliction, confinement, frustration, and rage, as I tried to find a personal connection to the layers I saw in the character.

Was there anything you used specifically from the comic books?

The script for the movie could not contain the whole backstory of Doom, but I invested a lot in his past experiences as motivations for wanting to capture the cosmic energy source: the loss of his gypsy mother, her imprisonment in Hell, and Doom's vow to contact her through esoteric science, all gave another layer for me to play, even if it was just private. There is a moment in the film right before Reed and Victor try their experiment where I kiss a medallion around my neck. It wasn't in the script, but the director liked it and left it in. That was my little nod to Doom's connection to his mother and the mystic arts. Then, when things are starting to blow up, I don't leave my workstation but [instead I] start screaming, "I will not fail!" It shows his secret obsession and for me [it] was about his deeper motivation to save his mother. Mostly from the comic books I tried to use as many of his stylized physical gestures, his various poses, the booming voice, sometimes even the sorrow in his laughter, because you always sense there is something lonely about Doom's quest for ultimate power.

Is there anything you deliberately avoided?

I think mostly I wanted to avoid being static and falling into the trap of "naturalism." As actors we always want to be so real that we sometimes fall into a style of acting that is very natural but has no size or dynamic to it. I wanted to embody the original Doctor Doom in all his glory from those comics, and I had to let myself play in the sandbox like a three-year-old without self-consciousness. Some might say I went over-the-top, but you can be real, and be big and bold in your choices too. I think Doom and the film deserved as much power as I could give him, so I wanted to avoid "playing small" and go for the big guns.

What motivates Doom?

Like all great tyrant-kings, Doom is obsessed with power and control because he is unable to express his deeper wound in any other way. There are issues of revenge: the loss of his mother and the kingdom of Latveria when he was young, his vow to save her and claim his right to the throne, and with his perceived betrayal by colleague Reed Richards that left him disfigured. All these factors contribute to a kind of madness that knows no bounds. His disfigurement is more than skin deep; his soul is in torment. He is a wounded narcissist. He was driven and arrogant before the accident and then his wounds of failure push him over the edge. Doom is one of the great villains in the history of the genre. He has intelligence, wit, a sense of personal entitlement, determination and a lot of style, but Doom is also tortured so I always feel sorry for him and kind of wish he would win.

What part of yourself did you bring to the character?

One always has to feel around in the psyche a bit to connect to the role one is playing. I did choose to tap into some of my personal triggers of hurt and rage and the lust for power, which I saw in Doom. Actors do look for ways to channel their ghosts into their work if possible. Doom offered many opportunities for me to express some of my shadows. Most of all was the opportunity to dip into my sometimes wicked sense of play, which in life can push the boundaries, but in character was wonderfully appropriate for Doom. Other than his obvious rage and obsession, I tried to bring out some sensuality in a few places. It's almost sexual. I thought it would be interesting to see this villainous man in a metal suit with a sometimes gentle touch. He touches the victimized Alicia in a slightly invasive way. He even caresses his breast plate in one scene. It's very subtle, but adds a note of humanity to this maniacal tyrant.

Did the costume help you find the villainy inside of yourself?

The suit gave me intense motivation in playing Doctor Doom. It was a grueling experience, hot, and uncomfortable. It covered my body and I was encased in it for many hours. It was made of a very hard plastic and often cut into my skin, almost like a constant irritation. There was something masochistic about it and I thought Doom might thrive on this. More than any emotional memory, the physical sensations of confinement and discomfort gave me a feeling of rage and frustration that seethes out in the performance. After a few hours in the suit I wanted to dominate all life and annihilate others with glee. I could make others suffer as I had. It was also the limitations of the suit and the mask that made me work to articulate as many hand gestures, finger movements, and bodily positions, so I could try to show who Doctor

Doom was and how he felt. I couldn't rely on my face, except in the beginning scenes, so the suit forced me to be as creative as possible to get across the inner life of Doctor Doom.

How did you develop the voice you used?

Doom's voice had to be commanding, dictatorial, full of bravado and wrath to match his grand style. I experimented a little with sounding Germanic/Eastern European since he hails from Latveria, which I imagine is in that part of the world. But I wanted a broad appeal and not to make him too regional, so I had to go with something closer to an educated British accent, "Mid-Atlantic" I think we used to say. This gave me permission to sound imperious and condescending, as Doom often does, and to enunciate clearly in a menacing way. My model was my hero Albert Finney in *The Dresser* playing the Shakespearean tragedian: commanding, furious, outrageous, sometimes comical, yet tinged with sorrow.

While the film is not without its faults, I think the love the cast and filmmakers had for the characters came through. What did you think the movie did well? What elements did you think were lacking?

The cast and crew gave their all to this picture. We knew it was low-budget, we knew we didn't have elaborate special effects (and really good CGI was still a few years away) but we had a lot of heart, as they say, and we were excited to be the first ones to bring these characters to the screen. The parts were well-cast. The Thing looked impressive. Sue was hot and wholesome. The movie has a wonderful comic book feel, a nice blend of sincere sci-fi drama and tongue-in-cheek in the rights parts. It's a family film with a wide appeal. It doesn't try to be super hip and cool in the modern idiom. Oley Sassone [the director] did a wonderful job maintaining the tone. Of course, we all had moments of pause. I did get a little concerned when I saw the robotic bendy-arm for Reed, and I had no idea how they were going to pull off Johnny's fire (indeed they went with full animation in the end sequence), but these were B-movie elements that a Roger Corman film would be destined to have in 1993. So I took it in stride. I saw it once with an audience and they cheered and cheered and laughed in all the right places. So this was a film for a fan base of comic book lovers for sure, and many were willing to overlook the lack of effects and go with the story of the characters, which I think is far more engaging than the later big-budget versions.

The only thing that really disappointed me was the lack of good sound work for Doom. They could never get it right. Many of the scenes that use production sound were garbled and hard to hear due to the mask. We did re-record some of my dialogue, which sounds much better in some scenes and you can tell the difference. I would have done it all, but time and money were factors I suspect. If there is ever an official release of this film, I would come back and do my dialogue over just to make it perfect.

When you found out that the film wasn't going to be released that must have been devastating.

When it became clear that the film was not going to be released, I remember feeling very strange and disappointed. More confused than devastated. We had done Comic Cons promoting it, press interviews, the whole thing. I had seen the film, it wasn't that bad, why not release it? I put the whole thing behind me pretty quickly, because actors need to move on and not get bitter about how projects turn out. It was so ironic that the film became one of the most bootlegged videos of all time. Those producers lost a lot of easy money. I acquired a legion of fans for my performance as Doom who always shake my hand at Comic Con. I remain proud of my work as the first actor to play Doctor Doom on screen, and my son grew up watching the video and imitating my voice and mad laugh as he played with his Doom action figure, and that kind of makes it all worthwhile.

It's now just another strange piece of Hollywood lore. Some day it will be released and I hope I'm around to see it. Even as a special feature on [the 2005 or 2007] *Fantastic Four* DVDs, it really deserves to be seen and enjoyed! Now we could even go back and fix some of the special effects and make it even cooler, but you have to care enough. Who cares? The fans, that's who.

Did any aspect of playing Doom transfer onto you?

I would say that playing Doctor Doom gave me a wonderful sense of liberation and entitlement. Doom certainly has plenty of entitlement. I did enjoy playing a larger-than-life character. It allowed me to stretch my muscles both emotionally and physically, push the boundaries of what is acceptable, and put my own personal touches on the role. Did Doom's madness and narcissism overtake me? Or did he just let me exercise what was already there? Some roles let you dredge up the demons, and hopefully you get stronger and more resilient. No matter. Humility is waiting in the wings. You win. You fail. You win again. The actor always feels only as good as his last performance, so the journey never ends.

How has playing Doom changed you personally?

I'm considering world domination, but in a nice way.

Rebecca Staab played Sue Storm

How were you cast?

I went in and auditioned, then had a callback a few days later. Two things I remember from the audition were seeing a drawing of the Marvel Comics' Sue Storm on the wall in the audition room, and thinking to myself, "Great! I look like her!" And the director, Oley Sassone, thanked me after the audition for "dressing the part." I had worn a tight black turtleneck and black spandex pants.

Can you talk about your process for creating the character Sue Storm?

Initially, I just looked through several different Fantastic Four comic books, getting a feel for Sue. I read the script over and over. A very important factor about Sue is that her superpower to become invisible was based on the character flaw that she was shy and insecure. Her previous weakness became her greatest strength. With that in mind, I chose to underplay Sue, keeping her a bit hesitant, and timid, until, as a Fantastic Four team member, she became more confident and outgoing.

Her relationship to the other team members was very specific, as well. She had always been madly in love with Reed, ever since she was a child, and she continued to look to him with awe and affection. Her relationship with Ben was very dear to her; he was her gentle giant. Sue's relationship with Johnny was the most comfortable, jovial, and honest.

What makes her tick?

Sue is loyal to family and friends, extremely dependable, and nurturing. Sue loved having the team together. The Fantastic Four was her absolute family.

In what ways are you like Sue?

I am very much like Sue — loyal, nurturing, the "spoke" to the wheel, making sure everyone is cared for. I am also very adventurous and athletic. I started out as a dancer and therefore I've always been proficient at sports, not afraid to take risks and to keep achieving. I'm very close to my family and friends. I am usually the "cheerleader" that keeps everyone going.

The Fantastic Four are unique because they are family. Can you talk about that dynamic?

As a tree has branches, the Fantastic Four, as a family, each have separate roles that make them strong as a team. Reed was the leader; Ben, the muscle; Sue, the glue; Johnny, the passion.

When you first put on the costume how did you feel?

Well, the feelings were mixed. Obviously, our film's budget was lower than low. When I first saw our costumes, I was disappointed. I had hoped they would look more superhero-ish, and less "homemade," but what are you going to do? So you just accept it, and give the costume as much life and power as a character can. So that's what we did. I did like that the costumes were consistent with the comic book's version, which I thought was important.

Did you ever allow yourself to feel heroic or powerful in the costume?

As much as possible.

The movie seems as if it was made with love. What did you think the film did well?

The film was made with *enormous* amounts of love. I am very proud that the film was loyal to the comic book. The script and decisions made for the production put the comic book and its established fans first. I think that that was very important. In turn, the result was a very honest and heartfelt buddy film. Our version absolutely captured the *team*, which was the essence of the Fantastic Four. Our film demonstrates the love and honor that the characters have for each other. I think it was brilliantly cast because each of actors was so similar to our characters, that the bond of love and friendship, leadership, unity, humor, and adventure are all authentic. Every time I watch it, I get a little lump in my throat, because it really is one of those feel-good films. An absolute blessing to our film was the director, Oley Sassone. He was the captain who made every day at work exciting, precise, and respectful. He understood not only filmmaking, but also script analysis, character development, storytelling, and making the most of limited resources.

Where do you think it falls short?

As far as falling short, I just think that it's disappointing that there was such a small budget allocated for a film. That was very important, but the actual film had so much potential, which unfortunately was constantly haunted by monetary and time restrictions. Given a proper budget, which would have allowed a more realistic shooting schedule, this version of the Fantastic Four could have really excelled.

It must have been greatly disappointing when the film was shelved.

The news that the project was shelved came a bit out of nowhere. We had already done several promotional appearances, and were looking forward to the opening. It's heartwarming to realize that the film has such a loyal fan base, and that it still lives on, perhaps longer as an underground cult hit than it might have if it had been released commercially.

The most disappointing realization was that there wouldn't be any sequels, as originally had been buzzing around. Since our film deals with the characters literally from the very beginning of the story, as just regular civilians who become superheroes, we didn't have much of the film to be superheroes. We were all looking forward to the possibility of shooting either sequels, a television series, or even an animated version. It really would have been great to take the story and the characters on another marvelous ride!

In some strange way, do you think that the film has garnered more attention than it might have if it did receive a proper release? Has it been a mixed blessing of sorts?

I do think the film took on a different aura once it became "invisible." Ha! Pun. The fans want the film, and went to great lengths, and watched deteriorated versions of VHS copies of VHS copies in order to see it. They seemed to want it no matter what. At comic book conventions, the remarks were always positive. The fans understood how the budget limitations sort of shortchanged what they had been hoping to see on screen, but always complimented the film on it's fidelity to the comic book, and on the bond between the characters. I think the inaccessibility of the film definitely drew more attention and fueled its fan base.

Did any aspect of Sue Storm's character transfer over to you, and vice versa?

It was definitely a thrill having the chance to play a superhero. I still think of myself as "Susan Storm." It was really great to be the first actress to play that iconic character, and it's wonderful to be a part of Marvel history.

Something I've taken away from the film, that I try to share with others, is the inspiration of turning a weakness into a strength. It's true that the two qualities are not mutually exclusive, and more closely related than most people realize.

Adrianne Palicki is Wonder Woman

DC Comics' three most important characters are also amongst the earliest superheroes created. Superman debuted in 1938, Batman in 1939, and Wonder Woman, who was created by the polymath William Moulton Marston (writing as Charles Moulton) in 1941.[104] Superman and Batman's status has been bolstered by their appearances in dozens of films and TV shows depicting their exploits, yet despite her top-tier status Wonder Woman hasn't faired nearly as well. Only a handful of actresses have played Wonder Woman, including Cathy Lee Crosby in a 1974 made-for-TV-movie that took tremendous liberties with the character, Lynda Carter in the popular television series, and Adrianne Palicki in an unaired TV pilot in 2011.[105] As a result, only the broadest strokes of her legend are widely remembered – the golden lasso, the bracelets and the invisible plane – and the rest have been largely forgotten.

Notwithstanding her celebrity, I wonder how many casual fans can recall her origin story. For the uninitiated: On remote Paradise Island, which is populated exclusively by women, an Amazonian Princess witnesses an American fighter plane crash-land in the jungle. The Princess recovers the body of its barely-alive pilot Steve Trevor and carries the wounded warrior back to the palace. Unsure of what to do with the uninvited guest, the Princess's mother Hippolyta consults the spirits of Aphrodite and Athena for guidance. Aphrodite instructs the Queen to return the pilot to America so that he can continue fighting "the forces of hate and oppression."[106] Athena similarly advises, "You must send him with your strongest and wisest Amazon – the finest of your Wonder Women – for America, the last citadel of democracy, and of equal rights for women, needs your help."[107]

In order to determine who among her people is the most worthy, the Queen decides to hold a contest. Knowing that her overprotective mother wouldn't approve of her participation, the Princess enters the competition in disguise and wins the daylong tournament. At the end of the contest, the Princess takes off her mask and reveals her true identity to her mother who reluctantly, but proudly, calls her daughter a "Wonder Woman," and gives her daughter the alias Diana, "after your godmother, the goddess of the moon," and bestows on her the now famous Wonder Woman costume.[108]

It would take another six issues before her golden lasso would make its first appearance. In *Sensation Comics #6*, Wonder Woman's mother presents the lasso to her daughter. The lasso, which compels people to follow her commands and to tell the truth, was conceived by Marston, who also invented a blood pressure test, which led directly to the invention of the polygraph. Wonder Woman believes that the lasso will be a great tool in her fight for human rights: "With this great gift I can change human character! I can make bad men good and weak women strong!"[109]

It is difficult to discuss Wonder Woman without addressing her gender and her standing as a feminist icon. Wonder Woman's identity and popularity now seem almost inseparable from gender politics. William Moulton Marston was very outspoken about his intentions. In the 1940s, he wrote a letter to comic historian and cartoonist Coulton Waugh which said: "Frankly, Wonder Woman is psychological propaganda for the new type of woman who should, I believe, rule the world . . . I have given Wonder Woman a dominant force but have kept her loving, tender, maternal, and feminine in every other way."[110] Marston was equally direct about his intentions in his 1942 essay "Women: Servants for Civilization" where he argued:

> "If you conclude, as I do, that the only hope of permanent peace and happiness for humanity on this planet is an increased expression of love, and that women are the primary carriers of this great force, one of the problems we face is to provide women with more opportunity for using their love powers. The last 6,000 years have demonstrated quite conclusively, I believe, that woman under the domination of man can increase but meagerly the world's total love supply. Our obvious goal, then, must be to devise social mecha-

nisms whereby man is brought under the love domination of woman."[111]

Thirty years later, Wonder Woman would grace the cover of the first standalone issue of Gloria Steinem's *Ms.* Magazine (July 1972) with the headline: "Wonder Woman for President." Gloria Steinem, who pays tribute to Wonder Woman by wearing bracelets on both arms, wrote:

> "The trouble is that the comic book performers of such superhuman feats—and even of only dimly competent ones – are almost always heroes. Literally. The female child is left to believe that, even when her body is a as grown-up as her spirit, she will still be in the childlike role of helping with minor tasks, appreciating men's accomplishments, and being so incompetent and passive that she can only hope some man can come to her rescue. Of course, rescue and protection are comforting, even exhilarating experiences that should be and often are shared by men and boys. Even in comic books, the hero is frequently called on to protect his own kind in addition to helpless women. But dependency and zero accomplishments get very dull as a steady diet. The only option for a girl reader is to identify with the male characters—pretty difficult, even in the androgynous years of childhood. If she can' do that, she faces limited prospects: An 'ideal' life of sitting around like a Technicolor [sic] clothes horse, getting into jams with villains and saying things like 'Oh, Superman! I'll always be grateful to you,' even as her hero goes off to bigger and better adventures."[112]

During *Wonder Woman*'s three season run as a TV series (1975-1979), its star Lynda Carter's mousy alter ego Diana Prince spun around and transformed herself into the unstoppable Wonder Woman. As her theme song boasted, the self-confident Wonder Woman could: "Make a hawk a dove/Stop a war with love/Make a liar tell the truth."[113]

Carter was so successful at playing the hero that since the 1970s no other actress has played the character in a live-action movie or TV series. That changed when NBC hired David E. Kelley (who created *Ally McBeal*, *The Practice*, *Boston Public*, and *Boston Legal*) to create a new Wonder Woman series. In 2011, Kelley wrote a script for the pilot, which was directed by Jeffrey Reiner (*Friday Night Lights*).

Kelley's Wonder Woman is very different from Lynda Carter's. For starters, Palicki, who very effectively played an outwardly tough but inwardly tender high school student in *Friday Night Lights*, essentially plays three different characters in the unaired pilot. As Wonder Woman, she fights crime. Publicly she is Diana Themyscira, the head of the large corporation Themyscira Industries, whose profits fund Wonder Woman's war on crime; and as Diana Prince, her secret identity, she is seeking to "carve out any semblance of a normal life." As Diana Prince she would conceal her inner power so as to not threaten a series of unimpressive male suitors.

Although Christian Bale and Christopher Nolan explored the notion that *both* Batman and Bruce Wayne's callow playboy were false identities, the notion of a *triple* identity is largely unexplored territory in the superhero lore. As Wonder Woman's trusted advisor (played by Cary Elwes in the unaired pilot) points out, "Having an alter-ego is the equivalent of self-induced schizophrenia."

Lynda Carter once described her Wonder Woman as a "promoter of peace" and a woman who demonstrates "modesty" regarding her power and her sexuality. Palicki's Wonder Woman champions the same tenets but takes a strikingly different approach. Her Wonder Woman is less interested in upholding the rules of law than she is in dispensing her own brand of rough justice. Over the protests of the police she forcibly takes a suspect's blood sample without a warrant or his consent. In another scene she beats information out of a suspect who is convalescing in the hospital.

In the pilot and presumably in future episodes Wonder Woman's aggressive methods come under critical scrutiny. One outraged character protests that what Wonder Woman did was "criminal," and continues, "At what point, do we say, 'Enough?' This woman, she knocks down doors without warrants, she wire taps, that lasso? You just can't go above the law. I don't remember anything in the United States Constitution, which says that a woman in a costume is exempt from the Bill of Rights. Even if her costume is red, white, and blue." Another character complains that she "Abu Ghraibs her quarry," a reference to the illegal interrogation methods, which included torture, used by American military personnel and other agents in the Iraq war.

David E. Kelley retained the bracelets, which deflect bullets, and the golden lasso, though he abandoned the invisible jet and replaced it with a small but visible one-person aircraft. But it wasn't the reimagined jet that caused a stir; it was Wonder Woman's wardrobe.

Kelley and his team redesigned Wonder Woman's famously bare outfit. Rather than sticking exclusively with Carter's short shorts, Palicki's Wonder Woman wears a costume with pants. Though the outfit was formfitting, it showed a lot less skin than Carter's costume, which was faithful to the character's attire in the comics.

News outlets as diverse as the *Hollywood Reporter*, London's *Daily Mail*, *New York Magazine's Vulture*, and AOL News all weighed in on the modifications. The negative reactions were so widespread and intense that DC Comics was forced to respond. Seeking to mollify the fans, a spokesperson for DC issued a statement: "All of the classic symbols - patriotic (stars, eagle) and heroic (lasso, bracelets) - are ever present."[114] Lynda Carter was supportive of the new series and the new costume. Carter told *The Hollywood Reporter*, "What's not to like? Adrianne looks gorgeous . . . ."[115] Although for much of the pilot, Palicki wears the long pants, in the final showdown against a gang of twenty goons, Wonder Woman kicks butt in her famous short shorts.

Overlooked in the media storm was the fact that Palicki's costume was very similar to the new look for Wonder Woman in the comics, which had been established during the previous year. However, the character's new look (though also controversial) never penetrated the zeitgeist. When novelist Jodi Picoult, who penned the five-part series *Wonder Woman: Love and Murder*, wanted to change the look of the character she, was met with similar resistance. In an article for *Playboy*, she wrote:

"When DC Comics approached me in 2006 to write several issues of the *Wonder Woman* comic book, my first order of business was to get that poor girl a functional outfit. After all, any woman who is even marginally as well-endowed as Wonder Woman knows you can't fight crime – much less go about your more mundane daily activities – while you're worried about your top falling down. I had visions of her off-panel, tugging up that glittery spandex corset. *Could we just add some straps to her bustier?* I asked and I was politely told that the costume had been around for sixty-odd years for good reason." [116]

After the first episode was shot, edited, and temporary special effects were added, NBC executives screened the pilot and then deliberated. Palicki, David E. Kelly, the creative team, and Wonder Woman fans anxiously waited as NBC decided the fate of the series.

It was during this period that Lynda Carter once again came forward to demonstrate her support. In a promotional appearance at Barnes & Noble that I attended, Carter said, "I think David Kelly, who created *Alley McBeal,* is a great writer. I think the young actress who's been cast as Wonder Woman is beautiful. I really want the series to succeed. I do want the story to be told to my daughter's children. I want Wonder Woman to continue. She is a great role model and it's a great story. [A new version] doesn't take anything away from me. I did the first one and it will always be there." After decades of being the only ambassador for the character, Carter felt it was time to give another actress a shot. She told the *New York Times,* "I really do think that the baton needs to be passed.[117]

Neither Carter nor Palicki would get their wish. NBC decided not to go forward with the series. In talking to *The Hollywood Reporter,* David E. Kelly (who is married to Catwoman/Michelle Pfeiffer) reflected on his *Wonder Woman* pilot:

"I still believe it's viable for a television series. I think it's ripe to do it. We made mistakes with ours. My only regret is we were never given a chance to correct them. We had

Adrianne Palicki as Wonder Woman. © NBC/Warner Bros.

a lot that was right about it and a great cast. In time, we could have fixed what we had done wrong, we just didn't get that chance. All of my series have been a work in progress to a certain extent where you figure them out by episodes three, four or five. This one actually gelled sooner than any that I have had in the past. We would have gotten there and I wish we were afforded a little more time. I do believe in the potential of the series and I wish them well with it. I think it could be a great success . . . Just learning the storytelling - - the genre was very different for me and I had a lot to learn; my learning curve probably would have gotten better. I'm sad we didn't get to do it . . . ."[118]

Eventually another version of Wonder Woman will be made. It's important for our daughters, and our sons, to see powerful women who are every bit as formidable as their male counterparts. As Jodi Picoult writes: "As long as little girls dress up in those red boots and that tiara for Halloween, as long as we all hope for good to triumph over evil, there will always be a place for Wonder Woman. Whether you admire her because she can kick through a brick wall without messing up her hair, or because she can (literally) fly circles around the guys, she represents what we all know: Absolutely nothing can stand in the way of a strong woman."[119] Adrianne Palicki, who plays superheroine Mockingbird (AKA Bobbi Morse) on Marvel's *Agents of S.H.I.E.L.D.*, has not previously said much publicly about her experience playing Wonder Woman.

THE INTERVIEW

Can you talk about your experience playing Wonder Woman?

Playing Wonder Woman was incredibly nerve-wracking. She was one of my biggest heroes growing up, and I knew they were very big shoes to fill. Once I accepted that not everyone was going to like what I did with her, I was able to relax and make her my own.

No one had played a live action version of Wonder Woman since Lynda Carter. That must have been intimidating.

Lynda Carter is a huge icon, and many people identify the character with her portrayal. I could never copy what she did, nor would I want to. You have to leave well enough alone. She was brilliant! The version I played was much more hardened to the world. She was lonely and had a bit of sadness about her.

Lynda Carter's Wonder Woman is a gentle ambassador of peace. Your Wonder Woman is very different. More like a hawk than a dove.

I wanted to make her strong, powerful and warrior-like. There were definitely some tongue-in-cheek moments, but for the most part she was very tough and not quite as empathetic as Wonder Woman in the earlier comics. I think, in our pilot, she fights for peace and justice, because she feels like she has these gifts, so she must. She may not really want that life for herself. She fights because it also brings her closer to home.

What motivated your Wonder Woman?

I definitely think justice is Wonder Woman's key motivation. She sees things in black and white, good and bad.

How are you like her?

I connect with some of the inner strength that Wonder Woman has, but I'm personally much more of a gray type of person, sometimes empathetic to a fault. In this version she has some of that, but in the end, justice will always prevail.

Did wearing the costume help you get into character?

The costume! Oh, the costume, the costume, the costume! So, much talk and speculation and judgment about the costume! It was pretty crazy to see. As a comic book fan myself, getting to wear that thing, let alone getting paid to wear that thing, was one of the most memorable, surreal times in my life. My inner child was dancing! When I put on that costume, I was able to fully immerse and lose myself in the character.

What did the show use from the Wonder Woman comics and what did it discard?

The difference between the Wonder Woman in the comic and the one in the show was that the world knows Diana Themyscira not only as the head of a multi-million dollar corporation, but also as Wonder Woman herself. The world knows she runs this corporation, mainly selling her own merchandise, to fund her extracurricular activities. That is, saving people. Diana Prince, however, is the alter ego that allows her to lead a somewhat "normal" life.

Your show would also have been a critique of the tendency to sexualize female superheroes. In the pilot, she takes a toy maker to task for their depiction of Wonder Woman.

I was very happy that David wanted to bring up the sexualization of female superheroes in the show. In the pilot, there's a Barbie made in Wonder Woman's likeness. It's pretty close, except for the "ginormous" breasts on the doll. Diana pretty much goes "apeshit" on the male employee that created it. It's a funny moment, at the same time, poignant. It's pretty hard not to sexualize female superheroes when they're wearing only spandex, and their upper half is spilling out of their shirt!

Looking back, what are your thoughts about the pilot?

Looking back, getting to play Wonder Woman, if even for a second, truly was one of the best moments of my life! She, Supergirl, and my brother's encouragement, made me the comic book fan I am today. My brother is a comic book writer. He and I are actually writing a comic together now, with a kick-ass female hero, of course!

PART SEVEN:
NOT ALL HEROES ARE SUPER

Leonard Nimoy is Spock

Leonard Nimoy is Spock.

Leonard Nimoy is not Spock.

Which statement is accurate? Based on the titles of his two memoirs, one might assume that even he doesn't know the correct answer. In 1975, Nimoy wrote the book, *I Am Not Spock*. Twenty years later, in the 1995 follow-up *I Am Spock*, Nimoy seemed to have changed his mind.

The truth of the matter is that the underlying message of both books is essentially the same. In both tomes Nimoy pleads, kids with, and cajoles his readers his readers to understand that while he admires the fictional Mr. Spock, that is just one of many parts that he has enjoyed playing. His point has frequently been misconstrued by those who are fixated on the book's title.

When *I Am Not Spock* was published, even much of the press focused primarily on the title of the book, paid scant attention to its content, and failed to convey Nimoy's reasonable thoughts. The result was that fans who hadn't yet read the book erroneously assumed that Nimoy was rejecting his association with the character, with *Star Trek* and, by extension, the fans themselves. In *I Am Spock*, Nimoy concedes that: "I made an enormous mistake in choosing the title for the book."[120]

Both books include conversations between Nimoy and Spock. In *I Am Not Spock*, Nimoy writes:

NIMOY:

Spock . . . this competition between us is silly.

SPOCK:

I am not aware that one exists.

NIMOY:

Well, it does. And it's silly. Don't forget that I'm real, and you're only a fictitious character.

SPOCK:

Are you sure?[121]

In the same book, Nimoy reflects, "I am not Spock. Then why does my head turn in response to a stranger on the street who calls out that name? But if I'm not, who is? And if I'm not Spock, then who am I?"[122]

In both books, Nimoy tries to answer that existential question, "Who am I?" The uncertainty is also at the heart of the mysterious alchemy between a talented actor and a cherished character. Where does one end and the other begin?

In his polemic *I Am Spock*, Nimoy ultimately concludes that on some level he and Spock are one and that their association has allowed them both, as the Vulcan salutation goes, to "Live long and prosper."[123]

Leonard Nimoy has played his signature character many times. He played Spock on TV in seventy-nine episodes of Gene Roddenberry's *Star Trek* (1966-1969); in twenty-two episodes of the animated series *Star Trek* (1973-1974), which reunited most of the original cast including William Shatner as James Kirk and DeForest Kelley as Dr. McCoy, and the most preeminent writers of the original series; and in two highly-rated episodes of *Star Trek: The Next Generation* (1991), where Spock helps forge an uneasy alliance between the Vulcans and the Romulans, who despite their shared lineage are warring tribes.

In movies, Nimoy reprised his role of the half-human, half Vulcan in *Star Trek: The Motion Picture* (1979); in *Star Trek: The Wrath of Kahn* (1982); in *Star Trek III: The Search for Spock* (1984), which he directed; in *Star Trek IV: The Voyage Home* (1986), which he directed; in *Star Trek V: The Final Frontier* (1989); and in *Star Trek VI; The Undiscovered Country* (1991).

He also played Spock in *Star Trek* (2009), in which Zachary Quinto plays a younger version Spock, who was born in a different timeline but encounters his older self as a result of a quirk in time travel, and again in a cameo in *Star Trek Into Darkness* (2013), where he gives Quinto's Spock insight into defeating an enemy.

Nimoy has also provided the voice of a Spock in the video games *Star Trek: Anniversary Enhanced* (1992), *Star Trek: Judgment Rites* (1993), and *Star Trek Prime* (2012), and as the Spock action figure in two dream sequences in the fanboy-friendly sitcom *The Big Bang Theory* (2012).

Besides directing two *Star Trek* movies the actor turned director also helmed several features films, including the hit comedy *Three Men and a Baby* (1987) with Ted Danson, and the drama *The Good Mother* (1988) with Liam Neeson, Diane Keaton and Jason Robards.

Unfortunately, aside from an occasional cameo appearance and voice-over work, Nimoy has retired from acting and directing. These days he seems to be focused on expressing himself through other means – including his photography. He displays and sells his work through R. Michelson Galleries.[124] His work is diverse and provocative, including *The Full Body Project*, photographs of plus-sized women in the nude, and *Secret Selves*, in which his subjects were encouraged to reveal their "alternate identities," display a part of their personality that is usually hidden from the world.[125] As I discovered during our conversation, playing Spock allowed Nimoy to reveal an aspect of his secret self.

Getting back to the original question about which title is more accurate – *I Am Not Spock* or *I Am Spock* – I have concluded, both paradoxically and logically, that both titles are equally accurate.

THE INTERVIEW

How did you create the character of Spock?

The essential ingredient was that the character was a half human, half Vulcan. Therefore, he had an internal combat between his emotional and logical selves. The logic of the Vulcans warring with the emotions of the Humans. That was the basis of the character.

How did putting on the uniform and the ears inform how you played him?

It was a society where Spock could find a home. He was not at home on Vulcan where he was half human or on Earth where he was half Vulcan. He found a home in Starfleet wearing that uniform.

How do your costume and makeup inform the role?

Leonard Nimoy as Spock. © Paramount Television

The intention of the look is to remind the audience constantly that he was not a human. That he is a person from another planet. That he is an alien.

Would you say that Kirk, McCoy and Spock represent the id, the ego and the superego?

It's a bit too Freudian for me. There is a triumvirate here. The Spock and the McCoy characters are opposite poles of an approach to an issue. Those two collaborate to bring an idea, an attitude, or an insight to Kirk who can make a decision somewhere along the spectrum of how he wants to function.

Does Spock owe any debt to Sherlock Holmes? Both characters are very logical and keep their emotions in check.

That's something you'd have to ask the writers about. I wasn't thinking in those terms when I was playing the character.

He is a character who is without fear or judgment of the unknown.

For Spock it is all about curiosity.

Yes.

"What is it? What is it?" was Spock's ongoing question.

I wasn't intending to ask you this next question. Something about the way you are talking about Spock made me think of it. Would you say you love this character? Do you love Spock?

It's a very subjective term isn't it?

Do you love him on any level?

[Laughing] That's a very funny question.

How so?

I would think that if I said yes it would seem narcissistic, wouldn't it?

I wouldn't think so.

[Laughing] I am very pleased to be identified with the character.

How has playing Spock changed you as a person?

I am much more rational than I was when I took on the job.

Where do you connect and differ emotionally?

I was much more emotionally oriented as an individual and as an actor. I had to refine my own responses to play the character and therefore I took on some of the aspects of the character. The character has had a very profound impact on my life. I'm not just talking about celebrity or opportunity or any of that. I am talking about my internal life, which has changed as a result of the character.

That statement is one of the central ideas behind this book.

[Laughing] You got it. You got it.

Could you elaborate please?

Put that in caps and make it big. You got it!

What's it like to be at the center of this *Star Trek* storm, to be the stone that caused the ripple in the water?

Are you suggesting that is me or us? What did you have in mind?

You, William Shatner, DeForest Kelly, and to a certain other extent the other four original cast members.

I can't speak for all the actors. I set out to make a contribution in hopes that people would be entertained and enlightened, and that life on this planet might somehow be improved by the work that was being done. I had a very altruistic attitude about what I was hoping to be a part of. I think *Star Trek* and Spock have had a very profound affect on a lot of people and I'm very proud of that.

What would you say is the worst part about being associated with the character?

I don't think there is a worst. There have been times that I have had some frustration – and I'm talking thirty years ago – where I was highly identified with *Star Trek* and Spock – and I was trying to get some work because there was no *Star Trek* production taking place. So, that was frustrating, but that was way in the past. I have no complaints.

How did you get from frustration to no complaints?

In 1979 we made another movie.

So, the only frustration was not being able to channel that energy?

Exactly. There was a lot of *Star Trek* interest but no *Star Trek* product.

They used to advertise "Sean Connery *is* James Bond".

Right.

Even though fans know Connery is an actor playing a role, on some level they want Connery to actually be Bond. Do you get that feeling from fans?

There is a new film in which another actor is playing Spock [in his early years]. People are going to have to come to terms with that. I certainly hope they will. Zachary Quinto is a very, very talent young man and I think he is doing a brilliant job. Now we're going to have to be thinking in terms of: "Zachary Quinto *is* Spock."

What ideas about the character did you share with Zachary Quinto?

Zachary did his homework. He watched *Star Trek* episodes, he watched *Star Trek* films, and he had a script to work with. We had some very good and useful conversations. I think he's going to come off very well in this film.

In the upcoming movie, you play Spock in his later years. You thought you had retired the character in 1991. How difficult was it for you to step back into the role after an eighteen-year separation from the character?

It's complicated. I wouldn't say it was difficult. It was complicated. My spock in [the Star Trek reboot] is somewhat different. He has a different role in the story than I had played in previous performances. The function of Spock is different. The challenges are those that any actor takes on when he reads a script and says, "I've got to go to work and do a performance in this character." Nothing extraordinary. A lot of nostalgia involved in coming back to a character after so many years. Some emotional adjustment to get back to find a way back into the character. To find a way to relate to all the young actors playing all the younger characters – Scotty and Kirk and so forth.

You know that sometimes when you hear a song on the radio and it takes you back to another time in your life?

Yeah.

Similarly, you put on the costume and are asked to go back emotionally to who you were many years ago when you first played him. That must have been a tricky emotional task to navigate.

It's an intriguing question. I can't elaborate too much without writing a book about it. I can tell you it was very moving, challenging, and finally very rewarding.

Why do you think we are so fascinated by these larger than life characters?

Look. You're talking about – what I consider to be a work of art. If that sounds pretentious so be it. A work of art is supposed to make us think about our secret selves. And I think *Star Trek* does that. Spock does that.

If you knew then what you know now you would still do it, wouldn't you?

No question.

Do you know what Spock's legacy is?

That's for you to decide. You are the audience. I do the work; you experience the result.

With the exception of _Star Trek_ and a few cameos, you've retired from acting and have concentrated on photography. In _The Hand Series_, you combine your love of photography with your signature character. In two of your photos, you play with the iconography of Spock's greeting. You took the familiar Vulcan salute and created a new idea. Were the hands in the photos your hands?

Yes.

It looks like a self-portrait.

Those images are a treatment of a sign. They are a treatment of an iconic image. Again, they are works of art – not necessarily explainable. Why did I photograph them a certain way? Why did I print them a certain way? Why did the artist use red here and yellow there? Why did he chop of the person's head in a portrait? Why did he have the person facing profile as opposed to facing the camera or the viewer? These are all questions that don't have answers. These are all artistic choices. Why paint in the abstract? Why not show us real things? Why paint minimally? Why not put everything on the canvas? Why use a brown frame instead of a black frame? These are all subjective choices.

There are so many action figures of your character, not just as Spock at one particular age but through his/your entire life. What's your take on the physical interpretation of your character?

You know this has been going on for over forty years. I think it's time that I put it in its proper place – which has to do with merchandising and celebrity. I don't dwell on it. I'm usually sent these things to look at them for execution of the work. Do I think it's successful? Do I think it needs some help? Is it ok? Do I find it offensive in some way? Does it need to go back to the artist to be worked on in some way?

But it's all part of the business, isn't it? It's all about a way for the studio or the merchandising company to create some commerce based on the fact that there is a celebrity involved. That's true of any celebrity. Whether it's a photograph or someone's cast-off clothes or furniture. It's all a part of the business. I keep it in its proper perspective, or try to.

When I compare Spock to many of the other characters (and actors) I'm speaking to, it strikes me that many of them are noted for their actions and their physical prowess, whereas Spock is noted for his intellect.

Think about this. Spock is all about his hands.

That is one of my questions.

Spock is all about his hands.

His hands are for greeting, mating rituals, and communicating. When did you make that discovery?

A long time ago.

Is there more for you to discover about Spock?

I'll find out if they ask me to perform it again.

In his book, *Up Till Now*, William Shatner talks about his being identified with Kirk. It's not about being typecast -- "branded" was the word he used. Do you relate to that notion?

Sure.

In what way?

I think it's absolutely true. There are certain cases where an actor plays a character who becomes indelible and people will always associate that actor with that character. Clark Gable in *Gone With The Wind*. [Imitating Gable] "Frankly my dear, I don't give a damn." These are iconic moments. Humphrey Bogart in *Casablanca*. You can go down the list. There are certain actors who are identified with that moment. It's indelible. It's indelible.

Actors might go on to play other characters and have a full career playing all kinds of assorted characters. But very often there's just one character that an actor is identified with and audiences will never forget.

That's not necessarily a negative thing. I think it can sometimes simply be about the delight an audience feels.

I don't think it's a negative thing.

I know the press always writes about "typecasting" and . . .

Typecasting doesn't bother me. I've never complained about typecasting. Typecasting means people know how to use you. The same way people know how to use ketchup. That's why people buy ketchup; because they know how to use it. [Laughs] I have no complaints about typecasting. It means that people know how to use you. If you want to break the type you work at it. Bill Shatner has done it. He's gone from playing leading men to playing characters, and he's doing it extremely well. He's done it very successfully.

If I were to speak to Shatner, what should I ask him?

Ask him when is he going to find something to do with his life. That's what I always ask him. "When are you going to find something to do for God's sake? I think on Sunday afternoon between three and four you don't have a job."

Who would win in a fight: Spock vs. Kirk?

Oh, please. [Laughs] No contest. No contest.

George Lazenby is James Bond

James Bond aficionados often cite George Lazenby's solo outing as the secret agent in *On Her Majesty's Secret Service* (1969) as the most underrated film in the long-running series. In his seminal book, *The James Bond Bedside Companion*, Raymond Benson, Bond scholar turned nine-time Bond novelist[126], wrote that the film is an "artistic triumph" and that Lazenby's "performance is the most honest and sincere of any of the actors who have played Bond."[127] Steven Soderbergh, the Oscar-winning director, wrote, "Lazenby has a vulnerability that Connery never had."[128]

On Her Majesty's Secret Service [OHMSS] is the film in which Bond, an inveterate womanizer, defies audience expectations by falling in love with and marrying Teresa "Tracy" Draco, the daughter of the head of a crime cartel. Because Bond must remain a perpetual bachelor, their relationship is doomed. In the end, Bond sees his new bride gunned down by an old enemy. In his book *The Man With The Golden Touch*, Sinclair Mckay observes that the "emotional stakes are raised very much higher than they are in any other Bond movie save 2006's *Casino Royale*." [129]

OHMSS concludes with a deeply shaken and stirred Bond cradling his wife's lifeless body, holding back the tears, and trying to convince himself that "It's all right. It's quite all right, really. She's having a rest. We'll be going on soon. There's no hurry, you see. We have all the time in the world."

Lazenby effectively strips down Bond's macho exterior, revealing a caring, sensitive soul inside, and he reminds viewers that 007 is not only a ruthless spy. McKay argues, "What everyone tends to forget now is that the literary Bond was not some form of callous automaton; very from it. In the opening chapter of *OHMSS*, Bond even has a flashback to childhood seaside holidays. This is the fledgling Bond that we see portrayed by George Lazenby – a man who can outfight anyone, but whose heart is bigger and more open than anyone might think." Lazenby's understated performance is all the more remarkable when you consider that prior to being cast as the world's most famous spy, Lazenby was a model, who had no formal training or acting experience.

Besides anchoring one of the best Bond films, and despite the film's disappointing box office performance, Lazenby contributed something of great importance to the Bond franchise in particular, and by extension, to superhero films generally: Lazenby's performance proved that another actor could take over a lead role that had become closely associated with another actor. Even though many enthusiasts of the Bond movies enjoyed identifying Connery with Bond, Lazenby's performance demonstrated that if a character is complex enough, the part doesn't belong to any individual actor.

In other words, despite Connery's blistering screen presence, the star of the 007 films was really Bond, not Connery. The character is bigger than any individual performer. As Albert R. "Cubby" Broccoli, the Italian immigrant who along with Harry Saltzman co-produced all of the official Bond films until his death in 1996, explained in his autobiography, "There was some brief media hysteria predicting that Connery's abdication would force the 007 empire into oblivion. It didn't happen, because of one fundamental truth: Jack Bond 007 is the real star. It is always one notch bigger than the actor who plays him. It is like a space station – it stays in orbit whichever hero is up there at any given time."[130]

Lazenby's performance paved the way not only for Roger Moore, Timothy Dalton, Pierce Brosnan, and Daniel Craig, it also provided the precedent for Val Kilmer, George Clooney, and Christian Bale to follow Michael Keaton as the Dark Knight, and for Dean Cain, Brandon Routh, and Henry Cavill to succeed Christopher Reeve as the Man of Steel.

To celebrate the release of Roger Moore's autobiography, *My Word is My Bond*, *The New York Times* organized an event at which the paper's film critic A. O. Scott interviewed the seventime Bond. During the interview, Moore stopped the proceedings and informed the audience that fellow Bond actor, George Lazenby, was seated among us. Lazenby stood up, and the packed crowd greeted him with warm applause. We were all delighted by the rare opportunity to be in the presence of two different

George Lazenby on the set of On Her Majesty's Secret Service (1969).
© Eon Productions.

Bonds. The following day, the normally reticent Lazenby agreed to do this interview with me.

THE INTERVIEW

What do you think motivates James Bond?

Bond is the personification of male desire. His drive to be the best. To be the winner. To accomplish whatever he sets out to do. He represents the male ego.

What is your view of his character?

James Bond is a villain, and a murderous one. He deals with villains and he has to outsmart them. So, he has the villain's essence in his make-up. He'd be a pretty good villain himself. He knows how to out-connive, out-spy, out-charm, out-kill. The guy basically gets away with murder.

Did you take anything from Ian Fleming's novels to inform your performance?

I did. The end scene in particular. When I read the novel originally, it made me cry. I had the book on my lap and I read it right before I did the scene. I wasn't an actor before the film started but [during the making of *OHMSS*] I had nine months of on-camera training. [Laughs] By the time we shot that scene, I was really starting to get into it.

But whatever insecurities you had as an actor didn't appear in the film. Your Bond is above all confident.

I did the best I could. I felt that I had to copy Sean Connery in a sense. Connery could just be himself and let his personality emerge. Because I was following in his footsteps, I felt that had to copy Connery's energy. I was at a bit of a disadvantage because it's much stronger when you're being yourself. Whoever first plays the character has the advantage of establishing the energy of the character.

Can you think of a specific example of that?

Normally, I swagger when I walk. I'm not as precise in my speech. Of course, I'm Austrian and I don't normally speak with an English accent. But to evoke Connery, I had to change my walk, my speech, and my attitude. I'm certainly not always this charming.

Your performance doesn't come across as a Connery clone. Did you remember a time when you said, "I'm going to break away from Connery's interpretation and be my own Bond"?

Yes, when I cried at the end. The director said, "James Bond doesn't cry." I had full on tears on the first take. During the second take, I didn't cry but I kept the emotion."

I don't think Connery's Bond would have cried in that circumstance.

No, he wouldn't.

George Lazenby as James Bond. © Eon Productions

What made that scene especially effective is how Bond for the first time in the series, opens up.

Ian Fleming did it for me. He gave me that emotion out of the book.

What do you like about Bond?

It depends on the situation. If I'm in a casino, I love to win. If I'm in a fight, I love to win. If I don't like somebody, I'd love to shoot him. [Laughing] You know what I mean? He can do all these things that I can't. Then I have the other side of myself, which is the peaceful side and I don't like anything about Bond. I just want to be quiet. Look into my own feelings and thoughts. Bond is not into that. Bond isn't into mediation, for example. I am.

Bond is not an introspective character.

No, he's not. Bond's just a charmer and he's very efficient at what he does. He gets away with a lot of bad behavior because he's the best at what he does. You wouldn't fire him no matter what trouble he gets himself into. In that way, he's like a used car salesman, which I was.

What do you think motivates your Bond more, his job or his self-gratification?

I think for Bond they go together. You can't make him do something that he doesn't want to do. He enjoys what he does. Otherwise he wouldn't feel so confident.

Where do your personalities most closely intersect?

That goes back to the male ego. That's what's attractive. He lives the life most of us would love to live.

Did you ever allow yourself to feel the power of playing Bond?

That comes naturally. Everyone started to call me "sir," whereas before I was Bond they called me "asshole." [Chuckles] It changes your persona. It's a big image to uphold, and I didn't handle it very well.

What is the biggest perk and downside of having been Bond?

To me the downside was being recognized when you don't want to be. The biggest perk was getting tables in restaurants. When you go into restaurants, they change tables around for you and you get the table you want. It's a different life altogether. But when I stopped playing Bond that changed a bit. I remember when it was announced that I was not going to be playing Bond anymore they took my photo down from a nightclub I used to go to. There was a restaurant that I used to go to and in the restaurant there was a sign that read "George Lazenby is a Premium Bond," but then that was taken out, too. I thought, *Oh, being James Bond* does *mean something*.

How did women respond to your Bond persona? Did they respond to you as James Bond?

Yes. After playing the part, I met a different class of women. Many of them were – what should I say – were "society climbers." Prior to doing the part, I spent more time with the average girl on the street. I found the average girl on the street to be much funnier, more real, sexier, and I missed them. That's why you'd see me going out with a girl on the street rather than an actress I was working with. I still find that.

How has playing this part affected your personally?

I lost myself. At first it took me away from the self that I thought I knew – but didn't. It made me into a new self, which I didn't know either. I was just playing another character in life. Now I'm beginning to understand life and I'm studying my own personality. I know that I am not who I think I am.

Who have you become?

I think I am a very fortunate human being who is a lot happier than I used to be. Now I'm happier knowing that there is something greater than me inside me.

One last question. Who would win in a fight, your Bond or Sean Connery's?

Sean's too old to fight me today. [Smiles] If we were both eighteen years old, you'd have to toss a coin.

Roger Moore is James Bond

Talking to Roger Moore when he's wearing a tuxedo is like trying to hold a conversation with Leonard Nimoy while he's wearing
Spock ears. Your rational mind knows you're talking with an actor
but your fan instinct can almost trick you into thinking that you're
talking to the real James Bond.

Moore and I met at a gala diner where he was invited to talk
about his work for UNICEF, the charity that provides aid to needy
children. Moore became a Goodwill Ambassador for UNICEF at
the suggestion of Audrey Hepburn, and since 1991 he has traveled
the world meeting ill and impoverished children and raising both
money and awareness for the organization.

At the gala, diners listened politely as Moore spoke about his
ties to the charity. However, there were many others who, like me,
were there less to see and admire Roger Moore the philanthropist than to rub shoulders with James Bond. After his speech,
the moderator opened the floor to questions. Moore responded
to all of them knowledgeably and passionately, but it wasn't until
I asked Moore about his work as the super spy did the gathering
turn festive. Moore knew his audience wanted him to acknowledge his on-screen counterpart, and he did not disappoint.

Prompted by my question, Moore self-effacingly explained
(probably apocryphally) how he was cast in the role that earned
him international stardom. "Harry Saltzman and Cubby Broccoli, the producers, and I used to gamble. They owed me a lot of
money. They thought it would be cheaper to put me in a movie."

Moore talked about taking over the role of Bond from Connery.
He said, "People would ask, 'Aren't you nervous about taking over
for Sean Connery?' And I'd respond, 'No, not really. There have
been four thousand actors who have played Hamlet, and this certainly ain't Hamlet.' There's not much to say in the role apart
from, 'My name is Bond.'"

It could be argued that Connery was so successful and beloved
as Bond that only an actor of great confidence could assume the
mantle. Moore's bravado and fearlessness are not unlike Bond's.

Furthermore, Roger Moore is suave, erudite, and witty, words that have been used to describe James Bond himself.

Later on, Moore admitted to having a few trepidations in taking over the part that Connery seemed to define indelibly. "I did get nervous when I was on my way to London for the first screening of *Live and Let Die*. I felt like I was in a delivery room waiting to have a baby. The baby's going to come out and that's it! There's nothing you could do about it."

Moore's fear about taking over for Connery, at least the one that he'd admit to, manifested itself in a most unlikely way - in Bond's drink of choice. Fearing that he could not order a "martini, shaken not stirred" without a Scottish burr, Moore's Bond goes without his preferred beverage. "I never ever said that in any of my Bond movies. But every waiter, every barman in the world knew that I wanted a martini shaken, not stirred."

During the course of discussing how he prepared for the role, Moore singled out a thought that initially troubled him. "How I approached Bond was I asked myself, *What sort of spy is he? Everybody knows him!*" Moore's point was the absurdity of Bond being a world-famous "secret" agent. If an operative is to be effective at his job, his true identity must remain hidden. Moore finally decided that Bond's audience had long ago suspended its disbelief about matters of this kind.

While Moore is demure about his popularity as Bond, he still enjoys the association. In an article for *The London Times*, Moore recently wrote, "I am an aficionado of James Bond – both the books and the films – and of course have a vested interest in the franchise. But more than that, I have a vested interest in the character. I feel protective towards him."[131]

After initial apprehension, the public embraced Roger Moore's interpretation of James Bond; his Bond was so popular that he played the part in seven consecutive movies. Moore's Bond was very different from Connery's. Connery was lethal, unkind, cruel, and he introduced the world to Bond's sadistic tendencies. During the 1960s, Connery seemed to be the only possible Bond (and for many, including former and current Bonds, Moore, Pierce Brosnan, and Daniel Craig, he will always be the gold standard).

In the 1970s and 1980s, Moore's Bond radically redefined the part. Some fans argued that Moore's interpretation was more faithful than Connery's to Fleming's original vision of the character. Moore, like Bond, was upper class whereas Connery (who once made a living as a milkman) was working class. (Though Bond's social class matters little to Americans, it is integral to England's understanding of and pride in the character.) Moore told me that he believed Bond did not like killing; and he added that his interpretation of Bond as a reluctant assassin was the insight that proved to be the linchpin of his approach to the part.

On the surface, suggesting that the world's most lethal spy would actually loathe killing is a little like arguing that the world's best chef hates eating. In Bond's world, killing is simply an essential part of the job description. Secretaries type, racecar drivers drive, and secret agents kill; they even have a government-issued license to do so. (Where do they keep that license anyway? In their wallets between their library and Costco cards?)

While the Double-O prefix is thought of as an exotic indicator of a spy's myriad arsenal of skills and knowledge spycraft, agents are automatically given the status after killing two targets. That's all. Nothing more meaningful than that. These days, two kills hardly seem very impressive. Matt Damon's Jason Bourne can kill two thugs with a rolled up magazine before breakfast. Moore's Bond killed while holding one hand on his Walther PPK and the other over his nose.

Connery on the other hand looked like he enjoyed killing. In his interview for this book, three-time Bond screenwriter Tom Mankiewicz described the differences between Connery's Bond and Moore's. "The difference is if you have Sean at a nightclub table with a beautiful girl opposite, he can either lean across the table and kiss her or he can take his steak knife and, under the table, stick it in her gut. He could then say, 'Excuse me, waiter. I have nothing to eat my meat with.' The audience will accept him doing either one. Roger could kiss the girl, but if he tries the knife thing, he'd look nasty. Roger looks like a nice guy. Sean looks like a bastard. Meaning, there's a twinkle in Sean's eye. There's violence in Sean's eye, and there isn't in Roger's." Mankiewicz didn't intend his observation of Moore as a criticism; it was merely as a statement of fact.

Mankiewicz's thoughts are echoed by Moore in his article for *The London Times*, "How did I differ from Sean? Being a coward, I hated guns and would far rather have tried to disarm an opponent with a flippant remark, whereas Sean would knock them out cold. That was the difference in our characters."

For Moore's Bond, killing was what he had to do so that he could travel to remote, romantic locales to meet beautiful woman and bed them. Moore's Bond carried out his assignments for the audience's vicarious enjoyment. Moore once remarked, "I basically said [to the audience], "I'm have a good time doing this, and I hope you're having a good time watching me have a good time."

Moore's Bond is having the best time when he's seducing his nubile costars. Instead of relishing the violence, Moore's Bond capitalizes on the audience's sexual fantasies.

I used to bristle when Moore detractors suggested that he made Bond into a Playboy-scoundrel. I would argue that if Moore didn't make audiences believe that he was the world's most able spy (and not merely a wisecracking ladies' man) then the films wouldn't work. The spy-as-gigolo-paradigm only works if it's played for cheap laughs – as it is in the Austin Powers films. It's not a concept that could have been sustained over Moore's seven-film reign as Bond. While I haven't changed my mind, after my interview with Moore I've come to the conclusion that he is not completely resistant to that interpretation himself. He seems most comfortable talking about Bond's more dashing, less dangerous side.

Neither Connery nor Moore's interpretation seemed to invite scrutiny about Bond's motivation. Surprisingly, even after about fifty hours of screen time, audiences don't know much about James Bond's personal life. They knew what he likes to drink and how he likes it prepared (shaken and not, you know, the other way). They knew the order in which he likes to say his name (last name, first name, last name again.) More avid fans recall that he was once briefly married but, before he could consummate his vows, he was widowed by the guy who played Kojak. Not until

Daniel Craig's "rough trade" Bond did the general public begin to wonder about the man behind the number.

From the books and films, we knew that at age eleven Bond became an orphan when his parents were killed in a mountain climbing accident. An aunt became his guardian and he schooled at Eton (a prestigious boarding school for boys) before he was expelled due to an incident involving a maid. Apparently, even at a tender age, Bond was already a lothario. After college, Bond joined the navy, rose to the rank of Commander, was recruited by Her Majesty's Secret Service, and became their best (i.e., most lethal) agent.

Audiences didn't seem to have much interest in the private life of a character they so loved. It probably seemed to his fans that what Bond did before his first onscreen adventure was irrelevant and perhaps, comparatively speaking, mundane.

For over fifty years, in twenty-three adventures (and counting), Bond movies have been escapist entertainment of the highest order. They are meant to "transport" us (as Marc Foster, the director of "Quantum of Solace" argues) out of the drudgery of our lives and distract us from our woes about, say, the economy or fears about wars (both cold and hot). Sean Connery concurs. He once remarked, "Along comes this character who cuts right through all that like a very hot knife through butter, with his clothing and his cars and his wine and his women. Bond, you see, is a kind of present-day survival kit."[132]

And men, particularly young men, live vicariously through the novels and movies about the dashing, sophisticated, fearless, capable, woman-seducing agent. Raymond Chandler put it simply: "Bond is what every man would like to be."[133]

In the public's mind, there used to be only one true Bond. In the 1960s, movie posters promised and audiences believed that "Sean Connery IS James Bond." Seven actors (including Barry Nielson who played Jimmy Bond in the TV version of *Casino Royale*) have had the privilege of officially assuming the mantle. Even Ian Fleming wished he could be his Bond. Before Fleming was a novelist, he worked in Naval Intelligence during World War II. When the war ended, Fleming returned to civilian life and

Roger Moore is dressed to kill. © Eon Productions.

wrote twelve books about the spy he never was. The plot of *Casino Royale* was based on an incident in Fleming's own life, when on leave in Portugal he tried to bankrupt a few German agents (and, in turn, the entire German government) at a casino. Fleming told *Playboy* in 1964, "I thought it would be a brilliant coup to play with them, break them, take their money. Instead, of course, they took mine. Most embarrassing. This incident appears *in Casino*

Royale, my first book, but, of course, Bond does not lose. In fact, he totally and coldly vanquishes his opponent."

While Moore has said he is not Bond, there might be a small part of him that wishes otherwise. Let's revisit Moore's statement that every bartender in the world knows Bond's favorite drink. It should be noted that in none of the movies dobartenders offer Bond an unsolicited martini. Perhaps, Moore's Freudian slip suggests that he is confusing his own off-screen adventures with Bond's onscreen ones.

With all due respect for Roger Moore's personal views, to audiences, Moore transformed himself into James Bond. In turn, men in the audience dream that we too could reinvent ourselves in Bond's image. The men imagined that if Moore can take Connery's title then perhaps they can too.

Of course, most of us never come close. In his eighties, Moore looks better and more like Bond than most men do. Standing next to him in my tux, I felt like a Trekkie wearing a Star Fleet Uniform while standing next to William Shatner at a Star Trek Convention – it's a little bit thrilling and a little bit preposterous.

Moore was the Bond that we "realistically" could hope to be. Moore's Bond was our wish fulfillment. Most of us knew that Connery's cool was way out of reach, but Moore humanized Bond just enough that we thought we had a shot of being like him.

Connery's Bond was a little too virile for an adolescent's nascent fantasies. Connery's Bond was too hard-edged and hairy for a teenage boy to relate to. Don't doubt for a moment that the teenage boy inside us is an important factor in appreciating Bond. It takes a fourteen-year-old's mentality to laugh without embarrassment at such common Bond movie touches as the title of Moore's sixth outing, *Octopussy*, or at the name of Bond-girl Holly Goodhead.

One got the sense that Connery's Bond wouldn't want to spend any time with you. Moore on the other hand was Bond as your pal. Bond as your protector. Bond as your wing-man. Bond as your daddy figure. With his disarming approach to the part, Moore welcomed you into his world of glamour and intrigue. He welcomed you on his adventures and he invited you to be just as

Roger Moore on the set of Live and Let Die (1973). © Eon Productions.

Bond-ian as he. Ian Fleming never wanted Bond to be a superhuman. Quite the opposite; he chose the name because, to him, it sounded bland. Today, the mere mention of James Bond sparks a visceral thrill in the gut of the teenager who continues to reside in many of us fans.

Moore retired his license to kill in 1984 after bedding Tanya Roberts and killing Christopher Walken in *A View To A Kill*. Since then, three other actors have gone on to "become" Bond.

Though Bond is no longer Roger Moore, Roger Moore will always be James Bond.

THE INTERVIEW

What was the key to understanding Bond's character? Can you give a practical example of how as an actor you applied that insight to a specific scene, moment or line?

When I first took on the part, I read Fleming's books. There was little offered in them about the character. However, I remember reading one line that said Bond had just completed a mission - meaning a kill. He didn't particularly enjoy killing but took pride in doing his job well. That was the key to the role as far as I was concerned.

[Author's Note: Moore is referring to the passage in the novel Goldfinger, in which Ian Fleming writes: "It was part of his profession to kill people. He had never liked doing it and when he had to kill he did it as well as he knew how and forgot about it. As a secret agent who held the rare double-O prefix – the license to kill in the Secret Service – it was his duty to be as cool about death as a surgeon. If it happened, it happened. Regret was unprofessional — worse, it was a death-watch beetle in the soul."[134]]

While there is deservedly much discussion about how suave and funny you were as Bond, you were also very good at making him cold-blooded and lethal. How did you approach those scenes?

Well if you read the Internet blogs, they agree I was funny, but they're not so sure I was suave and certainly they don't regard me as having been cold-blooded. There was one scene in *For Your Eyes Only* where I had to be rather cold-blooded in killing a villain. They say that scene changed the series tone for my films, but I wasn't comfortable with it, if truth be known. I was rather cold-blooded and mercenary on Fridays though. That's the day I received my paychecks.

What was your approach to saying "My name is Bond, James Bond," 007's signature line? Audiences eagerly anticipate the line. Seems like an actor can go a bit mad thinking about it.

Oh goodness, I spent many, many hours committing that line to memory! Guy Hamilton, the director on my first Bond, said, "Don't say the line with a Scottish accent and we'll be fine." Words I heeded.

From the movies, we learn so little about Bond personally. What do you imagine his private life is like?

It's probably one bar to another bed. I'd imagine his private life to be rather limited as he's seemingly always on the job.

When people meet you on some level (perhaps an unconscious one) they believe that they're actually meeting James Bond. Are you aware of that? What's that like for you? Do you feel any pressure to meet those expectations?

Oh, I don't think they think I'm Bond. Well, ok, maybe. I sometimes get comments like "Hello, Mr. Bond" and such like. I smile and keep walking, but if someone comes up to me and says "Hey, you're James Bond!" I'll say, "No, I am Roger Moore, I used to play James Bond." I don't pretend I am the character. Therefore, I have no expectations to meet other than those of meeting Roger Moore. I am, of course, charming, polite, and courteous.

Where do your and Bond's personalities converge and diverge?

Well, when I played the part he looked and sounded like me. That's where the similarities and differences begin and end!

Men the world over have dreamed of being as suave, capable, masculine, and as appealing to women as Bond. Most of us come up a bit short. When you were in character did you ever allow yourself to actually feel like Bond? How did that feel?

How does Bond feel? I don't know. I never really absorbed myself in a role like some actors do. Many take the roles home with them and live the part. I'm quite happy to leave mine at the studio and return home as I left, simple old Roger Moore. I guess it would be easy to think I'm invincible and live as charmed a life as 007, but that would be foolish, wouldn't it?

You've played a wide variety of characters in scores of movies. You've also starred in memorable television shows including *The Saint* and *The Persuaders*, but the character you're most associated with is James Bond.

Without doubt you are recognized for the last role you played. When I was Bond, I was recognized as Bond. Before that I was recognized as Lord Brett Sinclair, The Saint, Beau Maverick, Silky Harris and Ivanhoe. Bond was later than those other parts, and perhaps bigger, too.

What are the positive and negative aspects of the association?

The positive aspects of Bond? A bigger paycheck. The negative aspects? A coward having to pretend he is brave, and trying not to blink when explosions go off.

Canyoupleasegiveussomeadviceonhowtobeascoolas Bondin our daily lives?

Stay in bed . . . with a pretty lady.

How has playing James Bond affected you personally, not professionally, not publicly, but personally?

Personally, it has given me financial security. It has also provided me with a certain celebrity, if that is the right word, which has enabled me to work as a Goodwill Ambassador for UNICEF.

Speaking of UNICEF, how has playing Bond been an asset to meeting children in your travels for UNICEF?

It is a great asset. After all, who would want to meet a jobbing actor? But meeting an actor who once played James Bond, that opens doors. I find I'm able to meet with presidents, prime ministers and people who make decisions. Bond has afforded me a great personal passport, which I use for UNICEF.

What question should I ask my next interview subject?

My question for your next interview: How do you keep your head when all about you are losing *yours*?

Why do you think the films have remained so popular for fifty years and counting?

The films are hugely popular because they are entertaining. The producers never cheat audiences; the money goes on the screen.

To what do you attribute the character's popularity?

Every man wants to be James Bond; every woman wants to be bedded by him!

What drives James Bond?

He obviously feels a sense of duty and thrives on it.

Is Bond essentially a hedonist of sorts, who's primarily in pursuit of pleasure?

He takes pleasure along the way, and uses it to great advantage at times in extracting information from certain ladies, but hedonist? No, I don't think so.

What do you think are the most significant ways the *character* of Bond has changed?

He has had six different faces! Each Bond is right for that generation. I'm sure my Bond wouldn't work today; just as Daniel Craig's 007 probably wouldn't have worked for 1970s audiences. The producers move and adapt with the times. They are very clever.

Until recently, the Bond movies have deliberately avoided exploring Bond's psyche. Would you have enjoyed exploring those elements?

Me? Act and think deeply? No thanks! I wouldn't say they avoided exploring his psyche, but I guess after twenty-odd films you reach a stage where we know so much about the character without knowing that much about the man and it's interesting to take a look.

Can you talk a little bit about how you found the right note to play Bond?

Guy Hamilton, [who directed Moore's first outing as 007], told me to play it my way. We avoided some of the lines closely associated with Sean such as ordering a vodka martini, but otherwise I just played myself, as always.

Bond's movement appears effortless. Can you talk about how you approached the physicality of the part?

I never thought about it. I had doubles to make me look good!

There are some great moments in the films where you show Bond's vulnerable side. How do you approach those scenes?

I honestly don't read into it. I look at the script, speak to the director, and just say the lines.

Over the course of your seven Bond films, you experimented with different approaches to the part – from the tongue-in-cheek to the more realistic. What is your favorite approach?

I never really enjoyed the hard, gritty side of Bond. I much preferred being a lover and being a giggler.

Were there any moments in the Bond films that made you uncomfortable?

As I say, my Bond was a lover and giggler. I didn't think he should hit a woman, nor kill a man in cold blood. The storyline called for it, I know, but I personally don't feel comfortable with those types of scenes.

What do you see as the main difference between Sean Connery's Bond and yours?

Sean's Bond was a tough character who could fight his way out of a corner; my Bond would charm his way out of a corner.

What made Connery's interpretation distinctive?

Sean was the first Bond. He created and defined the part. He was distinctive in that there was no one else to compare him with.

What about George Lazenby?

George's film is a damn good movie. He could have been a great Bond and could have made quite a few movies, but it wasn't to be. We are friends.

Timothy Dalton?

Not long ago, I sat down to watch *The Living Daylights* for the first time and thought it a terrific movie, and Timothy, who I've known for years, is a bloody good 007 and a great actor. I was genuinely surprised by how much I enjoyed the film.

Pierce Brosnan?

Pierce played it much like me, though I did feel his films got a little too far-fetched . . . *invisible cars*?!

Daniel Craig?

Daniel is certainly the best actor to ever play 007, and I think he will go on to become the best ever Bond.

What about that actor who played Bond seven times, Roger Moore? What did you admire about his approach?

Oh, he was very handsome, charming, talented, and modest.

Who is the best Bond?

Sean, because he was the first.

For the final question, I ask all the people I interview some version of this "VS" question. Granted it's very, very silly, but here goes. Who would win in a fight, your James Bond vs. Sean Connery's?

Just after I had been announced as Bond, I took my eldest son, Geoffrey, to lunch at the White Elephant in London. He looked around the room and said, "Dad, could you beat up everyone in here?" I looked around. They looked a pretty frail bunch of folks, so I said "Yes, sure." He then asked, "What about James Bond?" I explained that I was going to be James Bond. "No!" he protested, "I mean the real James Bond, Sean Connery." It's a wonder my son grew so tall.

Clark Gregg is Agent Coulson

How does an actor with a cameo role in *Iron Man* and a supporting part as a character without super powers in *The Avengers* transform himself into a fan favorite who not only serves as the connective tissue between the increasingly complex and intertwined story lines in the Marvel Cinematic Universe but also has become the lead actor in *Marvel's Agents of S.H.I.E.L.D.*, (Marvel Studio's first foray into live-action television), even though his character was killed?

The answer lies with Clark Gregg's scene-stealing interpretation of Agent Phil Coulson, a high-level agent in S.H.I.E.L.D., the secretive agency created to deal with superhuman and human threats. Gregg has built a thriving career by imbuing his characters with distinctive personalities, even with just a few scant lines. He memorably played Agent Casper in Aaron Sorkin's *The West Wing*, a mysterious stranger in Sorkin's *Sports Night*, and a secret agent who helps Val Kilmer's operative search for the President's kidnapped daughter in David Mamet's absorbing political thriller *Spartan* (2004). All of these characters, like Coulson, keep their cards close to their vests; they're not prone to long flowery speeches or over-wrought displays of passion. "The Vulture" section at *New York Magazine*'s website observed, "His capable, ironic, slightly detached professionalism offered a nice human break from all the superheroics [sic]."[135] *Entertainment Weekly* opined that Gregg "somehow managed to make bureaucracy sexy."[136]

Prior to Gregg's appearance in *Iron Man*, Agent Coulson didn't exist on-screen or in the comics. In fact, he was created merely to deliver exposition and to introduce Robert Downey's Tony Stark (and the audience) to the world of S.H.I.E.L.D. But when the filmmakers witnessed the unique chemistry at play between Clark and Downey, they shrewdly decided to build up his character in that film and include him in *Iron Man 2* and *Thor*, two of Marvel's subsequent feature films. Audiences would learn a little more about his character in each film. Clark Gregg told *The Los Ange-*

les Times, "It's always been the case that it's a little bit of a chain letter. Every director and writing team add more facets to Coulson. There's an amazing Kurt Vonnegut story about a guy who's only alive when he's acting. It's called "Who Am I This Time?" I always think of that title. Every time it's a different world, a different superhero in the movies. I always sit down and wonder, Who is this version of Phil Coulson?[137]

When Joss Whedon wrote the script for the blockbuster-in-waiting The Avengers, Gregg's role was greatly expanded and additional dimensions of his character were explored. The film marked the first time Iron Man, Captain America, Thor, and the Hulk appeared together on the big-screen, and despite Nick Fury's commanding presence, the superheroes initially do not work cohesively as a team. It is only after Gregg's Coulson is killed in action that the heroes find a common sense of purpose, put their egos aside, and band together for the greater good. You would think that the impending destruction of the planet would be sufficient reason for the heroes to put aside their petty differences and unite, but it takes Coulson's death to galvanize them by personalizing the stakes and providing them with something to avenge.

Coulson's death, the most poignant moment in The Avengers, made the fans love the character more. They refused to accept the loss of the character. Soon, fans spray-painted the words "Coulson Lives" on public spaces around the world. The phrase was soon embossed on T-shirts, sweatshirts, baseball caps, key chains, buttons, bracelets, and bumper stickers.

The fans demanded attention, and Marvel took notice. They resurrected the character for their first venture into a live-action television series, Marvel's Agents of S.H.I.E.L.D.. The decision was a tricky one: no one associated with the new venture wanted to diminish Coulson's sacrifice. So they created the conceit that his death was real but that Nick Fury, director of S.H.I.E.L.D., "moved Heaven and Earth" and used "procedures that no good doctor would ever allow" to bring Coulson back to life. Eventually, when Nick Fury is forced to go into hiding to maintain the ruse that he's been killed in action, the one-eyed super spy steps down as

Clark Gregg as Agent Phil Coulson. © Marvel Television/ABC Studios.

director and names Coulson as his replacement. In this surprising turn of events, Agent Coulson becomes Director Coulson.

Gregg (who like many superheroes lost his father at a young age) voiced the character of Agent Coulson, in the animated series *Ultimate Spider-Man* (2012-2013), in the video games *Marvel Heroes* (2013) and *Lego Marvel Super Heroes* (2013), as well as in the short films *Marvel One Shot: A Funny Thing Happened on the Way to Thor's Hammer* (2011) and *Marvel One Shot: The Consultant* (2011).

Clark Gregg also directed *Choke* (2008), which he adapted from Chuck Palahniuk's novel of the same name, and *Trust Me*

(2013), for which he wrote the screenplay. Gregg also wrote the screenplay for the Hitchcock-esque *What Lies Beneath* [2000]. For five seasons, Gregg played the ex-husband of Julia Louise Dreyfus' title character in *The New Adventures of Old Christine* (2006-2010).

After a fair amount of begging, I was lucky enough to acquire tickets to the New York premiere of *The Avengers*. Robert Downey, Jr., Chris Hemsworth, Tom Hiddleston, Mark Ruffalo, and Clark Gregg were on hand for the opening. The event took place just blocks away from the World Trade Center's Ground Zero, so it was fitting when the actors took to the stage that Downey, on behalf of his co-stars, dedicated the night to the real heroes of New York, the police and fire departments; and members of both distinguished institutions were in attendance. After the lights went down, I noticed that Gregg and Ruffalo were being ushered to seats across the aisle from me. As the film unspooled, I watched the action and occasionally glanced over at the actors. Ruffalo nearly fell out of his chair as he witnessed the Hulk, his on screen avatar, toss a villain around like a rag doll. Gregg watched the movie with glee. Gregg's enthusiasm and his palpable enjoyment of the film were indistinguishable from the audience's. You would have thought he was just another Marvel fan. Turns out, he is.

THE INTERVIEW

Unlike every other actor I've talked with for this book, you couldn't rely on the comics to inform you how you would play the part. How did you create the character?

It was created along the way. There was very little about him in the very first *Iron Man* script. I don't even think he even was named Coulson at first. The character was just called Agent. I was very fortunate in that they realized that there was a need for a character like that in that world and that they wanted to perhaps start setting up S.H.I.E.L.D. [in the movies]. The first script I had didn't really hint at any of that, but by the time I showed up on set, they had already started to add that element into the script. And after they saw a scene between Coulson and Tony Stark, who were verbally sparing and giving each other a hard

time, pretty soon I was saying "The Strategic Homeland Intervention Enforcement Logistic Division." I went over to Jeremy Lat-
cham [senior Vice President of Production and Development] at
Marvel and I said, "Is this S.H.I.E.L.D.? Am I from S.H.I.E.L.D. and
he said, "Yeah, you are." It just kept on expanding. Then they
wrote a great joke where I say, "We've got to work on that name."

Then they decided to put Coulson in *Iron Man 2*. In *Iron Man
2*, I was doing a scene and they said, "Tell him you have to go to
New Mexico."

I did a couple takes and then I asked, "What's in New Mexico?"

They said, "Oh, god. Hasn't anyone spoken to you? You're going
to New Mexico because you're the one who finds Thor's hammer."

I said, "This is spectacular." I wasn't a full-on life-time-reading
comic book nerd but I definitely had grown up reading Marvel
comics. It was really exciting for me. I knew where I was.

There was also a little bit of buzz with fans saying, "Who is this
Coulson? He's not anywhere in the comics. We can't find him
anywhere." I actually thought for a second that was going to get
me killed-off right away, but instead Marvel started to add him to
the comics.

**Then it goes from Iron *Man 2* and *Thor*, to a pivotal role in *The
Avengers*.**

I was at Comic Con about to do the panel for *Thor*. I had been
to Comic Con right around when the first *Iron Man* was coming
out and on that visit I was able to walk the floor and buy up a
bunch of old Warlock comics, Iron Fist Comics, and some Avengers comics. So, when I went back to Comic Con for *Thor* and saw
a lot of people dressed up as Agent Coulson, it was actually kind
of great. I was backstage at the green room waiting to go out for
the panel for *Thor* and I turned to Joss Whedon, [who wrote and
directed *The Avengers*], who was standing next to me, and he
said, "I've been meaning to call you. You have a big part in *The
Avengers* and I'm about to surprise the audience with the whole
cast. Can I introduce you as part of the cast?

I nearly fainted on the spot. I said, "Yeah, that would be OK with
me." The next thing I know I was standing in front of 6,000 screaming nerds and there I was the happiest nerd in the place.

I thought that Agent Coulson would come in and give someone a Jamba Juice and get out of the way of all those amazing actors. I didn't know Joss wasn't going to make him a pivotal character. Then I get a call from Kevin Feige [President of Production at Marvel Studios] saying, "Listen Joss wasn't kidding you have a really great part in *The Avengers*."

I said, "That's unbelievable. I really don't know what to say."

He said, "Yeah, what happens to you is what brings the Avengers together."

I thought, *Oh, no. Oh, no. Oh, no!* I asked Kevin, "This is my last Marvel movie, isn't it?"

He said, "Well, just wait until you read it. I think you'll be very happy because you really go out in a blaze of glory."

Of course he was right. It was magnificent. I couldn't have been happier about it. I thought Joss had written me not only one of the great death scenes but also some of the best stuff anyone had ever written for me.

I showed up [on the set of *The Avengers*] and I had scenes with everybody. I couldn't have been any happier. Then it came to the day to shoot [the death scene] and I found myself quite emotional. I realized I didn't want to stop playing this guy. I really had enjoyed it. I made a couple of jokes to the camera for the gag reel like, "Are you really sure you want to do this? Because people say he's the glue to the Marvel universe." But it kind of fell on deaf ears because the next thing I know I'm bleeding out on the old Helicarrier deck, but it was really over.

Then somebody posted somewhere that Agent Coulson's funeral was going to be in *Thor 2*. I sent a text to Kevin Feige saying, "I think I have to do business with this." The people made a lot of jokes saying, "It's a comic book universe. How dead can he possibly be?" I thought, *If there's a funeral, he might be really dead.* Kevin didn't respond to my text and he had been really good at responding before. I thought, *Aw man, he got rid of my number. He knew I was going to be a nerd stalker.*

About a week later, I got a call from Jeph Loeb [Executive Vice President, Head of Marvel Television] and then from Joss saying,

"No, you're not dead. We think you're coming back to life for a television series."

I got on the phone with Joss, and I said, "I'm really excited about this, but I don't want to undo anything that we did in *The Avengers*."

He said, "No, neither do I. That was my big concern." Then he told me the big idea, which is that Coulson has one pat version of his close call with Loki and that was used by Nick Fury as a way of duping The Avengers into working together, but, in fact, the truth is much darker and more complex.

Can you elaborate on your and Joss Whedon's collective concerns about not diminishing Coulson's sacrifice in *The Avengers*?

I got the word that I was going to be killed off and I called up Joss and I said, "The script is magnificent. I didn't know how anyone was going to pull it off. I love what you've done with my character. Not only is it great pay-off for that character, I also think if you make a movie like this where there is no pain and there is no sacrifice then it almost feels irresponsible, especially if you really want to explore the themes of sacrifice and fighting for something even though you can die for your beliefs."

He was gratified to hear that. He said, "Everyone thinks this is my idea because I'm famous for killing off characters [on *Buffy the Vampire Slayer, Angel,* and *Serenity*] and it really means the world to hear you say that."

I wanted him to know that I supported it. Marvel championed the idea of losing *somebody* and I believe it was Marvel's idea that it be Coulson more so than it was Joss's. They certainly can afford to lose Coulson much more so than they can afford to lose one of their franchise characters. [Laughs] Even that proved to be something that the fans weren't happy about.

When the idea was on the table to bring Coulson back, we didn't want to say to the fans, "I know you were really moved by his death in *The Avengers* but it didn't *really* happen. When Joss described the scene that's in the pilot, he explained that Coulson believes one story and we very quickly learn that he doesn't know about his own survival and that there is a darker secret about what really happened. It's a dark enough secret that they don't want him to ever know the truth. As soon as I heard that I knew we were on the same page once again. In mythology you don't get to go to the afterlife and come back unscathed. As soon as I realized that this isn't the same Phil Coulson, who's had one of these near-death or full-death experiences without coming back different altered, having lost something. As soon as I realized that was where his mindset was, I knew it wouldn't be a cheat and that it would *enhance* the mythology of *The Avengers*.

Had you created an imaginary backstory for Coulson by the time you got to *The Avengers* set?

Yes. The fun thing about it is that I have a backstory and I have a lot of character ideas where I know who he is and what he's been through. But every time I get a script from another writer on one of these films, I find out something else about him. When I got Joss's script, I found out that he's a nerd, which made perfect sense to me. He's a nerd who has his own Captain America trading cards. He's a little obsessed with Captain America in an awkward and magnificent way. He's probably been to Comic Con. I discovered that he had a girlfriend, who was a cellist who probably got frustrated with his clandestine work and moved back to Portland. I fill out as much of it as I can, and when I get a new script which contradicts my imaginary backstory, I have to go back and do a lot of rewriting. The same is true of the television series where each new script I get I find out a new detail about his past, about his relationship with the other characters and about what he's into.

In the imaginary backstory you created to help you build the character, how did he get into this line of work?

You're going deep into the actor's process. I have a couple of different versions because I've altered them and used different ones at different times. But I always thought, and my hunch was confirmed once I saw *The Avengers* script, that his obsession with the heroism and patriotism of Captain America had lived side by side with him growing up in the 1970s and 1980s and the cynicism that went with it and that's how you got the duality of Phil Coulson. That he went into some elite versions of military and security work but his hobbies were very much off that grid.

Can you expand on the duality of Coulson?

On one hand, it's very clear in some moments that he functions with a kind of idealism and a belief in the principle of sacrifice for the greater good. At the same time, he came of age at a time when Americans were growing wary of secretive institutions. So he has to wrestle on a daily basis with the idea of keeping secrets from the public, who are the people he works for essentially, and dealing with the self-absorbed mentality of rock star divas, which is what many of these superheroes resemble. But at the same time he sees them risking their lives and doing these extraordinary things to protect people. He gets to see the whole part of the process. I think doing *Marvel's Agents of S.H.I.E.L.D.* in a world after some of the revelations about the NSA and Julian Assange makes it very much a dilemma of the moment. There are secrets, which need to be kept for the greater good, but at the same time, there are people who manipulate us using some of those secrets. I don't think that's something that is lost on Phil Coulson, and I don't think that his idealism equals blindness.

He's a cynical idealist, or an idealistic cynic.

One or the other.

Which is probably not unlike Joss Whedon's artistic point of view and that's what makes his work interesting.

I agree, and I think that's probably the foundation of where my connection with his work comes from.

Superheroes have a consistent look. Coulson, though not a superhero, has a consistent look as well. What are you trying to convey with his outfit?

It's funny because I had to really get into that for the TV series because he's maybe not the same person that he was before he was killed now that he's back alive. I felt that there was so little I could do within the constraints of what I understand. But he does have a uniform. He's always wearing his well-tailored suits. On one hand, the Men in Black suits have been done, but Agent Phil Coulson does operate in the suit. There's some very funny stuff in the third episode when he gets off a raft on a two-man commando mission and he's wearing a suit, even though the young S.H.I.E.L.D. agent with him is in full combat gear. That's Phil

Coulson's uniform. Yet in another episode, Agent Phil Coulson is working out, and he's not wearing a suit, and it felt strangely naked to me. It's fun that he has a look and people know what his outfit is. I don't wear suits very much; when I'm not working, I don't wear a suit, but I think there's something about the way that Agent Coulson wears a suits that speaks to who he is and shows how he functions within a very rigid structure, and yet within that there's increasing latitude to express who he is that is a little less cloaked than it has been in the movies.

Does putting on the suit help you get into character?

If I'm not, then the minute I put the suit on it certainly gets me a lot of the way home.

Does Coulson have faults?

Tons. I think the authorities see him very much a bull in a China shop. I think there's been a time in his life where he was willing to accept the company line unquestioningly and has done some things that he now has deep questions about. As far as I can tell, that seems to be deeply ingrained in his journey in *Marvel's Agents of S.H.I.E.L.D.*.

What parts of yourself did you bring to the role?

As much as I love the comics and as much I have enjoyed the darker versions of The Dark Knight, I live for the comedic parts of material. As much as I get to do the action and the drama and still have lines where I get to be sarcastic with superheroes and have funny takes on stuff, that's what really makes it delicious for me. There are times when I'm very serious, passionate, and tortured, but most of the other times I'm still able to survive all that because I can connect to what's silly about the world and about myself. That feels very close to who Coulson is. To a certain extent the character has evolved to that because that's who I am. It's a tailored suit at this point. Very talented people have done exquisite tailoring on it.

The use of Coulson has changed over time. At first, he was the connective tissue to link the disparate Marvel films together. Then he served as the reason for The Avengers working together. With *Agents of S.H.I.E.L.D.* he's being used to both expand on the concept of S.H.I.E.L.D. and as a bridge between

the Marvel Cinematic world and Marvel's first foray into a live action series.

I think he functions in different ways at different times for different chapters in the Marvel universe. His function was very clear in *The Avengers* but he's always been a bit of a shape-shifter. He moves undercover in plain sight. In *Iron Man*, he appeared to be a pesky bureaucrat where in truth he has much larger forces at his command then Tony Stark or Pepper Potts begin to realize. In some ways, he's an advance man for Nick Fury.

I can only look at what he's called upon to do today. What's really interesting about doing *Agents of S.H.I.E.L.D.* is that people with no superpowers and people who work for S.H.I.E.L.D. are not usually the protagonists or the focus of the story. They are there very much to enhance or conflict with the journey of the main protagonist who in these movies is a flawed superhero. Coulson is the "hero" of the show, to use that term. He's also very much an avatar for the people watching.

I think the entire "Coulson Lives" movement took Marvel a little bit by surprise. It certainly took me by surprise because Marvel found a magnificent way to make superheroes that are vulnerable and flawed and the audience can connect to them and fantasize themselves *into* that superhero role. But apparently there was a hunger for a character that could just show up and do his job even if he doesn't always have to like it. A human face in the superhero world. The audience really connected to that and they understand the crap that Phil Coulson puts up with from people. It really touched a nerve that he's the guy who has to go to the locker and take out the Destroyer weapon because the superheroes are too busy bickering with each other. The fact that he shows up at Comic Con and buys Captain America cards really drove the point home. To have a character like that at the core of the show is really a bold move by Marvel and it's something that the fans seem to be embracing. I think it really speaks to how much there was a need for an avatar for the audience in this world. Honestly, it's an honor to represent those people because that is me. Although Phil Coulson does have a skill set that makes him far from an ordinary person, he really is an everyman.

Because the role is so personal and meaningful to you, did you mourn his loss and the idea that you could no longer play this unique character again when he died in *The Avengers*?

Yes and no. I definitely felt the loss. As I said I was surprised by how moved I was shooting those last scenes. When I was putting on the suit for what I thought was my final time I was thinking about my daughter. I started playing the role when she was tiny and now she is more grown up and I wasn't going to do it anymore. Not only did I think I would miss playing the character but it's not often that you get to play a character that people connect with so much. I wondered if I was ever going to play another character that did connect with so many people around the world in this way.

On the other hand, I've had such a terrific and fun career and the most interesting roles are the ones that are coming to me lately. I've recently done five independent films including *Much Ado About Nothing* with Joss, and I've directed two films of my own that I really loved doing, so I wasn't hurting for opportunities, but there was something that made me very happy when the phone call came saying I would get to play him again. It meant a lot.

You played Agent Casper on *The West Wing*. Although Casper is different from Coulson, he could probably relate to Coulson on a professional level.

You know my memory is not terrific, from playing so many contact sports and getting hit on the head, but I feel that Agent Casper on *The West Wing* was such a good part because Aaron Sorkin had written him with so many funny lines. I feel like at some point that [*Iron Man* director Jon] Favreau mentioned to me that he enjoyed Agent Casper on *West Wing*, and that was the reason that I popped into his head for that role, even though we were neighbors. There is a lot of speculation out there in the fan universe suggesting that Phil Coulson was Agent Casper and was working under a different name earlier in his career.

Kevin Feige runs Marvel Studios, and he oversees a diverse group of superhero films. What does he understand about how to make superhero films?

I've gotten to be front row center to watching him work. I admire Kevin tremendously. He should write a book about management. He oversees every element of these films and has pioneered this model. At the same time, he has brought on really terrific, talented filmmakers, many of whom couldn't point to a similar tent-pole movie that they made to show that they were up to the task of making an ambitious superhero film. Like Jon Favreau. Kevin really trusted Jon. Jon deserves a lot of credit as well. He really championed Robert Downey when everyone thought that was a crazy idea. He also championed Gwyneth [Paltrow] and Jeff Bridges and really changed the model. That's also true for Kenneth Branagh. *Thor* was the hardest one as far as I'm concerned. The same is true of Joss. You don't look at *Serenity* and say, "This is the guy who should do *The Avengers*."

When Feige got a huge promotion he bought Star Wars action figures. He loves the material so much. He is in many ways like Phil Coulson and gets to do his dream job and he loves it. He is very interested in the people he works with. He hires great people and gives people the opportunity to do their best and helps them do their best.

I'm a fine example of this. He took advantage of a rare situation where in my opinion something was really clicking with Agent Coulson and Tony Stark and the way Agent Coulson fit into that world. As the script was evolving Jon and Kevin decided to take what was working and expand on it. It's obvious what that has meant to me. I think most people would have just stuck with the script that they had and wouldn't have seized on the opportunity. Agent Coulson has worked for me and I think that Agent Coulson has worked for them. That is a testament to the kind of artist Kevin is.

What is the most personally satisfying aspect of playing Coulson? Is it how the character connects with people?

Yes. When people started sending me pictures of Coulson Lives scrawled on a bridge pylon or on beaches in Africa, I was really touched. I got really moving letters. There is a tremendous artist from Vienna, who sent me this beautiful series of Coulson drawings. Her husband had died at a very young age from cancer and she had stopped drawing. She stopped doing her art. She really grasped everything I love about Agent Coulson. There was something about his stoicism and his willingness to show up and just do his job no matter what that connected with her and got her drawing again. I've gotten a lot of those kinds of strange packages from people, which really knocked me down and moved me. That part has been amazing. I get to take my twelve-year old self to work everyday and be handed an action figure. There's not a lot of guys who are fifty who get their own action figure.

Do you have a Coulson room in your house?

I don't need a room yet. I do have a pretty large closet with some particularly spectacular stuff in it.

Final question. Who would win in a fight between Agent Coulson and Nick Fury?

There's a reason Nick Furry has been around so long. You can't underestimate him. I would hate for that day to come because he's one of the few people Phil Coulson trusts something like absolutely. But the reason I think Phil Coulson is still around is that it's never a good idea to bet against Phil Coulson.

PART EIGHT: CONVERSATIONS ABOUT SUPERHEROES

Remembering Captain America's Creator, Joe Simon
A Conversation with JIM SIMON

Joe Simon created Captain America with his partner Jack Kirby. The character was an overnight success. Almost immediately after the first issue hit the newsstands in 1941, Captain America became a highly sought-after title. In speaking with comic book historian Les Daniels for the book *Marvel*, Joe Simon explained the phenomenon. "Captain America was exceptional, a sellout . . . We were up to, after the first issue, close to the million mark, and that was monthly."[138]

To put Captain America's remarkable circulation figure into further perspective, Daniels writes, "As a contrast, consider that the weekly circulation of *Time* magazine during the same period was 700,000 . . . We were entertaining the world,' Simon says."[139]

Simon's work in the field of superheroes established his well-deserved reputation, but Simon was equally adept at writing other types of stories. Simon, along with Kirby, created the romance comics genre, which were aimed squarely at adults, and they also wrote humor, crime, and horror comics.

During World War II, Simon, like his fictional creation, enlisted in the army. He served in the United States Coast Guard.

With his son Jim, who is a writer and a publisher, Simon co-wrote the book *The Comic Book Makers*, about the history and creators of many of the most popular and enduring comics, including among others, Superman, Captain America, Spider-Man, Archie, and Captain Marvel. Simon's autobiography, *Joe Simon: My Life in Comics*, was published in 2011.

Joe Simon passed away on December 14, 2011 at the age of ninety-eight.

Shortly before New York Comic Con's Memorial Celebration for Simon, I interviewed Jim Simon about his legendary father's enduring creation.

THE INTERVIEW

What was your father's initial inspiration for creating Captain America?

My father came from the newspaper field before he entered the "new" field called comic books. With the success of Superman and Batman, everyone in comics was looking to create the next big thing. That included my father. Working in comics, he wanted to create a comic book character that would be bigger than Superman and Batman. Being the innovative person that he was, he was aware that Superman and Batman were based on pure fantasy. He would take a different route. As a former newspaperman, he took the route where he created a character based less on fantasy and more on reality. In Europe, the Nazis were marching. Hitler and his Storm Troopers splashed across the headlines daily. News dispatches [reported] the persecutions, the concentration camps, and the incredibly cruel Gestapo tactics.

As he recalled in *The Comic Book Makers*, the book I wrote with him about his eyewitness account of the early days of comics. "It was a time of intense patriotism. Children played soldiers, shooting war toys at imaginary soldiers. Wouldn't they love to see him [Hitler] lambasted in a comic book by a soldier, a meek, humbling private with muscles of steel and a colorful, star-spangled costume under his khaki army uniform."

The creation of Captain America, I suppose, was my father's way of fighting ... of making a mockery of the Nazis and their mad leader. A lot of my father's comic book creations, though fantastical, were based on events in real life. He lived in the moment, even with his work.

Talk about how he came up with the character's name?

The name, "Captain America," just fit. According to what he told me, the name came to him as he was developing the sketches and story. There was no "brain-storming" for a name. He did not want another comic book character with "Super" in the name though he briefly considered it. My father always tried to do his own thing.

Unlike Superman or Batman who put on a "costume," Captain America, who was a soldier, wore a "uniform." Talk about the

look of the character and the decision to dress him in some version of the American flag.

Again, like the name, the costume was a natural for a patriotic comic book. The way my father designed him, Captain America was a powerful figure, both physically and symbolically: the costume draped the character's athletic figure in a chain-mailed armor jersey, with bulging arm and chest muscles, the American flag-colored skin-hugging tights, gloves, and boots, the star on the costume's chest, and stripes from the belt to a line below the star. The design worked as the muscles of the torso rippled gallantly under the red and white stripes. Here was the representation of the ideals of America, symbolized by a ready-for-action hero proudly wearing the red, white and blue colors of our flag.

The shield is also unique. It is not something that most people would think an army would issue to a soldier. Yet, of course, it works. How'd that come about?

The shield came about because my father wanted Captain America to have something unusual to use in battle. Remember, the original Captain America did not have a gun or other typical weapon. All he had was his exceptional athletic power and "never-give-up" heart and ideals. The shield was very important, then, especially for an action hero. The army wouldn't want their most fearsome weapon going into battle without some kind of defensive or offensive object, which, like the uniform, was also a symbol that put fear into the enemy.

Also, my father was a big reader as a kid. He loved to read books about King Arthur and the Knights of the Round Table: they always had shields, and as a child, my father had been hung up on shields, actually barrel tops, which were good defensive weapons against [the] stones [thrown by kids] in a tough neighborhood.

Another genre-defying aspect of the character is that unlike Superman and Wonder Woman, Captain America didn't really have super-powers. He was more like an _enhanced human._ What was your father's thinking about that?

Superman, an all-powerful crime fighter, was the basic pattern for the early successful comic book heroes, but I doubt if my father would have been happy creating another Superman knock-off to fight the good fight. Again, my father's instinct was to do things his own way and his coming into comics from a newspaper background based his thinking more along the lines of reality.

Yes, Captain America enhanced his strength via the super soldier serum, but the serum only enhanced what Cap had to start with. Captain America did not, like Superman, fly or come from another world or was impervious to bullets. He did not, like Wonder Woman, have an arsenal of weapons such as the Lasso of Truth or indestructible bracelets or an invisible airplane. No fun gimmicks.

Captain America, especially as Steve Rogers, for a comic book hero, was more believable. To many of his readers during World War II, it was more possible to identify with Captain America. He was one of us.

Comic book historians posit that some Jewish comic book writers who were immigrants found a way to explore their own personal issues of assimilation through their characters. Does that theory apply to Joe Simon and Steve Rogers/Captain America?

I never heard my father say anything like that. He was very proud of who he was, of being Jewish, even though he was not religious. I saw no interest in him exploring issues of assimilation through his characters, although he did play with the idea in several stories during his long career in comics.

Captain America was created during World War II, during a time that the country was unified in their support of the war. At the time, was he intended to be an advocate for American policy?

The reality was that not all Americans were in support of the war. I think that Captain America at the time my father created him was not specifically intended to be an advocate for American policy. I would suppose that my father came up with the character because my father was against the inhumanity, the barbaric behavior of Hitler and Hitler's followers. Did my father want the U.S. to get directly involved in the war and destroy Hitler? I am sure he did.

My father, as did Jack Kirby, who put such passion into helping produce the early issues of Captain America Comics, enlisted and joined the war effort against Hitler and the Axis forces.

Has the function of the character changed over time?

While I have not kept up with all the comic book stories based on Captain America, I doubt the basis of the character has changed much, if at all, over time. The stories may have taken different directions but the core of the character has been respected, I believe, by the many wonderful writers and artists and fans who have kept Cap going over the years.

Captain America famously punched Hitler. Today, it would be hard to imagine Captain American hitting a known terrorist. What do you think changed?

It depends on who is in charge of publishing Captain America. Some publishers would have no problem with Cap punching out a known terrorist.

Is the way that American readers perceive Captain America influenced by changes in the politics of American leaders?

If the character is done right, if the stories stick to the original basis of who Captain America is, America's interest in Captain America would not be changed by how our nation's leaders act.

What did your father think of the various film incarnations of Captain America - the Matt Salinger film, and the newer film staring Chris Evans?

He was always disappointed until the Chris Evans' *Captain America* movie, which he enjoyed immensely. He did think Matt Salinger looked a lot like Captain America.

Did he give Chris Evans any advice on how to play the character? If so, what?

Not that I know of. He loved Chris Evan's interpretation and portrayal of the character. I do know that my father and the movie's producer, Stephen Broussard, talked quite a bit. Mr. Broussard was and continues to be really terrific. The whole movie cast and crew were terrific.

What is your favorite Captain America comic book cover, and why?

Captain America Comics #1, the issue where Cap explodes across the cover and delivers a haymaker to Hitler's jaw. It was, with Jack Kirby, my father's first big success in comics, and that's why.

Comic Book Legend
A Conversation with STAN LEE

Stan Lee created or co-created more beloved superheroes than any other single creator in comic book history. His iconic characters include Spider-Man, Iron Man, Thor, The Fantastic Four, Daredevil, the Hulk, and the superhero super group, The Avengers.

His contribution to the creation and acceptance of comic books in popular culture cannot be properly summarized within the confines or scope of this book. However, failing to include Stan Lee would have left a gaping hole in this book (and made me sad), so I am very grateful to Stan Lee for the opportunity to conduct this short interview with him.

THE INTERVIEW

How did you attract audiences' interest in the ostensibly ordinary person when that character is not performing incredible acts of bravery as a superhero?

By giving that character realistic traits and attributes. What are the character's weaknesses, his hopes, dreams, desires? What frustrates him? What motivates him to do what he does? Note: When I say "him" in such cases, obviously I mean him or her.

Can you please talk about a few superhero conventions that you subverted?

In *The Fantastic Four*, I tried to avoid costumes because I always felt that no one, in real life, would put on a costume just because he has a super power. But most characters still have secret identities because the fans definitely like them. I also tried to use real names and places wherever possible. For example, Forest Hills rather than Gotham City; New York rather than Metropolis.

When creating a superhero, which comes first: the name, the power or their personality traits?

It could be either the name or the power. The personality traits come last.

Besides escapism, what function do the best superhero stories serve?

Hopefully "inspiration," which many readers need, and perhaps they also serve as role models.

Given the huge popularity of superhero movies, why is it that more moviegoers do not read comic books?

Most "grown-ups" think of comics as kid stuff and I don't think that impression will change for years, if it ever does.

Daredevil's father was murdered. Spider-Man's uncle was killed. Why do so many superheroes have family tragedies at the center of their creation myths?

It often makes an origin story, or any story, more dramatic and more realistic.

I understand you spoke with Robert Downey about Tony Stark. Specifically, what insights did you give him into Stark's character?

I modeled Stark after Howard Hughes. I told Robert to think of himself as an adventurous, inventive genius with a taste for the good life and a love of beautiful women, who also has a wry, rather sharp sense of humor.

What question should I ask the next superhero I speak to?

The only question I ever ask actors is: How can you stand all the boredom of playing a scene over and over and over and over again and then waiting around for hours while the lights are changed and set up for the next scene? I sometimes think being an actor is the most boring job in the world, except when you're in front of the camera. But most of the time is spent in just waiting around. Of course, if one is a star, the money more than compensates for the boredom.

Nicholas Hammond, who played Spider-Man, told me he believes your teenage self was the basis for Peter Parker. Is that so? If not, which character is most like you?

I guess there's a little of Peter Parker in every teenager. He was insecure, not much of a stud or a girl magnet, had to worry about his schoolwork, etc. As to your second question, I don't know that any of my characters are really like me. Perhaps Reed Richards [of The Fantastic Four] comes closest except I'm not as smart.

Hammond also told me that Spider-Man is so popular because when he's in costume he isn't identifiable as being of any specific race or nationality. What do you think is essential to his popularity?

Nick Hammond is right insofar as their international appeal. Of course, the most essential thing for any character's popularity is simply to give him traits that will make him interesting to the reader or an audience. I call him Spidey, you know.

Because you're friends with him.

The Marvel comic books were the only ones to give our character's nicknames. I made up a nickname for everybody. No one called Superman, Supey, or Batman, Baty, or the Green Lantern, Greeny, but all of our characters had nicknames. We had Spidey. I called Thor Goldie Locks, and on and on. It's amazing, none of the other companies ever caught on that. They never bothered to use that informality.

That wasn't the only difference between Marvel and other comic book companies. Your characters were often more flawed than the traditional superhero.

Well, I'm a very flawed guy so it was very easy for me to write that sort of thing.

Did you relate to one character more than others?

Whatever character I was writing at the time that was the one I related to.

How did the idea of using costumes for superheroes come about? Did that come out of necessity? Or out of your imagination?

It came out of fan mail. I've never understood the reason for costumes. I know if I had a superpower I wouldn't run out and get a costume. Which is not to say that I don't have a super power; don't misunderstand me.

I'll tell you what happened. When I did *The Fantastic Four,* which was the first of Marvel's big famous superheroes, I decided not to give them costumes because I figured I wanted to try to be more realistic. So, in the first issue, they didn't have costumes. The book sold so well and we got so much fan mail, and yet almost every letter said, "We love the book so much but if you don't give them costumes, we'll never buy another issue." Well, I don't need a house to fall on me. I realized that for some reason, which I do not understand, the fans of superheroes like their heroes to be wearing costumes.

Your heroes sometimes didn't have secret identities.

Well, that's true, in the case of The Fantastic Four, anyways. In my comic book adaptation of William Shakespeare's *Romeo and Juliet*, Romeo and Juliet don't have secret identities.

Your comic book version of Romeo and Juliet does have more robots than any William Shakespeare's play.

[Laughs] Yes, we have more robots and Cyborgs and medically advanced humans. What we did, of course, is take the whole plot of Shakespeare's *Romeo and Juliet*. There's no way you can improve on Shakespeare, but you can make it different. We set the story in the future, when there are Cyborgs and when you can have medically advanced humans. We played up the war, the hostility, and the conflict between the Montagues and the Capulets. We played up that [war] even more than Shakespeare did because we do have our comic reading audience to think of, but it's basically the Shakespearean written by a top comic book writer for today's audiences. I forget what we're charging for it but I know it isn't enough.

You've always been a Shakespeare enthusiast. I read an interview with you that dates back to the 1970s when you said you were reading his work as early as eight years old.[142]

Oh, he was wonderful. Even as a kid, I read him. I probably didn't understand most of it, but I loved the language, the poetry, the "What ho, Horatio" type of things that he used to write. I loved the fact that everything was bigger than life and the fact that all his characters were so beautifully delineated.

When Kenneth Branagh was directing the feature film *Thor*, he used *Henry V* for inspiration. I wonder if Peter Parker and Hamlet share a similar DNA.

I certainly wasn't thinking that consciously, but Shakespeare was such an indescribably magnificent writer that it's hard to write anything at all that you can't, in some way feel, "Well, this is a little bit similar to a theme that Shakespeare wrote." [That's] because he wrote everything.

There's that one Shakespeare line that says, "The fault, dear Brutus, is not in our stars, but in ourselves." That line speaks to how you write. You always like to write about the character's faults, and you still make us root for them because of their faults.

Well I think that makes for more interesting reading and interesting movie viewing. If you have a character that is perfect, then he really is uninteresting, but if you have a character that is flawed and is still trying to do the right thing, then an audience can relate to him because that's the way most people are. I mean, I hate to admit it, but even I am not fully perfect.

[Laughing] No, say it ain't so, Stan.

I try my best.

Your writing seems as if it was an act of defiance. If people traditionally did one thing then you would do the opposite. You would say, "You don't think a teen can be a superhero – well, I'm going to write a teen."

It makes it more fun to write. You never want to write things that have been written before. Of course, it's hard to find something that hasn't written before, but you're quite right. I, and I'm sure many other writers, were always trying to say something in a different way and to present something that the reader hasn't read before. That's what makes what we do so much fun.

Who would win in a fight between Spider-Man and Iron Man? What about Hulk vs. Iron Man?

Inasmuch as they're all fictitious characters, the winner would be whomever the writer chooses him to be!

As much fun as some of the new superhero films are, I think that some of your ideas are best represented in comic book form.

Well, modesty forbids me from agreeing but I think there's a lot of merit in what you say.

I thank you for all your comics, and I thank you for talking to me.

Hey, I've never enjoyed myself so much. You're a great interviewer. We should do this more often.

I'll call you tomorrow at the same time.

[Laughing] Okay, I'll be waiting.

SUPERHEROES ON TV
A Conversation with KENNETH JOHNSON

Before working on *The Incredible Hulk*, Kenneth Johnson wasn't particularly interested in telling stories about superheroes. He thought yarns about men in spandex were too juvenile. Johnson had already made a name for himself writing for *The Six Million Dollar Man*, a television series staring Lee Majors as Col. Steve Austin, an astronaut who after a near-fatal crash is surgically "rebuilt" with cutting-edge hardware at the instigation of a top-secret government agency. The procedures turn him into the first "bionic man," giving him many superhuman attributes.

That show started with the now classic refrain, "Steve Austin, astronaut, a man barely alive. 'Gentlemen, we can rebuild him. We have the technology. We have the capability to build the world's first bionic man. Steve Austin will be that man. Better than he was before. Better. Stronger. Faster.'" Many of the younger fans of the show, including myself, would pretend to have bionic powers. To illustrate bionic prowess, kids would sing out loud the bionic audio effect, "Na-na-na-na. Na-na-na."[141]

Johnson was hired to write for *The Six Million Dollar Man* so that he could introduce a bionic love interest for Austin. He created Jaime Sommers, played by Lindsay Wagner. Johnson then wrote, produced, and directed her spin-off series, *The Bionic Woman*.

When Universal acquired the rights to five characters from the Marvel universe — The Human Torch, Captain America, The Man From Atlantis, Miss Marvel, and The Incredible Hulk — they offered Johnson the chance to create a show around any one of them. At first, Johnson was reluctant to accept the offer. He was looking for a change of pace. With a background in Shakespeare and Strindberg, Johnson didn't have any interest in the superhero set.

Nevertheless, he considered the offer. While mulling over a concept for the show, Johnson recalled a book that his wife had given him, Victor Hugo's novel *Les Miserables*. He thought he could transfer the idea of the relentless Inspector Javert chasing

Jean Valjean to the Hulk series. The characters of Javert and Valjean eventually became Jack McGee, a tabloid newspaper reporter, chasing after Bill Bixby's Dr. David Banner.

Johnson completely reworked the origin myth. For starters, the title character's name was changed from Bruce Banner to David Banner because Johnson didn't like comic book alliterations. In the comics, Bruce Banner becomes the Hulk after he is exposed to gamma radiation while saving his friend. In the series, David Banner is haunted by his inability to save the life of his wife who died in a car wreck. Plagued with guilt, Banner experiments with accessing the superhuman strength that people sometimes display in life-or-death, "fight or flight" situations. His tests go awry, and hereafter whenever Banner becomes sufficiently angry, he turns into the Hulk.

Johnson also wanted to change the color of the Hulk from green to red because "the color of rage is red, not green."[142] However, after changing Banner's origin tale, he didn't feel that he could get away with another significant change without potentially alienating hardcore fans of the comics.

Rather than have Banner's metamorphosis into the Hulk take place off camera, the way Clark Kent stripped off his business attire to become the Man of Steel in *Adventures of Superman*, Johnson wanted the transformation to occur on screen. These "Hulk Outs" as Johnson called them, became a highlight of the show. As Banner's body gradually enlarged, his now bulging muscles tore through his clothing. The effect of the muscles bulging was created rather simply by having off camera crew members tear the shirt.

Despite the show's fantastic premise, Johnson always tried to keep the show grounded in reality. In one episode, the Hulk fights a bear. Stan Lee, creator of the Hulk character, suggested to Johnson that the Hulk's adversary should be a robotic bear. Johnson nixed the idea as being simply too fantastic.

Johnson also injected wit into the show. He wrote Banner's now classic line of portentous understatement, "Don't make me angry. You wouldn't like me when I'm angry."

From week to week, Banner went to new towns, as he sought a cure for his affliction while at the same time evading the tenacious pursuit of Jack McGee (Jack Colvin). During his travels, he usually befriended people who were grappling with demons of their own. The dramatic premise of the show gave Johnson an opportunity to deal with serious issues; child abuse, alcoholism, and domestic violence are some of the concerns that Johnson explored during the course of the series. At the end of each episode, Banner always left his new friends or his new love interest behind as he continued his lonely quest. A sparse piano tune perfectly captured the melancholy and the isolation of Banner's plight.

Unfortunately, the network chose abruptly to cancel the series, depriving Johnson and the show's loyal fans of a fate-resolving final episode.

Kenneth Johnson with Bill Bixby and Lou Ferrigno. Photo courtesy of Kenneth Johnson.

The show ran for five seasons from 1978 to 1982, and it remains one of the longest running series based on a comic book character.[143]

THE INTERVIEW

In adapting the comic to television, you completely revised the Hulk's origin story. Originally, he came into being after Banner was infected by a dose of radiation from a "gamma bomb." In that version, the Hulk is essentially born from America's fears about the nuclear age.

And it worked okay in the comic book, but that took it into the realm of Big Government mobilizing and chasing him. I sought a far more simple and personal story. I believe I was right, particularly after seeing the feature version.

In your version, Banner's wife dies because he failed to save her. As a result, Banner begins experimenting with controlling the fight or flight impulse. You changed the Hulk legend and suggested we all have an inner Hulk inside, our own inner demons. Please explain how your new origin tale functioned to create a new Hulk myth and enabled you to tell the type of stories you wanted to tell.

The pilot film begins with the title card, "Within each of us, at times, dwells a mighty raging fury." And it does. We've all felt that. Look at the road rage that is being acted out more and more. I wanted to connect David's experiences with those of everyday people. We also used the idea that the Hulk manifests itself in different ways. With David, his demon was anger. With someone else it might be Lust, Greed, Obsession, Fear, etc. We used that thematic element to run through every episode. We would think about the plot, we'd ask ourselves what is this episode about?

Which Classic Hero Myth best mirrors David Banner's journey in your show?

I never thought about it as being a mirror of a specific Classic Myth. Other than the classical underpinnings of Hubris, which was driving David's experimentation, just as it did Stevenson's Dr. Jekyll or Shelley's Frankenstein. Certainly there are elements of Victor Hugo's Jean Valjean pursued by Javert, and the notion of a struggling journey that the hero must take as defined by Joseph Campbell.

I think children relate more to the Hulk than they do David. They wish they were as powerful as he. Adults relate more to David's struggle. Why?

Seems pretty obvious: kids are more apt to act out while adults struggle against their desire to act out. Did you know the audience demographics? The largest segment was adult women, then adult men, then teens, then lastly kids. We always wrote and produced the show with a psychological and character approach that would appeal to an adult audience.

Kenneth Johnson directs Lou Ferrigno. Photo courtesy of Kenneth Johnson.

What advice did you give Lou Ferrigno about playing the Hulk, and what were some of his early ideas about the character that, while valid, didn't fit into your concept?

Louie had no early ideas and totally followed my lead. I told him that the creature had pretty much the mentality of a small child. Once the tantrums were past, then a childlike curiosity prevailed.

When confronting someone, Hulk often flexes his arms. Did that develop because Lou came from bodybuilding world, where poses like that are common, or was there another reason that had to do with character?

The pose came primarily from observing the world of animal confrontation and conflict. The rearing up, displays of musculature for the purposes of intimidation are classic. Body builders do it for the same reason: to show off and intimidate their judges and competitors. Even if Lou hadn't been a body builder, the approach would've been the same.

What specifically were the limits or the rules regarding the Hulk's powers?

We basically figured that he was about as strong as three or four men.

Kenneth Johnson and Lou Ferrigno on location in New York City for the episode "Terror in Time Square." Photo courtesy of Kenneth Johnson.

Hulk isn't pure beast. He's able to reason. In the pilot, he knocks down a tree to save a little girl in the water.

A twist on Mary Shelley. Frankenstein's monster threw a little girl in a lake because he'd seen her throw a flower in.

In the episode "Terror in Time Square," the Hulk races to stop David's boss from killing someone. Please explain the guiding philosophy behind Hulk's consciousness and intelligence and how the design of the Hulk's look fit into that concept.

He was driven by primal passions and urges. If David Hulked out because he knew someone was going to be killed and he needed to prevent it, then the creature would carry on that primal drive.

Do you think that the Hulk progressed or learned as a character at all, or is he the same after each episode? Should he change? Why's that?

Since he always represented the unschooled side of David's mind, he never remembered a past experience as a guide for his current behavior.

The show worked under the assumption that the Hulk would do only what Banner would do in his conscious state. In particular, the Hulk doesn't kill anyone. What was the reason for this decision? To keep the audience sympathetic to the creature and, in turn, David?

Partly that, but also not to have him face a murder rap, although I recall doing one show where David thought that had happened and was appropriately grieved. Also, the Hulk physically beating up on a person was just too easy and obvious. Additionally, I was anxious to keep the violence quotient as low as possible. It seems almost humorous given the nature of the beast, but nonetheless we tried to keep the action to property damage as much as possible.

David's failures are addressed full force. He couldn't save his wife. He was limited, as we all are. You could have "softened" his failure by creating mitigating circumstances for his inability to protect her, but you didn't.

I wanted David to feel the enormous burden of guilt for his wife's death. That guilt was always percolating just beneath the surface, fueling his ongoing frustrations at not understanding how some people had risen to amazing feats of power under seemingly identical circumstances, yet he failed. Softening that guilt would've taken him off the hook.

Kenneth Johnson with Bill Bixby, who is wearing contact lenses that help mark his transformation into the Hulk. Photo courtesy of Kenneth Johnson.

David is continually being bullied. Were you and Bill Bixby mindful of stopping short before David became a victim?

One of the great challenges of creating the Hulk Outs in the series was not simply to have him beaten up. Indeed, the first metamorphosis occurs because of a flat tire. The second because of his dream of guilt. The third because he couldn't get in to the burning lab to save Susan Sullivan. One of my favorites in the series was because he didn't have the right change to make a phone call. We were always looking for reasons that average people could identify with and feel the same frustrations over.

CBS abruptly cancelled the show. This prevented you from writing a series finale. What would have happened? Would Banner have been caught and gone on trial for killing Elaina Marks? Would he have been found guilty?

There were never specifics worked out. All I knew was that it would be important for an audience to have a sense of closure, that David's long, arduous, and classic odyssey had reached a successful conclusion.

In that episode, would Banner have found a cure?

Yes.

Steve Austin's stories were very different from Banner's. Even though both Austin and Hulk are in some way Franken-stein stories about people with great power, the shows didn't cover the same territory. What was the metaphor for *The Six Million Dollar Man?*

I didn't create the show but came on when I wrote *The Bionic Woman*. My personal approach was that despite the electronic appendages that Steve and Jaime had they were first and fore-most humans, neither of whom, particularly Jaime, was happy about their reconstruction at first. To paraphrase Shakespeare, "Some people have bionics forced upon them."

What was the main underlying issue that the show sought to resolve?

I never felt there was an overall mission, such as David had, but rather an ongoing adjustment to bionic life and the appropriate use of the power that came from it. In the episode titled "The Seven Million Dollar Man," Monte Markham, who played Bar-ney Miller, the second bionic man, became equally as bionic as Steve.[144] Psychologically, emotionally, and honorably he proved an unfit recipient of the gifts. This emphasized the unique, heroic nature of Steve Austin.

For the most part, Austin enjoyed his powers. He's not as conflicted as Banner was. Banner thought it was a curse. Aus-tin seemed empowered by it.

You're right. It had much more of an upside than a downside. Jaime on the other hand hated it at first and slowly grew into it. Although there were times such as in my "Doomsday" episode where her bionic legs were gravely injured and malfunctioning which emphasized the dilemma of having to rely on mechanical limbs. Jaime also used her bionics with a bit more humor, such as opening her tuna cans with a bionic thumb, or peeling potatoes at bionic speed.

What was Jaime Summer's archetype?

I had no specific classic reference in my head when I created her. The head of [the Department of] Psychology at Boston University, among others, felt that Jaime *herself* was the archetype.

What do you think the new "Jaime archetype" is?

I think she represented a superheroine who, though reluctant at first, rose to the extreme challenges and resolved to utilize the gift (curse?) that had been placed upon her for the benefit of others who were weaker and in need. Her humanity was always first and foremost the most compelling innate drive within her character.

Jaime Sommer's backstory is very different from Steve Austin's. She's a tennis pro turned teacher; he's an astronaut. He's more analytical, she's more instinctive. He's right brained; she's left brained. Seems as if you were trying to write his opposite.

True. I wanted a character that was both worldly and traveled, the tennis pro, a funny choice since Lindsay used to laugh about her total lack of sports prowess. When I was asked to turn it into a series, I wanted her to be a character that everyone, and kids particularly, could feel an easy access to. Hence, she became a teacher with a sense of humor. In the opening show she tore a phone book in half to get her students' attention.

You've said that you want to be mindful of just how powerful Jaime Summers was. When you wrote for the show, she didn't hit people; instead, she'd pull the rug out from beneath them. If you wrote for the show today, would that be necessary? Why?

I'd still play it that way, because as I said, merely hitting is just too easy, a lot less fun, much more harsh and intimidating.

Regarding the difference in powers between Jaime Sommers and Steve Austin, was it a fairly logical choice to give Jaime a bionic ear? Bionic nose would not have worked well. What other powers did you contemplate, and why did you reject them? How did the powers you selected support the archetypes?

I went for the ear because I didn't want her exactly the same as Steve and I knew the ear would open up possibilities for eavesdropping, etc. Also there's the subtext that "she'll really listen to you."

Why do you think fans associate the superhero character so closely with the actors who portray them?

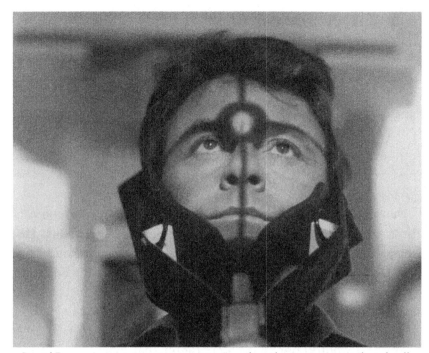

David Banner's experiment is going to "awaken the raging spirit that dwells within him." This still was made from Kenneth Johnson's original film negative. Photo courtesy of Kenneth Johnson.

That happens with all characters, not just superheroes. There are people out there who don't realize the actors on soaps aren't really the characters they play. Perhaps superheroes stand out a bit more because of the powers they have.

Do you think the type of superhero the actor plays alters fan's reactions? Did Bill Bixby's fans react differently than Lou's fans because Bixby's character was the human, non "super" identity?

Yes, of course. Bix was already an established star who just got the jibes of people saying, "We won't make you angry." Lou was virtually unknown and therefore much more connected to the creature.

What about the fans of Lee Majors and Lindsay Wagner?

Lee had a well-known persona prior to *The Six Million Dollar Man*, but so thoroughly embraced the Austin character that people believed him to be the squeaky clean ex-astronaut. He was a good guy, but squeaky-clean wouldn't be the appropriate description. Lindsay was swept into stardom by the role and had trouble adjusting at first. It's very intimidating to be an overnight star. As she herself later confessed, she got a bit seduced by it and didn't handle it all that well.

In researching this book, it was a pleasure to be able to go back and watch the old episodes. As I go over my mental rolodex of some of those images, such as the Hulk cradling his (Banner's) now dead wife, Steve Austin despondent over the death of his wife, Steve Austin frustrated that Jaime doesn't remember they were in love, Banner and McGee working together to get out of the wilderness, Steve fighting Bigfoot and then befriending him, there's a theme that runs through all these stories. It's about people trying to connect with each other. Their attempts to connect with others were heroic even if they frequently failed on a human level.

I couldn't agree more. More than anything I hope my personal legacy is one of Humanism, of trying to break down prejudice, encourage tolerance, and increase the human connections between people.

Who would win in a fight, the Hulk or the Bionic Man?

You must ask yourself why you didn't include Jaime in the contest. I think they'd all just shake hands and agree to disagree. They are, after all, heroes every one. [Author's Note: I didn't include Ms. Sommers in the battle royal because the limits of her powers were tested against them both in the two-part episode "The Return of Bigfoot."]

Crafting James Bond and Superman
A Conversation with TOM MANKIEWICZ

The celebrated screenwriter, Tom Mankiewicz, died at the age of sixty-eight on July 31, 2010. He was a widely respected craftsman whose wit was the trademark of his writing. His father was writer-director Joseph Mankiewicz (*All About Eve*) and his uncle was screenwriter Herman Mankiewicz (*Citizen Kane*).

Mankiewicz is cherished by James Bond fans for his screenplays for *Diamonds Are Forever*, *Live and Let Die*, and *The Man with the Golden Gun*, as well as for his uncredited work on *The Spy Who Loved Me* and *Moonraker*.

In fact, the producers of most of the Bond films, Albert R. "Cubby" Broccoli and Harry Saltzman, were so impressed by the work he did on *Diamonds Are Forever* they hired him to pen the next Bond film, *Live and Let Die*, while *Diamonds Are Forever* was still in production. For *Live and Let Die*, Mankiewicz met another challenge: he tailored the script to accommodate the flair for playing light comedy of the new James Bond actor, Roger Moore.

For *The Man with the Golden Gun*, Moore's second Bond film, Mankiewicz devised Roger Moore's favorite one-liner. As Bond trains a rifle at the crotch of a hostile weapons maker from whom he has to extract information, he demands, "Speak now or forever hold your piece."

Bond isn't the only iconic screen hero that Mankiewicz helped shape and define. When director Richard Donner needed to rewrite the unwieldy and excessively campy scripts for *Superman* and its sequel, he turned to his old friend Tom Mankiewicz. Mankiewicz conjured up just the right tone and the delicate balance of humor, heart, action and romance for the first two Superman movies. Though Mankiewicz was officially credited as a "creative consultant," Donner has often sought to make it known that Mankiewicz was the primary writer on both films, which are universally considered to be the best.

It is clear that Mankiewicz was very proud of his association with both the Superman and Bond franchises.

THE INTERVIEW

What was the key to understanding Superman's character? What did you have to keep in mind when writing for him?

The fun thing is writing for Clark Kent, not letting anyone know that he's Superman. That's the fun of the character. If Superman didn't have the Clark Kent alias, he'd be pretty boring. What I tried to do was to give him a sense of humor.

The thing that finally made the movie work was the scene where Superman landed on Lois's balcony. In the original script, it was about two pages long, but it was missing something. Late one night, it hit me. I called Dick [Richard Donner] in the middle of the night and I said, "After she interviews him, he takes her flying." He said, "My God, that's it. That's what we're looking for." I expanded it to about nine pages. That's more important than the explosions and rockets. He takes her flying. If you make Superman a romantic figure– he has a crush on Lois – the character has greater dimension and he becomes more appealing.

But he also has a higher duty from his father and his planet to be there for "truth, justice, and the American way." There's no way Superman can be married to anybody or to have a steady girlfriend. He's got a job to do.

Dick had a motto for the film, which was "verisimilitude." We had signs in our office saying "verisimilitude." If you write it like it's really happening, the picture is going to work. It is too easy to stand back and show the audience that you're smarter than the material. That's camp. The old *Batman* series on television was camp. It can work for twenty-two minutes on television, but it has never worked for a two-hour dramatic movie. You can't make fun of your characters. You've got to treat them seriously, especially Superman, who is a piece of American mythology.

Was it tricky to justify and provide context for the mythology?

I said to Dick one night, and this was the 1970s, and I loved my Jack Daniels, and Dick would have a joint or two. We were in the car (with a driver by the way) and I said, "Why does Superman have an S on his chest?"

Dick said, "What?"

Christopher Reeve played Superman not as a "strange visitor from another planet" but as a "friend." © Warner Bros.

I said, "I know the S stands for Superman, but it can't stand for Superman up on Krypton because up on Krypton he's not Superman."

So, we devised this thing – if you look at the Council of Elders – everyone has a different letter on their chest. We decided it was a family crest. So, Jor-El has an S on the middle of his chest inside an inverted triangle. The others have Es or Ls or whatever.

I remember at the time we were talking to Brando about it, and I said, "Yes, it's going to be a family crest."

And Dick said, "Superman, as everybody knows, has a spit curl. So, you're going to have a spit curl too."

He said, "Oh, no. There's where I draw the line. I'm not going to have a spit curl." He finally relented and he does have a spit curl just like Superman's. We decided that it was a family trait. In that sense they are very real people.

How malleable is Superman as a character?

It's interesting because Chris, who was a wonderful, wonderful guy and was very idealistic in many ways, really thought that the mantle had been passed to him to make something out of this character.

[Richard Lester's 1983] *Superman III* was not as successful as the two we did. Terry Semel and Bob Daily at Warners came to Dick and me and said, "Would you guys do the next one and put it back on track?" I explained to them that the biggest problem with *Superman III* is that it's a Richard Pryor movie - not a Superman movie. It's got to be about Superman." Even though it was going to be terrifically lucrative for us to make the movie, we decided not to do it because we thought that we had done everything in the first two.

Then as Chris got more control over the film because he was Superman, he did that very ill-advised movie *Superman IV: The Quest for Peace*, which was a dud. While they were still writing the script, I said to Chris, "Here's what you got to look for Chris, don't ever mess with anything that Superman can take care of on his own. You want total elimination of nuclear devices? Superman can do that in an hour. He can just hurl them all out into space. If you're writing about Superman, don't put in a sequence of a tsunami. He can stop a tsunami. All those people don't have to die. Don't talk about famine. Don't talk about poverty because he could fix that. So, you've got to be very careful when you write to do the kind of things that he can handle. So, I said, "Chris, it's not going to work. As much as I'd like it to work, as it's an honorable thing to be talking about, you got to look out at what your characters can do."

One of the problems with *Superman IV: The Quest for Peace* is that it becomes an overtly political film.

That's just anathema. That should never be. Superman has never been about politics. You might say, "Well, during the Second World War he might have been a hero for America," but Superman never went and fought the Nazi's in Germany for a very good reason. Superman could have won World War II in one day. So, you don't involve him in that. Literally. Because you don't care how large the German army is or how many Messerschmitts they have. He could do it all in one day. So, don't get near that. If Superman has a political view, Superman can make that political view a reality by himself, and that's why you shouldn't touch it.

The minute you give him a social cause, say Superman wants to help the homeless, well, I sit in the audience and I say, "Superman, well you lazy son of a gun. You can build homes for all the homeless in one day. You can just get the trees, build the homes, furnish the homes, and put the homeless in them." And I don't care if there's a hundred million homeless, Superman could do it. So, don't let the audience say, "Jesus, why doesn't he just go do this himself?"

Do you believe that the true identity of the character is Superman or Clark Kent?

See that's something that Chris, Dick, and I would talk about a lot. Obviously, the real person is Superman because that's the person that arrived on Earth. The little baby that held up the car is Superman, but that little baby who grew up, went to school, who met Lana Lang, who moved to Metropolis and became a reporter. That's Clark Kent. We never wanted to get into one of those anxiety-ridden, "I have a split personality" situations; we wanted it to make it more fun. He exists in the everyday world as Clark Kent, but who knows what happens when he goes into the bathroom? Does Superman shit? I don't know. He does eat that meal, but he's not human. There are questions along these lines that it's best to stay away from.

Superman seems to want Lois to like him as Clark.

I think so. We are getting a little too deep psychologically. I once ran the film and someone said, "Superman, of course comes from the Nietzsche concept." I said, "I think you're reading a little more into this film than is there." I think he wants her, absolutely wants her to like him, but he also has fun with it. For instance, after she comes back from flying. There's a great shot that Dick did after they return from their flight around Metropolis. Superman puts her back on the ground, says "Goodbye now," and then flies away. As Lois walks into her apartment, Clark comes in right through the door. It's the same shot with a cut. It was absolutely impossible for him as an actor to have changed clothes in time. It was a sleight-of-hand trick of Donner's. If you are Superman you must have a great time being Clark coming through the door. You know you've had a great time taking her flying but you don't even mention it to her. He's having a good time with it, but to come back to the crucial point, when he loses his powers, he loses his sense of mission, too.

How did Christopher Reeve differentiate between Superman and Clark Kent and make them two separate characters?

Chris very honestly said he stole a lot from Cary Grant to play Clark. Cary Grant used to have this wonderful little stutter that he could do. Chris studied it. It helped him a lot. I'm not sure if anybody ever noticed that. I'm not sure that it is that striking, but as we were discussing, this is where the fun is. It's in the fact that Lois is desperately in love with Superman, and there's Clark Kent right in front of her. She, of course, uses him. She dominates him, sometimes takes advantage of him. "Oh, Clark, do this." Because you're not doing a huge make up job you have to create huge difference in personality.

How about physically?

When you watch him walk down the hallways as Clark Kent, he's got a little slouch. He is ungainly. There's the scene where he tries to open the champagne and he can't do it. Then, he sprays it all over people. When he gets his coat caught in the ladies room door, he is Clark, the bumbler.

And Chris had great fun with the character of Clark Kent. And, as I mentioned, he walked differently; he really made a big difference between Clark and Superman. Because if Clark arrives looking great, with his hair nicely done and standing totally erect, he'd look so much like Superman that if Lois Lane didn't recognize him, she'd have to have an IQ in single digits.

Because the glasses aren't going to do it.

That's right, the glasses aren't enough. It needed just what Chris gave it: the bumbling, the subtle stuttering, and the slight slouch.

What was Christopher Reeve's reaction to being cast as Superman?

It's amazing that he was thinking about it at the time because the film had not come out and he had only been in one other movie in a supporting part. His first concern was – and it's a young actor's concern – "Am I going to be Superman for the rest of my life?" He wanted me to get him in touch with Sean Connery because I had done *Diamonds Are Forever* with Sean and I knew him pretty well. He said, "Sean Connery will know about typecasting because he doesn't play Bond anymore. I've got to talk to him." He was so earnest.

One night there was a party. I knew Sean wouldn't want to talk to him about it in that way. Sean could be a prickly guy too. Well, we were there and there was Sean. Chris said, "Oh, please. I've got to talk to him."

I went up to Sean and said, "The kid playing Superman is over there and he wants to talk to you about typecasting."

Sean said, "Ahh, geez, Boy-o." Sean used to call me "Boy-o."

I was only twenty-seven when I wrote *Diamonds Are Forever*, so I was "Boy-o" to him, but I persisted, "Do me a favor and just talk to him."

He agreed finally and then he said to Chris, "In the first place, if Boy-o wrote the script it's probably not going to be a fucking hit." He loved to take the Mickey out of me. He said, "So, you don't have to worry about that. Now, if it is a hit, then find yourself something completely different to do right away." Which I guess was why Chris did *Somewhere in Time*, a love story. Then Sean added, "By the way, if it is a big hit, get yourself the best fucking lawyer in the world and stick it to them." Then, the favor granted, he walked away.

I said to Chris, "Well, there's your advice."

Then the films came out and they were very successful. At that point, how do you think he felt about being so closely identified with that character?

A blessing and a curse, and I'm confident that Chris understood that it was a blessing and a curse. We talked about it a couple of times. When he first came here for the opening of Superman, he didn't have any money; he didn't have a pot to piss in. He was paid very little money for *Superman.* I remember taking him to a poker game I played in. He was a bad poker player. I remember he was in some big pot and he lost it. The guy he lost it to said, "Well, at least it shows you really don't have X-ray vision." I paid his poker bill that night.

But once he became Superman, it *was* a blessing and a curse. And Chris was certainly accurate: Sean Connery was the greatest example of that. Still, even today. My God he's made so many wonderful pictures since he's been James Bond and has given so many wonderful performances, but the Bond roles stay with you forever.

I was deputized to try to get him back for *Live and Let Die.* He came back for *Diamonds Are Forever* after missing *On Her Majesty's Secret* Service with the understanding that this would be his final Bond movie. The reason he came back was because he made a deal with United Artists that enabled him to make any two pictures of his choosing. That was one of the reasons he came back. He gave away most of his salary to the Scottish Educational Society. Cubby Broccoli said to me, "Have lunch with Sean. Tell him about the script you're writing."

I said, "Sean, we've got alligators, and a big boat chase."

He said, "Listen, Boy-o, one of the things I always hear is that I owe it to the public to play Bond. I've done six fucking movies. When do I stop owing it to the public? It's not a question of being kind or unkind. What, after the twelfth or fifteenth? After they stop making money anymore and people say, 'What, that's all he plays? How much do you owe after six films?'"

I understood completely. If he didn't get out then, he would just be James Bond. His other films wouldn't be taken seriously.

I'll give you a good example. When Chris did *Monsignor,* he played a character who's posing as a priest and he falls in love with Geneviève Bujold. I watched it in a theater in Westwood in the afternoon and there must have been only twenty people in the theater. At the moment, he's going to reveal himself to Genevieve Bujold, he says, "Darling, I have a terrible secret." Someone in the theater yelled out, "I can fly!" That's gonna stay with you. I must confess, I laughed.

Do you think it requires a certain type of actor to play a superhero? For instance, do you agree with A. O. Scott, who wrote in *The New York Times* that an actor playing a superhero must "has enough charisma to embody the role but without the kind of excessive individuality that would overshadow it."[145]

I think that's very true. Dick Donner made a perceptive remark at the beginning of the picture when he said to Chris, "Let the suit do most of the work." In other words, "You are Superman. If you also try to be incredibly idiosyncratic as Superman or overwhelmingly thunderous as Superman it doesn't work." One of the reasons, I think, that Chris works very well as Superman is that even as Superman he seems very shy. And I wrote it that way, but Clark Kent is a completely different deal. That's mostly acting. How do you want to get your coat caught in the door? Do you want to trip and do a pratfall?

When people go see a Bond film, they go because they personally like the character and want to spend some time with him. The plot is almost irrelevant to them.

Absolutely. You're absolutely right. It's the character of Bond that makes the movie. After George Lazenby played Bond in *On Her Majesty's Secret Service*, Sean came back with *Diamonds are Forever*. One night he said to me, "I couldn't understand the fucking script. Could you? You wrote it."

And I said, "Sean, all I know is at the beginning Harry Saltzman said to me, 'What's Blofeld's ultimate threat? I said, 'Harry, he's going to destroy the world.'"

I swear to God Harry said, "It's not big enough."

But when you look at the rules - and start with the rules - who are you writing? You're writing a guy who every man wants to be and every woman wants to fuck. No woman wants to marry James Bond. I'm sorry - even though it's a very heartbreaking thing in *On Her Majesty's Secret Service* when the Diana Rigg character dies.

Every woman who goes to see Bond thinks about spending a weekend with him. How would you like to go to Rio with Bond? How would you like to go to the Bahamas with Bond? You don't want to stay too long. He's every woman's one-nighter, two-nighter, three-nighter fantasy. Once you know that, Bond can be as cruel as you want him to be. I don't mean actively cruel, but that wonderful line in *Thunderball* when Luciana Paluzzi is shot in the back when he's dancing with her and he says, "Do you mind if my date sits this one out? She's just dead." Then he puts her down at a table full of people and the audiences laugh. Because you've established that character so well. If a normal character did that on screen you'd think, "What a despicable, horrible human being." But it's James Bond.

Of course during my time writing Bond, Bond was becoming more like a Disney picture. That car in *Goldfinger* changed James Bond forever. The ejector seat, the squirting of the oil, the machine guns. The audience just loved it. So the pressure was on to get more and more stuff, but Bond should have remained the same. Bond should have been a smoker, although they outlawed it. Sean smoked for the first five or six movies. There was a limit to how much he could drink on screen. It became more of a family movie. Bond's original character got a little softer towards the end of Roger's run; and with Timothy Dalton they tried to bring back the tougher guy.

Do you think the audience should see only a limited amount of his personal life?

His personal life is never really dealt with in the books except in *On Her Majesty's Secret Service*. By the way, the novels are a lot of fun to read. In terms of his private life, I think it's always been verboten to get into that.

Bond's personal life is a cipher to me. I don't see that he has a personal life. I mean he's always on the move. He's always checking into a hotel suite. He's always got the good girl and the bad girl. Usually two bad girls. There's the bad girl that he turns around and makes a good girl. The bad girl who tries to kill him

Sean Connery as James Bond. © Eon Productions.

that he winds up killing, but essentially it's Bond faces the world as opposed to Bond sits at home.

By the way, Sean once came to me to write his unofficial Bond movie, *Never Say Never Again.* I was very close to the Broccolis and I said, "I can't do that."

Then after the picture was made and they had to reshoot, he asked me to come see it and to give him suggestions. I called Cubby and said, "Is that all right with you?"

Cubby said, "Oh, absolutely. Absolutely." He said, "By the way, it would have been alright with me if you had written it."

I never asked him because I didn't want to put Cubby in that position.

Bond shouldn't be an introspective or self-reflective person?

I don't think he can be introspective or self-reflective. Also, he cannot be involved in a serious relationship with a woman who he truly loves and continue to be James Bond because it's totally irresponsible. Here's a guy who gets caught inside coffins and thrown out windows. You couldn't say, "This is my wife and I love her," or "This is my wife and kids" and continue to put yourself in harm's way as James Bond always does.

I had said to Sean back then, if you want to do a completely original film, and I talked to Cubby about it, "We should do a James Bond where you are in the Caribbean or wherever and you're on the heels of an assassin, and you are one step slower. You realize that your time is up. He outmaneuvers you. It's only through your wits that you finally kill him. During the film, you fall in love and we'd cast a big movie star." I was thinking of Sophia Loren back then, who would be about Sean's age, and they'd sail off into the sunset.

Cubby said, "That's great except there'd be no more fucking Bond movies and I want to keep making them."

What is the difference between writing for Sean Connery and Roger Moore?

As a writer, I always said the difference between Sean and Roger is that Sean used to throw away the throw-away lines, and Roger, because of his RADA [Royal Academy of Dramatic Arts] upbringing, *played* them. So, I wrote dialogue for Roger to really play those quips. The difference is you can put Sean at a nightclub table with a beautiful girl opposite him, and he could just as easily lean across the table and kiss her or use his steak knife under the table to stick it in her gut, and then say, "Excuse me, waiter. I have nothing to eat my meat with." The audience will accept him doing either one. Roger can kiss the girl but if he tries the knife thing, he would look nasty. Roger looks like a nice guy. Sean can look like a bastard. Meaning, there's a twinkle of violence in Sean's eye, that just isn't there in Roger's.

Roger Moore with Madeline Smith in Live and Let Die. *© Eon Productions.*

In *The Man with the Golden Gun*, Moore as Bond does rough up a woman. Do you think it wasn't that successful for the reasons you described?

Yeah, that's right. First of all, they were trying to make Roger more physical. In the beginning of *Live and Let Die* – and Roger's just a wonderful, wonderful man and has become a great friend – the first scene we filmed was him running for the double-decker bus that eventually gets shaved off during his car chase.

Guy Hamilton said, "When we start, Roger, you run for the bus and hop on."

Roger said, "There's something you oughta know about me Guy, I can't run."

Guy said, "Can't run?"

Roger said, "I look like a twit when I run. I have such long legs." He said, "Watch." And he ran and he looked like Bambi. So, you had to adjust.

Guy said, "Right then. Roger, *walk* briskly towards the bus and get on."

You know, of course, every actor has his strengths and weaknesses.

It was a huge deal for Roger to take over for Sean. When he did, we were down in Jamaica, where there was an enormous press conference. Someone said, "Why are you doing this?"

Roger said, "When I was a young actor at RADA, Noel Coward was in the audience one night. He said to me after the play, 'Young man, with your devastating good looks and your disastrous lack of talent, you should take any job ever offered you. In the event that you're offered two jobs simultaneously, take the one that offers the most money.'

Roger said, "Here I am." He's wonderful. He's a terrific guy.

Do you recall any other script notes that either Moore or Connery gave you about their character?

Sean wanted to have a meeting when he arrived in Vegas to do *Diamonds are Forever*. I was so pleasantly surprised that about half of his notes were for other characters. He would say, "Are you sure she should say this here? Wouldn't it be stronger if she did something?"

I thought, *Good for him. He's really read the script and he's thinking about everybody in it.*

I'm sure he thought, *Don't worry about me, I've played this part before.* He would say, "Can I get something funnier here?"

When Lana Wood appears at the crap table and says, "Hi, I'm Plenty." Bond says, "Why, of course you are." She says, "Plenty O'Toole." He asked me if he could respond, "Named after your father perhaps?"

I said, "It's a great line." But the very fact that he asked me – I was only twenty-seven years old – shows you the kind of way he goes about his work. He's totally professional. Any other actor would just have tried it right in the take. I was amazed. It's a good line. It's *his* line.

Sean Connery with Lana Wood as Plenty O'Toole in a scene from Diamonds are Forever (1971). © Eon Productions.

When Roger Moore told the Noel Coward story, he was obviously being self-deprecating. He brought a lot to the role.

Oh, absolutely. Roger is very smart. Besides his natural modesty, he was self-deprecating because he understood that people love Sean and that Sean is a legend. It was exactly the right thing, the graceful thing to do. Especially at that particular press conference since there wasn't a foot of film yet with him as James Bond.

I think he got a bit of a bum wrap over the years.

Of course, he has. It's because he followed such a big act. Sean was the *only* guy at the time, as George Lazenby found out, that people would accept in that part. The fact that Roger stayed on for so many of them is a real tribute to him, and he did it really well.

Do you think that the character of Bond in *Diamonds Are Forever* is consistent with his character in *Live and Let Die*?

No. Roger's character in *Live and Let Die* is a much more urbane Bond. I played to his strength. For instance, one of my favorite lines in there occurs when he's taking the little old lady for the flying lesson and, because they're being chased, they fly around in the plane half-destroying the airport. The little old lady is so frightened by the end of the chase that she nearly passes out. He looks at her and says, "Same time tomorrow, Mrs. Bell?" Now, Sean wouldn't have played that well. I would have found another line for him, but Roger had this urbane kind of cheeriness about him that you can do that. It's just an instinct. You know who you're writing for.

You spoke earlier about Connery's uneasy relationship with the part. How did Moore feel about playing Bond? Moore seemed more comfortable with it, a little more at ease.

I think Roger is very comfortable in his own skin. He really is. And I think that shows. So when you give him a part to play that suits him, he is just awfully good at it. He's a real pro. That's a wonderful quality for an actor to possess, especially when you know you're playing something that you are absolutely right for. If you cast Roger as a crazed killer because you thought, *Boy, this is gonna be great because you're casting Roger against type,* I think you'd probably be disappointed. I don't know if Roger plays that very well. I suspect he'd be uncomfortable playing so dark a character.

Do you have a favorite one liner?

The Best Bond quip maybe that I ever wrote, and I wrote hundreds of them, was cut out of *The Spy Who Loved Me*. It's when Roger meets Barbara Bach at the bar. He knows that she's a Soviet Major or something, and she knows he's 007. Anyway, he says, "I must say, you're prettier than your pictures Major."

She responds, "The only picture I've seen of you, Mr. Bond, was taken in bed with one of our agents – a Miss Tatiana Romanova." She's the girl in *From Russia with Love*.

Roger then said, "Was she smiling?"

And Barbara Bach answers, "As I recall, her mouth was not immediately visible."

Roger retorts, "Then I was smiling."

Master of the Marvel Comic Book Universe
A Conversation with JOE QUESADA

With Marvel Comics' enormous but relatively recent success in creating blockbuster superhero films, it's sometimes easy to overlook the fact that Marvel continues to publish comic books. For more than a decade as the editor-in-chief of Marvel Comics, Joe Quesada, who also wrote and illustrated comic books, oversaw virtually all aspects of Marvel's vast comic book empire.

When Quesada first assumed the position in 2000, the house built primarily by Stan Lee, Jack Kirby, and Steve Ditko was nearly in ruin. Marvel had narrowly avoided bankruptcy and was creatively stagnant. Quesada infused the comic book company with new creative energy by hiring untried but inventive artists and by spearheading fresh and sometimes controversial comic book events. One popular arc was *Civil War,* a story in which superheroes debate and battle each other after the United States government passes a law declaring that all caped crusaders must reveal their true identity and register themselves as "living weapons of mass destruction."

Other memorable storylines under Quesada's reign include *One More Day,* where, in an effort to save his Aunt May's life, Spider-Man makes a deal with supervillain Mephisto to wipe his (and the world's) memory and essentially expunge his marriage to his long-time love interest Mary Jane, and *Fallen Son: The Death of Captain America,* in which Captain America is assassinated or, at least, appears to be. Captain America remained "dead" for over two years until he returned in a series entitled *Captain America: Reborn.*

By the time Quesada was named Chief Creative Officer of Marvel Entertainment in 2010, Marvel had conquered the world of comics, and together with the success of its movies and other ventures, which includes TV programs, theme parks, and video games, the company was worth $4 billion to the Walt Disney Company, which acquired it in 2009.[146]

THE INTERVIEW

Why are superheroes so popular now?

I think there is a new breed of movies that has been very true to the source material. There's something else at work though. There's a new level of respect for comics by a new breed of film-makers who have come of age reading comic books.

Are the superheroes we see on film the same characters we see on the page? What gets lost in the translation?

What films do well is use the essence of the character. What gets lost, and rightly so, is decades and decades of continuity and minutia. The filmmakers try to distill the forty, fifty, sixty years of history for the neophyte, who might be seeing the characters for the first time not in a comic book but in a movie. Also, the time constraints of the movie require you to get in everything in two hours. The minutia gets lost and you have to do everything in broader strokes. When it's done well, you've lost really nothing of the essence of the character

I'm going to ask you to distill the essence of many of Marvel's most popular characters. What is the essence of Spider-Man?

The essence of Spider-Man like all really good Marvel characters is not Spider-Man. The essence is Peter Parker. At the end of the day, you can put Spider-Man on the screen with a suit that harkens to a spider, but Peter Parker must remain Peter Parker. He must still be the loveable, nebbish guy who has dozens of problems in his life. He's not perfect and he doesn't always make the right decision, but he tries to do the right thing. As long as you've nailed that and the mantra for Spider-Man, which is "with great power comes great responsibility," then you've nailed it. Everything else is window dressing.

Iron Man?

Iron Man is about Tony Stark. He's a brilliant scientist, who gets lost in what he invents and learns tragically about the error of his ways. He is a quintessential hero in that in his origin he wasn't necessarily the most likeable guy. However, in true Hollywood fashion he learns from his mistakes and becomes a great hero. He's quick-witted and has brainpower. As long as you preserve that you have the essence of the character.

The Hulk?

Bruce Banner is a victim of technology. He's not necessarily the bravest of souls but he's managed to contain the monster within so that he can be something greater than himself.

Does Hulk work best as a hero or as uncontrolled id?

I think the beauty of the Hulk is that he can work in a number of incarnations. The toughest of them to pull off is to make the Hulk a pure hero. He works best as id gone mad. What people enjoy about the Hulk is that he represents the child inside us. We all get mad sometimes and just want to hit a wall. We hold back, but the Hulk just hits that wall. That's what attractive about the Hulk.

I was a fan of *The Incredible Hulk* TV series. I even admired Ang Lee's *Hulk*, which was not well received by the fans. Why do people have such a hard time capturing what makes the Hulk fun?

I think that's because people see so many things in him. Ang Lee saw something very different in the Hulk from the people who produced the TV show. The people who made the TV show went for the hero angle as opposed to Ang Lee who saw the character as a misunderstood monster. I agree with you that Ang Lee's movie worked though.

What made the TV show so immensely popular was Bill Bixby as David Banner. Bill Bixby arguably had one of the highest Q ratings in the history of TV. [The Q Rating or Q Score is a measurement of the popularity and appeal of a subject.] He was one of the most likable guys. He exuded such warmth and empathy.

Relatively speaking, the Hulk was barely in the show. Banner "hulked out" twice a show but was on screen for relatively little time. The emphasis was always on Banner.

The Hulk was always there to provide a little violence – just enough to do the right thing. It was masterfully done. That's why the Hulk has endured. When people talk about who is the most recognizable character on a worldwide basis, Spider-Man's popularity has eclipsed the Hulk's, but prior to *Spider-Man* (2002), the Hulk might have been the most recognizable. That show has been syndicated into dozens of different languages all around the world.

I agree. Spider-Man's worldwide popularity is relatively new and it is a direct result of the movie version.

In the United States, he's always been recognizable. Kids always loved Spider-Man, but on a worldwide level, he just wasn't as recognizable as the Hulk. Bill Bixby and The Hulk were just the most recognizable.

Lou Ferrigno takes pride in playing the Hulk. What did he bring to the role?

What Lou brought to the role is that there's something very charming in someone who takes great pride in playing the character. How often do you see someone who has been cast as a genre character that is so overwhelmed by the casting that they feel bitter about it? Lou's a guy who truly enjoys the recognition he gets for playing the Hulk. People see Lou and they say, "There's the Hulk." You can see his love for the character and the fact that he loved playing the monster. If you see Lou at a convention today, you can see how much pride he has in it.

It used to be that unknown actors played superheroes but that's no longer the model. What changed?

It's interesting because the iconic characters like Batman never had any problems getting a mainstream actor to play them. Michael Keaton wasn't a mega-star at the time but he was a very established actor. Who was next?

Val Kilmer, then George Clooney, and then Christian Bale.

Batman is a marquee superhero, who has always been able to attract actors of caliber. With Superman, it was tough to attract an established actor because Superman is really the star. A major league actor might shy away from that. It's the kind of role that can makes a star. In the case of *Iron Man*, I thought it was really inspired casting. I thought it was a brilliant choice for Robert Downy Jr. to do the character because it had so much potential. Now the actors are starting to see the career-building potential of playing these characters. Iron Man has never had a movie but he has a forty-year history in publishing with an immense popularity. They have to think, *If these characters have been around so long it must be because there's something there.* And as we comic books fans knew, there *was* something there.

Do you think there's the one actor for one hero?

No, I think there are only a handful of actors who are right for any particular hero. When I think of Iron Man, I can personally only think of two or three actors who can play that part. Same thing with Captain America. Same thing with Spider-Man. Same thing with Batman. Every once in a while, you get interesting casting. Most people wouldn't have thought of Michael Keaton as Bruce Wayne, but he's arguably the best Bruce Wayne up until Christina Bale. I would even argue that he might be better.

I think you ask any fan at a convention, "Who is your dream Iron Man? Who is your dream Wolverine?" and they'll give you three or four different examples. Invariably when fans make those "dream team" selections, it's based on which actor happens to look like the comic book character, whereas a producer and a director have to worry about who can really play the part. Are there actors out there who might look the part perfectly? Sure, but I don't think there's a single actor out there who can *embody* the part better than Downey, and that's the magic in making these movies and casting them properly.

In comics, it might take Superman fifty years to marry Lois Lane or for Spider-Man to be unmasked. However, it only took two movies for both of those events to take place. Why the difference in story telling?

Understand that in comic books we put out a story every single month. Publishing is the great Sisyphus boulder. We roll the comic up the hill, we put it out and before we know it we have to roll the next one up the hill. In publishing it's a constant grind of material and reinventing the characters. With respect to the movies, there will only be one Spider-Man movie every two years or so and only one Iron Man movie every two years or so. In movies, they have to move the characters around in an accelerated pace.

The truth of the matter is that you have to take the franchise to the greatest possible story end with each film. The stakes must get higher with every movie. So, you accelerate through the timeline.

The other thing is that even within the forty years of publishing, we can probably distill Spider-Man's story into ten hallmark moments in his life. Ten things that audiences just absolutely remember. Chances are those are the ten things that the filmmakers will try to get across in the first three or four movies. It's a matter of hitting certain time points and hitting the best story telling moments.

Are costumes an outer extension of their inner personality. Is that who they are?

It's interesting because costumes can contain a multitude of meanings, secret identities and what they represent. Costumes can be two different things in respect to a Marvel character and a DC character. For a Marvel character, the costume is another persona that they put on. Peter Parker is Peter Parker and he puts on the spider costume to become someone other than who he is in order to fight crime. Whereas for characters like Batman or Superman – and in their case Bruce Wayne and Clark Kent – the costumes are facades. The "real" person is actually a facade and the superhero is actually the "real" person. It's who they are. It makes them a little less honest than a character like Peter Parker.

In the case of Tony Stark as Iron Man, there was a point when I became editor-in-chief at Marvel where I said, "I don't understand why a character like Tony Stark would have an alter-ego. It wouldn't make sense. You know, I understand why Peter Parker puts on the costume and becomes a masked vigilante. It's because he doesn't want to endanger his friends and family by having the villain find out who he is and then having the villains hunt down the weaker members of his entourage.

In the case of Tony Stark, he is already a multi-millionaire and is a public figure. Judging by the world we live in, the richest people and their families have to travel around with security. They are always in danger of kidnapping.

In the world of Tony Stark he is already a marked man and his family and friends need protection. If I were Tony Stark I'd walk around in a suit of armor saying, "Don't fuck with me, and don't come after to my family because I have this suit of armor." That's one of things we did in his comic book. It was a great twist at the end of the first movie when he said, "I am Iron Man." Here's a superhero who doesn't have an alter ego. He can use that to his advantage as a businessman and in his private life. It's different strokes for different characters.

I am now an Iron Man fan, but when I was younger, I didn't relate to the character because I couldn't see his face. It was completely obscured. I saw only the suit of armor and not a person. Same thing with Spider-Man, as opposed to Superman.

In respect to Spider-Man, some people found that very appealing, especially if you were Hispanic or African-American. Because he wears the mask he can be anybody, he can be me. That might be part of his initial appeal. When he puts on the full body suit and fully covers his face he can be anyone. No matter what your skin color, he can be you.

If you applied real world logic, do you have to be slightly insane to be a superhero?

[Laughs] I think so. You'd have to be unhinged to fight crime in a unitard, but when you look at this post 9/11 world, where we saw those firefighters who were running up the World Trade Center buildings as people who worked in them were rushing to get down, you see that the line between the firefighters and Spider-Man is wafer thin, separated only by a unitard. What's the difference at that point?

I think you can understand the real insanity of a superhero if you stand at the top of a building in New York City and look down. Then you begin to understand how insane the idea is of throwing a cable across to another building and swinging over to it. How absurd it is! But I'm not an extreme athlete, so who knows? What's interesting about the world today is that superheroes become more and more plausible when you see what extreme athletes can do. I'm not sure if you're aware that there are a sizable number of people who are creating their own superhero costumes and claim that they are going out and fighting crime. I don't know about you but that scares the hell out of me. It really does.

It's comforting in comics, but not so comfortable in real life. The Guardian Angels were controversial for doing just that in New York City.

I was a little kid when the Guardian Angels were making it big in New York, and I remember people were protesting against them. They said, "This is how Hitler started with the Nazis." I was like, "Wow!" Any police or security force that's not sanctioned by the U.S. government is going to make people nervous.

Given that, what moral authority are superheroes working under? They are, as you say, vigilantes.

It's part of the mythology of superheroes. It's part of the acceptance of what you think the world should be. You dismiss that part of the logic from your brain. I see superhero stories as modern day morality plays. They are modern day versions of when hunters sat around the fire telling stories or cavemen carving stories on cave walls of the great hunt or God of the great hunt, or listening to stories of Norse gods or the Greek pantheon or the Roman pantheon — they all sound great. When you think about the stories logically, you say, "Well that doesn't work at all," but before you do that you can get so caught up in the fantasy of it and the realities of the particular world that you've established that you accept it. You accept that the characters have such a great moral barometer and somehow whatever decision they make about crime and punishment tends to be the right one. They are judge and jury all in one.

Is modeling good behavior the purpose of superhero stories?

I think it's aspirational. That's the great part of it. Regardless of where we come from, our sex preferences, religion or ethnicity, at our core we all have a moral barometer that is relatively consistent with all of us, a certain sense of right and wrong. In superhero stories, we see so much of that in its purest form, and even in the case where superheroes might come from the wrong side of the tracks or haven't always done the right thing, there's always that point when they will have a crisis of conscience. They will have to face themselves and realize what they have done is wrong, and they have to turn their lives around to change it. At their core, superhero stories are about extraordinary people doing extraordinary things under very difficult and extraordinary circumstances.

Do you think adults enjoy comic books the same basic way that a kid does?

I think there are many levels to the stories. There is no doubt that when Stan Lee took over and ushered in the Marvel Revolution, the stories became much more sophisticated. So, they worked on numerous levels. Kids respond to "Let's get the bad guys" and it's very action-packed and black and white. Adults understand the grays and nuances, the relationships between characters and the subtext in the writing. When comic books work well, they work on all those levels.

Why do you think so many heroes are orphans?

That has to do more with the product of the times. Particularly the older characters, characters like Superman and Batman, who were created by Jewish immigrants who had some fears of abandonment, or who actually lost parents and family during the War. I think that goes to the heart of the creators. That's cyclical. That changes from time to time. Marvel characters in particular either lost their parents or have *serious* daddy issues. That's often what inspires them to greatness.

Parental issues seem to be at the core of many comic books.

It's part of an important family dynamic. If you look at children's literature, much of it has to do with search for your parents or abandonment by your parents. That strikes at a very primal early childhood fear that we all have. Looking back at my childhood, that was always a fear of mine. "What if Mom and Dad weren't here? What if they separated?" There's so much that can happen in a fragile, little unit. That's what speaks to those issues, hence so many of these origins.

It's possible that Stan Lee created an Aunt and Uncle dynamic as a change of pace for the father/son relationships that were the cornerstones of Superman and Batman's mythology.

That's a great question.

What misconceptions do you think there are about comic books

I think the most basic misconception is that comic books are nothing but a child's medium. So, many people are not aware of the great levels of sophistication that comic books have achieved. There is a real artistic and literary sophistication to so many of these stories that anyone who hasn't read a comic book in a while will be very surprised by. We have some great writers who are working in comic books. Stephen King is working in comic books.

Misconceptions about comic book fans?

There's always been that cliché comic book store fan guy like the Comic Book Guy character in *The Simpsons*. While there are nerds among us, you can say that about any group that centers on one interest. I'm a huge baseball fan and there are baseball nerds out there too. But let's face it, nerds are loveable and sexy these days. There's a new face to comic book fans. One of the nice things about the New York Comic Con was seeing how many female fans we now have who are really enjoying comics. It's a growing industry and a growing and ever-developing genre. Like it or not, it is affecting all aspects of modern entertainment. We are everywhere.

It's funny that you say that because I was in Duane Reade the other day and they still have these Hulk Valentine cards. It occurred to me that so many different products are simply "delivery systems" for superheroes.

[Quesada laughs]

If it weren't a Valentines Day card, it could have been a toy truck with a superhero on it. If it weren't a toy truck, then it could have been a notebook.

The reason people are licensing our characters is that they realize that people are attracted to them, find them fun, find them entertaining. There is a lot to it. This is why you see our characters on so many products. The Superman emblem alone is put on so many things. It's worn as clothing and occasionally it's tattooed on people's bodies, sometimes even by people who don't even read Superman comics, because they like what it stands for.

A FOUNDING FATHER OF THE MARVEL CINEMATIC UNIVERSE
A Conversation with JON FAVREAU

Jon Favreau was an unlikely choice to helm Marvel's *Iron Man* (2008), the first film in Marvel Studio's ambitious strategy to feature individual superheroes in standalone films and later bring the superheroes together as an all-star group in a separate, concurrent franchise. Before *Iron Man*, Favreau, best known for writing and starring in the independent film *Swingers*, had directed only a handful of films, including the Will Ferrell comedy *Elf* and the children's film *Zathura: A Space Adventure*. Marvel had a lot riding on the success of *Iron Man*: if *Iron Man* failed at the box office, then Marvel Studio's other films including *Thor, Captain America: The First Avenger, The Avengers, Thor: The Dark World, Captain America: The Winter Soldier*, and *Guardians of the Galaxy* (2014) might not have gotten made.

Favreau cast Robert Downey, Jr. as the "genius, billionaire, playboy, philanthropist." In his pre-Tony Stark days, Downey's off-screen personal troubles occasionally overshadowed his immense talent. At a time, when Tim Burton's dark and edgy Batman films were considered to be the gold standard of superhero films, Favreau eschewed conventional wisdom by taking a page from the early Bond movies as he refashioned the superhero film into a sophisticated and witty romp.

In his *New York Times* review, A. O. Scott wrote:

"What is less expected is that Mr. Favreau, somewhat in the manner of those sly studio-era craftsmen who kept their artistry close to the vest so the bosses wouldn't confiscate it, wears the genre paradigm as a light cloak rather than a suit of iron. Instead of the tedious, moralizing, pop-Freudian origin story we often get in the first installments of comic-book-franchise movies – childhood trauma; identity crisis; longing for justice versus thirst for revenge; wake me up when the explosions start – "Iron Man" plunges us immediately into a world that crackles with character and incident."[147]

466 HOW TO BE A SUPERHERO

Marvel's faith in Favreau paid off. *Iron Man* connected with both comic book fans and the general audience. The nearly $600 million that the film earned at the global box office is especially impressive, considering that at the time Iron Man was regarded as a second-tier hero. *Iron Man 2* (2010), which Favreau also directed, solidified Iron Man's reputation as a first-string superhero and earned almost $625 million. By comparison, *Superman Returns*, a film boasting what the *New York Times* described as "the most famous fictional character ever created in cartoon form," didn't crack $400 million worldwide.

Favreau also played Matt Murdock's friend and law partner, Franklin "Foggy" Nelson, in *Daredevil* (2003), and appears as Happy Hogan, Tony Stark's friend and bodyguard, in all three films staring the Armored Avenger, including the Shane Black directed *Iron Man 3* (2013).

THE INTERVIEW

Did you have any interest in superheroes as a child?

Not more than your average kid. It wasn't like I had every issue of every comic, but certainly in grade school I dug the characters a lot. I used to draw them. Then in high school, we used to go down to Forbidden Planet, which was a comic book shop near Union Square, for the science fiction and fantasy books, as well. I wasn't a comic book nut. That really wasn't my thing, but I have a pretty good awareness of them and their origin stories. I'm pretty literate, but comics began to become very serialized by the time I was a teenager, and either you're all in or you couldn't follow the story lines. So, I wasn't an avid comic book reader by then.

Sounds like you weren't a big Iron Man fan. You might have read a few stories but didn't follow his books seriously.

No. No. I read it as part of the origin stories, and I had bound collections of the older Don Heck stuff [Heck co-created Iron Man with Stan Lee, Larry Lieber and Jack Kirby]. I was aware of Iron Man, but at the time as a kid he wasn't an appealing character for me. He really wasn't relatable. He was a little full of himself. He wasn't that appealing a character to a kid. Not like a Spider-Man or a Hulk.

Given that background, what prompted you to say, "This film is for me."

Coming to him as an adult, I found him more compelling because he is a complex character. Here I am, a grown up. Most leads in movies are younger than me. Most things they are dealing with are going to be issues that are no longer relevant to me. I don't relate to situations about being single, or dating, or high school. The idea of Tony Stark, as a guy dealing with fame, money and power, and responsibility, was very appealing to me. It also allowed me to hire a lead that I was more interested in and more interested by.

The other aspect that made it interesting to me was that it allowed the movie to be a little more grounded for me because he was a self-made hero and he was tech-based. I didn't have to account on a big mystical buy or a magical buy to accommodate the audience. It freed me to make a film that was based a little more in realism. That was compelling. The technology was there to show him as a hero. While CGI [computer-generated imagery] still falls short in creating realistic looking humans, CGI is very effective in creating characters with hard, metal surfaces, like Iron Man.

Talk about defining the character.

I knew the character. That was equally as important. I thought it was important to stick to the mythology of the books. On one hand, Iron Man was part of Marvel's pantheon of original books. That gave him a little more – how should I put it – gave him a little more weight than the latest IPs [Intellectual Properties] that are coming out of comics, which aren't part of our cultural memory. Part of what's fun about Iron Man is that he's been around for so many years. But even avid Iron Man fans don't gravitate towards any one villain or story line. That was never the strong suit of Iron Man. He never had a great run compared to some of the other superheroes in Marvel and DC.

So I really wasn't restricted by plot or story. As long as I hit a couple of touchstones, I could reflect on the books without making the mistake that has been made so often and that has been resented so much in the past. That is, too often when studios have acquired the rights to comic books, the filmmakers throw out a lot of the stories' histories to make movies based on whatever current trends appear to be the most interesting to the movie-going public. I think what happens is that you wind up alienating your core fans. Although the core fans alone can't make a movie a hit, you don't want to alienate them because if you keep them happy and make a good movie at the same time, you can really cut through the clutter in the marketplace. The core fans are pretty vocal. And in the case of Iron Man, they were virtually the only ones who heard of him. They were pretty important to us.

If the core fans can't make a movie a success by themselves, why is it important to cater to them?

Part of the answer reflects my personal preference. I relate to that group. I think there were a lot of movie people who, not so recently, perhaps ten years ago, or maybe even five years ago, caused resentment among the hard-core fans. Too often the film-makers ignored the serious comic book fans at best and were weirded out by them at worst. It's almost like high school groups – and they were like the popular kids who don't like the nerds. So often when you were in meetings with the people in Hollywood, you'd find them shaping their movies to appeal to backers and distributors, and you would find that they really didn't consider that group. They were more interested in making the movie sexy. They would co-opt and transform the comic book material by re-constituting it in the mold of an action movie, which tended to go for sexy casting, sexy music, sexy costumes, sexy violence. It was just designed to get a movie made, something that they thought enhanced their chances of selling their projects to the studios.

But the appeal was never that there was a base of support for the comic book genre. I guess, Superman busted through years ago but that was a very identifiable IP. That wasn't because it was a comic book; it was because it was Superman. You can really say the same thing for Batman, and Tim Burton just made it really interesting. But other than those two properties, no one cared about superhero movies at all until Marvel really began its campaign to bring its characters to the screen in a more accurate way. I think X-Men was the first franchise to do so. *X-Men* (2000) was a real turning point. It took a group of superheroes that was very well-known and beloved by the fans. I mean X-Men was the coolest, most interesting book to read or own or reference when I was in high school. I think it was a turning point in the vibe of that group. It took the premise of a comic book that was already interesting and offbeat and it carried it to the next level. Wolverine became the poster boy for the more complicated, more unexpected version of a superhero.

They took it and they started a formula where you hire a person who has cut his teeth in independent film – as was the case with Bryan Singer, who made *The Usual Suspects*. They brought an essentially unknown cast together; they stayed fairly close to the books. They couldn't help themselves, of course, and they had to stick them in leather motorcycle racing outfits, which I guess is a small price to pay to enter the mainstream. It went from a group of comic book characters that no one but the fanboys had ever heard of and by making a quality movie, it broke through, exceeding all expectations, and it became a mainstream phenomenon, as well, while still satisfying the fanboys, albeit with certain misgivings about the interpretation of the costumes. Prior to the X-Men movie, iconic elements of the characters were used or discarded at the pleasure of the studio.

Michael Chabon wrote an essay for *The New Yorker* in which he said that a superhero's outfit is really the "secret skin," or the true identity, of the character -- it is inextricably linked to the hero.

I don't know if I agree with that. It depends on which hero it is. There are certain heroes, like Superman, where I think that's true. The first question you have to ask yourself when you make one of these comic book movies is: Who is the real character and who is the alias? Is the character Superman or is the character Clark Kent? Is Superman his disguise, or is Clark Kent his disguise? In the case of Superman, the character is Superman and the disguise is Clark Kent. In the case of Iron Man, I think the character is Tony Stark and the disguise is Iron Man.

It's the tension that exists as the character transitions from one to another. It's not a constant. It's a continuum. In the Spider-Man movies, when you start off, I'd say the character is Peter

Parker. In the sequels, after *Spider-Man 2*, I'd say Spider-Man is the character and Peter Parker is the disguise. He might be talking on a more mythical level. That might be true if you look at it as allegory – more like Joseph Campbell, but in the specific ins and outs of actual crafting one of these movies it's not always a given that that's the case.

What would you say is Tony Stark's psychological profile? Who would you say he is deep inside?

I can only infer the answer from the books, but we've made certain decisions in our process because that's the nature of fleshing things out. Tony Stark's a guy who on the most superficial level represented the military industrial complex because, at the time, we were on the brink of the Vietnam War. He was fashioned after Howard Hughes and embodied some of the more anachronistic aspects of the bachelors from the 1950s and early 1960s, not unlike the characters from the show *Mad Men*. At the time, it didn't seem odd, but now it seems a little tongue-in-cheek. So in staying faithful to the way he was originally depicted, he's a little outdated right now.

But there are certain qualities and characteristics that we tried to maintain and update a bit. He's a guy who has chosen his career and his hedonistic streak over family and stability and security. He's not married and he has no children, but he's in his forties. He's older than most of the other superheroes. Most of them seem to be in their twenties, if not their teens. He's a guy who is a full adult. He's a guy who was famous and successful in his own right long before he took on the persona of Iron Man. He's a guy who invents the suit – symbolically manifesting his transition from one life to another. He goes from a life of moving forward ambitiously with blinders on, who enjoys the trappings of his fame and fortune, to become a guy who lives an anonymous life and a life of service. He uses all of his abilities and resources to be of service to others and that seems to fit the superhero paradigm whether it's Batman, Spider-Man, or Iron Man.

Tony Stark is arrogant and narcissistic, and you didn't soften that.

We were fortunate to have Robert Downey, who is able to remain likeable. In the hands of a different or less thoughtful actor the effect would have been much different. We would have had to do a lot of things differently.

Would you have been able to do the same plot five or six years ago when America was more hawkish?

I think so. I think so. Because Tony Stark is certainly more hawkish than the Hollywood establishment, and we didn't try to pull back on that at all.

Yes, but he has a change of heart about his profession as an arms dealer.

He's not handing out flowers. He goes in, makes a judgment, and he brings to bear all of his military resources and technology to effect the outcome of a situation, not just in America but around the world. He can be attacked for being a manifestation of American hegemony, but I think the transition he does go through by not sticking his head in the ground is to realize that there is a responsibility that goes along with that power and it should be exercised only in the name of justice and not arrogance or ignorance. So, in my opinion, his transition is not going from being a hawk to being dove, but rather he is transformed from being powerful and unconcerned with the consequences of his inventions and actions to someone who actually sees the human dimension and consequences of it all. He realizes that there is a responsibility that goes along with exercising that power. Not unlike the Spider-Man catchphrase, which is "With great power comes great responsibility." The same can be said of Tony Stark, except that he had great power before he became Iron Man, but only later does he come to terms with the responsibility that should accompany that.

One of the things I've found in interviewing actors who have played superheroes is that the actor seems to find the superhero that they are most like. How is Downey like Tony Stark?

There are two sides to that coin. One side is that as I'm sifting through headshots and flipping through pages of resumes and thinking about what the story is going to be, I'm looking for a clue, for some sense of clarity about a path, or a game plan, for two years as a filmmaker, where I'm going with it. Ultimately, I'm the one who is going to be steering the ship through the whole process and I have to understand where the lighthouse is. That has to come together in number of ways. It's not like the other movies I've worked on where the script comes first and other things fall into place. Here I have a pile of comic books, I have different versions of an outline. I have reams of storyboards and set pieces and villains. It all has to come together.

When I met with Robert, I understood what the movie was all about. What the tone was. How to balance humor with action, and how it fits in among the glut of other superhero movies. How it can be distinct yet familiar. I understood what I had to do as a director once I had Downey starring.

Downey, on the other hand, understood the role and the history of the character as depicted in the books and saw a way to apply his life experience and bring that to bear on the role. He understood how to make a transition into the mainstream and to be able to attack the role without compromising any of his integrity as a performer, and also to play into the fanboy streak that he has.

He attacked it from one end and I from another. There was great resistance to both of our desires. It was only through his unflagging determination to get the role and mine to continue supporting it and to push it through on my end did it finally come together. What seems to be kismet now was pretty precarious at the time.

He grew up the son of second-generation Hollywood. His dad was a pioneer in independent film. He grew up in a long shadow. His father seems to have been pursuing a dream. He had to share his father with that dream. That's a blessing and a curse. You are basking in this wonderful, creative, energetic atmosphere, yet you're sharing your dad, who you selfishly want to keep for yourself. You're sharing him with the rest of the world. Robert was recognized very young. He was nominated for an Academy award [for *Chaplin* (1992)], I think in his twenties. [Downey was twenty-six when he was nominated.] He grew up on the outside faster than on the inside. Suffered for it. He became recognized, famous, and wealthy before he found out – truly – who he was. Because he was a celebrity, his mistakes became public, whereas most of us make our mistakes in relative privacy. Difficulties accompany that. He and Tony Stark, the character he plays, are considered geniuses in their own fields. So, there's a cockiness and confidence that comes with that. That can be a two-sided coin. If you're laughing at or condemning them, you see them as cocky. If you are inspired by them or believe in them, you see it as confidence and poise. I discovered that when you plug in Robert Downey, Tony Stark is a lot more interesting than the Tony Stark I read growing up. I thought it was a very favorable trade. I thought we traded up.

Did you have to tell Downey that he'd forever be identified with the role?

No, I didn't have to tell him. He's been around a lot longer than I have. He was telling me more things than I was telling him to be honest with you.

A. O. Scott of the *New York Times* wrote that an actor who plays a superhero has to have "enough charisma to embody the role but without the kind of excessive individuality that would overshadow it."

Yeah, that's traditionally been the case. That's one of the reasons that Marvel was so resistant to Robert, who was a bigger name than Iron Man. But we threw that out the window. Maybe now that's changed, but that was certainly true when we hired him. It was scary at the time for the studio, which was releasing its first movie and they were betting the whole farm on a name and image. They took the leap. I think Robert upstaged *Iron Man*, and he made it a huge success.

I think that's true. I think that's why audiences saw the film. Seeing Downey's attitude and demeanor is what probably sold the general public on coming out for another superhero film.

Yeah. *The Dark Knight* (2008) is a much different movie and differently inspired, especially the performance of Heath Ledger [as the Joker]. I asked Justin Theroux, who wrote *Iron Man 2* (2010), what he thought of the movie. He said, "You know what's great, our superhero is the Joker. He's not the villain." That's a fun different twist. Certainly in the Batman pantheon, you have the very stoic central figure of Bruce Wayne/Batman and you have a kaleidoscope of colorful villains that revolve around him in this carousel of insanity. Those movies are always as good or as bad as their bad guys. In the case of this one, with Heath Ledger, they really came up with something very fertile and rich and off-putting. They hit the tone that no one else was going for just right. Then you have your Riddlers and Penguins and the sexuality of Catwoman, all these twisted mythic archetypes, enlivening the movies through this hyper-real urban redo of noir and pulp crime fiction. It's some weird cross between comic books, and the Sunday funnies. It's this weird surreal world with weird surreal villains.

Marvel's approach has always been: It's New York City. It's the real place. It's real people. They can't pay the rent. They bicker. They run into each other. There's public opinion that has to be dealt with. You're dealing with politics, wars, and the things that are in headlines. There's much more realism. You can't play in the world as much. You can't take as much liberty without breaking the tone of the piece. It suits me a little more as a filmmaker. I like to comment on what I see a little more. As opposed to inventing things from whole cloth.

There are other aspects that allow us to borrow things from reality and twist them a little more. It has a bit of a satirical bent. I prefer an easier ride. I prefer entertainment that's a little more fun and a little less gut-wrenching. I try to present the kind of entertainment I like to watch. Fortunately, with the superhero genre, there are now subgenres that are developing. Now, with the huge first weekend that *The Dark Knight* had, it's clear that the genre is not tapped out by any stretch. There is a lot of room for a lot of success. It will be interesting at the end of the summer to see them line up the movies and to start drawing comparisons between movies based on comic book superheroes and the others which aren't, and I think you'll see that superhero movies claim the lion's share of the box office.

How do superheroes work on us?

Every superhero story has its roots in what Joseph Campbell calls "The Hero's Journey." It's a very specific structure, whereby a character from an ordinary status has an extraordinary experience that elevates him to a heroic status. In every story you are trying to find the heroic aspect of your lead. Sometimes the heroism can be literal, like a guy becoming a Jedi Knight. Many believe that the more you feed into the hero's journey structure the more people like it, and as a result, the more successful the film is commercially. [George] Lucas is a great example of that, especially in the first *Star Wars* film. Sometimes it has more subtle forms. Even in *Swingers* we were asking ourselves, "What is the heroic nature of this character? How does he change and transform?" The reason a superhero movie works so very well is that you have the big screen, the big characters, the big costumes, special effects, and super powers to exemplify that journey. Whereas 10,000 years ago, you would draw a guy throwing a spear at a buffalo on a cave wall, you can now show guys flying through the air and blasting people with their repulsion beams. It's a bigger than life depiction of the very relatable story of facing adversity and being transformed through overcoming obstacles, of becoming your higher self. What's nice about the superhero movies is that they are serialized and you can revisit those themes over and over again as the heroes face different adversaries and greater challenges.

Why do you think father/son conflicts are such a key part to so many origin myths?

I think that the closer you stick to the ancient themes and archetypes, whether you look at Aristotle's *Poetics* or the handful of story lines that you find in Shakespeare's comedies and tragedies, the more likely you are to connect powerfully with people's psyches. That theme has always been a part of our culture. It goes back to the Greeks with the Oedipal stories.

They are always touching very basic primal fears and desires that we share. You try to tap into these things. That being said, you can't sit back and say, "Where's the father figure? How can I retell the story of Oedipus?" You have to simply write your song because you want the kids to dance. You don't think in those terms, but when you look back at it it's amazing how repetitive thematically these things turn out to be. But nobody I know thinks about it from the perspective of a theme when they are being creative. They are simply telling a story that they enjoy or are interested by. Then when you look back you see these themes emerge, but I never hear anyone who is good at making movies approach things purely from a thematic sense. You tend to recognize or analyze your themes when you're done. Those patterns emerge in the stories people like to tell and like to hear. It's for the students, the professors and the critics to bat themes around, but the people who make the movies aren't really thinking about that – except later on reflection.

Can you attribute any meaning behind Iron Man's suit?

I was looking at the Golem, that old story set in Prague about the little town that is being oppressed by the government. The peasants magically create this Frankenstein monster out of clay that fights off the oppressors. That's one paradigm that seemed to apply. Another is the Old Testament story of Joseph being cast in the pit. He emerges from being held captive, is inspired by Godly visions, and then reinvents himself. *Joseph and The Amazing Technicolor Dreamcoat* is probably the most famous pop culture reference to that tale.

There's certainly a lot of Batman in Tony Stark. Because I think he was a knock-off of Batman when he was created. They used to borrow a lot back and forth, DC and Marvel. I think it was definitely a reaction to Batman, which is interesting because here we are trying to share the same marketplace with Batman and we're trying to create our own personality. Tonally, we tried to be completely different and to exist completely separately.

Still, they are both self-made, mortal billionaires. Both are bachelors who have secret identities as crime fighters, and they are men of great intelligence, tremendous wealth, with unlimited available resources, and they have big companies supporting them.

There are a lot of influences on Iron Man. One of them is the life of Howard Hughes, who seems to have parallels with Stark. We try to consider all these things on some level.

Based on the popularity of the Batman films, I would have thought the impulse would be to draw a more direct line between Batman and Iron Man, to emphasize their similarities. Your film is more breezy and lighter.

Yeah, we tried to keep it more fun and young. I also have a six-year-old son and a five-year-old daughter, and I wanted something they could see. My tastes are a little bit softer and more hopeful as I get older. I like my work to reflect that in some way. I think they have to be stories of escape and hope and yet it's important to address the scarier events of our time (however obliquely) and try to defuse some of the anxieties, tensions, and the sense of powerlessness that we might feel -- to have this invented character who is uniquely suited to deal with these issues and make short work of them. Whether it's war or the economy or crime or technology, here's a guy who can cut through all of that and make the world a better place.

How powerful is Iron Man? If you made him too powerful you'd minimize the drama by taking away any sense of jeopardy.

Sure and that's part of the problem of the books. The suit varies. He can fly, blow stuff up. He's super strong. If you look at the way he's defined by the Marvel summary of him he seems to have no weakness. But making his power source that's related to his heart condition a weakness, and also exploring his character flaws, that creates balance. You have to create balance within a hero, otherwise they are unstoppable, and we are completely unable to relate to them.

This is a superhero film that's not too dark for kids.

I tried to make a movie that was smart enough for grown ups, without having anything in it that could cause anyone to feel irresponsible for bringing kids to see it. It's a little bit weirder for parents because of some of the stuff between the lines. Some of the weirder stuff is stuff that only parents notice, but there are no blood squibs, and you really don't see people die close up.

What question should I ask the next superhero I speak with?

How much did they have to think about and practice the voice of the superhero? As I've watched and worked on these types of movies, I've noticed that the actors who normally come from a very internal place seem to audition voices for themselves in a way almost like trying on the costume. The costume does so much and the voice is so important. I'd ask actors about their process for finding the physical voice of the character.

Who would win in a fight, Iron Man vs. Spider-Man? Iron Man vs. The Hulk?

Iron Man would win both. Iron Man could create the "Hulkbuster" suit. He's smarter, less powered by emotions that the Hulk, he has more resources than the Hulk. And Spider-Man, I think he'd beat Spider-Man, as well. Though that's a tough one, I'd say that Iron Man would win because I have to root for the home team.

What about Iron Man vs. Superman?

I think Superman beats everyone. Unless you have Kryptonite. Superman wasn't created as a balanced character. Unless we could make a suit out of Kryptonite, I think we have problems. I don't think anyone can beat Superman.

APPENDIX:
WORLD'S GREATEST HEROES

World's Greatest Heroes
Part One: The Formative Years

For various reasons, a number of actors who have played superheroes whom I had hoped to interview for this book were unavailable. Because I think it is valuable to include some of their thoughts, I have culled published comments of theirs from many sources. Some of the actor's quotes have appeared in multiple articles, and in such cases I have attempted to credit the earliest appearances. I am indebted to the writers who conducted the original interviews.

Part one of the appendix highlights the era that began with the Batman and Superman serials of the early 1940s and continued through Christopher Reeve's *Superman* feature films, which started exceptionally strongly in the late 1970s but concluded weakly in the late 1980s. In this period, superhero films were still in a nascent stage and the actors who played them were often unfairly typecast.

Kirk Alyn – Superman

Kirk Alyn played Superman/Clark Kent in two serials, *Superman* (1948) and *Atom Man vs. Superman* (1950). He appeared in a cameo role as Lois Lane's father in *Superman* (1978). His 1971 autobiography is appropriately titled *Kirk Alyn: A Job for Superman*.

Kirk Alyn on playing Superman: It was great fun playing Superman. When I was a little child, my father never let me play cops and robbers. Now, there I was playing Superman. I was getting it all out of my system. It was marvelous.—*Starlog*, 1979.[148]

Kirk Alyn on his approach to the part: I had to do everything very seriously so that the kids would believe it. I didn't dare lampoon anything or make fun of it.—*Superman: The Comic Strip Hero*, 1981.[149]

Kirk Alyn on performing some of Superman's heroic deeds: Many times I felt very ridiculous doing some of the things. It's not the ordinary kind of acting. You do it and you wonder how the heck am I going to pull it off ... We must have done [a scene where Superman picks up one criminal and bashes him into another] four or five times because I couldn't stop laughing.—*Superman: The Comic Strip Hero*, 1981.[150]

Kirk Alyn on typecasting: I couldn't get a job in Hollywood. I was permanently typecast as Superman.—*Starlog*, 1979.[151]

Sean Connery - James Bond

Sean Connery played James Bond in *Dr. No* (1962), *From Russia With Love* (1963), *Goldfinger* (1964), *Thunderball* (1965), *You Only Live Twice* (1967), *Diamonds are Forever* (1971), and in *Never Say Never Again* (1983). Connery, who said that above all Bond must appear to be "competent," kept his promise to never say never again when he provided the voice of the secret agent for the video game adaptation of *From Russia With Love* (2005).

Long-time friend Michael Caine provided insight into Connery's feelings about 007 when he said, "If you were Sean's friend in those days then you didn't mention the subject of Bond. Never."[152]

Sean Connery on what he likes about Bond: His redeeming features, I suppose. His self-containment, his powers of decision, his ability to carry on through till the end and to survive.—*Playboy*, 1965.[153]

Connery's description of Bond: He is really a mixture of all that the defenders and the attackers say he is. When I spoke about Bond with Fleming, he said that when the character was conceived, Bond was a very simple, straightforward, blunt instrument of the police force, a functionary who would carry out his job rather doggedly. But he also had a lot of idiosyncrasies that were considered snobbish. But if you take Bond in the situations that he is constantly involved with, you see that it is a very hard, unusual league that he plays in. Therefore he is quite right in having all his senses satisfied - be it sex, wine, food or clothes - because the job and he with it may terminate at any minute.—*Playboy*, 1965.[154]

Connery on being typecast as Bond: Let me straighten you out on this. The problems in interviews of this sort is to get across the fact, without breaking your arse, that one is not Bond, that one was functioning reasonably well before Bond, and that one is going to function reasonably well after Bond. So, you see, this

Bond image is a problem in a way and a bit of a bore, but one has just got to live with it.—*Playboy*, 1965.[155]

Sean Connery on playing Bond: I don't think a single other role changes a man quite as much as Bond. It's a cross, a privilege, a joke, a challenge, and as bloody intrusive as a nightmare.—1971 Interview.[156]

Sean Connery eighteen years later: I'm not quite as branded or destroyed by the association with Bond as I once was. There's no question it was getting in the way of my decisions to do anything else. The strange thing was how long it hung around, but it doesn't bug me as much as it used to.—*Lucasfilm Fan Club*, 1989.[157]

Burt Ward – Robin

In addition to playing Robin during the three seasons of the *Batman* TV series, as well as in the feature film, Ward played Robin in the animated series *The New Adventures of Batman* [1977]; and in two trivial 1979 TV specials, *Legends of the Superheroes: The Challenge* and *Legends of the Superheroes: The Roast*.

Ward performed the voice of Robin on a spoken-word record entitled *Boy Wonder, I Love You* [1966], which was produced by the adventurous and eclectic musician Frank Zappa, and on an episode of *The Simpsons* [2002].

Ward also appeared as a fictionalized version of himself in the TV-movie *Return to the Batcave: The Misadventures of Adam and Bruce* [2003], where he appeared alongside Adam West, Frank Gorshin (Riddler), Julie Newmar (Catwoman), and Lee Meriwether (Catwoman from the 1966 feature film *Batman*).

On being cast as Robin: The producers said to me, "Burt, we're going to explain to you why we're selecting you out of 1,100 people, why we've chosen you to play this role."

I said, "Why's that?"

They said, "Because in our minds, Burt, if there was really a Robin, we believe that you, personally, would be closest to what Robin would be. We don't want you to take on some characterization of the character. We really want you to be yourself, and to be enthusiastic." That was what they required. —Hollywood.com, 2012[158]

On wearing the costume: When they would have the scene with Adam and I as Bruce Wayne and Dick Grayson inside Commissioner Gordon's office, and then we say we have to leave, and five minutes later there's a call for Batman and Robin and there we are again, as Batman and Robin. Nobody in the world would believe that we're not the same people. I learned a heck of a lesson by going to conventions because when I would go out and make personal appearances in costume, people would fight over my paper drinking cup as a souvenir. Four-and-a-half hours of people waiting in line. By the time parents got up there, their kids were asleep in their arms, and they would just go nuts. And after the appearance, I could go back and change, and come out ten minutes later, and people were still milling around, and I can walk like I was invisible. — Hollywood.com, 2012 [159]

On the impact of playing a superhero: I mean when you come into the set at 7:30 in the morning and you come out of make-up and the first thing you know, the ladies start coming into our dressing rooms at 7:45. We're talking about wild times in the dressing rooms, on the set, between the shots, in the lunch wagon. When we got home at night after fourteen hours on the set, I think we redefined the meaning of the word pleasure pad. And then of course, doing the personal appearances on the weekend, that's where it really got wild. And I have to be honest with you, we became like sexual vampires. On our show, I must tell you, it was . . . the 1960s were a period of time when everything was free love. People made love to each other. It was a very open life, you know? So, it wasn't as though we were out soliciting or anything. We were the ones being chased. — CJAD 800 AM, 1995[160]

Frank Gorshin – The Riddler

Frank Gorshin played the Riddler in ten episodes of the *Batman* TV show, in the feature film *Batman* and in two episodes of *Legends of the Superheroes* (1979). He also played supervillain Professor Hugo Strange in three episodes of the animated series *The Batman* (2005).

Frank Gorshin on the Riddler's laugh: When I got the role I thought, *I'm going to laugh a lot.* I remember reading the comic book and it was indicated that he would leave these riddles and laugh. So I knew the laugh was going to be an import thing. So I started fooling around with all these laughs. Big laughs, little laughs, machine gun laughs, and I thought, *Wait a minute.* I remembered Richard Widmark in the picture *Kiss of Death* when he pushed the old lady down the stairs when he did it. That's really what set him apart from the others. And it wasn't so much the sound of his laugh, it was the fact that he was laughing when he did something so evil. That's what made his character so terrific. I thought, *It's really not the sound; it's just got to be an honest laugh.* So I started listening to myself laughing and when something was really funny I found that I have this high pitch laugh. [Does the laugh] And that's it.—Personal appearance at Chicago's Hero-Con, 1991.[161]

Cesar Romero – The Joker

Cesar Romero played a very jovial Joker in twenty-two episodes of *Batman* (1966-68) and in the feature film *Batman* (1966).

Cesar Romero on playing the Joker: It's a lot of fun. We had a lot of fun doing the show. It's a part, you know, that you can do everything that you've always been told not to do as an actor. In other words you can get as hammy as you like and go all out. It's great fun and I enjoy it.—CBS Affiliate interview, 1966.[162]

Cesar Romero on the odds of Joker defeating Batman: Oh, you can't win. The villain can't win. We always win, you know, on Wednesday night [when the first of the two-part episode airs]. At the end of the show on Wednesday night, we're winning, but then comes Thursday night, we lose.—CBS Affiliate interview, 1966.[163]

Burgess Meredith – Penguin

Burgess Meredith played the Penguin in twenty-one episodes of the television program *Batman*, as well as in the 1966 feature film *Batman*.

Burgess Meredith on the Penguin's laugh: I didn't smoke at the time. And the Penguin had to smoke all the time. And I said to [producer] Bill Dozier, "If I start smoking again, I'll sue you." And he said, "Go ahead. It'll get us a lot of publicity." I had that [cigarette] and it used to choke me. And that's how the laugh started.

Because we didn't have many takes in those days; you had to get it [right] pretty fast. So if I began to choke from the cigarette, I would go [demonstrating Penguin's cackle]. But I was really choking. It was quite accidental, but every time I would walk out into the street kids would cough at me."—*CBS This Morning*, 1989.[164]

Eartha Kitt – Catwoman

Eartha Kitt played Catwoman in five episodes of *Batman*. She was the first African-American woman to play the character.

Eartha Kitt on the ongoing appeal of Catwoman: She has a tremendous sense of humor. She likes teasing. You never know when she's going to leap at you [or] when she's going to caress you.—*USA Today*, 2004.[165]

Van Williams – The Green Hornet

Van Williams played Britt Reid/Green Hornet in twenty-six episodes of *The Green Hornet* (1966-67), which was produced by William Dozier, the producer of Adam West's *Batman*.

Van Williams on his assessment of the series: I felt my role was very one-dimensional as there were two characters [Green Hornet and his alter ego Britt Reid] that had to be dealt with. When I had my first meeting with Bill Dozier, my main complaint was that the show should have been done as an hour. I told Dozier that the only way I would play the role was as straight and honest as I could make it and I would not do anything like they were doing to *Batman*. I received some criticism because of the way I played it, but that was how I felt it should be played.—*Polar Blair's Den*, 2006[166]

Van Williams on the ongoing appeal of the show: I did six series, [plus appearances in scores of] TV shows, and [three] movies, and the thing I am remembered for the most is *Green Hornet*. It is still playing and I still get a lot of fan mail from all over the world. I think it has become a cult of some sort. It is amazing how the fans remember things about the show that I had totally forgotten. One of the things I remember most was how many cops would come up to me and say, "I became a cop because of what you did with your life." That is something to be remembered for.—*Polar Blair's Den*, 2006.[167]

Van Williams on *The Green Hornet* (2011) starring Seth Rogen: I wasn't happy at all with the movie. He [Seth Rogen] played it completely wrong. Made it into a joke, a comedy. My friends who saw it when it first came out said I was going to hate it, which is what my reaction was. My friend, Adam West, lives out here [in Idaho], heard about the film while it was being made and was pushing to get me a role of some kind in it. As it turned out, I had a flare-up with my back and when they called I couldn't shoot anything so I'm not in it. And glad now that I'm not.—*National Enquirer*, 2011.[168]

Lynda Carter – Wonder Woman

Lynda Carter became a source of inspiration to her many fans when she played Diana Prince/Wonder Woman in sixty episodes during the three season TV run of *Wonder Woman* (1975-79).

Lynda Carter on her approach to the character: The way that I approached the character, I really tried to give her humanity, which is why I think it worked. It's that she was just a regular person who happened to do all these things and everyone else goes crazy. But I think that must have been a chord that was struck in the eyes of a lot of the viewers, and I have to say that I have had a tremendous career and I still work.—*The Larry King Show*, 2002.[169]

Lynda Carter on the appeal of Wonder Woman: I think it's the goddess within us, the secret self.—*New York Times*, 2007.[170]

Lynda Carter on still being associated with Wonder Woman: I was comfortable back when I did it and I'm comfortable with it today. I'm still doing what I do and part of the reason people come to see me is because they liked her. It's not something I can get away from, nor would I want to. What's not to like about Wonder Woman?—*Out*, 2012.[171]

Lynda Carter on being a sex symbol: I never meant to be a sexual object for anyone but my husband. I never thought a picture of my body would be tacked up in men's bathrooms. I hate men looking at me [in that lascivious way] and thinking what they think. And I know what they think. They write and tell me."—*US Magazine*, 2013.[172]

Lynda Carter on the location of her costume: I will never tell. I can't give up that secret. But I have it. It's safe. Some of it spends some time at the Costume Institute in New York on display. Don't ask me, but I'll tell you anyway, I never put it on again. But, I've got the whole deal still.—*Adelante* Magazine, 2009.[173]

Lynda Carter on a fan's gesture: I was talking with a fan that I've known since he was quite young who had somehow gotten his hands on one of [my costumes], and he very kindly said, "I'd like you to have it." I have two children. So now I'll have one for each of them and I won't have to cut it in half.—Personal Appearance, 2011.[174]

Lynda Carter on the appeal of Wonder Woman in the GLBT [Gay, Lesbian, Bisexual, Transgendered] community: If you are liked by the gay and lesbian population, you've really made it. It's like that kind of loyalty. I think part of the appeal is the secret self of Wonder Woman. The secret's out – the one that other people can't see, the whole of you.—*Metro Weekly*, 2009.[175]

Bill Bixby - David Banner

Bill Bixby played the soulful and empathetic Dr. David Banner for six seasons in *The Incredible Hulk* (1978-82) and in three reunion films, *The Incredible Hulk Returns* (1988), *The Trial of the Incredible Hulk* (1989) and *The Death of the Incredible* Hulk (1990).

Bill Bixby on reading the script for the pilot episode of *The Incredible Hulk*: I didn't even like the title. I wanted to make fun of it because of its name. I told my agent, "You've got to be kidding!' when he suggested I might be interested in it. He said, "Read it!" and so I took it home and thanks to his intelligence, I did read it. Right away I knew this could be done in the style of the monster pictures or the creature films of the 1940s. But one advantage we enjoy over the previous monster pictures is that the Hulk is not evil.—*Birmingham News*/Alabama, March 12, 1978.[176]

Bill Bixby on his approach to the show: We don't make fun of the characters. That would cartoon it. From the beginning we decided to make it an adult show that kids are allowed to watch, rather than a childish show adults are forced to watch.—*The Los Angeles Times*, 1993.[177]

Bill Bixby on the symbolism of the Hulk: The Hulk is the personification of the enemy, which lurks under the surface of us all. We have to control that enemy within ourselves, or we can't control the conduct of the world.—*New York Newsday*, May 7, 1978.[178]

Bill Bixby on relating to the Hulk: I remember when I was in high school with a girl I wanted to date for a year but she was surrounded by football players. I wanted to turn into the Hulk.—*Beaver County Times*, September 10, 1978.[179]

Bill Bixby on the vicarious pleasures of the Hulk: A song in the musical version of *Candide* had lyrics which essentially said, "It gave a harmless outlet for the emotions which could lead to war and social agitation." That describes the Hulk, the show's a catharsis. It's interesting to watch adults watch the Hulk. It isn't Bill Bixby they're watching. It's themselves."—*Beaver County Times*, September 10, 1978.[180]

Bill Bixby comparing the Hulk to his cancer: In the show, my character had this creature in me that I did everything to suppress and keep from coming out. Now in my real life, I have this creature inside of me that I'm obligated to overcome.—AP story printed in *The Albany Herald*, Feb 11, 1993.[181]

[Note: A little over nine months after this AP interview that ran in the Albany Herald on November 21, 1993, Bill Bixby died of cancer at the age of fifty-nine.]

Christopher Reeve – Superman

Christopher Reeve ushered in the modern superhero film when he played Clark Kent/Superman with a twinkle in his eye in *Superman* (1978), *Superman II* (1980), *Superman III*, (1983) and *Superman IV: The Quest for Peace* (1987).

Christopher Reeve on defying conventional wisdom about superhero films: The decision to play Superman was probably the most courageous career decision that I made because, at that time [in 1977 when Reeve was cast], the idea of a Superman film was laughable to many people. So the challenge was to turn around their expectations. I remember feeling that the odds were very much against trying to pull off that first movie. But I also believed that by working together, we would be able to make a character out of this, and make it romantic rather than macho; make it funny rather than pompous or one-dimensional. People were really thinking it would be a joke. I think that converting the people who laughed at the idea was quite an achievement. I was doing well in theatre at the time, so to go into films as Superman was a pretty bold choice.—*Starlog*, 1987.[182]

Christopher Reeve on reading Superman comics: Back in 1977, I read a few, but they weren't really that helpful. It's so stylized when you have four panels on a page. It doesn't help to make a three-dimensional film character. So I did a little research, then filed it all away and started from what *I* wanted to see in Superman. You can only really play what's inside you—what you know and feel and care about. I try to bring all that to the role instead of worrying about comic-book history.—*Starlog*, 1987.[183]

Christopher Reeve on his inspiration for making Superman and Clark Kent two distinct personalities: I remember seeing George Reeves on TV in the 1950s and wondering why Lois Lane didn't instantly recognize Clark Rent as Superman. How could a thick pair of glasses substitute for a believable characterization? Right away I saw a great opportunity: I would attempt to create more of a contrast between the two characters. After all, Lois shouldn't have to be blind or dim-witted.—*Still Me*, 1998.[184]

Christopher Reeve on his approach to Superman: Superman is a big fish in a small pond. He's Superman on Earth only because he's in a different solar system. If he'd grown up on Krypton, if Krypton had not been destroyed, he might have been average, nothing special about him. That allowed me to underplay the character and make him quite casual.—*Esquire*, 2003.[185]

Christopher Reeve on the basis for Clark Kent: I based the character of Clark Kent on the young Cary Grant. There's a wonderful scene in *Bringing Up Baby* in which he plays a paleontologist working on a dinosaur, and he's up on a ladder that this is rocking back and forth. He looks terribly awkward and afraid, while Katherine Hepburn looks brash and fearless as she comes to his rescue. He has a shyness, vulnerability, and a certain charming goofiness that I thought be would be perfect for Clark Kent. He even wears the same kind of glasses. Of course I knew I couldn't be Cary Grant, but there was nothing to prevent me from stealing from him.—*Still Me*, 1998.[186]

Christopher Reeve on wearing the costume: I wasn't quite sure what I would do as Superman, so I decided that I would simply let the costume do most of the work. The technology was developed to make me look incredible, but that made it easier in that I could underplay the part. So I thought, *The thing to do is not do too much. Don't pose or overact. Just be Superman.*— *The Mirror*. Unpublished interview put online June 2011.[187]

Christopher Reeve on how to convincingly portray flying: The actual flying is completed in one's own mind. They used to ask, "How come the stuntman doesn't look real?" And I said, "Because the flying happens in the eyes." The flying comes in the conviction that you know where you are, what the altitude is, what speed you're doing, and you know what you're looking at. If that's not supplied by the actor, it doesn't happen.—*Starlog*, 1979.[188]

Christopher Reeve on playing the role: I think I was the right actor for the part at the time I played it, but I think the role is larger than any particular actor and should be reinterpreted from generation to generation.—*Still Me*, 1998.[189]

Christopher Reeve on the meaning of Superman: Superman is a strong visual representation of a thought common to every citizen of Western culture. Namely, how do I function as an individual in a society where I feel like a mouse? However, we mustn't pump this up into being pseudo-mythology. Superman should be left up on the screen or on the page. The questions that people have come up with about the symbolism of Superman are really quite frightening. Religious figures have called me up and asked if I'm aware of the responsibilities of being a contemporary Christ figure. Hey, I'm an actor from New Jersey; I can't be responsible for that."—*Omni*, 1983.[190]

Christopher Reeve on the real identity of Superman: I look at *Superman IV* as the unmasking of Superman, with the emphasis on Kal-El the being from Krypton. It becomes clear in the film that both of his identities – both Superman and Clark Kent – are personae that he has to become for other people. At the film's heart, what we really pay attention to is who he is underneath, which is Kal-El.—*Starlog,* 1987.[191]

Christopher Reeve on typecasting: After the success of *Superman,* one of my greatest problems as an actor was that my agents and many Hollywood producers wanted me to be an action hero, which didn't interest me. Sometimes I got the sinking feeling that I had inadvertently closed the door to my future as a legitimate actor. Over the next few years, I discovered that *Superman* had actually opened many doors; the question was how to make the best use of these opportunities.—*Still Me,* 1998.[192]

Christopher Reeve on Superman memorabilia: I have kept one item from my ten-year history as Superman. And that is I cut out the "S" out off of the back of the first cape that I ever wore and framed it. It's in my son's bedroom.—Interview with John C. Tibbetts, 1987.[193]

Terrence Stamp - General Zod

Terrence Stamp played the villainous General Zod in *Superman* and *Superman II.*

Terrence Stamp on his classic line: Rarely a day passes when I don't have somebody looking at me strangely - to which I say, "Kneel before Zod, you bastard." It generally gets a big laugh. I haven't been smacked recently, anyway.—Shortlist.com, 2013.[194]

World's Greatest Heroes
Part Two: In the Shadow of the Bat

A new era of superhero films began in the late 1980s with Michael Keaton's damaged and thrilling interpretation of the Dark Knight and ended in the late 1990s with George Clooney's smug and hollow Batman. The superhero movies made during this period were often ersatz *Batman* films, merely lighter or darker variations on the approach that Keaton and director Tim Burton so effectively established.

Michael Keaton – Batman

Michael Keaton played Bruce Wayne/Batman in *Batman* (1989) and *Batman Returns* (1992). Keaton's two films made over $675 million worldwide.

Michael Keaton on his initial reluctance to play Batman: I was dumbfounded when he first called me. I think I tapped the receiver a few times and said, "You sure you have the right number?" But that didn't last long because it was Tim [Burton], so I knew there must be something to it. I said, "Yeah, of course I'll read it," thinking no way would I do it. I pictured Batman as one of these arms-akimbo superheroes. If he'd been written that way, I would have been first to admit I was the wrong guy, and one other thing: I had always wanted to work with Jack Nicholson, and I thought, *Damn, if this is going to be my only shot, I don't know if I want to take it.* I felt that it would be better to work with Jack where we're two people dressed in some sort of normal garb. But when I read the script, it made sense to me. It was pretty damn good.—*Playboy*, 1992.[195]

Michael Keaton on his approach to Bruce Wayne: When I talked to Tim again, I said, "I don't think you're going to agree with this, but here's my take on Bruce Wayne: He's essentially depressed and a little nuts, real dark, and a couple of steps off. Yet, at the same time, he's not off at all . . . and he's focused. Bruce Wayne gets real focused when he sees a woman he's interested in. In the first movie, it was Kim Basinger as Vicki Vale, and in this one, it's Michelle [Pfeiffer], who plays Selina Kyle, the Catwoman. That focus doesn't always last because Bruce Wayne has a lot of other things on his plate, which is why he's always a little absentminded and preoccupied. Tim agreed with my take on Bruce Wayne.—*Playboy*, 1992.[196]

Michael Keaton on acting in the Batsuit: You can't really hear clearly and your peripheral vision is limited, and you can't move very well. It's very constricting from actually the top of your head to the tip of your toes. That works for the character in terms of finding [his] isolation, which was great. I noticed while in London on the first one, I was on the set and I felt very far away from everyone and I thought, *This is kinda* cool. So I let myself disappear because the character is actually someone who hides behind things. And even Bruce Wayne keeps himself at a distance. Because of his background he is a very isolated and distant man.—BBC, 1992.[197]

Michael Keaton on advice from Jack Nicholson: We were both getting made up in our suits. He just looked at me and said [imitating Nicholson], "Well, we just gotta let the wardrobe do the acting, kid." And it's true.—*Late Night With David Letterman*, 1989.[198]

Michael Keaton on Batman's gravely voice: Bruce Wayne is a man about town, a luminary, having to go to social functions and make public appearances, so people know his voice. So I came up with dropping his voice down, as Batman it comes from a lower thing that he drops down into, a place he has to reach to become a quasi-vigilante. That's where that whole voice thing came from and it's just to protect himself, it's part of the transition inside of him from one thing to another thing.—*Los Angeles Times*, 2011.[199]

Michael Keaton on why he didn't make a third Batman movie: The reason they weren't interesting was the reason I didn't want to do them anymore. I read the script [for *Batman Forever*]. I wasn't into it, but how I wanted to do the third one is what they did in [*Batman Begins*]. I read an article about how they were going about it and I said, "That's exactly what I thought should be done.—MTV.com, 2008.[200]

Jack Nicholson – Joker

Jack Nicholson gave a tour de force performance as the Joker (created in 1940 by Jerry Robinson and Bill Finger) in *Batman* (1989), created by Jerry Robinson and Bill Finger.

Jack Nicholson on playing the Joker: Well, the Joker comes from my childhood. That's how I got involved with it in the first place. It's a part I always thought I should play.—MTV.com, 2007.[201]

Jack Nicholson assessing his own performance: I was particularly proud of my performance as the Joker. I considered it a piece of pop art.—Esquire.com, 2003.[202]

Jack Nicholson on his onscreen persona: Around the time of *Batman*, I realized I was fooling around career-wise. It was great work and a great film but I didn't want to be seen as this crazy, Joker figure anymore. I think I had a conversation with myself, a real heart-to-heart, and decided I didn't like people thinking of me as a fool.—TotalFilm.com, 2004.[203]

Jack Nicholson on playing the Joker only once: Let me be the way I'm not in interviews. I'm furious. I'm furious. [He laughs] They never asked me about a sequel with the Joker. I know how to do that. Nobody ever asked me. Maybe it's not a mistake. Maybe it was the right thing, but to be candid, I'm furious.—MTV.com, 2007.[204]

Dick Durock – Swamp Thing

Dick Durock, the stuntman turned actor, played the antihero, Swamp Thing, in Wes Craven's *Swamp Thing* (1980), *The Return of the Swamp Thing* (1989), and in seventy-two episodes of the TV series *The Swamp Thing* (1990-93).

Dick Durock on the Swamp Thing costume: Well, the makeup and costume, I got used to that. The first time it took about four hours to put it all together, the second two hours, and by the time we got to the series we had it down to forty-five minutes. But it was still tough. At the end of the day you're wearing eighty pounds of wet latex, plus all the chemicals on your face. It sure isn't sunglasses and autographs, I'll tell ya."—Icons of Fright.com, 2008.[205]

Warren Beatty – Dick Tracy

Warren Beatty played Chester Gould's creation in the 1990 film *Dick Tracy*, which he also produced and directed. Beatty also played the detective in the unaired thirty-minute TV retrospective on the character, *Dick Tracy Special* (2010), which he wrote and directed and that was reportedly made so that Beatty could continue to control the rights to the fictional character.

Warren Beatty on his childhood memories of Dick Tracy: It was the first comic strip I got involved with as a kid. You know, Dick Tracy was the first non-funny comic strip. People got shot, times were tough in the Depression, things had to be done, and he went and did them.—*Los Angeles Times' Hero Complex*, 2011.[206]

Warren Beatty on the character Dick Tracy: He's an honest man. He knows what he wants to do. He knows bad is bad, good is good. He'd liked to have a family; he doesn't know that he can live up to the responsibilities that it entails. He's tempted. He's really, really tempted.—*Entertainment Tonight*, 1990.[207]

Danny DeVito – Penguin

Danny DeVito portrayed the misunderstood Penguin in Tim Burton's *Batman Returns* (1992).

Danny DeVito on the Penguin: The Penguin is quite an intelligent man. If Oswald's parents had taken time to accept him as a human being despite his deformities he might have grown up to be Albert Einstein, but because he was thrown away, and because of who and where he was raised, he became something totally different, totally evil.—*Starlog*, 1992.[208]

Danny DeVito on how the Penguin outfit influenced his performance: In a very odd way, it did help me [get into character]. Usually as an actor, you're given the luxury of hiding behind a character, playing the game and acting and reacting any way you want. With the Penguin, that proved to be even more the case. Once I put the mask on, I felt I could do *anything*.—*Starlog*, 1992.[209]

Danny DeVito on staying isolated on the set: I felt that for this character to work, I couldn't break with his identity, even for a moment. So, I decided that I wouldn't let anybody visit me while

I was in makeup. No family, no kids, no studio executives. And it really didn't work out too badly.—*Starlog*, 1992.[210]

Danny DeVito on the importance of playing the Penguin: I'm very proud of my performance in *One Flew Over the Cuckoo's Nest*, but my teenage self would be most impressed that I played the Penguin in a Batman movie. He has the comic book on his bed. I'd have to tell him that it would turn out a bit different from the comic though, because of this crazy thing called Tim Burton.—Big Issue.com, 2012.[211]

Michelle Pfeiffer – Catwoman

Michelle Pfeiffer played Catwoman in *Batman Returns* (1992). In her review for the *New York Times*, Janet Maslin wrote: "Selina metamorphoses thrillingly into Catwoman, in a sequence that ranks with the most captivating moments Ms. Pfeiffer has spent on screen. Fully inhabiting this vixenish character, she turns Catwoman into a fierce, seductive embodiment of her earlier dissatisfaction. 'Life's a bitch,' she slyly declares. 'Now so am I.'"[212]

Michelle Pfeiffer on Julie Newmar: I used to watch the *Batman* TV series when I was a kid and I had a real fascination for Julie Newmar as Catwoman. For me, she was breaking all the stereotypes of what it meant to be a woman at that time. She was allowed to do the forbidden things. She could be bad and good, mean, and vicious. I was also at the point where I was coming into my own sense of sexuality, so it was fascinating to watch Catwoman always trying to get back at Batman because she was in love with him and he did love her back. I found Catwoman a thrilling character to watch.—*Starlog*, 1992.[213]

Michelle Pfeiffer on the physical training for the film: I believe I really cemented my take on Selina as a woman about to make a power move during the physical training. When I was performing the kicks and cracking the whip, I could suddenly feel what Selina Kyle must have felt as she was transforming from this mousy secretary to the fearsome criminal. And boy I sure liked the sound the whip made!—*Starlog*, 1992.[214]

Michelle Pfeiffer on wearing the costume: The costume was no bed of roses. The boots were built very high and weren't re-

ally designed well. Every time I stood up, I would kind of tilt forward. They hadn't thought about how I was going to go to the
bathroom, so they had to fine-tune it to take care of that problem. The costume was very tight. The strap was cutting into my
vocal chords, and the mask was so tight on my ears that I had
trouble hearing, and because Tim had the soundstages air-conditioned down to thirty-five degrees, I would sweat inside the suit
and then get incredibly cold. I was kind of miserable the first few
weeks but I got used to it.—*Starlog*, 1992. [215]

David Hasselhoff – Nick Fury

David Hasselhoff played the superspy and director of the secret government agency Supreme Headquarters International
Espionage Law Enforcement Division in *Nick Fury: Agent of
S.H.I.E.L.D.* (1998), a TV movie written by David Goyer, one of the
writers of Christopher Nolan's *Dark Knight* trilogy and Zack Snyder's Superman movie, *Man of Steel.*

David Hasselhoff on playing the original Nick Fury: I love Sam
Jackson [who has played the character], but you know, my Nick
Fury was the organic Nick Fury that was written and discussed
with Stan Lee before anyone got in there to change it. Nick Fury
was written to be tongue-in-cheek, and he had a cigar in his
mouth, he was a tough guy—he was cool."—*Movieline*, 2012.[216]

David Hasselhoff on Stan Lee: The greatest compliment I ever
received was when Stan Lee was on the set and said, "You are
Nick Fury. You are exactly what I imagined him to be."—MTV.com,
2009.[217]

Mark Hamill – Joker

Mark Hamill provided the voice of the Joker in *Batman: The
Animated Series* (1992-94), in *The New Batman Adventures* (1997-
1999), and in *Justice League* (2002-09). He also provided the
voice of the Clown Prince of Crime in the animated feature films
Batman: Mask of the Phantasm (1993), *Batman Superman Movie:
World's Finest* (1997), and *Batman Beyond: Return of the Joker*
(2000). He also played the Joker in the video games *Batman:
Vengeance* (2001), *Batman: Arkham Asylum* (2009), *Batman:
Arkham City* (2011), and *DC Universe Online* (2011); in the first epi-

sode [and unaired TV pilot] of *Birds of Prey* (2002), and in the animated short film *Batman: New Times* (2005) opposite Adam West's Batman. Hamill also made a cameo appearance as the character in *Static Shock* (2002) and in several episodes of the TV series *Robot Chicken*.

Mark Hamill on playing the Joker: What I liked about doing the Joker was his villainy. I thought, you know, I could use this laugh almost as a vocabulary. Instead of having it be one continuous laugh, I could use it like color on a canvas. There could be sinister laughs, there could be joyful, gleeful, maniacal laughs, there could be malevolent and evil laughs. There are so many different colors that you can give him, so that kids will have more than one laugh to mimic on the playground. I do have to thank the people at *Batman*, because this work opened up an entire new career for me.—*Animation World Magazine*, April 1997.[218]

Val Kilmer - Batman

Val Kilmer has made almost a separate career playing iconic figures including Jim Morrison, Mark Twain, Doc Holiday, Elvis Presley, and Moses. What concerns us here is that he played Bruce Wayne/Batman in *Batman Forever* (1995).

Kilmer spoofed his history with Batman when he appeared as himself, alongside his former *Willow* co-star Warwick Davis, on the comedy series *Life's Too Short* (2013). In the show, Kilmer tells Davis, "I've got a routine that I always do and it kills" and then produces Batman's cowl. Davis enters his office alone and tells his secretary that he has a surprise for her. Now wearing the cowl, Kilmer enters the office. Davis asks his secretary to guess the actor's identity, and as the actor stands there the secretary fires off a list of actors who played the Dark Knight but she fails to remember Kilmer.

I worked as a production assistant on *Batman Forever* for about a week in New York City before the production moved to California. One of my responsibilities was holding up a large cardboard sign to obscure Kilmer in his costume so that the press couldn't catch a glimpse of the new Batman. I remember being fixated on his Batsuit, which had a kind of hypnotic effect on everyone who came to the set.

Another one of my duties was to serve as an off-camera stand-in for Tommy Lee Jones, who was playing Harvey Dent/Two-Face. You can see my essential contribution to the movie in the scene in which Kilmer's Batman stands on the ledge of a building and with fire in his eyes watches Two Face's dramatic escape. The Dark Knight is actually glaring at me.

Val Kilmer on how he was cast: It turned out that while they were discussing me as the next candidate for the role, I was re-searching a film about an African adventure. On the day that Warner Bros. called my agent and said, "Yeah, he's who we want," I was in a cave of bats in South Africa.—*The Cinematic Sage of the Dark Knight- Reinventing a Hero*, 2005.[219]

Val Kilmer on how wearing the Batsuit made him feel like an old man: You need help getting dressed. It takes about forty-five minutes to get undressed. This is true. You need help going to the bathroom. You can't hear anymore because [the Batcowl] is plastic and then when you call out for help no one comes. In between takes, you're like a mannequin and you're immobile in a kind of a lounge chair and you're like, "Daisy, can I have some water?" You have to be fed through a straw.—*Conan*, 2013[220]

Chris O'Donnell - Robin

Chris O'Donnell played Dick Grayson/Robin opposite two dif-ferent actors playing Batman: with Val Kilmer in *Batman Forever* (1995) and with George Clooney in *Batman and Robin* (1997).

Chris O'Donnell on playing Robin: The two questions I get asked most in my life at this point are: "What is it like to work with Al Pacino [in *Scent of a Woman*], and weren't you Robin in the Batman movies?" I tend to like the first question a little bit better.—*AFI Lifetime Achievement Award for Al Pacino*, 2007.[221]

Chris O'Donnell on the failings of *Batman and Robin*: It just felt like everything got a little soft the second time [I played Robin in *Batman and Robin*]. On *Batman Forever*, I felt like I was making a movie. The second time, I felt like I was making a kid's toy commercial.—*Shadows of the Bat: The Cinematic Saga of the Dark Knight*, 2005.[222]

Jim Carrey - The Riddler

Jim Carrey played Dr. Edward Nygma/The Riddler in *Batman Forever* (1995).

As a production assistant working on *Batman Forever*, I observed that Carrey tirelessly practiced manipulating the Riddler's scepter. He was steadfast in his quest to master the prop and to use it as an extension of the character.

Jim Carey on the Riddler: I tried not to do a Frank Gorshin, because he was so strong in it. He was The Riddler. I didn't try to outdo him or anything like that. I approached this like me. *What I would do, where I would go.* I just did The Riddler like when Elvis went to Vegas.—1995.[223]

Billy Zane - The Phantom

Billy Zane played Kit Walker/The Phantom, a role the actor said he was "destined" to play, in *The Phantom* (1996).

Billy Zane on the character: He doesn't have super powers or the biggest, baddest gun. The point isn't how many people you can kill or how you kill them. He is there to fight piracy, greed, and cruelty in all their forms on land and sea. The Phantom is a Zen cowboy and you have to realize that he was originally marketed to women, in a women's magazine, in fact.—Film Scouts, 1996.[224]

Michael Jai White - Spawn

Michael Jai White became the first African-American to star in a superhero movie when he played Al Simmons/Spawn in *Spawn* (1997).

Michael Jai White looking back at Spawn: *Spawn* was before its time. It was an edgier type of film and we always battled with going all the way there. I always felt, as [did] Todd McFarlane [Spawn creator], that Spawn should have been rated R. If we do another one, it certainly will be. It's about a guy from Hell! You don't do [it as] a PG-13 film. [*Spawn* was rated PG-13.] Studios get scared because they want lots of kids to come and they think they know what's best. The kids are more sophisticated and they like edgier things. The reason why the comic book was the number one comic book for so long was because it had that edge. In the same way people were attracted to the comic book, the movie should have been a reflection of that. For it not to be that way invites criticism. There is a need for people to have this antihero that is really dark. When they give an edge to Spider-Man and give an edge to Batman, you see how many great benefits they reaped from that. Well, it seems to be common sense. You have the darkest of the characters. With Spawn, it really can quench an audience's desire for truly how badass a superhero could be.—Black Film.com, 2008.[225]

George Clooney – Batman

George Clooney played Bruce Wayne/Batman in *Batman and Robin* (1997). The pun-filled movie is so dreadful that it helped to dampen audience's appetite for comic book movies for eight years.

George Clooney on playing Batman: With hindsight, it's easy to look back at this and go, "Woah, that was really shit, and I was really bad in it."—*Total Film*, 2011.[226]

George Clooney on finding out he was going to play Batman: The truth is, my phone rang, and the head of Warner Bros said, "Come into my office, you are going to play Batman in a *Batman* film." I said "Yeah!" I called my friends and they screamed and I screamed and we couldn't believe it!—*Total Film*, 2011.[227]

George Clooney on making the movie: I just thought the last one had been successful, so I thought I was just going to be in a big successful franchise movie, and in a weird way I was. Batman is still the biggest break I ever had and it completely changed my career, even if it was weak and I was weak in it. It was a difficult film to be good in. I don't know what I could have done differently, but if I am going to be Batman in the film *Batman & Robin*, I can't say it didn't work and then not take some of the blame for that.—*Total Film*, 2011.[228]

George Clooney on the Batsuit: They put nipples on the Batsuit. I didn't know why they would do that. If Batman had to wear the suit that [I] had to wear, everyone would die. You're lying on a board like this and you can't move and they just prop you up and you're like, "I'm Batman."—Barbara Walter's Special, 2012.[229]

George Clooney on the quality of his Batman movie: I may have buried that franchise. I look at is as a bit of a black eye.—*Los Angeles Daily News*, 1997.[230]

World's Greatest Heroes
Part Three: The Superhero Boom

A new era of superhero films began in the twenty-first century when the one-two punch of *X-Men* and *Spider-Man* demonstrated to audiences that talented actors working with inventive filmmakers could make films that could be as stimulating and rewarding for adults as they were for children.

In this period, superhero films earned respect as a genre that was regularly transcending outdated stereotypes. As A. O. Scott wrote in *The New York Times,* "Their ascendancy in Hollywood is a triumphal chapter in a seventy-year epic during which comic books have moved from the disreputable, juvenile margins of pop culture to its center. The superheroes demand to be taken as seriously as they have always taken themselves."[231]

Wesley Snipes – Blade

Wesley Snipes played the vampire antihero and martial arts expert in *Blade* (1998), *Blade II* (2002) and *Blade: Trinity* (2004); David Goyer was a writer on all three *Blade* films and he directed *Blade Trinity.*[232] The first *Blade* film straddled two different eras. In one respect the film, which was released just one year after *Batman & Robin*, was a product of the post-Tim Burton/Michael Keaton era, but it was also the first superhero film that was based on a Marvel character to receive distribution. [Neither *Captain America* (1990) nor *Fantastic Four* (1994) were released theatrically.] Although *Blade's* $131 million worldwide box office take was robust for a mostly unknown superhero, it didn't really have any significant mainstream cultural impact. The entire trilogy earned $415 million worldwide.

Wesley Snipes on preparing for the part: Because I've been doing martial arts and yoga and mediation, and following a good diet, it doesn't really take me too much time to be in shape and ready for a film like this. When you have a regular health discipline, your body stays in shape all the time. I've been lucky to never stop exercising, and in this film it's cool to have incorporated all kinds of fighting and physical styles, from a Hong Kong style in the opening, to a more "Wesley style" which is more ju-jitsu, African, kick-ass whatever I feel like, so it was intense but fun.—Cranky Critic.com, 2002.[233]

Wesley Snipes responding to a reporter who said *Blade* "kick-started" the superhero trend: Thanks for saying that. Some people forget or overlook my/our contribution to this current trend. The "Gaming" community knows and the streets give us credits, but the movie world frequently plays us like the "ugly step child" or the "kitchen help," especially when the conversation revolves around the "boys in tights" or "the bat."—IGN, 2011.[234]

Hugh Jackman - Wolverine

Hugh Jackman has played Wolverine seven times: in *X-Men* (2000), *X2* (2003), *X-Men: The Last Stand* (2007), *X-Men Origins: Wolverine* (2009), in a cameo in *X-Men: First Class* (2011), *The Wolverine* (2013), and *X-Men: Days of Future Past* (2014).

Hugh Jackman on Wolverine's temperament: Wolverine is really not a good guy at all. Well, he's good, but he's not nice"—*Entertainment Weekly*, 2013.[235]

Hugh Jackman on empathizing with Wolverine's sense of alienation: Around the age of ten or so, after my mom left, my dad was bringing us up, but he had to travel, and we were sent off to different friends' homes. It was very unusual for the mother to leave, and I remember knowing people were looking at me differently. I wished I had come from a normal family. I hated feeling like we were the weird ones on the block.—*Playboy*, 2008.[236]

Hugh Jackman on Wolverine's character: What happens is that Wolverine is a warrior by nature, a man whose weapons and strength are not pretty, [they're] more instinctive, a little more brutal. . . I used to watch a lot of Mike Tyson videos, looking at him as an early boxer. That's what I tried to model Logan on. And what happens in this story, following the comic book arc, is that he realizes, actually, being a warrior doesn't always work for him and that somehow the calmer, more efficient, more disciplined approach of the samurai is more effective.—*Bleeding Cool*, 2013.[237]

Hugh Jackman on Wolverine's rage: If you took away all their powers, I'm pretty sure, of all the X-Men, Wolverine's the one you don't want to piss off. He's the one you want on your side, and definitely not against you because he just won't stop until he's dead, or you're dead. You'd be dead first, usually. I definitely know that internal rage. I think one of the things I always loved about the comics was this idea that, this character, when he goes into what they call "Berserker Rage," when he goes berserk, that white blind rage which he has, it makes him incredibly powerful. But it's also a great flaw. It's almost like he loses consciousness of what he's doing, and during that, he can do great damage as well. I can remember feeling like that vividly, at times. Usually, and luckily, that took place for me on a rugby field where it was somehow sanctioned, all this violence.—*Bleed Cool*, 2013.[238]

Hugh Jackman on his feelings towards the character: I love the character, he's kind of like a best friend to me, and I don't ever want to take [him] or the fans for granted.—*Entertainment Weekly*, 2013.[239]

Hugh Jackman on the finite number of times he can play Wolverine: There's only so much chicken breast I can keep eating.[240]

Halle Berry – Storm

Halle Berry played Ororo Munroe/Storm in *X-Men*, *X2*, *X-Men: The Last Stand* and *X-Men: Days of Future Past*.

Halley Berry on identifying with her character: Everybody can relate to the subject matter. Everybody has felt like an outcast and always will on some level I think. Whether you are black or white or pink, you can relate to what that is and it is seductive. Everybody can relate to being unfairly judged, especially being judged by the things that are totally out of their control.—Sci-Fi Online.com, 2006.[241]

Halley Berry on not reading the comics to prepare for the part: You know, I didn't. Bryan [Singer, the director] didn't want it. The people who didn't grow up with the series, he didn't want us to. He wanted us to read the script and read the backstory that he provided us. Because all the characters changed from decade to decade, and they sort of went off in different directions. So he thought [reading the comic books] would be really confusing and he thought it would be easier, and I think rightfully so, not to go back and read all the comic books. I read some that pertained to the way he wanted Storm to be played. Those were the ones he suggested that I read and he gave me.—*Venice Magazine*, 2002.[242]

Halley Berry on the meaning behind X-Men: They're all sort of living with some sort of struggle, and a lot of it is very internal, trying to find a way to fit into this society. I think that's what the basis of the comic book is, and that's what everybody in life deals with, which is why I think this comic book series is so appealing to so many people, and resonates, and hits home with almost every human being. Because we've all been ousted, or isolated, or forced to make tough decisions [in order] to accept who we are. And do we change who we are to benefit our lovers, our friends, our family, society, do we change? Or do we say, do we have the problem or do they have the problem? I think that's a question people continue to ask themselves.—CinemaSource.com, 2008.[243]

Tom Welling – Clark Kent

Tom Welling played Clark Kent in 217 episodes of *Smallville* (2001-11), but it wasn't until the series finale that he finally got to play Superman.

Tom Welling on what appealed to him about *Smallville*: It wasn't *Lois & Clark*. It wasn't *Superman*. It was about a high school kid. Going into that first audition, I didn't know how anyone could prepare to play this role, and as I was waiting in the room to go in to the audition, I realized that you have to take everything that makes this kid a superhero, and throw it out the window. I had to do it just like a normal kid. The special effects and everything else would help fill in the blanks, and that's how I've tried to attack this material, even now.—*Smallville: The Official Yearbook*, 2004.[244]

Tom Welling on playing Superman: I really think people are really going to like what we did. I mean, when *I* think about it, I get excited. The last image of Clark Kent ripping off his shirt to reveal his Superman costume underneath. For me, it gave me goosebumps.—TV Line.com, 2011.[245]

Tobey Maguire – Spider-Man

Tobey Maguire played Peter Parker/Spider-Man in *Spider-Man* (2002), *Spider-Man 2* (2004) and *Spider-Man 3* (2007). The three films collectively earned nearly $2.5 billion.

Tobey Maguire on the Spider-Man comics: I read the first four years of the comic books in preparation for the first film, so I am pretty familiar with the character.—*At the Movies*, 2004.[246]

Tobey Maguire on his approach to Peter Parker: I think the aspects which shape Peter Parker are those very common to young people who go through a whole series of existential doubts and conflicting desires about who they are and where they stand in their world. It's about identity and self-discovery and figuring out a little more about who you want to be and who you think you should be. That's what's so intriguing about the Spider-Man concept – the fact that Peter Parker openly raises his doubts so that the readers of the comic strip could share his worries and fears. He's not an all-powerful, all-knowing cardboard superhero. He's not a superhero at all, by that standard. He's very mortal, someone who agonizes a lot about his role in life. For an actor, being able to get into those areas is what you dream about.—Cinema. com, 2002.[247]

Tobey Maguire on his approach to playing Spider-Man: You have to act in a very different way when you have that suit on, using a very different kind of body language as the character. Sam [Raimi, the director] and I talked a lot about keeping the audience with the character even though you can't see his expression.—Film.co.uk, 2002.[248]

Tobey Maguire on how playing Spider-Man changed his life: So much shifted in my life the weekend the movie came out. It was shocking. I'd been making movies for a while, so I had experienced some attention, but then, all of a sudden, the Sunday after it was released, I remember I went to lunch with my little brothers and there were all these people outside and photographers. It was a lot more attention than what I was used to.—*VMAN*, 2002.[249]

Tobey Maguire on the location of his costume: I actually don't have a suit. I have had many offers to show up for kids' parties.—*Blunt Review*, 2007.[250]

Tobey Maguire on who would win in a fight between Spider-Man and Wolverine: I don't know; I think Spider-Man would probably win, right? Wolverine? He's got metal or steel all over his skeleton. I'm not really scared of the claws. I kind of think Spider-Man is going to win that fight.—*Wizard*, 2002.[251]

Ben Affleck - Daredevil

Before being cast as Bruce Wayne/Batman in the 2016 Superman-Batman team-up film, Ben Affleck played Matt Murdock/Daredevil, the blind superhero, in *Daredevil* (2003). The film made nearly $180 million worldwide. Affleck reprised his role as Matt Murdock in *Elektra* (2005), a spin-off movie about Daredevil's ex-lover turned assassin, but his cameo was cut from the film.

Ben Affleck on the impact of *Daredevil* on his career: I made a bunch of movies that didn't work. I was ending up in the tabloids. I don't know what the lesson is, except that you just have to find your compass. I liked *Sum of All Fears*. *Daredevil* I didn't at all. Some movies should have worked and didn't. At a certain point, it's just up to the movie gods. Anyway, this image becomes a self-fulfilling prophecy. And I just said, "I don't want to do it anymore. This is horrible. I don't want to be in this spotlight, this glare, in this way. It's tawdry, it's ugly, it's oppressive, and it's inane. So I'm going to try to get away." And most of the way I did that was by not acting. I said, "I'm going to steer myself toward directing. I'm going to do something that takes me toward a place where the work that I do is reflective of what I think is interesting dramatically".—*Details*, 2012.[252]

Nearly seven years before it was announced in 2013 that he was going to star in a new Batman movie, Ben Affleck on not wanting to play another superhero: By playing a superhero in *Daredevil*, I have inoculated myself from ever playing another superhero. Wearing a costume was a source of humiliation for me and something I wouldn't want to do again soon.—IGN, 2006.[253]

Eric Bana - Bruce Banner

Eric Bana played Bruce Banner in Ang Lee's esoteric *Hulk* (2003), a film which went on to earn slightly more than $245 million worldwide.

Eric Bana on the tone of the film: It was the first of the "dark" takes. Make no mistake.—*Huffington Post*, August 2013.[254]

Eric Bana on his feelings about the film: I'm proud of what it tried to do. I apologize to all those people who were so angry about it. I'm fascinated by the people who hated that movie and feel compelled to watch it again, which *always* blows my mind. But, yeah, it is what it is and I certainly don't regret doing it.—*Huffington Post*, August 2013.[255]

Eric Bana on how the film, which got tepid reviews and was a box office disappointment, was actually good for his career: I would have had a completely different career, right? I feel very blessed to have been given the opportunities that I've had the last 10 years, so I wouldn't want to change that for anything. Everyone's career is different and I'm not saying it wouldn't have been exciting; it would have been a different thing. I don't know that I would be sitting down here talking to you about "Closed Circuit." So yeah, it's just different, and I've really enjoyed my ride. [My career] would be less eclectic, and, make no mistake, if I had done three Hulks, it would have wiped out [opportunities to do other films], and it always takes a long time to do those movies. So it would take six of my movies off the table.—*Huffington Post*, August 2013.[256]

Ron Perlman - Hellboy

Ron Perlman played Hellboy, the spawn of a demon and a witch, who is doing everything in his power to avoid fulfilling his supernaturally ordained destiny, which is to bring about the end of the world, in *Hellboy* (2004) and *Hellboy II: The Golden Army* (2008). He also voiced the character in the animated films *Hellboy Animated: Sword of Storms* (2006) and *Hellboy Animated: Blood and Iron* (2007); in the animated short *Hellboy Animated: Iron Shoes* (2007) and in the video game *Hellboy: The Science of Evil* (2008).

Ron Perlman on his characterization of Hellboy: So much of my aesthetic was formed by my dad. He was into Cagney, Bogart, and Errol Flynn, Gable, Spencer Tracy, and John Garfield. To this day, I have one TV in the room that I occupy most in my house exclusively on Turner Classic Movies, when it's not on MSNBC, because the political process is quite epic and entertaining at this juncture.—*Vulture*, 2008.[257]

Ron Perlman on the time-consuming task of getting into his Hellboy costume: I think I've reached a point where the idea of putting on extensive makeup doesn't appeal to me anymore. I'm crusty, I'm curmudgeonly. It begins to hunch my shoulders, the idea of it. I'm not against it – look, it's been one of the greatest friends I've ever had in my career and some of the greatest projects I've had to work with were heavily makeup-laden. But I'm older now and maybe a little more impatient and it's not as easy to sit in the chair. Having said that, when a project has a glow to it, like a Hellboy does, there's nothing that one has to do that's too much or you feel put upon in any way. I hope Hellboy will be the one-and-only part that I ever have to sit in the makeup chair for three or four hours before I get on the set. This character is worth whatever pains one has to go through to play him, and always has been.— ComicBookMovie.com, December 15, 2008. [258]

Ron Perlman on dressing up as Hellboy while meeting a sick child: We did put the makeup on at the request of the Make-A-Wish Foundation for this kid who had leukemia—who still has leukemia—who had just spent hundreds of hours in chemotherapy, and the only way he got through it was by watching the Hellboy movies. He requested to meet Hellboy, and I said, "That should be easy." And the guy who requested it was like, "He doesn't want to meet Ron; he has no desire to meet Ron. He wants to meet Hellboy." So one thing led to another, and we gave him his wish, but it was gratifying to see people's response to what a made-up character can do for a person who is actually fighting for his life.—The Onion's AV Club, 2013.[259]

Halle Berry – Catwoman

Halle Berry played Catwoman in the dreadful *Catwoman* (2004). The film and her performance won Worst Film and Worst Actress at the Golden Raspberry Awards. She endeared herself to fans by personally showing up to accept the dubious honor.

Halle Berry on her Raspberry Award: I want to thank Warner Bros. Thank you for putting me in a piece-of-shit, God-awful movie. It was just what my career needed. I was on top and *Cat-woman* plummeted me to the bottom.—Razzie Channel, 2005.[260]

Thomas Jane – Punisher

Thomas Jane played Frank Castle/The Punisher, the vigilante superhero, in *The Punisher* (2004) and again in the short self-made fan-film *Dirty Laundry* (2013).

Thomas Jane on the tone of *The Punisher*: It was definitely an uphill battle because Marvel had made all their money off much cuter movies. In a lot of ways we succeeded in bringing some of the darkness, but in a lot of ways I failed. I was bringing in movies like *Rolling Thunder* and *Death Wish* and *Taxi Driver* to the production meetings, saying I really think fans of this Punisher guy, they like these kinds of movies. We'd hit a nerve if we were to emulate them, go down this road. *The Dark Knight* hadn't come out yet, so a lot of what I was saying fell on deaf ears.—Entertainment Tonight.com, 2013.[261]

Thomas Jane on the Punisher's inner struggle: What [the cold-blooded murder of his family] challenges is Frank's ability or lack thereof to reconnect to society and to humanity and to a sense of right and wrong. Whether or not he's successful, or how successful he is, that struggle is to me what subverts the genre because so many times you get a revenge film where the protagonist is already formed. He is what he is and he does what he does, and then he pays the price for going down that road, hopefully. [In] any good vigilante film, there's a price to be paid for going against the law and for taking the law into your own hands, and operating outside of society. That's what it is in our movie.—About.com, 2004.[262]

Thomas Jane on his fan-film *Dirty Laundry*: For me it was a kind of swan song, a way to say goodbye to the character, by doing it some justice before saying goodbye, just me expressing what I loved about him. It was vindicating to find out a lot of folks felt the same way."—*Tampa Bay Times*, March 20, 2013.[263]

Michael Chiklis – The Thing

Michael Chiklis played the lovable monster Ben Grimm/The Thing in *The Fantastic Four* (2005) and *Fantastic 4: Rise of the Silver Surfer* (2007).

Michael Chiklis on growing up on the Fantastic Four: I'm the only one of the four that was a real, avid Fantastic Four fan. That shows my age. When I was thirteen or fourteen years old I used to go down to the corner store and get the latest Fantastic Four issue.—BBC, 2005.[264]

Michael Chicklis on Ben Grimm: Ben Grimm is the everyman that's the reluctant hero. He's the one in the Fantastic Four that doesn't want these powers, doesn't want to be the Thing. Certainly he can't switch back and forth, so he's really got the biggest problem of all of them, and he's a curmudgeonly kind of a guy. I really admire the strength of character of this character, and that's what sort of drew me to him. He's the heart and soul of this group.—Radio Free.com, 2005.[265]

Michael Chiklis on his costume: The last face that I wore is in my office, but it's sort of like the Raisin Thing, because it shrivels in the air.   I didn't realize that after a number of weeks, it sort of starts to shrivel, and it kind of looks disturbing at this point.—Radio Free.com, July 6, 2005.[266]

Jessica Alba – The Invisible Woman

Jessica Alba played Sue Storm/The Invisible Woman in the undercooked *The Fantastic Four* (2005) and *Fantastic 4: Rise of the Silver Surfer* (2007).

Jessica Alba on the frustrations of acting in Fantastic Four: Tim Story, the director, told me, "It looks too real. It looks too painful. Can you be prettier when you cry? Cry pretty, Jessica." He was like, "Don't do that thing with your face. Just make it flat. We can CGI the tears in." I'm like, "But there's no connection to a human being." And then it all got me thinking *Am I not good enough? Are my instincts and my emotions not good enough? Do people hate them so much that they don't want me to be a person? Am I not allowed to be a person in my work?* And so, I just said, "Fuck it. I don't care about this business anymore."—Elle, 2010.[267]

Christian Bale – Batman

Christian Bale played Bruce Wayne/Batman in *Batman Begins* (2005), *The Dark Knight* (2008) and *The Dark Knight Rises* (2012).

Christian Bale on acting in the Batsuit: The very first time I put on the Batsuit was actually for the screen test, so it wasn't my specific Batsuit, built for me. [I believe it came] from, I don't know, *Batman Forever* or something from before. It was very constricting because it was smaller; it was too small on me so I can hardly breathe in it, but you got your first impression about the heat of it. But also for me, it became clear that I just could not wear that Batsuit and feel anything but an ass unless I really became like a beast within it, and that he became somewhat demonic. Because to me, like just standing there in the Batsuit, I felt like an idiot on his way to a Halloween party, and that's the way he's often been portrayed, and the way that it had gone with some of the movies with these kind of one-liners and quips and things. It just wasn't savage enough for what to me that Batsuit felt like it had to be. It was his demonic incarnation and the way that he channeled all of his negative emotions and rage so that he was able to function in regular society as Bruce Wayne.—*BlackFilm*, 2005.[268]

Christian Bale on Batman's true identity: I think because he channels his rage so much into the Batman character and creating that as a creature and a kind of monster, that in a way it's demonic therapy. His negative emotions can go into that character so that he is able to function in his everyday life. He's a good actor. He performs most of the time. The only person who knows who he really is Alfred. With everybody else, he's got some kind of facade and a wall that he's putting up whether it be as the wastrel playboy character or the angry young man, but he's never really letting anybody inside at all. I like very much the relationship with Alfred and him. It has its duality because he's his servant, he's his butler, but also he's the closest thing he has to a father figure and the only person who truly knows him. I think it's one of the most important parts of the movie.—IGN, 2005.[269]

Christian Bale on his approach to Batman: If you think about the obsession that somebody must have to retain the pain and anger from an incident that happened twenty years previously and is still in the forefront of his mind. You know that's an incredible obsession. I mean, that's an unhealthy obsession. So concentrating on the fact that he's attempting to take his pain and his guilt and his anger and the rage and do something good with it, even though his impulses are that he does just want to rage and break bones and do damage. So there's always that conflict, and remembering that I never wanted to appear to be Bruce Wayne in a Batsuit when I was playing the Batman. That he just *becomes* [Batman], that it is an alter ego completely.—About.com, 2005.[270]

Christian Bale on Batman's mental health: I think probably some psychiatrists would say, yes, [he's insane] for hanging on to that pain intentionally, keeping hold of it and letting it rule much of his life. I wouldn't say he's schizophrenic or something, like it's an actual or multiple personalities [that] he's unable to control. He can control it, but it's intense discipline that he's learned to be able to function in everyday life. And in many ways, the Bruce Wayne character, the playboy, the cad, etc., the businessman, he's actually the mask. He *is* the performance. Nobody would say it would be a healthy state of mind to be in, but I'm not suggesting that he's actually got multiple personality disorder or anything like that. Although, personally, I think that'd be quite an interesting way to take it if you wanted to really go to extremes with him.—About.com.[271]

Christian Bale on the meaning of Batman: I think that the general notion of trying to attempt to use negative emotions: anger, resentment, whatever the hell it is that everybody feels, and trying to turn it into something positive is something that I can relate to.—IGN, 2005[272]

Michael Caine - Alfred

Michael Caine played Alfred in *Batman Begins* (2005), *The Dark Knight* (2008) and *The Dark Knight Rises* (2012).

Michael Caine on Alfred's backstory: I'm a method actor, I'm Stanislavski and all that stuff, there is a backstory to my character. For instance, I play Alfred the butler in [*The Dark Knight* trilogy] and I wanted him to be a tough butler, and I wanted him to be an ex-soldier. The voice, the voice is the first Sargent I ever had. Because I was a soldier, and I had this voice of this Sargent and that's his [Alfred's] voice. And I always imagined him to be SAS, which is our special forces. He was wounded, and didn't want to leave the Army, and went to work in the officer's mess behind the bar, and Batman's father came in and he saw him and said, "Would you like to be trained as a butler?" And he said yes, and he went with him to America and was trained as a butler and that's his backstory.—*Screenrant,* 2012.[273]

Brandon Routh - Superman

Brandon Routh played Clark Kent/Superman in *Superman Returns* (2006), which was an unofficial sequel to *Superman* and *Superman II* with Christopher Reeve.

Brandon Routh on following in Christopher Reeve's footsteps: Well, the film is written to be the vague sequel to the first two films. Inheritably in the script there are many homages in the character, especially written from that character, so there are similarities because of that. The only thing that was done, really, to mimic Chris' performances, was pushing the glasses up with the forefinger. I did that sometimes. Sometimes Bryan [Singer, the director] would love a shot and I didn't do it. [Sometimes he'd] tell me to do it because it fit in a certain shot, or sometimes I adjusted the glasses like that.—About.com, 2012.[274]

Brandon Routh on shooting his first scene as Superman: I think I probably did some mental relaxation and took some deep breaths in my dressing room before I went out. The first scene that we shot, if I remember correctly, is actually not in the film anymore, but it's in the *Daily Planet*. Some of the crew had seen me in passing for costume tests, and we'd done small things like this. But this was the full crew and actually there were all of the people in the *Daily Planet,* all of the extras and they couldn't look and turn around. We didn't want anyone taking pictures or shots. A photo hadn't been released yet, and so everybody had to keep their backs turned. These 100 extras, you're in the *Daily Planet,* so that was kind of cool. Just to know the first time it was on camera, it was really powerful. That was kind of the final piece that I needed to be secure in the role, was to actually have some footage in the camera and to know that day was marked and I had become the character.—About.com, 2012.[275]

Brandon Routh on humanizing Superman: You know, that has to do with the script. I mean it allowed me to do that, which was fantastic because we really get to see the character mature and deal with some things that are, that I think as an audience member, really pull us in. I think Superman's journey is to become comfortable on earth. Of course he's got his role as earth's greatest protector, but he also wants to be as happy as he can. If that happens to be with Lois, then he's going to find a way. It might not be easy but he'll do [it]. That's the journey, so it was great to be able to play that.—About.com, 2012[276]

Brandon Routh on interacting with fans: People come up and they love the character, and as much as they may have loved me in the role – I'm just the vessel being able to put that guy up on screen.—MTV Geek, 2013.[277]

Daniel Craig – James Bond

Daniel Craig brought James Bond back to his literary roots when he played the personally flawed but professionally unmatched secret agent in *Casino Royale* (2006), *Quantum of Solace* (2008), and *Skyfall* (2012). The Bond series is the longest-running franchise in movie history, with a combined box office take exceeding $6 billion for the twenty-three official films.

Daniel Craig on his reluctance to play James Bond: It was going to be a life-changing thing if I said yes. It was going to change everything. It was going to change how I was perceived in the world and I suppose I was very nervous about that.—*60 Minutes*, 2012.[278]

Daniel Craig on why he finally accepted the part: Some things come along and you just have to try them. I thought, *I can't be afraid of it.* I was very brave or very stupid – I don't know which. I did think it through as much as possible. It took about eighteen months for me to decide. At first I thought, *I can't do this.* Then I thought, *In ten years I'll be sitting in a bar, drinking, and I'll think, I could have been Bond.* I just couldn't turn down the opportunity.—Playboy, 2008.[279]

Daniel Craig on the vicarious pleasure of playing Bond: I get a huge thrill out of it, a schoolboy thrill, which is about being an action hero on top of a train, which is so far removed from who I am. But I'm getting to live out a few fantasies.—*60 Minutes*, 2012.[280]

Daniel Craig on typecasting: Everybody says, "Oh, wait a minute. You're going to be typecast." That's obviously true. I'm now forever always going to be known as James Bond. But that's not a bad thing. That's not a bad label to have.—*60 Minutes*, 2012.[281]

Nicholas Cage – The Ghost Rider

Nicholas Cage played antihero Johnny Blaze/The Ghost Rider, the devil's reluctant bounty hunter, in *Ghost Rider* (2007) and *Ghost Rider: Spirit of Vengeance* (2011). The two films together grossed over $360 million worldwide.

Nicolas Cage on Ghost Rider fighting his personal demons: That's what is really exciting about it. In this case, the kids are going to want to go see *Ghost Rider* and their minds are so impressionable. So what I wanted to make clear was that no matter how much trouble you get into you can always take a negative and turn it into a positive. That's the spirit of Johnny Blaze. He's a man who's dealing with the worst kind of trouble. His soul has been abducted by the devil. I mean, that's as big as it gets, and yet he's figuring out a way to turn it around and turn it into something positive. I was thinking that with kids who might be going to the principal's office and they know that they're in a world of trouble they can find some way to make the best out of it and do something good from it no matter how bad it gets.—*Movies Online*, 2007.[282]

Nicolas Cage on identifying with Ghost Rider: Well, I think that I identify with him because he's a scary character, and I was trying to comprehend how something scary could also be good, like I said earlier. As a boy I grappled with nightmares and things like that. So I was trying to get control of the nightmares by maybe making friends with them. So *Ghost Rider* was like the perfect way to do that because here was a nightmare who was also a friend.—*Movies Online*, 2007.[283]

Nicolas Cage on his costume: On my costume, my leather jacket, I would sew in ancient, thousands-of-years-old Egyptian relics, and gather bits of tourmaline and onyx and would stuff them in my pockets to gather these energies together and shock my imagination into believing that I was augmented in some way by them, or in contact with ancient ghosts. I would walk on the set looking like this, loaded with all these magical trinkets, and I wouldn't say a word to my co-stars or crew or directors. I saw the fear in their eyes, and it was like oxygen to a forest fire. I believed I was the Ghost Rider.—*Empire Magazine*, 2011.[284]

Nicolas Cage on the challenges of playing Ghost Rider: I compared him to a cop, or a paramedic, who develops a dark sense of humor to cope with the horrors he has seen. But Blaze has also caused the horrors, so he's hiding out because he doesn't want to hurt anyone else.

Ghost Rider was an entirely new experience, and he got me thinking about something I read in a book called *The Way Of Wyrd* by Brian Bates, and he also wrote a book called *The Way Of The Actor*. He put forth the concept that all actors, whether they know it or not, stem from thousands of years ago – pre-Christian times – when they were the medicine men or shamans of the village. And these shamans, who by today's standards would be considered psychotic, were actually going into flights of the imagination and locating answers to problems within the village. They would use masks or rocks or some sort of magical object that had power to it.

It occurred to me, because I was doing a character as far out of our reference point as the spirit of vengeance, I could use these techniques. I would paint my face with black and white make up to look like an Afro-Caribbean icon called Baron Samedi, or an Afro-New Orleans icon who is also called Baron Saturday. He is a spirit of death but he loves children; he's very lustful, so he's a conflict in forces. And I would put black contact lenses in my eyes so that you could see no white and no pupil, so I would look more like a skull or a white shark on attack.—*Empire Magazine*, 2011.[285]

Nicolas Cage on reading comics as a child: At the time I was having nightmares, and Ghost Rider was a way of getting control of the bad dreams, to have them for you instead of against you.—*The Guardian*, 2007.[286]

[Note: In the mid Nineties Tim Burton cast Cage as the Man of Steel in *Superman Lives*, but Warner Bros. cancelled the project citing escalating costs.]

Nicolas Cage on almost playing Superman: I am a big believer that the right character is the one that ultimately happens, and while I enjoyed Superman I think Brandon [Routh] was the right choice for that part, and I absolutely believe that *Ghost Rider* is the right choice for me to play. It's a better match, I am glad it worked out this way.—WebWombat, 2007.[287]

Robert Downey, Jr. – Iron Man

Robert Downey, Jr. played billionaire industrialist and brilliant inventor Tony Stark/Iron Man in *Iron Man* (2008), as a cameo in *The Incredible Hulk* (2008), *Iron Man 2* (2010), *The Avengers*, (2012), *Iron Man 3* (2013) and *Avengers: Age of Ultron* (2015).

Robert Downey, Jr. on auditioning for Iron Man: [It was] a spiritual/ritualistic process. The missus says she could've woken me up in the middle of the night and I'd have recited the audition dialogue in double time. It was all shock, awe, conquer. It was about devastating the competition. Right before the first take I felt like I almost left my body, a sudden surge of nerves. Then, all of a sudden, it was like coasting downhill on an old Schwinn Cruiser, like I could do no wrong.—GQ.com, 2013.[288]

Robert Downey Jr. on what he likes about the character: His superpower is his mind. His superpower is his ability to invent and I think that's something that all of a sudden makes it applicable to every man, woman and child who will see it. I love this phrase that "There's nothing more serious than a child at play." I know that that's true for me. I think everyone has their thing. I ask around and make it my business to ask someone, "When you're following your joy, what is it?" It tends to be several things but it usually has to do with tinkering with no particular aim, or it's a hobby that's not a hobby at all. It's a complete spiritual endeavor for that man or woman or kid. I think that ultimately, that's what saves his ass in the simplest form of the story is his ability to create out of desperation or loneliness or out of industrialism or patriotism.—*Superhero Hype*, 2008.[289]

Robert Downey, Jr. on playing Iron Man: If there's ever been a character in the history of my career that I would be happy to kind of meld with and associate myself with, it's Tony Stark, because it's the coolest job I've ever had.—Joblo.com, 2008[290]

Robert Downey Jr. on how playing Iron Man changed him: When you're looking at the back nine, and you're not a kid any more, you start to realize how you share things with a character like Tony. I will never be more like Tony than I was three weeks before we started shooting the first one when it was all the promise. Back then, I was like, "Wow, look at this role I get to play." But, that was a long time ago. As Iron Man has become more real and more kind of out there in his own way, I become just moderately more humble and more humanized.—*Digital Journal*, 2013.[291]

Robert Downey Jr. on his thoughts about not playing Iron Man anymore: At whatever point I'm done with this, I'm going to have a bit of a crisis, because I probably haven't even fully ingested how much I've enjoyed it, how much it's meant. It so came out of kind of relative obscurity as this second-tier character from the Marvel universe, and I feel I was part of making it something more. But it also to me was just good filmmaking.—GQ, 2013.[292]

Samuel L. Jackson – Nick Fury

Samuel L. Jackson played Nick Fury, head of S.H.I.E.L.D, the meaning of which has been changed from the Hasselhoff film and now stands for Strategic Homeland Intervention, Enforcement and Logistics Division, in *Iron Man, Iron Man 2, Captain America: The First Avenger, The Avengers,* in *Marvel's Agents of S.H.I.E.L.D., Captain America: The Winter Soldier* and *Avengers: Age of Ultron.* Even before Jackson was cast in the films, the Marvel artists had started drawing Nick Fury in his likeness.

Samuel L. Jackson on the comics: I've been reading the Fury comics since I was a kid. I remember when it was Nick Fury and his Howling Commandos in the War World II comic books. That's when I was introduced to him, and then I moved on. Then all of a sudden, I pick up an Avengers comic book and I was like, "Hey, that's me!" It's amazing. It's great.—*The Age*, September 6, 2012.[293]

Samuel L. Jackson on working on *The Avengers:* It's kind of funny to stand around in a room and see everybody. Thor is standing there in his costume. Captain America. Sometimes he's dressed and sometimes he's not. Scarlett [Johansson] is there as Black Widow. Robert Downey is there. He very seldom has his Iron Man costume on when he's just hanging around with his buds. It's just amazing to look around the room and see all of those guys there and go, "Okay. This is cool."*–BBC Newsbeat*, 2011.[294]

Heath Ledger - Joker

Heath Ledger posthumously won the Best Supporting Actor Academy Award for his fearless performance as the Joker in *The Dark Knight* (2008).

Heath Ledger on preparing for Joker: I sat around a hotel room in London for about a month and I just locked myself away and formed a little diary and experimented with voices and I'll answer your question (laughs).... I ended up making him within the realm of a psychopath, kind of like zero empathy or very little to no conscience towards his acts, which is fun because there's no real limits on their boundaries to what he would say or how he would say something or what he would do. So yeah, that. I don't know, it's always a very personal process in terms of how you land in your characters shoes, so to speak, and it's a combination of reading all the comic books I could and the script, and then just really closing my eyes and meditating on it, you know? Chris [Nolan] and I very much saw eye to eye on how the character should be played, and that was evident from the first meeting we had on the project. We both had identical images in our minds, and so I went away, found it, came back.—FHM, 2008.[295]

Heath Ledger on getting into the mindset of evil: I think we all have it in us. For awhile there I was thinking that sometimes I'll connect some exterior thoughts, I'm kind of eating raw meat and what that does to your mouth and to your eyes and simple little visuals like that that can kind of twist your mind a little bit and it feels evil when it's not necessarily an evil thought, but it may look and come across as evil. I don't know, I guess the rest is just trusting your research and trusting all the definitions of these words, a psychopath, and, you know, then just running with it.—FHM, 2008.[296]

Christopher Nolan directed Ledger in *The Dark Knight*: Like a lot of artists, he would sneak up on something. So, you couldn't really sit and go, "Okay, you're going to do the Joker. You're going to show me what it's going to be." You had to sort of say, "Let's read this scene. Don't act it, just read." And he'd sit with Christian and there would be a line or two where his voice was a little different, throw in a little bit of a laugh. And then we would film hair and makeup tests and try different looks, and in that, he'd start to move, and we'd have these rubber knives and he'd choose what weapon and explore the movement of the character. We weren't recording sound, so he felt quite able to start talking and showing some of what he was going to do. And in that way he sort of sneaked up on the character.—Lincoln Center Film Society Event, 2012.[297]

Michael Jai White worked with Ledger on *The Dark Knight*: He was incredible. He was a really nice guy. I noticed one day he was in his full Joker gear and he wasn't going to be filmed that entire day. It was all on the other guys. Heath could have came in dressed in jeans and a t-shirt if he wanted to, but he dressed like that for the benefit of the other actors to play off of him. Here's a guy who was very successful, and puts himself through hours of prosthetics and wearing uncomfortable clothes just to help out other actors; and no one would have blamed him if he just wore jeans and a t-shirt.—Black Film.com, June 2008.[298]

Terry Gilliam directed Ledger in *The Brothers Grimm* in (2005) and in the actor's final role, which Ledger didn't live to complete, *The Imaginarium of Doctor Parnassus* (2009): Heath was exhilarated by playing the Joker. He said, "I'm able to do things I never believed were inside me." He's working with great actors, like Gary Oldman, and Aaron Eckhart, and he'd say, "I go into these scenes, and they can't do *anything* to me!" He used to just giggle that he had found a character that was impregnable. They could beat him, hit him, and it wouldn't make a difference because he was so utterly wacko. It freed him up and got him out of that uncertainty after *Brokeback*. It was just, "Let's go. Let's fly." And he flew.—*Entertainment Weekly*, 2009.[299]

Edward Norton – Bruce Banner

Edward Norton played Dr. Bruce Banner in *The Incredible Hulk* (2008). The movie grossed about $263,000 worldwide, about $18 million more than Ang Lee's version, which was released five years earlier.

Edward Norton on why he didn't make another Hulk film: I couldn't do it for a variety of reasons - personal and professional. I had a blast doing *The Hulk*. I don't mean to sound snotty, but I don't aspire to spend that much time in my life doing those types of films. I have a lot of other things I want to do.—*Metro*, August 10, 2012.[300]

Edward Norton on passing the baton: Hulk is kind of one of those wonderful things that already at least three people had played it before me. Bill Bixby, Eric Bana, and now Mark Ruffalo has done it, and Mark's an old friend of mine, a great, great actor and great guy. And we both thought it was the greatest, both of us. He has kids and they love it. It's really fun because Hulk is maybe like Hamlet; lots of people can play it and do their own interpretation.—BBC, 2012.[301]

Jackie Earl Haley – Rorschach

Jackie Earl Haley played the psychopathic superhero Rorschach in Zack Snyder's faithful adaptation of Alan Moore and Dave Gibbon's groundbreaking graphic novel *Watchmen* (2009).

Jackie Earl Haley on Rorschach: Rorschach's been in incredible pain, I think, his entire waking moment of every day, just, you know, absolute psychological pain. And he finds himself and his own identity in becoming Rorschach. I think every lash-out at injustice, every punch, every kick is a lash-out against his mom and the horrible upbringing, the neglect, the beatings that tweaked him. And if it wasn't for that upbringing, he wouldn't have lost his identity in the first place—that he needed to go out and come up with this black-and-white sense of justice just to survive. So his soul is a very, very dark place and gazing into that abyss for months upon months upon months is an unsettling place to be.— Groucho Reviews.com, 2009.[302]

Jackie Earl Haley on playing a completely masked character: As an actor, I had to live and breathe and feel to let it be this natural Rorschach, but at the same time perhaps throw in some external layers so that it's also coming through. Some days I felt like I was animating the suit, and that's what needed to be done.— Watchmen Comic Movie.com, 2009.[303]

Ryan Reynolds - Green Lantern

Ryan Reynolds played Hal Jordan/Green Lantern, a superhero whose energy is derived from his power ring, in *Green Lantern* (2011). The CGI-heavy film, which reportedly cost $200 million to produce, earned about $230 million worldwide.

Ryan Reynolds on Hal Jordan: We are not playing him as a fearless guy at all. The reason that the ring chose Hal Jordan is because he has the ability to overcome fear. He is as baffled by this decision that these cosmic entities have made as anyone else. He doesn't understand why he was chosen. He's afraid to admit that he is afraid. That is kind of his challenge throughout the film. It's finding that footing and finding that ability to overcome it. That is what is deep within him. That is the reason why he becomes the greatest Green Lantern of all because fearlessness is insanity. Courage is an amazing trade. It's noble and it's a virtue that everyone wants. So that is what it is that he has to find within himself. He is one of those guys that is trying to be fearless when he meet him and we realize that he is going in the exact wrong direction.—*Collider*, 2011[304]

Ryan Reynolds on the film two years after its release: I saw how difficult it is to make that concept palatable, and how confused it all can be when you don't really know exactly where you're going with it or you don't really know how to access that world properly. That world comic book fans have been accessing for decades and falling in love with. So at this point I have very little interest in joining that kind of world. A great script and a good director can always turn that around. I believe that Joss Whedon [director of *The Avengers*] is the guy that just nails it and

Christopher Nolan obviously nails it. So if they were gonna do it,
like that, it would be an interesting thing to do.—*Empire*, 2013[305]

Mark Strong – Sinestro

Mark Strong gave a delightfully sinister performance as Green
Lantern's reluctant partner Thaal Sinestro in *Green Lantern*. The
film recounts Hal Jordan's origin story and it concludes before
Hal Jordan and Sinestro become mortal enemies, as they are in
the comics.

Mark Strong on Sinestro: He is an alien, you know? In the
movie, you have to decide as an actor how you are going to give
a character like that presence. You can't really move, walk, and
talk like yourself. . . [S]o you have to find something "other." So
any backstory and all of that is always useful. The knowledge that
Sinestro goes to where he goes to is useful, but I am trying not to
foreshadow it. But having said all of that, he has a kind of presence, which is undeniably strong. So what I am trying to create
is that he goes to the dark side not because he is inherently evil,
but because he is a kind of control freak. He is a dictatorial mili-
taristic guy who wants to keep order. So, for him, all that happens
. . . tips over into him keeping the people in his sector under his
thumb. He decides that even the Lantern Corps are no longer
worthy. So, he goes off and forms his own corps in order to kind
of perversely attack the Lanterns to try and make them better
than they are, but he loves the corps and he is the greatest Green
Lantern. I am trying to just give him a presence and weight that is
worthy of that. I think that probably prefigures, and you will see
in there that he is a guy that you don't mess with, and who can
easily go the other way.—*Collider*, 2011.[306]

**Mark Strong on how to act in the heightened world of *Green
Lantern*:** Well, first of all, you create the character yourself like
you do normally. So as an actor I am aware of his character traits,
the physicality of the prosthetic, and the lines he is speaking. You
know, he is talking about a corps that has protected millions of
worlds for countless millennia. These are massive concepts. I'm
trying as an actor to incorporate all of that and use the physicality of the prosthetics and everything to kind of — I don't know,

it's almost Shakespearean. That is the best way I can describe it. It's like when you are in a theater, and you are playing on a stage, and you need to fill a room. The best way I can describe it is that we were always taught that you don't gesture like you do in normal life. When you gesture, you did this and that, you know? To actually lift your arms and gesture properly when you are saying something is much more powerful and stronger. There is a scene in which I have a speech to all of the Lanterns, and I just try to use a bit of that. It's not naturalistic, but I think the whole thing will work together to give a strong character. That is my hope anyway.—*Collider*, 2011.[307]

Seth Rogen - The Green Hornet

Seth Rogen played Britt Reid/Green Hornet, the superhero outlaw, in the action-comedy *The Green Hornet* (2011).

Seth Rogen on Green Hornet's relationship with his sidekick Kato: The real reason we did this movie was that we wanted to make a movie about a hero and his sidekick, and about these two guys trying to work out their relationship. But it's funny, people are like, why didn't you do a serious version of this movie, and I like literally can't imagine the serious version of this movie.—*Long Island Press*, 2011[308]

Seth Rogen two years after the film's release: We got excited about the prospect of having that opportunity to make a big, mainstream film that we did it, being completely naive as to exactly how much of what makes us good would be basically stifled and evaporated, merely by signing on to do a movie of that budget and that rating. And really it was a combination of hubris, actors and filmmakers both working far outside their comfort zone, and the general machinations of studio movies where it always seems the focus is on the wrong places.—*WTF Podcast*, 2013[309]

Chris Hemsworth - Thor

Chris Hemsworth played Thor, the God of Thunder who has to learn humility, in *Thor*, and in *The Avengers*, *Thor: The Dark World* and *Avengers: Age of Ultron*.

Chris Hemsworth on his Thor audition tape: My audition was me in a kitchen with my mum shooting on this little video camera

– we literally did it in two minutes. It's funny, you can spend hours preparing for a role and work your ass off and not get the part, and then you do a two-minute video shoot by your mum and suddenly you get a massive role. I'm not sure what the moral of that story is.—*Empire*, 2010[310]

Chris Hemsworth on Thor's character arc: Thor is this brash, cocky young warrior who's about to inherit the keys to the kingdom and he has to learn some humility along the way.—*Empire*, 2010[311]

Chris Hemsworth on the Shakespearean elements of Thor: When we first started, Ken [Kenneth Branagh, the director] gave me a copy of *Henry V* and made me do a monologue from it, partly to play with language but also to show me that the Asgardians are essentially the royal family from that play – Thor is Henry V in space.—*Empire*, 2010[312]

Chris Hemsworth on preparing for Thor: To prepare for the role, I read the comics and noticed the character was ten times bigger than me. Early on, when my name first came up for the part, I read the blogs and comments of fans saying, "He's too skinny. He'll never be able to do it." That provided the motivation to get into the gym and prove them wrong. In fact, preparing for the role was harder work than the shoot itself. The routine was nothing fancy. It was a lot of old-fashioned bodybuilding and force-fed nutrition. We used a lot of pulling exercises, and Kenneth set up a wood-chopping area for me to prepare. Those were important to wield the hammer correctly. We would also add yoga work for flexibility, but I'd stop that when Natalie Portman would arrive. She can't see that. I'm Thor. I have to be smashing something.—*Ask Men*, 2010[313]

Chris Hemsworth on Thor's hammer: We tried different versions of the hammer at the beginning. If it was too light a prop, it looked like I was swinging a toothbrush. It needed weight to it to force my back and legs into the swing. We looked at footage of chopping and punching athletes to study how the body moves, looking for that sort of Mike Tyson open-chest-full-momentum swing.—*Ask Men*, 2010[314]

Chris Evans – Captain America

Chris Evans played Steve Rogers/Captain America, the all-American hero, in *Captain America: The First Avenger*, *The Avengers*, in a cameo in *Thor: The Dark World*, and *Captain America: The Winter Soldier*, and *Avengers: Age of Ultron*.

Chris Evans on the costume: It's an amazing costume. Given the fact that his costume is red, white, and blue, and it's tight, and it could be kind of flash and over the top and given the fact that the movie takes place in the 1940s and 1950s. They've done a really good job of making it look really cool. I think everyone that's going to see it is going to say, "Okay, well done. Well done. I think they got the costume right. The casting they completely ruined, but the costume they nailed!"–*Empire*, 2010.[315]

Chris Evans on getting into character: I think wardrobe in general is a pretty big deal for any character. Whenever you put on the clothes of the characters it always helps bring them to life. Of all the characters I have played, superhero or not, I was most excited about putting this one on. It absolutely lent itself to the role. There was a lot of build-up for me, more than anything else I've done, and deciding to do it involved a lot of sleepless nights. You know that if your body rejects the suit, it's too late, but it felt fantastic. I loved it and never want to take it off.–*Empire*, 2010.[316]

Chris Evans on preparing for the movie: Obviously I went and read any comic books I could find, but the most helpful thing in the comic book world was finding out who he was before. This is kind of an origins tale and I think at the end of the first film you still see little skinny Steve, the guy you relate to, and that's the guy you always see in Steve Rogers. That's what the audience will like. Well, that's certainly what I'd like. I have a friend who's a comic book nut and he loves when I say this. He is the best human being I know. He is an eagle scout. I don't know if you know what an eagle scout is, but it's basically a boy scout that stayed way too long [Laughs]. He is just a good man who does the right thing and would rather not even tell a white lie. His morals are intact and I'm amazed people like that can exist. Even his demeanor is noble and honorable. He *is* Captain America, so I told my buddy I was basing it on him. I wish I could do his reaction. It's hilarious.

It's what Steve Rogers would say if you called told him you were going to base a movie on him. So, on a personal level it's him I'm ripping off, but obviously the comic books are the best.—*Empire*, 2010.[317]

Chris Evans on holding the shield: It's tricky. They have a bunch of different shields: some are the real heavy legit shields that look fantastic on film; some are kind of rubbery for when you're doing dangerous stuff and you don't want to get your face [hit] with it. Each has a different weight to it. It's always strange, but it's always great sliding it on. It just feels cool. It's strange seeing the stunt-man dressed up and being like, "Is that what I look like? Alright!" [Laughs]. You know you can often forget. The shield is the icing on the cake.—*Empire*, 2010.[318]

Chris Evans on his reluctance to play Captain America: I would have been fine playing a superhero if it was one movie and I would have been fine playing a superhero maybe if it was my first time around. The reason I was scared was because initially it was nine pictures, then it came down to six movies. Even six movies, that's ten years, dude. I mean, I could be doing this until I'm forty. To make a decision, I don't know what I'll be passionate about tomorrow. What if I just don't want to do this anymore? What if it gets weird or too much or I fall in love with writing or something else and I just want to do something else? Or I just want to move to the mountains, whatever. My freedom is gone if I do this movie. You're signing something away and I just guess I wasn't 100 percent positive that the end game in my life was to be a gigantic movie star. And if you're not 100 percent committed to that goal, making this decision is kind of scary. That, mixed with it's a big lifestyle change, too.—Collider.com, 2010[319]

Mark Ruffalo – Bruce Banner

Mark Ruffalo played Dr. Bruce Banner, as a man more in control of his rage than in previous incarnations of the character, in *The Avengers*, in a cameo appearance in *Iron Man 3*, and *Avengers: Age of Ultron*.

Mark Ruffalo on preparing for the Hulk: I think you go right back to the beginning and dust off your first issue of *Avengers* and I've been doing that. I've been watching the 100 hours of Bill Bixby's Hulk, and I've been really thinking about the inception, the original motivation of that character and why they came up with that character. He's a cross between Doctor Jekyll and Mr. Hyde and Frankenstein. [Note that none of these fictional associations is with a hero.] I'm finding a lot of stuff there, and I'm actually going to be physically playing the Hulk. No other actor's ever done that. So, I've been getting into Tai Chi and Pilates and doing a lot of movement stuff. I don't know what I want to do with it exactly, but I've been working physically to bring the leviathan alive.—IGN.com, November 17, 2012.[320]

Mark Ruffalo on Banner's rage: Rage is an intense thing. It's big; it's huge. It's your whole body, and so I'm not going to compare myself to any other Hulks. I just know that I want that rage to be as real as possible. I want that when he goes off that you feel it in me. That it happens to me first and then it becomes Hulk. I don't think it's simultaneous. It's interesting. It takes some people quite a bit to get to rage.—IGN.com, November 17, 2012.[321]

Mark Ruffalo on the original Hulk series: When I was offered the role, I talked to writer-director Joss Whedon about it. He said he wanted to return to the Bill Bixby kind of world-weary charm of a man who is on the run but still trying take time to live his life and falling in love and having a sense of humor about himself, and I like that, but I also liked the idea that I would be the first actor to play both Banner and the Hulk. That was probably the most exciting thing to me.—Contact Music.com, 2012.[322]

Mark Ruffalo on the difficulty of making a Hulk movie: It's hard to watch a movie with a guy who doesn't want to be there.—IGN. com, 2012.[323]

Mark Ruffalo on how *The Avengers* is a metaphor for the United States: You have all these disparate egos, superheroes in this and that, and they refuse to give up some of their positions in order to make a more perfect union and to join the team. That's really what the whole movie is about: subjugating your own best interest momentarily to further that of the whole. These movies reach a lot of people, they're our modern mythology. I think a lot of the beliefs I have and cherish were fostered by the decency of our superheroes, and what they were about and what they were fighting for.—Wall Street Journal.com, 2012.[324]

Mark Ruffalo on having the CGI Hulk resemble him: Yeah, well, it was a big fight. Marvel in the past did not want to use an actor's face in the Hulk, did not want the Hulk to resemble the actor, and Joss and me were really pushing to see Banner inside this beast. There was always this disconnect when you're watching the movie and all the sudden we're in a CGI movie, and it's animation and the continuity and just the subtlety of rage and all the different gradations of rage and all that is hard to capture in animation.—Fandango.com, 2012[325]

Mark Ruffalo on playing a fully digital character: There's this algorithm that digitally puts 2,000 pounds of muscle onto my body. It's weird. I wear this skinny little suit with reflective balls all over it. When we shot the stuff, I was actually standing in a warehouse with a couple of cardboard boxes and some foam mats, but when I looked at the monitor there I was as the Hulk in this landscape with cars and boulders and hills.— *Telegraph*, 2011.[326]

Mark Ruffalo on his inspiration for the way his Hulk moves: Believe it or not, I looked at a lot of gorillas. Just because they had this kind of lumbering thing that becomes explosive, you know. I like that. Plus, when you do the motion capture, you put the suit on and then you go into a room where they have monitors all around, and so you step in front of this monitor and there's the Hulk. It's literally like putting a costume on but it's the Hulk. Every move I make, the Hulk is making - a very rudimentary version of him - and all of a sudden, you start looking at that and you're like, *Moving like that isn't honest to that character.* All of a sudden, the image of the Hulk starts telling you how to move. He doesn't move quickly. He has this kind of lumbering thing and his shoulders are a little rolled over, you know.—Collider.com, 2012[327]

Anne Hathaway – Selina Kyle

Anne Hathaway played Selina Kyle/Catwoman in *The Dark Knight Rises*. Hathaway's character is never actually referred to as "Catwoman" in the film.

Anne Hathaway on how actress Hedy Lamarr inspired her interpretation: I know this sounds odd, but her breathing is extraordinary. She takes these long, deep, languid breaths and exhales slowly. There's a shot of her in [the 1933 film] *Ecstasy* exhaling a cigarette, and I took probably five breaths during her one exhale. So, I started working on my breathing a lot.[328]

Anne Hathaway on how her Catwoman is different than previous incarnations: What's come before doesn't limit or even affect this new version. It doesn't affect me because each Catwoman – and this is true in the comics as well – she is defined by the context of the Gotham City created around her. Catwoman is so influenced by Gotham and whoever is creating Gotham at the time. Michelle Pfeiffer's Catwoman was informed by Tim Burton's Gotham and Eartha Kitt was informed by Adam West's Gotham. You have to live in whatever the reality of the world is and whatever Gotham is.[329]

Kal Urban – Judge Dredd

Kal Urban played the antihero Judge Dredd in box office failure *Dredd* (2012), a film that despite capturing the flavor of the grim comics grossed only $35 million worldwide.

Karl Urban on Judge Dredd: I guess one of the things that attracted me to this character was the definition of his heroism, his brand of heroism is very human. He's not a superhero, he doesn't have super powers. He's just a man with an extraordinary skill set, a cool bike and a versatile gun. More importantly he is the type of guy walking into a building when everybody else is running for their lives in the opposite direction. So the opportunity to play that kind of man was something that I was hugely attracted to.— *Wired*, 2012.[330]

Kal Urban on the comics: When you take on a character you have to go through many different doors in order to define him. I read every *Dredd* comic that I could and obviously a huge basis for the character was what was on the page.— *Wired*, 2012.[331]

Andrew Garfield – Spider-Man

Andrew Garfield played Peter Parker/Spider-Man in *The Amazing Spider-Man* (2012) and *The Amazing Spider-Man 2* (2014).

Andrew Garfield on Peter Parker: I always felt stronger inside than I looked on the outside, which got me into trouble. I related to Peter Parker so much because I felt like someone else inside. I love the comic books and the animated TV series, and I even dressed as Spider-Man as a kid. My brother was Superman.—*Entertainment Weekly*, 2011.[332]

Andrew Garfield on wearing the Spider-Man suit for the first time: It's bizarre and I have to not look at my face. It's strange and surreal to be wearing it and I won't lie, I actually shed a tear when I first wore the spandex for the first time. I didn't expect to get so emotional but I did.—Capital FM Interview, 2010.[333]

Andrew Garfield on Spider-man's universal appeal: Spider-Man stands for everybody: black, white, Asian, gay, straight, lesbian, bisexual. To me, love between two consenting adults is love. To me, that *anyone* would bat an eyelash at what I said is interesting.—Comic Con, July 2013.[334]

Andrew Garfield on Spider-Man's sexuality: I was kind of joking, but kind of not joking about MJ [Mary Jane, Peter Parker's girlfriend], and I was like, *What if MJ is a dude? Why can't we discover that Peter is exploring his sexuality? It's hardly even groundbreaking! So, why can't he be gay? Why can't he be into boys?*—*Entertainment Weekly*, 2013.[335]

Andrew Garfield talking to Tobey Maguire in 2012 interview for *VMAN* magazine: Peter Parker is such a positive character—he's pure wish fulfillment, an underdog. I grew so much from him when I was a kid, from the comics all the way up to the first movie you were in. I was nineteen when I saw [*Spider-Man*]. I got a pirated DVD at Portobello Market with my friend Terry McGuiness and we went back to my skanky apartment in North London and we watched it twice in a row and then practiced your final line in the mirror! Terry has this thick accent and every time I would recite that line he would laugh this very distinct laugh and say, "No, man, you could never be fucking Spider-Man. You'll never be fucking Spider-Man!" I was so humiliated and upset. But, um, fuck you, Terry!—*VMAN*, 2002.[336]

Andrew Garfield on the importance of comic book movies: I feel like comic books are our Greek mythology. I kind of equate the themes, and I think a lot of people would agree that themes that Stan Lee was writing about in his comics are the same themes you'll find in Shakespeare or in Aeschylus or in Greek tragedies. I feel like the same human themes are in there, it's just under a different kind of guise.—BBC Breakfast, 2010.[337]

Henry Cavill – Superman

Henry Cavill played Clark Kent/Superman in *Man of Steel* (2012), which treated Superman's arrival on earth as a "first contact" story between humans and an alien being.

Henry Cavill on the responsibility of the role: It's important to do the role justice. There are a lot of people relying on me to do this well. I gladly accept that responsibility, and it's a great one to have because it's a wonderful opportunity. I don't let the pressures get to me because that's going to hinder my performance and, therefore, let people down. So, I choose to ignore the pressure side of it and focus on doing justice to Superman.—*Cineplex Magazine*, 2012.[338]

Henry Cavill on typecasting: Superman is a bigger-than-life role, and I can't imagine anything else that comes along is going to compare to it. That said, professionally, there's always a worry that you might get typecast. But that all depends on how well you choose the movies in-between. You can't live in fear of that. No matter what your profession is, you can spend your whole life worrying about what might happen or what could've happened.—Ask Men.com, 2013.[339]

Henry Cavill on Superman's cool factor: Is Superman cool? It doesn't get any cooler. He has all the cool superpowers. He's cool. People say, "Is Superman cool?" What, because he does the right thing all the time? How is doing the right thing not a cool thing to do?—*Nightline*, June 2013.[340]

Henry Cavill on Christopher Reeve's Clark Kent: If you saw Christopher Reeve's Kent walking around in the real world, you'd be like, what's wrong with that guy? Go to bed!—GQ, 2013.[341]

Henry Cavill on his approach to movie: We wanted to base this whole story on realism, to modernize it, to make the character easier to associate with. Personally, I wanted to apply a very real world feeling of that loneliness. We've all felt lonely at one stage or another. Whether it be for long periods of time or short periods of time, and that's what Clark experiences. He's spent his entire life without one person empathizing with him. His two adoptive parents sympathize but they have no answers, they have no idea how he feels. That's what I applied to the character.—*Katie, 2013.*[342]

Henry Cavill on his approach to Clark Kent: I think over complicating it and making it anything but hiding in plain sight would change the honesty of the character. Now that Clark needs a secret identity, it's just a matter of him adapting to a new environment as opposed to changing or playing a new character.[343]

Henry Cavill on humanizing Superman: It's in the comic books. In past live action movies, it's always been taken for granted that he's an invulnerable alien who saves cats from trees – of course he's going to the right thing. It's never been put into question why he does the right thing. Or what if he didn't? Or that this guy has lived a certain life which must be quite lonely, and these are all aspects that which haven't asked before, and through asking them we immediately provide a human angle to this incredible being.—*Moviehole, 2013.*[344]

Henry Cavill on his redesigned costume: [Having Superman wearing his "underpants" on the outside] is a dated look. When the original suit was conceived, it was very much during the era of Victorian strongmen and circus strongmen. I think I it was important to bring a new look which kids would find cool because *Man of Steel* is just as much for the new generation as it is for the older generation.—*The Showbiz 411, 2013.*[345]

Henry Cavill on wearing the suit: The suit wasn't incredibly comfortable, but they went to great lengths to make sure it was as functional as possible. The cons do not outweigh the pros at all. I got to wear a Superman suit every day. The suit had this magnificent energy to it. So, it was ok. Yes, slightly uncomfortable every now and then. But who cares?—*Moviehole, 2013.*[346]

Henry Cavill on what he's he planning to do after an interview: I'm going to go fly around a bit. Maybe save some lives.—*USA Today, 2013.*[347]

Chris Pratt – Star-Lord

Marvel's most unconventional superhero film to date stars Chris Pratt as the rapscallion pilot Peter Quill/Star-Lord, who leads a team of misfits and unlikely heroes in *Guardians of the Galaxy* (2014), with a cast that also includes Zoe Saldana as Gamora, Academy Award winner Benicio Del Toro as The Collector, and Academy Award nominee Bradley Cooper as the voice of Rocket Raccoon.

Chris Pratt on the unconventional tone of *Guardians of the Galaxy*: I think tone is the major thing we have to accomplish, a consistent tone, going from silly and comedic to high-stakes drama and action, and everything in-between. It's really up to James [Gunn, the director], and I trust everything that he's doing. I think we're getting good stuff. I don't know what to say about it other than it might be . . .Oh! It's the greatest movie of the twenty-first century! That's what I'll say. It'll be the *Citizen Kane* of movies other than *Citizen Kane*.–IGN.com, 2013.[348]

Chris Pratt on comparing Star-Lord to Han Solo: He's also a rogue kind of dude in space who is only after his self-interests and has to learn to care about someone else enough to sacrifice himself.–IGN.com, 2013.[349]

Chris Pratt on the dynamics of the group: This is something a little different from normal superhero films. It's a space opera. This isn't a single origin superhero movie. This is like *Bad News Bears* in space. This is a group of ragtag people, or aliens or beings that come together for the greater good. It's really a movie about these people finding their family. Each of these characters is in their own way a bit like orphans. They are alone and fighting for their own interest and then come together. It's a movie about family.[350] – IGN.com, 2013[351]

Ben Affleck – Batman

Ben Affleck has been cast as Bruce Wayne/Batman in *Batman v Superman: Dawn of Justice* (2016), which pits Batman against Superman.

Ben Affleck on the backlash to his being cast as Batman: Every kid should see their dad as a superhero, right? It's so awesome, man. I am so excited. Warner Bros. called me up and said, "Do you wanna do this?" And I thought, *Well, I'm not twenty-five man. Are you sure about this?* And they said come down we want to show you what we're doing and it was incredible.

Zack Snyder is directing. Zack [Snyder] had this incredible take on it. Obviously you can't do what Chris [Nolan] and Christian [Bale] did, those movies are amazing so he wants to do something different but still in keeping with that, so I thought, *This is a brilliant way to do this and I really know how to hook into this.* I said, "Ok, I want to do it."

The people from the studio were like "We're thrilled, we're so excited." They said, "Look, we want to talk to you because people go through this process, and it can be trying."

I said, "What do you mean?"

They said, "We want to show you the reactions that [other] people who have been cast have gotten, like on the internet and stuff.

I was like, "Really?"

They sent me reactions to people who were in these movies who did a great job and the public would say, "Kill him!" I was thinking, *But he was amazing.*

It doesn't matter what people think before the move comes out. It matters what they think when they see the movie obviously. I'm like, "I'm a big boy. You don't need to coddle me. I can handle anything."

They said. "Just don't use the Internet for a couple of days."

I'm like, "I handle shit. I'm very tough."

I saw the announcement, I look down at the first comment after the story that says, "Ben Affleck is going to be Batman," and the first one just goes, "Noooooooo!" I'm like, kids we're going to be Luddites for a while." I feel like I have a lot of opportunities now, which is really great. Some just come and go but this is something that's going to be really exciting.—*Late Night with Jimmy Fallon,* 2013.[352]

ACKNOWLEDGEMENTS

I would like to thank the many people who have supported me in a variety of ways while I wrote this book. At the top of the list is my family: Tracy Visceglia, Mark Visceglia, Gail Ravetz, Irving Shapiro, and Joan Shapiro.

I will always be enormously grateful to my mom, Sandra Edlitz, and my late father Robert Edlitz, for their love, for nurturing my imagination, and for always encouraging me to pursue my dreams.

I'm indebted to Elliot Ravetz – who has been a friend and a mentor to me. His insights and encouragement have immeasurably improved this tome. He's been there for me every step of the way (and not just on this book). I know he knows how much I love him but it's worth repeating.

I am also everlastingly thankful to my very dear and very creative friends Jerry Kolber and Adam Davis: Jerry for a lifetime of support and love, and Adam for, among other reasons, the innumerable laughs and for encouraging me to write. They are two of the best friends that anyone could hope to have.

I'd like to give thanks to Jim Graham, Teal Cannady, David Weiner, Vilma Vias, Shelly Oneida, Pamela Shaw, Kim Davis, Holly Gerace, Terry Gerace, Charles Salzberg, Paul Kean, Mary McCann, Ophira Eisenberg, Marika Condos, Renee Jamieson, Peter Lane, Jonathan Lyons, to the LC clan including Karin Weston-Brody, Ian Brody, and Peter Bergin, to the gang at Bastardos (including Clinton Bester, Rachel Zirkle, Mal Mallinson, Antonio Linares, Sherif Ibrahim, the late Gus Tsamas, and Michael Markiewicz), and to my longtime group of buddies including Libba and David. Additional thanks go to Arlen Schumer, Dr. Jeff McLaughlin, Benjamin Holcomb, and Raymond Benson. I would also like to express my deep feelings of gratitude to David Mamet.

I am grateful as well to the various websites that have published my work. Thanks go to *The Los Angeles Times Hero Complex*, *The Huffington Post*, *Empire* magazine, *Geeks Are Sexy* and *Superhero Cinema*. I would like to extend my thanks to Geoff Boucher and

Nev Pierce. Big thanks go to Summer Brooks and the gang at Sirius/XM's *Slice of SciFi.*

I greatly appreciate the confidence in this book and sound advice from my dedicated agent Ellen Scordato and for the support of her team at Stonesong.

I am very happy to have my first book published by Ben Ohmart and BearManor Media. Additional thanks go to Michelle Morgan, John Teehan, David W. Menefee and Robbie Adkins.

I love the cover design that Peter Romeo at Wooly Head Design dreamed up with the very talented Young Song.

I would like to thank all of the actors' personal assistants, agents, managers, friends, and publicists who didn't delete my emails or throw out my phone messages. If it weren't for them, this book would be a lot thinner. These wonderful people include Erin Gray, Gareth Owen, Patrick Jankiewicz, Emese Felvegi, Marni Anhalt, Leanna Levy, Richard Michelson, Toni Collins, who heroically made the Bob Holiday interview possible, Ashley Hanley, Jason Newman, Ari Lubert, Megan Messmer, Sal Abbinanti, Sarah Lampert, Peter Matteliano, Julie Civiello, Pam Susemiehl, Luke Windsor and Fred Westbrook.

I'm especially grateful to all the actors and actresses who spoke to me. All of them were very generous with their time and their insights.

My appreciation also extends to the many comic book shops that kept me flush with graphic novels – Midtown Comics, Forbidden Planet, St. Mark's Comics, Jim Hanley's Comics, and Mysterious Time Machine.

Every day that I get to spend with my kids Ben and Sophie is the best day of my life. You make me proud every single day.

Most of all, I eternally grateful to my beautiful, kind, loving, funny, wise, unflappable, and unfailingly supportive wife Suzie Shapiro. You are the perfect partner, and marrying you is the smartest thing I have ever done.

FOOTNOTES

1 David Mamet, Some Freaks, Penguin Books, 1991, p.179.

2 Michael Chabon, "Secret Skin: An essay in unitard theory.," The New Yorker, March 10, 2008.

3 Chabon has written a book about a superhero aimed at children called The Astonishing Secret of Awesome Man. The book is illustrated by Jake Parker.

4 Although part of the joke was the implication that Carell's character was so pathetic that Aquaman was his favorite superhero.

5 David Hochman, "20Q," Playboy, May 2006.

6 Will Brooker, Batman Unmasked: Analyzing a Cultural Icon, Bloomsbury Academic, 2011.

7 James Chapman, License to Thrill: A Cultural History of the James Bond Films Columbia University Press, 2000.

8 Robert Sellers, The Battle For Bond, Tomahawk Press, 2008, p.180.

9 John Glen, "For My Eyes Only: My Life with James Bond," Potomac Books, 2001.

10 Benjamin Svetkey, "He's Bond. He's Blond. Get Used to It!," Entertainment Weekly, May 24, 2006.

11 Fiona Cummings, "The Name's Bland, James Bland," Daily Mirror, October 15, 2005.

12 The casting of Ben Affleck as Batman faced similar negative feedback. In fact, someone petitioned the White House to "make it illegal for Ben Affleck to portray Batman (or any super hero [sic]) on film for the next 200 years.".

13 Steven King, "2006: My Top 10 Movies," Entertainment Weekly, February 2007.

14 David Edelstein, "Rachel Weisz and Daniel Craig on Getting Entangled in Betrayal," The Vulture, August 23, 2013, http://www.vulture.com/2013/08/rachel-weisz-and-daniel-craig-on-betrayal.html.

15 Jeremy Smith writing as Mr. Beaks, "Mr. Beaks and David S. Goyer Go In Depth on Man of Steel," Ain't It Cool News, June 14, 2013 http://www.aintitcool.com/node/62885.

16 Each "holy something" phrase is listed in the webiste HolySmokesBatman.com.

17 Michael Mallory, Marvel: The Characters and Their Universe, Barnes & Noble, 2004, p.130.

18 From Marvel Studios: Assembling a Universe, which aired on ABC on March 18, 2014.

19 In Les Daniel's book Batman: The Complete History, DC comic book editor Julius Schwartz recalled that the prognosis wasn't quite as dire as Kane remembered: "I wouldn't say they were going to kill it, but it certainly was being discussed."

20 Robert Greenberger, "Bats in their Belfries: The Proliferation of Batman," published in Gotham City 14 Miles: 14 Essays On Why 1960s Batman TV series Matters, published by Sequart Research & Literacy Organization, Location 367.

21 Adam West, Back to the Batcave, Berkley Publishing Group, 1994, p. 67.

22 Les Daniels, "DC Comics: A Celebration of the World's Favorite Comic Book Heroes, Billboard Books, 1995, p. 138.

23 Les Daniels, "DC Comics: A Celebration of the World's Favorite Comic Book Heroes, Billboard Books, 1994, p.140.

24 Unlike Batman, which was essentially an hour show that was aired in two parts, The Green Hornet was only a half-hour long and aired only once a week. In a rare interview with Wes Britton on Dave White Presents, Van Williams attributes the show's failure to the fact the thirty-minute episodes didn't give the show's producer and writer's sufficient time to properly flesh out their stories. The two-part interview with Williams can be found at AudioEntertainment.org.

25 Mark Hamill, famous for playing Luke Skywalker in the Star Wars saga, played the Joker. Hamill's interpretation is convincing enough to make audiences almost forget about Jack Nicholson's and Heath Ledger's interpretation of the Clown Prince of Crime.

26 I originally learned about the song by reading Michael S. Miller's appendix in Gotham City 14 Miles: 14 Essays on Why the 1960s Batman TV Series Matters. At the time of this writing, the song can be found on YouTube: https://www.youtube.com/watch?v=TvsmPPG7npc.

27 Les Daniels, DC Comics: A Celebration of the Word's Favorite Comic Book Heroes, Billboard Books, 2003, p.146.

28 Lauren Moraski, CBS News.com, November 29, 2011 http://www.cbsnews.com/8301-31749_162-57332940-10391698/spider-man-turn-off-the-dark-breaks-broadway-theater-record/.

29 George Gene Gustines, "Look! Up in the Sky! Hoping for Broadway!," The New York Times, June 29, 2010 http://theater.nytimes.com/2010/07/04/theater/04superman.html.

30 Bob Holiday's autobiography Superman on Broadway was co-written with Chuck Harter. Harter also wrote Superboy & Superpup: The Lost Videos, a book taking an in-depth look at two failed pilots made by Adventures of Superman producer Whitney Elsworth.

31 Quote taken from: JacksonBostwick.com/biography.htm. It originally appeared in Starlog Magazine in an article written by Kim Howard Johnson.

32 Walter Mosley, "Spider-Man: The Quintessential Black Male Hero," Playboy, December 2009, p. 112.

33 Jeremy Smith writing as Mr. Beaks, Ain't It Cool, June 14, 2013 http://www.aintit-cool.com/node/62885

34 Douglas Wolk, Reading Comics, Da Capo Press, 2007, p.97.

35 Austin Grossman, "Star-Spangled Schlemiel," The New York Times on March 17, 2007 in Section A, page 15.

36 Joe Simon and Jack Kirby, Captain America, #1, Timely Publications, March 1941, p.5.

37 Stan Lee and Jack Kirby, Strange Tales #114, Marvel, November 1963.

38 Stan Lee, Captain America #122, Marvel, February 1970.

39 Josh Bell, Las Vegas Weekly, "Chatting with Original 'Captain America' direction Albert Pyun, June 29, 2011 http://www.lasvegasweekly.com/ae/film/2011/jun/29/chatting-original-captain-america-director-albert-/.

40 CP Lorusso, You Bent My Wookie.com, June 21, 2011, http://youbentmywookie.com/features/ybmw-interview-captain-america-1990-director-albert-pyun-12902

41 TV Store Online.com, July 23, 2013, http://blog.tvstoreonline.com/2013/07/direc-tor-albert-pyun-talks-with-tv.html.

42 It turned out that Captain America wasn't really dead and he eventually returned.

43 Reported by Josh Tyler, "Goyer's Flash is Out of Time," Cinema Blend, February 2007, http://www.cinemablend.com/new/Goyer-s-Flash-Is-Out-Of-Time-4415.html.

44 Lewis Wilson played Batman fifteen times in the Columbia Pictures serial Batman (1943) and Robert Lowery matched that number in fifteen episodes of Batman and Robin (1949). Olan Soule provided the voice of Batman on a number of cartoons including Super Friends (both the 1973 and 1980 versions), The Batman/Superman Hour, The All-New Super Friends Hour, Challenge of the SuperFriends and The World's Greatest Super Friends.

45 It is widely known among Batman aficionados that The Caped Crusader has a self-imposed code that restrains him from killing his enemies. In an article at ComicsAlliance.com Chris Sims writes that in "1940's Batman #4, in a story by co-creators Bill Finger and Bob Kane -- which is about as definitive as you can get -- Batman reminds Robin that "we never kill with weapons of any kind." However, there are notable instances in the comics, before the rule was established, and on-screen when Batman has apparently forsaken his own principles. Batman kills the Joker in Tim Burton's Batman and a couple of Penguin's henchman in Burton's Batman Returns; and in Christopher Nolan's Batman Begins, he essentially kills Ra's al Ghul by not attempting to save him from certain death.

46 Other animated Superman adventures include the Fleischer Studios' Superman (1941-1942) starring Bud Collyer, Filmation's The New Adventures of Superman (1966-1967), The Superman/Aquaman Hour of Adventures (1967-1968), The Batman/Superman Hour (1968-1969) all staring Collyer and Superman (1988) starring Beau Weaver.

47 Including X-Men Origins: Wolverine (2009), X-Men: The First Class (2011) and The Wolverine (2013), the X-Men films have grossed over one billion dollars.

48 Richard Reynolds, Super Heroes: A Modern Mythology, University Press of Missis-sippi, 2004. Quote cited in an article by David Cox, "X-Men: First Class – Mutant Heroes of the Teenage Outsider, The Guardian," June 2011. http://www.theguard-ian.com/film/2011/jun/06/x-men-first-class-teenage-outsider

49 Douglas Wolk, Reading Comics, Da Capo Press, 2007, p.95.

50 As a tribute to Joe Shuster's first girlfriend Shuster and Jerry Siegel named some of their most important characters with the initials LL -- Lois Lane, Lana Lang and Lex Luthor. Although it should be noted that when Lex Luthor first battled Superman, he was know only as "Luthor." It would take another two decades before the super villain was given a first name. Other writers would continue this tradition and, over the years, the list of characters grew to include Linda Lee, Lucy Lane, Lewis Lang, Laura Lang, Lillian Luthor, Lionel Luthor and Lori Lemaris, Superman's mermaid love interest. Stan Lee employed similar approach when naming his heroes. However, his reasons were less romantic than Shuster's. Comic Book Resources reported that during a conversation Kevin Smith, Stan Lee said, "I have the worst memory in the world. So I finally figured out, if I could give somebody a name, where the last name and the first name begin with the same letter, like Peter Parker, Bruce Banner, Matt Murdock, then if I could remember

one name, it gave me a clue what the other one was, I knew it would begin with the same letter."

51 Cynthia Wang, People Magazine, July 11, 2007, http://www.people.com/people/article/0,,20045784,00.htm.

52 "'Dollhouse' and More First Looks," Entertainment Weekly.com, http://www.ew.com/ew/gallery/0,,20210536_20512354,00.html.

53 Roger Ebert, Chicago Sun-Times, July 14, 2000, http://www.rogerebert.com/reviews/x-men-2000.

54 Jodi Picoult, "The Paradox of Wonder Woman," Playboy, December 2009, p.115.

55 From Lou Ferrigno's biography, which is published on his website LouFerrigno.com.

56 Marvel: The Characters and Their Universe by Michael Mallory, Published by Barnes & Noble Books, (c) 2002, p.130.

57 Ibid, p.135-136.

58 Ibid, p.141 and IMDB.com

59 The Hulk Speaks by Amy Reiter, June 19, 2003, http://www.salon.com/2003/06/19/ferrigno_2/.

60 While Wilson Fisk is The Kingpin in the comics, he is never called by his alter ego's name in the film.

61 Jennifer Garner starred as the assassin in Elektra (2005), a spinoff film, which made a little over $56 million at the global box office. Affleck's cameo at Matt Murdock was cut from the final film but appears as an extra on the DVD release of the film.

62 Steve Gerber, "Howard the Barbarian," Howard the Duck, Marvel, January 1976.

63 Ibid.

64 Ibid.

65 Grady Hendrix, "One-Man Counterculture: How One Man Changed Comics with Howard the Duck," Slate.com, February 20, 2008, http://www.slate.com/articles/news_and_politics/obit/2008/02/oneman_counterculture.html.

66 Ibid.

67 Margalit Fox, "Steve Gerber, Creator of Howard the Duck, Dies at 60," The New York Times, February 14, 2008, http://www.nytimes.com/2008/02/14/arts/14gerber.html?_r=0

68 Cary James, "Screen: From George Lucas: 'Howard the Duck,'" The New York Times, August 1, 1986, http://movies.nytimes.com/movie/review?res=9A0DE4D81F31F932A3575BC0A960948260

69 Ibid.

70 Jane Galbraith "Review: Howard the Duck," Variety, August 6, 1996, http://variety.com/1986/film/reviews/howard-the-duck-1200427011/.

71 Sheila Benson, "'Howard' Bows As One Lame Duck," The Los Angeles Times, August 1, 1986, http://articles.latimes.com/1986-08-01/entertainment/ca-18936_1_howard-bows.

72 Nate Shelton, "Steve Gerber talks about his unexpected return to Howard the Duck," Diamond Previews Online, November 2001, as cited at SteveGerber.com.

73   Darren Schroeder, "Steve Gerber: The Dark Duck Returns," Silver Bullet Comics, July 20, 2001, as cited at SteveGerber.com.

74   In 1994, Coates played Ellen Lane, the mother of Terri Hatcher's Lois in Lois & Clark: The New Adventures of Superman.

75   Jackie Kelk played Jimmy Olsen for seven years on The Adventures of Superman. Jack Grimes took over the part and voiced the character for the show's final three years and, then again, for the animated series The New Adventures of Superman (1966).

76   George Reeves' faith in Mark Sandrich was well-founded. Sandrich directed Fred Astaire and Ginger Rogers in The Gay Divorcee, Top Hat, Follow the Fleet, Shall We Dance and Carefree. He also directed Holiday Inn with Astaire and Bing Crosby. Sandrich died of a heart-attack while directing Astaire and Crosby in Blue Skies.

77   The list of actors who have played Jimmy Olsen include Jackie Kelk and Jack Grimes who played Olsen on radio, Jack Larson, Michael Landes, Justin Whalin, Ryan Harder, Aaron Ashmore who played Olsen on TV, and Tommy Bond, Marc McClure and Sam Huntington who played Olsen in feature films.

78   The first two Superman films were shot at the same time. Richard Donner, the director of the first film, was originally intended to be the director of the second film. However, after the first film was entirely shot but before filming of the second film was completed, producers Alexander and Ilya Salkind asked Richard Lester to direct the remaining scenes in part two, so that Richard Donner could oversee the editing of part one. Using almost only footage that Donner shot, deleted scenes, screen tests and the ending from Superman, Superman II: The Richard Donner Cut is an attempt to show audiences what Donner's vision for the film might have been had he been given a chance to complete it.

79   Tommy Bond also played Butch in the Hal Roach produced Our Gang. The shorts were also known as The Little Rascals.

80   In the 1982 Sidney Lumet film, Reeve and Michael Caine play a couple who scheme to murder Caine's wife. It has often been reported that the onscreen kiss between Reeve and Caine hurt the film's box office returns. While the film didn't perform as well as the filmmakers' hoped, putting aside the Superman films, Deathtrap was actually one of Reeve's highest grossing films.

81   Mark Hamill's full quote was, "To be honest with you, sure. I'm human. I mean, I like ice cream, but I don't eat it three times a day. And I've forgotten a lot of it. If I was still working on it, it might be different, but I've put it in perspective. I want to be supportive without being critical, but it's not mine anymore."

82   In the first season the show was titled Superboy. It was changed to The Adventures of Superboy in season two.

83   Jerry Siegel, "How Luthor Met Superboy!," Adventure Comics #271, April 1960.

84   Ibid.

85   Jeff Jensen, "The Joys of Lex," Entertainment Weekly, June 16, 2006, http://www.ew.com/ew/article/0,,1204678,00.html.

86   Over the course of ten seasons literally dozens of characters learn Clark's secret. While most of those characters wind up dead, in prison or conveniently suffer memory loss, there are a surprisingly large number of friends and acquaintances that are entrusted with the truth and avoid a dark fate.

87 Lex learned Clark's true identity in the seventh season finale but the Fortress of Solitude collapses on him before he could expose Clark's secret. In season eight it was revealed that Lex was still alive but in hiding. The Green Arrow tracks down Lex and kills him. The Lex Luthor who confronts Clark in the series finale is actually a clone who shares all of the original Lex's memories.

88 Brian Peterson and Kelly Soulders, "Finale," Smallville, original air date May 13, 2011.

89 Later in the episode Lex will be exposed to a neurotoxin that will cause him to forget all of his memories - including Clark Kent's secret identity.

90 Roslyn Sulcas, "Thor's Nemesis Makes Some Thunder: Tom Hiddleston Gets Mythic for 'Thor – The Dark World,' The New York Times, November 6, 2013, http://www.nytimes.com/2013/11/10/movies/tom-hiddleston-gets-mythic-for-thor-the-dark-world.html?ref=movies.

91 David Mermselstein, "Shakespearean Kenneth Branagh talks about the challenge of directing 'Thor,' The Washington Post, April 2011, http://www.washingtonpost.com/movies/shakespearean-kenneth-branagh-talks-about-the-challenge-of-directing-thor/2011/04/26/AFDr4n6E_story.html.

92 Michael Chabon, "After Strange Gods," The New York Review of Books, September 22, 2005, http://www.nybooks.com/articles/archives/2005/sep/22/after-strange-gods/?pagination=false.

93 Chloe Fox, "Tom Hiddleston, interview: from Thor to a sell-out Coriolanus, The Telegraph, January 14, 2014, http://www.telegraph.co.uk/culture/theatre/10561842/Tom-Hiddleston-interview-from-Thor-to-a-sell-out-Coriolanus.html.

94 Bryan Cranston (Walter White from the drama Breaking Bad) and Hugh Jackman have both walked around conventions dressed up as their signature characters. However, Bryan Cranston wore a full head mask that completely concealed his face. From reports I gather that Jackman also wore a mask, which (at least) partially obscured his face. In both cases, Cranston and Jackman were hiding in plain site.

95 Alan Taylor, director of Thor: The Dark World, said that the additional photography should not be described as a reshoot: "To say 'reshoot' means 'you screwed up the first time and you've got to go back and get it right this time' and it was never that. I come out of TV where you never reshoot, because you don't have time. If you do reshoot it's because someone really screwed up...[It]'s my experience with the Marvel process that they save a portion of the budget for this." Germain Lussier, "'Thor: The Dark World' Director Alan Taylor," Slash Film, November, 14, 20013, http://www.slashfilm.com/film-interview-thor-the-dark-world-director-alan-taylor/.

96 Ibid.

97 Eric Larnick, "Kevin Feige, Marvel Studios Head, On Marvel's Next Risks, Tom Hiddleston's Bad Boy Appeal and Jack Kirby," Moviefone, September 24, 2012, http://news.moviefone.com/2012/09/24/kevin-feige-marvel-studios-interview/.

98 Chloe Fox, "Tom Hiddleston, Interview: From Thor to a Sell-Out Coriolanus, The Telegraph, January 14, 2014, http://www.telegraph.co.uk/culture/theatre/10561842/Tom-Hiddleston-interview-from-Thor-to-a-sell-out-Coriolanus.html.

99   Chris Hewitt, "Hello, Mr. Ambassador," Empire magazine, 2012.

100   Robert Ito, "Fantastic Faux!," Los Angeles Magazine, 2005, p. 108.

101   Roger Corman interview, "Roger Corman – With Great Power Extended Interview," http://www.youtube.com/watch?v=dR2sb9ZZvtw.

102   MJ Simpson, "Interview: Roger Corman," MJ Simpson: Film Reviews and Interviews, http://mjsimpson-films.blogspot.com/2013/03/interview-roger-corman.html.

103   Elle Magazine, 2010, as cited in Popeater.com, http://www.popeater.com/2010/11/22/jessica-alba-elle-full-interview-fantastic-four/.

104   Spider-Man, Thor, Iron Man, the Fantastic Four and the Hulk, who were established in the 1960s, are youngsters by comparison.

105   In 1967 Ellie Wood Walker played Diana Prince/Wonder Woman and Linda Harrison played Walker's more glamorous mirrored reflection of Wonder Woman in William Dozier's nearly five-minute long unaired pilot. Kathy Lee Crosby played Wonder Woman in a 1974 TV movie. In three episodes of Lynda Carter's series Debra Winger played Wonder Woman's teenage sister Wonder Girl.

106   William Moulton Marston, "All-Star Comics #8," DC Comics, 1941.

107   Ibid.

108   Ibid.

109   William Moulton Marston, "Sensation Comics #6," DC Comics, 1942.

110   Les Daniels, Wonder Woman: The Complete History, Chronicle Books, 2000, p. 22.

111   William Moulton Marston, "Women: Servants for Civilization," Tomorrow, February 1942, p 42-45, as cited by Michelle R. Finn in "Wonder Woman and the Persistence of Feminism in mid-20th Century America."

112   Gloria Steinem, in an introduction for the book Wonder Women, Bonanza, 1972, as cited by J. Caleb Mozzocco on EveryDayisLikeWednesday.com, http://everydayislikewednesday.blogspot.com/2010/03/gloria-steinem-on-wonder-woman-pt-1.html

113   Lyrics by Norman Gimbel, music by Charles Fox, 1973.

114   "Where are the stars and stripes? Adrianne Palicki's new Wonder Woman costume is 'devoid of American patriotism'," March 20, 2011, http://www.dailymail.co.uk/tvshowbiz/article-1368132/Adrianne-Palickis-new-Wonder-Woman-costume-devoid-American-patriotism.html.

115   "The Critics (and the Fans) of David E. Kelley's 'Wonder Woman' Costume," The Hollywood Reporter, March 22, 2011, http://www.hollywoodreporter.com/news/critics-fans-david-e-kelleys-170141

116   Jodi Picoult, "The Paradox of Wonder Woman," Playboy, December 2009, p.115.

117   Melena Ryzik, "A '70s Survivor With a Secret Identity," The New York Times, October 30, 2007, http://www.nytimes.com/2007/10/30/arts/television/30cart.html.

118   Lesley Goldberg, "David E. Kelley: 'Wonder Woman' Reboot Still 'Viable' for TV," The Hollywood Reporter, January 5, 2013, http://www.hollywoodreporter.com/live-feed/david-e-kelley-wonder-woman-408894.

119   Jodi Picoult, "The Paradox of Wonder Woman," Playboy, December 2009, p.116.

120   Leonard Nimoy, I Am Spock, Hyperion, 1995, p. 6.

121   Leonard Nimoy, I am not Spock, Celestial Arts, 1975.

122 Leonard Nimoy, I Am Spock, Hyperion, 1995, p.7 – citing I am not Spock.

123 Ibid, p. 330.

124 As of this writing, Mr. Nimoy's work can be viewed and purchased at http://www.rmichelson.com.

125 RMichelson.com, http://www.rmichelson.com/Artist_Pages/Nimoy/Secret-Selves/.

126 Raymond Benson wrote 3 film novelizations, 6 original novels and 3 short stories.

127 Benson was comparing Lazenby to Connery and Moore. Benson's book was published in 1984, pre-Timothy Dalton, Pierce Brosnan and Daniel Craig. Raymond Benson, The James Bond Bedside Companion, Dodd, Mead and Company, 1984, p.198.

128 Steven Soderbergh, "A Rambling Discourse," Extension 765.com, November, 1, 2013, http://extension765.com/sdr/2-most-irrelevant-no-1.

129 Sinclair McKay, The Man with the Golden Touch, The Overlook Press, 2008, p.123.

130 Cubby Broccoli with Donald Zec, When the Snow Melts: The Autobiography of Cubby Broccoli" Boxtree, 1998, p.212.

131 Roger Moore, "Bye Bye to Ian Fleming's James Bond?," The London Times, October 4, 2008.

132 Playboy, "Playboy Interview: Sean Connery," November 1965, Reprinted in 50 Years of the Playboy Interview: James Bond, 2012.

133 While the quote, which is attributed to Raymond Chandler, originally appeared on the back of certain editions of On Her Majesty's Secret Service, some Bond scholars believe the quote should be credited to Raymond Mortimer, who reviewed the book for The Sunday Times. For more on the topic, visit Edward Biddulph's James Bond Memes at http://jamesbondmemes.blogspot.com.

134 Ian Fleming, Goldfinger, Thomas & Mercer, 1959.

135 Scott Meslow, "Agents of S.H.I.E.L.D. Recap: A Step in the Wrong Direction," Vulture, October 2, 2013

136 "A Small-Screen Marvel," Entertainment Weekly, August 30, 2013, p.34.

137 Gina McIntyre, "'Agents of S.H.I.E.L.D.': Clark Gregg on Marvel, Joss Whedon mind meld," The Los Angeles Times' Hero Complex, September 24, 2013, http://herocomplex.latimes.com/tv/agents-of-s-h-i-e-l-d-clark-gregg-on-marvel-joss-whedon-mind-meld/#/0

138 Les Daniels, Marvel: Five Fabulous Daces of the World's Greatest Comics, Harry N. Abrams, 1991, p. 37.

139 Daniels, Marvel, p.37.

140 Stan Lee: Conversations, which is edited by Jeff McLaughlin, is a collection of interviews with Lee from 1968 to 2005.

141 With tongue-in-cheek, Dave Turner of the now shuttered The Nostalgia Center.com writes: "I always thought it extremely fortunate that Steve Austin damaged both his legs and only one arm in his crash. Had it been the other way (two arms and one leg) we would have had a bionic man who ran around in circles really, really fast!"

142 Michael Mallory, Marvel: The Characters and Their Universe, Barnes & Noble, 2002,p. 130.

143 Adventures of Superman ran six season; Smallville lasted ten.

144 Michael Mallory, Marvel: The Characters and Their Universe, Barnes & Noble, 2002,p. 130.

145 A.O. Scott, "Heroes vs. Stars: Revenge of the Nerds, " The New York Times, May 8, 2005.

146 Brooks Barnes, "Disney Swoops Into Action, Buys Marvel for $4 Billion," NY Times, August 31, 2009,

"http://www.nytimes.com/2009/09/01/business/media/01disney.html?_r=0.

147 A.O. Scott, The New York Times, "Heavy Suit, Light Touches," May 2, 2008, http://movies.nytimes.com/2008/05/02/movies/02iron.html.

148 Jeff Elliot, Kirk Alyn: Superman Remembers, Starlog, March 1979, p.49.

149 Superman: The Comic Strip Hero, BBC, 1981, http://www.youtube.com/watch?v=fJprUlmj_Ko

150 Superman: Comic Strip Hero, BBC, 1981.

151 Ibid.

152 Robert Sellers, Battle of the Bonds, Tomahawk Press, 2007 p.127.

153 Playboy, "Playboy Interview: Sean Connery," November 1965, Reprinted in 50 Years of the Playboy Interview: James Bond, 2012.

154 Playboy, "Playboy Interview: Sean Connery," November 1965, Reprinted in 50 Years of the Playboy Interview: James Bond, 2012.

155 Playboy, "Playboy Interview: Sean Connery," November 1965, Reprinted in 50 Years of the Playboy Interview: James Bond, 2012.

156 1971 Interview with Sean Connery as cited by Robert Sellers, Battle of the Bonds, Tomahawk Press, 2007, p.180.

157 Dan Madsen and John S. Davis, "Sean Connery: Discovering the Bonds Between Father and Son," Issue #9, 1989 as cited by Cinema Raiders.com http://cinemaraiders.blogspot.com/2012/09/sean-connery-interview.html.

158 Matt Patches, "Burt Ward on Robin: What It Takes to Bring Batman's Sidekick to Life," Hollywood.com, July 24, 2012, http://www.hollywood.com/news/movies/34931171/burt-ward-on-robin-what-it-takes-to-bring-batman-s-sidekick-to-life.

159 Ibid.

160 Peter Anthony Holder, "Transcript of the interview with Burt Ward from television's BATMAN," for CJAD 800 AM radio, Montreal, Canada, August 28, 1995, http://peteranthonyholder.com/cjad15.htm.

161 Personal appearance at Chicago's Hero Con, 1991, cited at 66Batman.com, http://www.66batman.com/cgi-bin/yabb2/YaBB.pl?num=1280259617.

162 CBS affiliate interview conducted by Jean Boone, 1966, http://www.texasarchive.org/library/index.php/Jean_Boone_-_Interview_with_Cast_of_Batman,_The_Movie_%281966%29.

163 Ibid.

164 CBS This Morning, 1989, http://www.youtube.com/watch?v=qtjxXEhp-bU.

165 Bill Keveney, "Holy Cluster of Catwoman," USA Today.com, March 16, 2004, http://usatoday30.usatoday.com/life/television/news/2004-03-16-catwomen_x.htm.

166   Blair Whipple, "The Green Hornet: Van Williams Interview," Polar Blairs Den.com, November 2006, http://www.polarblairsden.com/tvgreenhornetvwinterview.html.

167   Ibid.

168   Barry Levine, "Green Hornet Van Williams Heart Attack Terror," National Enquirer.com, October 28, 2011, http://www.nationalenquirer.com/celebrity/exclusive-interview-green-hornet-van-williams-heart-attack-terror.

169   Larry King, Larry King Show, March 5, 2002, as cited on CNN.com, http://transcripts.cnn.com/TRANSCRIPTS/0203/05/lkl.00.html

170   Melena Ryzik, "A '70s Survivor With a Secret Identity," The New York Times, October 30, 2007, http://www.nytimes.com/2007/10/30/arts/television/30cart.html.

171   Jase Peeples, "The Further Adventures of Lynda Carter," Out.com, April 24, 2012, http://www.out.com/entertainment/interviews/2012/04/24/lynda-carter-wonder-woman-tour-album?page=full.

172   US Magazine, 2013, cited on Huffington Post.com, http://www.huffingtonpost.com/2013/07/24/lynda-carter-wonder-woman-costume_n_3639923.html.

173   "Lynda Carter: An Interview with Wonder Woman," Adelante Magazine, April 2009, http://adelantemagazine.com/2009/04/lynda-carter-an-interview-with-wonder-woman/.

174   Personal appearance by Lynda Carter at a Barnes & Noble in New York City, May 2011.

175   Sean Bugg, "Lynda Carter Talks about Her New Album, Her Upcoming Show at the Kennedy Center and the Importance of Gay Rights," Metro Weekly.com, June 4, 2009, http://www.metroweekly.com/feature/?ak=4284.

176   Birmingham News, Alabama, March 12, 1978, as cited at http://articles.latimes.com/1993-11-23/local/me-60008_1_bill-bixby.

177   Myrna Oliver, Bill Bixby, Star of TV's 'Incredible Hulk': Dies, Los Angeles Times, November 23, 1993, http://articles.latimes.com/1993-11-23/local/me-60008_1_bill-bixby.

178   New York Newsday, May 7, 1978, as cited at http://members.tripod.com/jhh_2/QuotesHulk.htm

179   "Bill Bixby Jolly Over Green Giant's Success," Beaver County Times, September 10, 1978, http://news.google.com/newspapers?id=sBsvAAAAIBAJ&sjid=gdsFAAAAIBAJ&pg=2190,2005536&dq=bill+bixby+interview&hl=en.

180   Ibid.

181   "Bill Bixby Compares Cancer to TV's 'Incredible Hulk," AP Story as cited in The Albany Herald, February 11, 1993, http://news.google.com/newspapers?id=kd9EAAAAIBAJ&sjid=4LYMAAAAIBAJ&pg=1213,1674364&dq=bill+bixby+interview&hl=en.

182   Clifford Meth, "Man and Superman: An Interview with Christopher Reeve," Starlog, February 1987, as cited on Comics Bulletin.com, http://www.comicsbulletin.com/columns/4444/man--superman-an-interview-with-christopher-reeve/.

183   Ibid.

184   Christopher Reeve, Still Me, Random House, 1998, p.195.

185   Cal Fussman, "What I've Learned," Esquire, December 2003.

186   Christopher Reeve, Still Me, Random House, 1998, p.197.

187   David Edwards, "Christopher Reeve on how he approached the Superman role in previously unpublished interview, "The Mirror, June 2011,http://www.mirror.co.uk/tv/tv-news/christopher-reeve-on-how-he-approached-the-superman-135347.

188   Richard Meyers, "Superman: The Movie – How They Made The Legend Live," Starlog, March 1979, Issue 20, p.46.

189   Christopher Reeve, Still Me, Random House, 1998, p.200.

190   Ibid.

191   Kim Howard Johnson, "The Unmasking of Superman," Starlog, August 1987, Issue 121, p.40.

192   Christopher Reeve, Still Me, Random House, 1998, p.200.

193   TV Interview with John C. Tibbetts, 1987. http://www.youtube.com/watch?v=APeVihoDe6Q.

194   "Kneel Before Zod, You Bastard.," ShortList.com, 2013, http://www.shortlist.com/entertainment/films/terence-stamp.

195   Playboy, July 1992, as cited at Polar Blair's Den, http://www.polarblairsden.com/moviesbatman89pb.html.

196   Ibid.

197   Interview conducted by Terry Wogan, BBC, 1992 https://www.youtube.com/watch?v=e31HvyoW5HU.

198   Late Night With David Letterman, 1989,

199   Geoff Boucher, "'Batman': Michael Keaton on 'The Dark Knight' – and a Lost Scene from 1989 film," The Los Angeles Times' Hero Complex, May 16, 2011.

200   Josh Horowitz, "Michael Keaton Endorses Chris Nolan's Batman Flicks, Looks Forward to 'Dark Knight'," MTV.com, January 21, 2008, http://www.mtv.com/news/articles/1579979/michael-keaton-endorses-dark-knight.jhtml.

201   Josh Horowitz, "Jack Nicholson 'Furious' Over Heath Ledger Playing Joker in 'Dark Knight,' November 7, 2007, MTV.com, http://www.mtv.com/news/articles/1573617/jack-nicholson-furious-over-heath-ledger-playing-joker.jhtml

202   Mike Sager, "What I've Learned," Esquire, December 2.003, http://www.esquire.com/features/what-ive-learned/ESQ0104-JAN_JACK

203   "The Total Film Interview," March 1, 2004, http://www.totalfilm.com/features/the-total-film-interview-jack-nicholson.

204   Josh Horowitz, "Jack Nicholson 'Furious' Over Heath Ledger Playing Joker in 'Dark Knight,' November 7, 2007, MTV.com, http://www.mtv.com/news/articles/1573617/jack-nicholson-furious-over-heath-ledger-playing-joker.jhtml.

205   Mike C, "Fright Exclusive Interview," February 2008, http://www.iconsoffright.com/IV_DickDurock.htm.

206   "Warren Beatty Still Flirting with 'Dick Tracy' Sequel," The Los Angeles Times' Hero Complex, June 9, 2011, http://herocomplex.latimes.com/movies/warren-beatty-flirting-with-dick-tracy-sequel/#/0

207   Entertainment Tonight, 1990, http://www.youtube.com/watch?v=a84iUPZ-i54.

208   Marc Shapiro, "Demon in the Sewers," Starlog, Issue 183, October 1992, p.39.

209   Ibid.

210   Ibid, p.41.

211   Jane Graham, "Danny DeVito On His Marriage…And Hair Obsession," Big Issue. com, July 25, 2012

212   Janet Maslin, NY Times, June 19, 1992. http://movies.nytimes.com/movie/review?r es=9E0CEFDF1539F93AA25755C0A964958260

213   Marc Shapiro, "Night of the Cat," Starlog, Issue 183, October 1992.

214   Ibid, p. 44.

215   Ibid, p. 44.

216   Jen Yamato, "David Hasselhoff: I Was 'The Ultimate Nick Fury,' Movieline.com, May 25, 2012, http://movieline.com/2012/05/25/david-hasselhoff-avengers-nick-fury-samuel-jackson/.

217   Casey Seijas, "Former 'Nick Fury' David Hasselhoff Talks Samuel L. Jackson & Marvel's New Super-Spy," MTV.com, March 24, 2009, http://splashpage.mtv. com/2009/03/24/exclusive-former-nick-fury-david-hasselhoff-talks-samuel-l-jack-son-marvels-new-super-spy/.

218   Jacquie Kubin, "An Interview with Mark Hammil," Animation World Magazine. com, 1997, http://www.awn.com/mag/issue2.1/articles/kubin2.1.html.

219   The Cinematic Sage of the Dark Knight- Reinventing a Hero, 2005, as cited in Bruce Schivally, Billion Dollar Batman, 2011 .

220   Interview with Conan O'Brien, Conan, August 12, 2013.

221   Chris O'Donnell, "AFI Lifetime Achievement Award for Al Pacino, Chris O'Donnell Salutes Al Pacino at the AFI Life Achievement Award.

222   Shadows of the Bat: The Cinematic Sage of the Dark Knight, Warner Home Video, 2005.

223   1995, as cited in "Batman Forever," at Turner Classic Movies.com, http://www. tcm.com/this-month/article/153078|0/Batman-Forever.html.

224   Leslie Rigoulot, "Billy Zane on The Phantom," Film Scouts.com, 1996, http://www. filmscouts.com/scripts/interview.cfm?File=bil-zan.

225   Wilson Morales, "The Dark Knight: An Exclusive Interview with Michael Jai White," Black Film.com, June 25 2008, http://www.blackfilm.com/20080620/fea-tures/mjwinterview.shtml.

226   "George Clooney talk Batman and Robin," Total Film, September 30, 2011, http://www.totalfilm.com/news/george-clooney-talks-batman-robin.

227   Ibid.

228   Ibid.

229   Mark Julian, "George Clooney Once Again Expresses Regret Over Hit Bat-man Role, Says He Had No Idea About the 'Bat Nipples," Comic Book Movie. com, February 2, 2012, http://www.comicbookmovie.com/fansites/GraphicCity/news/?a=53860.

230   "Clooney Taking It Easier After Series of Film Flops," The Los Angeles Daily News, 1997, as cited in Bruce Scivally, Billion Dollar Batman, Henry Gray Publish-ing, 2011.

231   A.O. Scott, "Heroes vs Stars: Revenge of the Nerds," The New York Times, May 8, 2005, Sunday Arts and Leisure Section, p. 1, http://www.nytimes.com/2005/05/08/movies/moviesspecial/08scot.html

232 Goyer was also the executive producer and writer of Blade: The Series (2006), which starred Sticky Fingaz as Blade.

233 Paul Fischer, Cranky Critic.com, 2002, http://www.crankycritic.com/qa/pf_articles/wesleysnipes.html

234 "Daywalker Speaks: Wesley Snipes Interview," IGN.com, August 11, 2011, http://www.ign.com/articles/2011/08/11/the-daywalker-speaks-wesley-snipes-interview?page=2.

235 Nicholas Fonseca, "And Now For His Sixth Act..." Entertainment Weekly, May 31/June 7, 2013, page 47, and at EW.com, http://www.ew.com/ew/article/0,,20706365,00.html.

236 Michael Fleming, Playboy, December 2008, p.64.

237 Brendon Connelly, "On Set Interview: Hugh Jackman Pitches Us Vision Of The Wolverine," Bleeding Cool.com, July 8, 2013, http://www.bleedingcool.com/2013/07/08/hugh-jackman-set-visit-interview/.

238 Brendon Connelly, "On Set Interview: Hugh Jackman Pitches Us His Vision Of The Wolverine," Bleeding Cool.com, July 8, 2013, http://www.bleedingcool.com/2013/07/08/hugh-jackman-set-visit-interview/.

239 Lanford Beard, "Hugh Jackman on 'Wolverine' sequel, Neill Blomkamp' 'Chappie,' musicals he's eyeing," Entertainment Weekly, November 23, 2013.

240 Nicholas Fonseca, "And Now For His Sixth Act..." Entertainment Weekly, May 31/June 7, 2013, p.47.

241 Sci-Fi Online.com, 2006, http://www.sci-fi-online.com/2006_Interviews/06-05-25_HalleBerry.htm.

242 Terry Keefe, "With a Landmark Oscar For Her Searing Portrayal of the Gritty Belle of Monster's Ball, Halle Berry's On a Roll," Venice Magazine, 2002, as cited on The Hollywood Interview.com, http://thehollywoodinterview.blogspot.com/2008/11/halle-berry-hollywood-interview.html.

243 Michael Dance, "Halle Berry Interview for X:Men: The Last Stand," The Cinema Source.com, 2008, http://www.thecinemasource.com/blog/interviews/halle-berry-interview-for-x-men-3-the-last-stand/

244 Richard Matthews, "Smallviille Yearbook," Titan Publishing, May 2004, as cited on Superman Homepage.com, http://www.supermanhomepage.com/tv/tv.php?topic=interviews/tom-welling1.

245 Matt Webb Mitovich, "Tom Welling on Smallville Series Finale: 'People Are Really Going to Like What We Did'," TVLine.com, May 13, 2011, http://tvline.com/2011/05/13/tom-welling-smallville-series-finale/.

246 Tim Lammers, "Star Accepts Great Responsibility of Coveted Role In 'Sider-Man 2'," At The Movies.com, June 21, 2004, http://www.ibatom.com/atthemovies/3444062/detail.html.

247 "Spider-Man: Interview with Tobey Maguire," Cinema.com, 2002, http://cinema.com/articles/540/spider-man-interview-with-tobey-maguire.phtml.

248 "Doing Whatever a Spider-Man Can," IoFilm.co.uk, April 26, 2002, http://www.iofilm.co.uk/feats/interviews/t/tobey_maguire.shtml.

249 Elliott David, "The Amazing Andrew Garfield," VMAN Magazine, Summer 2012, http://www.vman.com/site/content/175/the-amazing-andrew-garfield.

250 "Tobey Maguire," Blunt Review, com, 2007, http://www.bluntreview.com/reviews/tobey.htm

251 Mike Cotton, Wizard Magazine, May 2004, as cited in Comic Book Movie.com, http://www.comicbookmovie.com/spider-man_movies/spider-man_2/news/?a=1234

252 Mark Harris, "Ben Affleck: No Apologies No Regrets. No Bulls#*t.," Details, October 2012, http://www.details.com/celebrities-entertainment/cover-stars/201210/ben-affleck-actor-cover?currentPage=3.

253 Stax, "Ben Affleck on Daredevil 2," IGN.com, September 3, 2006, http://www.ign.com/articles/2006/11/03/affleck-on-daredevil-2.

254 Mike Ryan, "Eric Bana, 'Closed Circuit' Star, Is A Lot Different Than You Probably Think He Is," Huffington Post.com, August 26, 2013,http://www.huffingtonpost.com/2013/08/26/eric-bana-closed-circuit_n_3816932.html.

255 Ibid.

256 Ibid.

257 Connor Kilpatrick, "Ron Perlman on Hellboy, Nicaraguan Cigars, and His Next-Door Neighbor Selma Blair," July 10,2008, http://www.vulture.com/2008/07/ron_perlman_on_hellboy_nicarag.html

258 Ed Gross, "I, Hellboy: An Interview with Ron Perlman," ComicBookMovie.com, December 15, 2008, http://www.comicbookmovie.com/hellboy/news/?a=5506.

259 Marah Eakin, "Ron Perlman on Clay Morrow, Hellboy, and His Crush on Ryan Gosling," The Onion's AV Club, June 4, 2013, http://www.avclub.com/article/ron-perlman-on-clay-morrow-hellboy-and-his-crush-o-98547.

260 Golden Rasberry Award, 2005, YouTube.com, http://www.youtube.com/watch?v=U-7s_yeQuDg.

261 Jarett Wieselman, "Thomas Jane: I've Never Fit the Hollywood Mold," Entertainment Tonight.com, March 12, 2013, http://www.etonline.com/movies/131606_Thomas_Jane_Interview_The_Punisher_Anniversary_Gasparilla_International_Career_Achievement_Award/index.html.

262 Rebecca Murray, "One on One with Thomas Jane from "The Punisher," About.com, 2004, http://movies.about.com/cs/thepunisher/a/pnshtj040904_2.htm.

263 Steve Persall, "The Punisher star Thomas Jane talks filming in Tampa Bay," Tampa Bay Times, March 20, 2013, http://www.tampabay.com/things-to-do/movies/the-punisher-star-thomas-jane-shares-memories-of-tampa-bay/2110155.

264 BBC.co.uk, July 2005, http://www.bbc.co.uk/films/2005/07/18/fantastic_four_interview.shtml.

265 Michael J. Lee, "Michael Chiklis" Radio Free, July 6, 2005, http://movies.radio-free.com/interviews/fantast1_michael_chiklis.shtml.

266 Ibid.

267 Elle Magazine, 2010, as cited in Popeater.com, http://www.popeater.com/2010/11/22/jessica-alba-elle-full-interview-fantastic-four/.

268 Ibid.

269 Jeff Otto, "Interview: Christian Bale," IGN.com, June 2005, http://www.ign.com/articles/2005/06/14/interview-christian-bale-2.

270 Rebecca Murray, "Christian Bale Talks About 'Batman Begins'," About.com, 2005, http://movies.about.com/od/batman/a/batman022005.htm.

271 Ibid.

272 Jeff Otto, "Interview: Christian Bale," IGN.com, June 2005, http://www.ign.com/articles/2005/06/14/interview-christian-bale-2.

273 Roth Cornet, Screenrant.com, 2012, http://screenrant.com/michael-caine-dark-knight-rises-alfred-back-story-rothc-120090/.

274 Rebecca Murray, "It's a Bird, It's a Plane, No, 'its Brandon Routh as Superman," About.com, 2006, http://movies.about.com/od/superman/a/superbr061906.htm.

275 Ibid.

276 Ibid.

277 Aaron Sagers, "Interview: Brandon Routh Talks 'Superman Returns' VS 'Man of Steel,' MTV.com, June 12, 2013, http://geek-news.mtv.com/2013/06/12/brandon-routh-superman-returns-man-of-steel/

278 60 Minutes, 2012. Available in online video at http://www.cbsnews.com/video/watch/?id=50150372n.

279 Playboy, "Playboy Interview: Daniel Craig," 2008, Reprinted in 50 Years of the Playboy Interview: James Bond, 2012.

280 60 Minutes, 2012. Available in online video at http://www.cbsnews.com/video/watch/?id=50150372n.

281 60 Minutes, October 2012.

282 Sheila Roberts, "Nicolas Cage Interview, Ghost Rider," Movies Online.com, 2007, http://www.moviesonline.ca/movienews_10831.html.

283 Ibid.

284 "Exclusive Nicolas Cag Webchat," Empire magazine online, 2011, http://www.empireonline.com/interviews/interview.asp?IID=1444.

285 Ibid.

286 Dorian Lynshkey, "You've Got To Be Able to Break the Wall," The Guardian.com, February 15, 2007, http://www.theguardian.com/film/2007/feb/16/1.

287 Clint Morris, "Interview: Nicolas Cage," Web Wombat.com, 2007, http://www.webwombat.com.au/entertainment/movies/nicolas-cage-ghostrider-int.htm

288 Chris Heath, "RD3," GQ.com, April 2013, http://www.gq.com/entertainment/movies-and-tv/201305/robert-downey-jr-profile-may-2013?currentPage=2.

289 Edward Douglas, "Robert Downey Jr. is Iron Man!," Superhero Hype.com, April 30, 2008 http://www.superherohype.com/features/articles/96459-robert-downey-jr-is-iron-man.

290 JoBlo, "Set Visiit: Interview with Iron Man Actor Robert Downey, Jr.," JoBlo.com, April 11, 2008, http://www.joblo.com/movie-news/set-visit-interview-with-iron-man-actor-robert-downey-jr.

291 Earl Dittman, "Robert Downey, Jr. Finds His Inner Superhero in 'Iron Man 3'," Digital Journal.com, May 3, 2013, http://digitaljournal.com/article/349424.

292 Chris Heath, "RD3," GQ.com, April 2013, http://www.gq.com/entertainment/movies-and-tv/201305/robert-downey-jr-profile-may-2013?currentPage=2.

293 Giles Hardie, "Samuel L. Jackson Q&A," The Age.com, September 6, 2012, http://www.theage.com.au/entertainment/movies/blogs/get-flickd/samuel-l-jackson-qa-20120906-25fxu.html.

294   "Samuel L. Jackson interviewed about playing Nick Fury in Avengers!" BBC Newsbeat, 2011, as cited by World of Superheroes.com, http://www.worldofsuperheroes.com/film-tv/samuel-l-jackson-interviewed-about-playing-nick-fury-in-avengers/.

295   "Heath Ledger's Last Interview," FHM.com, July 17, 2008, http://www.fhm.com/reviews/movies/heath-ledgers-last-interview-20080717.

296   Ibid.

297   Kristopher Tapley, "A Look inside Oscar winner Heath Ledger's Joker diary from 'The Dark Knight' HitFix.com, May 31, 2013, http://www.hitfix.com/in-contention/a-look-inside-oscar-winner-heath-ledgers-joker-diary-from-the-dark-knight.

298   Wilson Morales, "An Exclusive Interview with Michael Jai. White," Black Film.com, June 25, 2008, http://www.blackfilm.com/20080620/features/mjwinterview.shtml.

299   "Heath Ledger: The Untold Story," Entertainment Weekly, January 23, 2009, p.27, http://www.ew.com/ew/gallery/0,,20252991_20477938,00.html.

300   Andrew Williams, "Edward Norton: I Don't Aspire to Act in Films Like The Avengers," Metro.co,uk, August 10, 2012, http://metro.co.uk/2012/08/10/edward-norton-i-dont-aspire-to-act-in-films-like-the-avengers-530608/.

301   BBC Interview, "Edward Norton Compares Playing The Hulk to Hamlet," August 9, 2012, http://www.bbc.co.uk/newsbeat/19165274.

302   "Jeffrey Dean Morgan & Jackie Earle Haley – Watchmen," Groucho Reviews.com, February 28, 2009, http://www.grouchoreviews.com/interviews/289.

303   "Comic Con Interview with Jeffrey Dean Morgan and Jackie Earle Haley – Watchmen," Watchmen Comic Movie.com, 2009, http://www.watchmencomicmovie.com/080408-watchmen-jeffrey-dean-morgan-jackie-earle-haley.php.

304   Steve Weintraub, "Ryan Reynolds On Set Interview Green Lantern," Collider.com, 2011, http://collider.com/ryan-reynolds-interview-green-lantern-2/.

305   Ali Plumb, "Reynolds Not Keen On Justice League," Empire. Magazine, March 22, 2013, http://www.empireonline.com/news/story.asp?NID=36900.

306   Steve Weintraub, "Mark Strong On Set Interview Green Lantern," Collider.com, 2011, http://collider.com/mark-strong-interview-green-lantern/.

307   Ibid.

308   Prairie Miller, "Seth Roger Interview: The Green Hornet," Long Island Press.com, January 17, 2011

309   Marc Maron, WTF Podcast, 2013, as cited by Kevin Jagernauth, IndieWire.com, http://blogs.indiewire.com/theplaylist/it-was-a-dark-time-seth-rogen-speaks-candidly-about-the-failure-of-the-green-hornet-20130610.

310   James Dyer, "Valhalla Rising," Empire, November 2010, p.78.

311   Ibid, p.79.

312   Ibid, p.78.

313   John Scott Lewinski, Chirs Hemsworth Interview," Ask Men.com, 2010, http://www.askmen.com/celebs/interview_500/542_chris-hemsworth-interview.html.

314   Ibid.

315   Alastair Plumb, "Captain America Talks Costume," Empire, July 2010, http://www.empireonline.com/news/story.asp?NID=28293.

316   Helen O'Hara, "Chris Evans Talks Captain America," 2010, http://www.empireon-line.com/interviews/interview.asp?IID=1319.

317   Ibid.

318   Ibid.

319   Steve Weintraub, "Chris Evans Talks Captain America: The First Avenger, The Avenges, Wanting to Direct," Collider.com, 2012, http://collider.com/chris-evans-interview-captain-america-the-avengers/

320   Jim Vejvoda, "Ruffalo: Hulk is Like a Sex Scene," IGN.com, November 17, 2010, http://www.ign.com/articles/2010/11/17/ruffalo-hulk-is-like-a-sex-scene.

321   Ibid.

322   Rich Cline, "Mark Ruffalo, Interview," Contact Music.com, April 2012, http://www.contactmusic.com/interview/interview-with-mark-ruffalo-april-2012.

323   Jim Vejvoda, "Ruffalo: Hulk is Like a Sex Scene," IGN.com, November 17, 2010,

324   Barbara Chai, "'The Avengers' Has a Deeper Meaning. Just Ask the Hulk." Wall Street Journal.com, January 3, 2012, http://blogs.wsj.com/speakeasy/2012/01/03/the-avengers-has-a-deeper-meaning-just-ask-the-hulk/.

325   Todd Gilchrist, "Interview: Mark Ruffalo Talks Playing the Hulk," Fandango.com, May 1, 2012, http://www.fandango.com/movieblog/interview:markruffalotalksplayingthehulkexclusive-714139.html.

326   John Preston, "Oscars 2011: Mark Ruffalo Interview," Telegraph.co.uk, February 27, 2011, http://www.telegraph.co.uk/culture/film/oscars/8345218/Oscars-2011-Mark-Ruffalo-interview.html.

327   Steve Weintraub, "Mark Ruffalo The Avengers Set Visit Interview," Collider.com, 2012.

328   Geoff Boucher, "'Dark Knight Rises' star Anne Hathaway: 'Gotham City is full of grace.," Los Angeles Times Hero Complex, December 29, 2011, http://herocomplex.latimes.com/movies/dark-knight-rises-star-anne-hathaway-gotham-city-is-full-of-grace.

329   Ibid.

330   Nathan Barry, "Dredd Star, Writer Open Up About the Iconic Comic Character," Wired.com, September 14, 2012, http://www.wired.com/geekdad/2012/09/karl-urban-alex-garland-dredd/2/.

331   Ibid.

332   Chris Nashawaty, "Web Master," Entertainment Weekly, July 2011, p.35.

333   Capital FM interview, 2010, as cited by Corinne Heller, "Andrew Garfield Cried When He First Put on 'Spider-Man' Suit," On the Red Carpet.com, December 30, 2010.

334   Comic-Con, July 2013, as cited by Darren Franich, "Andrew Garfield: 'Spider-Man Stands for Everybody: Gay, Straight,' Entertainment Weekly, July 20, 2013, http://insidemovies.ew.com/2013/07/20/spider-man-gay-andrew-garfield-comic-con/.

335   Sara Vilkomerson, "Andrew Garfield on Spider-Man's sexuality: Why Can't He Be Gay?" Entertainment Weekly, July 10, 2013, http://insidemovies.ew.com/2013/07/10/andrew-garfield-spider-man-gay/.

336 Elliott David, "The Amazing Andrew Garfield," VMAN Magazine, 2002.

337 BBC Breakfast, December 29, 2010,

338 Bob Strauss, "Hero In Training," Cineplex Magazine, September 2012, p.30.

339 John Scott Lewinski, "Henry Cavill Interview," Ask Men.com, 2013, http://www.askmen.com/celebs/interview_500/535_henry-cavill-interview.html.

340 Nightline, June 2013, ABC.

341 Stuart McGurk, "Get Cape. Wear Cape. Fly." GQ.com, June 5, 2013, http://www.gq-magazine.co.uk/entertainment/articles/2013-04/29/henry-cavill-man-of-steel-gq-cover-interview/page/4

342 Katie Couric, Katie, June 13, 2013, ABC.

343 Simon Reynolds, "'Man of Steel' Henry Cavill Interview, " Digital Spy.com, June 14, 2013, http://www.digitalspy.com/movies/interviews/a490196/man-of-steel-henry-cavill-interview-i-fit-the-vision-of-superman-now.html.

344 Mandy Griffiths, "Moviehole Chats to Man of Steel," June 28, 2013, http://moviehole.net/201365839moviehole-chats-to-man-of-steel-henry-cavill.

345 The Showbiz 411, June 14, 2013, http://www.youtube.com/watch?v=KMp7_Ksdv48.

346 Ibid.

347 Bryan Alexander, "'Man of Steel' Star Henry Cavill Needs Nerves of Steel," USA Today, June 4, 2013 http://www.usatoday.com/story/life/movies/2013/06/04/man-of-steel-henry-cavill/2384785/.

348 Eric Goldman, "Chris Pratt Talks of Guardian's of the Galaxy's Tone and Potential Marvel Crossovers," IGN.com, August 29, 2013, http://www.ign.com/articles/2013/08/29/chris-pratt-talks-guardians-of-the-galaxys-tone-and-potential-marvel-crossovers.

349 IGN, July 21, 2013.

350 Scott Collura, "Comic-Con: First Guardians of the Galaxy Footage Shown," IGN, July 2013, http://www.ign.com/articles/2013/07/21/comic-con-first-guardians-of-the-galaxy-footage-shown

351 IGN, July 21, 2013.

352 Ben Affleck interview with Jimmy Fallon on Late Night with Jimmy Fallon, September 16, 2013.

INDEX
Numbers in **bold** indicate photographs

Adams, Lee 49-57
Adventures of Batman and Robin, The 129, 482
Adventures of Superboy, The (pilot) 299
Adventures of Superboy, The see *Superboy*
Adventures of Superman 21, 127, 141, 144-145, 154, 240, 262-288, **267**, **275**, **283**, 290, 292, 293-294, 430, 491, 551
Adventures of Superman, The (radio) 272, 273, 547
Affleck, Ben 243, 245, 510, 538-539, 543, 546
Akerman, Malin 218-228, **218**, **222**
Alba, Jessica 216, 338, 514
Alfred the Butler (character) 39, 132, 136, 186, 515, 516-517
Allen, Barry (character) 113-127
Alyn, Kirk 21, 262, 263, 269, 482-483
Amazing Spider-Man, The 2, 30, 31, 348, 534
Amazing Spider-Man 2 5, 534
Amazing Spider-Man, The (TV) 65-79, **66**, **70**, **73**, 118, 424
Andress, Ursula 12, 14
Aquaman (character) 5, 65, 145, 543, 545
Aquaman (TV) 5
Arrow 4
Ashmore, Aaron 289, 547
Atom Man vs. Superman 262, 482
Austin, Col. Steve 428-429, 436-439, 550
Avengers: Age of Ultron 100, 107, 521, 522, 528, 530, 531
Avengers, The (characters) 97, 406, 411, 423, 522, 531, 532-533
Avengers, The (movie) xii, 1, 31, 32, 33, 100, 230, 325, 327, 329, 402-414, 467, 521, 522, 523, 526, 528, 530, 531-532

Bale, Christian 4, 31, 128, 362, 383, 460, 461, 514-516, 539
Bana, Eric 510-511, 525
Banner, Dr. Bruce (character) see Banner, Dr. David

Banner, Dr. David (character) 26, 29-30, 113, 230, 235-236, 242, 429-431, 432-433, 434, 435-437, 439, 459, 489-490, 510-511, 525, 531-533, 545
Basinger, Kim 31, 494
Batgirl (character) 44, 65, 180-199, 200, 216, 311
Batman (character) 2, 3, 4, 5, 7, 10, 24, 26, 27, 30, 31, 37, 38, 39, 40, 41-42, 43, 44, 46, 47, 48, 58, 65, 94, 110, 113, 116, 117, 118, 128, 129, 130, 131, 132, 134-135, 136-137, 138, 139, 140, 144, 146, 148, 155, 160, 162, 163, 164, 185, 190, 191, 192, 194, 195, 196, 201, 204, 208, 216, 219, 220, 240, 297, 302, 304, 307, 309, 339, 349, 359, 362, 383, 411, 418, 425, 460, 461, 462, 465, 467, 472, 475, 478, 482, 485, 494-495, 498, 500, 501, 503, 515-517, 545
Batman (TV) 13, 26, 27, 28, 37-48, **40**, **43**, **45**, 50, 55, 67, 76, 113, 131, 143, 180-199, **181**, 302-311, **303**, **305**, 442, 484-488, 498, 543, 544
Batman (serial) 482, 545
Batman (1966) 39, 484, 485, 486
Batman (1989) xii, 17, 26-27, 31, 98, 113, 114, 116, 117, 174, 467, 470, 494-496, 545
Batman & Mr. Freeze: SubZero 129
Batman and Robin (serial) 545
Batman and Robin 27, 348, 494, 501, 503-504, 505
Batman: Arkham Asylum 129, 499
Batman: Arkham City 129, 499
Batman: Arkham Knight 129
Batman: Assault on Arkham 128
Batman Begins xii, 7, 114, 495, 514-517, 545
Batman Beyond (short) 129
Batman Beyond (TV) 129
Batman Beyond: Return of the Joker 128, 499
Batman Beyond: The Movie 129
Batman Forever 495, 500-502, 515
Batman: Gotham Knight 128
Batman: Mask of the Phantasm 129, 499
Batman: Mystery of the Batwoman 128
Batman: New Times (2005) 39, 128, 500

Batman Returns 27, 28, 31, 114, 116, 117, 174, 467, 470, 494, 497-498, 545

Batman: Rise of Sin Tzu 129

Batman: Strange Days 129

Batman/Superman Hour, The 545

Batman Superman Movie: World's Finest, The 129, 499

Batman, The (2005) 39, 485

Batman: The Animated Series 27, 39, 48, 76, 129, **133**, 155, 156, 201, 499

Batman: The Brave and the Bold (2010) 39, 302

Batman: The Complete History 37

Batmantis (character) 39

Batman Unmasked 10

Batman: Vengeance 129, 499

Batman v Superman: Dawn of Justice 510, 538-539, 543

Batson, Billy (character) 58-64

Beatty, Warren 497

Beck, C.C. 58, 62

Berry, Halle 4, 28, 217, 302, 507-508, 512-513

Bilson, Danny 114, 116

Bionic Woman, The 429, 436, 437-438, 438-439

Birds of Prey 500

Bixby, Bill 230-241, **234**, 242, 244-245, **428**, 429, **433**, 435, **436**, 438, 459, 460, 489-490, 525, 532

Black, Shane 468

Blade (character) 165, 505-506

Blade 505-506

Blade: The Series 555

Blade: Trinity 505-506

Blade II 505-506

Blaze, Johnny (character) 519-521

Blofeld, Ernst Stavro (character) 14, 15, 16, 449

Bond, James (character) 3, 5, 10-21, 25, 33, 173, 230, 255, 376, 381-401, 441, 446, 447, 449-456, 467, 483-484, 518-519

Bond, Tommy 292, 293, 547

Bostwick, Jackson 58-64, **60**

Boy Wonder, I Love You 484

Branagh, Kenneth 326, 330, 331, 332, 414, 426, 529, 548

Brando, Marlon 23, 305, 443

Bringing Up Baby 491

Broccoli, Albert R. "Cubby" 10, 383, 388, 441, 447, 451, 453

Brosnan, Pierce 10, 13, 16, 17, 19, 21, 383, 389, 400, 550

Broussard, Stephen 421

Brown, Reb 100, 342

Burton, Tim xii, 26-27, 31, 98, 113, 114, 116, 145, 174, 195, 337, 467, 470, 494, 497, 498, 505, 521, 534, 545, 562

Byrne, John 141

Cage, Nicolas 4, 145, 519-521

Cain, Dean 108, 141-154, **142**, **149**, **152**, 155, 279, 289, 383

Caine, Michael 12, 163, 483, 516-517, 547

Cameron, James 5

Captain America (character) 65, 95-112, 327, 338, 403, 409, 412, 417-421, 429, 461, 467, 523, 530-531, 545

Captain America (1944) 100, 246

Captain America (1977) 100, 342

Captain America (1990) 95-112, **101**, 421, 505

Captain America: Reborn 457

Captain America: The First Avenger 31, 32, 33, 100, 421, 522, 530-531

Captain America: The Winter Soldier 33, 100, 102, 421, 467, 522, 530-531

Captain America II: Death Too Soon 100, 336

Captain Marvel (character) 58-64, 417

Carell, Steve 5, 543

Carrey, Jim 4, 134, 502

Carter, Lynda 259, 359, 361, 362, 363, 364, 366, 488-489, 549

Casino Royale (book) 393-394

Casino Royale (1954) 12, 393

Casino Royale (1967) 12

Casino Royale (2006) 3, 5, 10, 12, 18, 19-20, 381, 518

Cassidy, Jack 51

Castle, Frank (character) 513

Catwoman (character) 27-28, 47, 188, 201, 220, 302-311, 364, 476, 484, 487, 494, 498-499, 512-513, 533-534

Catwoman 27-28, 512-513

Cavill, Henry 146, 150, 152, 154, 383, 536-537

Chabon, Michael xii, 3, 4, 326, 333, 471-472

Chiklis, Michael 338, 513-514

Christopher, Gerard 21, 81, 297, 300

Ciarfalio, Carl 336-358, **339**, **344**, **346**, **347**

Clift, Montgomery 280, 283-284,

Clooney, George 4, 48, 128, 150, 216, 288, 348, 383, 460, 494, 501, 503-504

Coates, Phyllis 262, 272, 274, 278, 279, 547

Comic-Con 3, 219, 327

Connery, Sean 10, 12-13, 14, 15, 16, 17, 18, 19, 25, 336, 337, 376, 381, 382-383, 384-385, 387, 388, 389, 390, 391, 393, 395, 400, 401, 446-455, **448**, **452**, 483-484, 550

Conroy, Kevin 27, 128-140, **130**, 197

Corman, Roger 336, 337, 338, 342, 354

Coulson, Agent Phil (character) 402-415

Craig, Daniel 3, 5, 10, **11**, 11, 12, 17-21, 383, 389, 392, 399, 400, 518-519

Craig, Yvonne 44, 180-199, **181**, **189**, **193**, **198**, 216

Craven, Wes 496

Crosby, Cathy Lee 359, 549

Culp, Joseph 336-358

Cumming, Alan 226, 254-260, **254**

Cyclops (character) 9, 165-177

Dalton, Timothy 10, 16, 19, 383, 400, 451, 550

Daly, Sam 150-151, 156

Daly Superman, The 155

Daly, Tim 150, 155-164

Daredevil (character) 4, 230, 240, 242-245, 423, 424, 510

Daredevil 243, 245, 348, 468, 510

Dark Knight, The xii, 2, 4, 114, 475, 476, 499, 513, 514-517, 523, 524

Dark Knight Returns, The (novel) 31, 131, 195

Dark Knight Rises, The xii, 2, 28, 114, 499, 514-517, 533

Davey, John 60-61

DC Universe Online 129, 499

Death of the Incredible Hulk, The 230, 236, 240, 489

Delaney, Dana 136, 155

De Meo, Paul 114, 116

Dent, Harvey (character) 501

DeVito, Danny 201, 497-498

Diamonds are Forever 15, 441, 446, 447, 449, **452**, 454, 455, 483

Dick Tracy 497

Dick Tracy Special 497

Die Another Day 17, 19

Dini, Paul 133, 155

Dirty Laundry 513

Ditko, Steve 65, 457

Doctor Doom (character) 336-358

Donner, Richard xii, 23, 24, 25, 173, 289-291, 441, 442-443, 444, 445, 449, 547

Downey Jr., Robert xii, **2**, 4, 216, 326, 402, 405, 414, 424, 460, 461, 467, 472-475, 521-522, 523

Dozier, William 38, 180, 183-184, 186, 486, 487, 549

Dredd 534

Dredd, Judge (character) 534

Dr. Manhattan (character) 113, 218

Dr. No 14, 483

Durock, Dick 496

Eichinger, Bernd 336, 337

Elektra (character) 243

Elektra 510, 546

Ellsworth, Whitney 267-268, , 286

Entertainment Weekly 2, 3, 17, 402, 506, 507, 525, 535

Entourage 5

Evans, Chris 100, 327, 338, 421, 530-531

Falcon, The (character) 97, 102

Fallen Son: The Death of Captain America 457

Fantastic Four 216, 338, 342, 343, 353, 513-514

Fantastic Four, The (characters) 4, 336-358, 423, 424, 425, 426, 513-514

Fantastic Four, The (1994) 336-358, **339**, **344**, **346**, **347**, 505

Fantastic Four: Rise of the Silver Surfer 338, 342, 343, 353, 513-514

Favreau, Jon xii, 216, 243, 413, 414, 467-480

Feige, Kevin 32, 327-328, 407, 413-414

Ferrigno, Lou 25, 230-241, **231**, **234**, 242, 245, 347-348, **428**, **430**, **431**, 433-434, 460

Finger, Bill 37, 180, 297, 302, 496, 545

Fisher, Carrie 75, 76

Flash, The (character) 42, 77, 93, 113-127, 180, 197, 227, 314

Flash, The (TV) 42, 77, 93, 113-127, 197, 227, 244

Flash, The (2014) 119

Fleming, Ian 14, 328, 383-385, 390, 393, 395, 396, 483

Forty Year Old Virgin, The 5, 543

For Your Eyes Only 16, 396

Foxx, Jamie 4, 46

From Russia With Love 14, 17, 456, 483

From Russia With Love (video game) 483

Fury, Nick (character) 31-32, 404, 408, 412, 415, 499, 522-523

Garfield, Andrew 30, 31, 65, 534-536

Garner, Jennifer 243, 546

Gerber, Steve 246, 247, 248-249

Ghost Rider 519-521

Ghost Rider: Spirit of Vengeance 519-521

Ghost Rider, The (character) 519-521

Glen, John 16

Glover, John 313, 320-321

Goldfinger 18, 396, 450, 483

Gordon, Barbara (character) 44, 180-199

Gorshin, Frank 39, 484, 485-486, 502

Gotham 4

Gough, Alfred 211, 312, 316

Goyer, David 7, 24, 81, 114, 499, 505, 555

Grant, Cary 206, 445, 491-492

Gray Ghost, The (character) 27, 39, 48, 138

Grayson, Dick (character) 296, 485, 501

Green Arrow, The (character) 4, 65, 548

Green Hornet, The (character) 38, 65, 487-488, 528

Green Hornet, The (TV) 38, 487-488, 544

Green Hornet, The (movie) 348, 488, 528

Green Lantern (character) 46, 65, 425, 526-528

Green Lantern (movie) 526-528

Gregg, Clark 402-415, **403**

Grimes, Jack 273, 547

Grimm, Ben (character) 336-358, 513-514

Gruffudd, Ioan 338, 343

Guardians of the Galaxy 33, 467, 538

Gustin, Grant 119

Hackman, Gene 4, 312, 315, 317-318, 323

Haiduk, Stacy 81, 297-300, **298**

Haley, Jackie Earl 525-526

Hamill, Mark 133, 134, 277, 295, 499-500, 544, 547

Hamilton, Guy 397, 399, 453

Hamilton, John 264, 268, **273**, 276

Hammond, Nicholas 65-79, **66**, 424-425

Harley Quinn's Revenge 129

Hartley, Justin 5

Hasselhoff, David 499, 522

Hatcher, Teri 141-154, **149**, **152**, 279, 547

Hathaway, Anne 4, 28, 302, 533-534

Heck, Don 468

Hellboy (character) 511-512

Hellboy 511-512

Hellboy Animated: Blood and Iron 511

Hellboy Animated: Sword of Storms 511

Hellboy: The Science of Evil 511

Hellboy II: The Golden Army 511-512

Hemsworth, Chris 405, 528-529

Henning, Bunny 299

Heroes 4, 297

Hiddleston, Tom 325-334, **329**, 405

Holiday, Bob 49-57, **49**, **52**, **54**, 542, 544

Horowitz, Howie 180, 183, 186, 187, 188

Howard the Duck 246-253, **250**

Hughes, Howard 424, 472, 478

Hulk, The (character) 4, 5, 25, 28-30, 79, 230-241, 347-348, 404, 423, 427, 428-439, 459, 460, 466, 468, 480, 489-490, 511, 525, 531-533, 549

Hulk 25, 29, 230, 240, 459, 510-511

Human Torch, The (character) 96, 114, 336-358, **339**, 429

Huntington, Sam 22, 289, 547

Hyde-White, Alex 336-358

Incredible Hulk, The (TV) 25, 28-30, 230-241, **231**, **234**, 242-245, 347-348, 428-439, **428**, **430**, **431**, **433**, **436**, 459, 460, 489-490, 532

Incredible Hulk, The (movie) 25, 31, 32, 33, 230, 327, 521, 525

Incredible Hulk, The (cartoon) 230

Incredible Hulk Returns, The 230, 242, 347, 348, 489

Injustice: Gods Among Us 129

Invisible Girl, The 114, 336-358, 514,

Iron Man (character) 3, 159, 162, 216, 403, 423, 427, 458, 460, 461, 462-463, 467-480, 521-522, 523, 549

Iron Man xii, **2**, 4, 31-32, 33, 216, 402, 405, 406, 412, 413, 460, 463, 467-480, 521-522

Iron Man 2 4, 31, 32, 33, 402, 406, 467-480, 521-522

Iron Man 3 2, 4, 33, 468, 521-522, 531

It's a Bird . . . It's a Plane . . . It's Superman 49-57, **49**, **52**

Jackman, Hugh 9, 165, 168, 217, 506-507, 548

Jackson, Samuel L. 31-32, 499, 522-523

Jane, Thomas 165, 513

Jimmy on Jimmy 289

Johnson, Kenneth 28-29, 230, 236, 428-439, **428**, **430**, **431**, **433**

Joker, The (character) 4, 27, 39, 113, 128, 134, 157, 249, 475, 486, 496, 499-500, 523-525, 544, 545

Jones, Tommy Lee 501

Jordan, Hal (character) 526-527

Jor-El (character) 21, 23, 24, 89, 150, 216, 443

Justice League 129, 314, 499

Justice League: Doom 128, 155, 314

Justice League: The Flashpoint Paradox 128, 150, 151, 155

Justice League Unlimited 129

Kane, Bob viii, 37, 131, 297, 302, 543, 545

Keaton, Michael 17, 26, 31, 106, 128, 204, 383, 460, 461, 494-495, 505

Kelk, Jackie 273, 547

Kelley, David E. 362, 363, 364-365, 367

Kent, Clark (character) 4, 7, 8, 21, 23, 25, 50, 51-52, 80, 81, 82, 83, 86-87, 88, 89-90, 94, 118, 141-154, 155, 157, 158, 201, 204, 206, 209, 211, 213, 244, 262, 269, 270, 275, 290-291, 292, 294, 295, 297, 300, 312-324, 430, 441-442, 444, 445-446, 449, 462, 471, 482, 490-493, 508, 517, 536-537, 548

Kidder, Margot 203, 269-270, 289

Kiel, Richard 230

Kilmer, Val 31, 128, 383, 402, 460, 500-501, 562

Kirby, Jack 95-112, 325, 330, 332, 336, 338, 417-421, 457, 468, 544

Kiss of Death 486

Kitt, Eartha 28, 302, 487, 534

Kyle, Selina (character) 28, 494, 498, 533-534

Lane, Lois (character) 8, 21, 25, 31, 51, 141, 142, 154, 155, 157, 191, 211, 262-271, 272, 274, 294, 295, 297, 299, 300, 442, 444-445, 446, 461, 482, 491, 518, 545, 547

Lang, Lana (character) 23, 81, 297-300, 444, 545

Larson, Jack 21-22, 264, 265, 266, 272-288, **273**, 289, 290, 292, 293-294, 295, 547

Lazenby, George 10, 13-15, 16, 19, 21, 381-387, **382**, **384**, 400, 449, 455, 550

Ledger, Heath 4, 475, 476, 523-525, 544

Lee, Ang 25-26, 29, 230, 240, 459, 510, 525

Lee, Bruce 38

Lee, Linda (character) 200, 201, 204, 209, 545

Lee, Stan xiii, 4, 8, 30, 65, 68, 71, 74, 106-107, 113, 168, 174, 230, 236, 242, 245, 325, 330, 332, 336, 338, 423-427, 430, 457, 465, 467, 468, 499, 536, 544, 545

Legends of the Superheroes: The Challenge 39, 46-47, 128, 484, 485

Legends of the Superheroes: The Roast 39, 46-47, 128, 484, 485

Lego Marvel Super Heroes 404

Les Miserables 29, 230, 251, 429

Lester, Richard 23, 443, 547

LeVine, Deborah Joy 141, 143

License to Kill 16

Lieber, Larry 325, 332, 468

Liebowitz, Jack 273, 285-286

Live and Let Die 15-16, 389, **394**, 441, 447, **450**, 453, 455

Living Daylights, The 400

Lois & Clark: The New Adventures of Superman 21, 39, 141-154, **142**, **149**, **152**, 279, 317, 508, 547

Loki (character) 325-334, 408

Lucas, George 246, 248, 249, 250, 252, 477

Luthor, Lex (character) vii, 22, 99, 113, 155, 157, 162, 312-324, 545, 548

Magneto (character) 166, 174, 175, 328

Maguire, Tobey 4, 65, 67, 77-78, 151, 509-510, 535

Majors, Lee 428, 438

Mankiewicz, Tom 15, 16, 26, 50, 290, 291, 390-391, 438- 456

Mannix, Eddie 284-285

Mannix, Toni 282, 284-285, 287

Man of Steel 24-25, 81, 114, 499, 536-537

Man with the Golden Gun, The 441, 453

Marsden, James 9, 165-177, **167**, **172**

Marston, William Moulton 359-368, 549

Marvel Heroes 404

Marvel One Shot: A Funny Thing Happened on the Way to Thor's Hammer 404

Marvel One Shot: The Consultant 404

Marvel's Agents of S.H.I.E.L.D. 4, 366, 402-415, 522

Maxwell, Bob 273

McCain, John 3

McClure, Marc 289-296, 547

McFarlane, Todd 502-503

McKellen, Ian 174, 328

Meredith, Burgess 486-487

Meriwether, Lee 188, 302, 484

Millar, Miles 211, 312, 316

Miller, Frank 8, 31, 131

Mister Fantastic (character) 336-358

Moonraker 16, 441

Moore, Roger 10, 15, 16, 17-18, 19, 20-21, 383, 388-401, **392**, **394**, 441, **450**, 451, 453-456, 550

Moulton, Charles see Marston, William Moulton

Mr. Spock (character) 340, 371-380, 388

Munroe, Ororo (character) 507-508

Murdock, Matt (character) 242-245, 468, 510, 545, 546

Mystique (character) 9-10

Neill, Noel 21-22, 262-271, **263**, **267**, 272, **273**, 279

Nelson, Barry 12

Never Say Never Again 13, 16, 451, 483

New Adventures of Batman, The (1977) 39, 128, 484

New Adventures of Superman 39, 545, 547

New Batman Adventures, The (1997) 76, 129, 499

Newmar, Julie 28, 47, 302-311, **303**, **305**, 484, 498

Newton, John 21, 67, 77, 80-94, **82**, 124, 196, 210, 297, **298**, 298, 300

Nicholson, Jack 4, 12, 494, 495, 496, 544

Nick Fury: Agent of S.H.I.E.L.D. (1998) 499

Nightcrawler (character) 254-260

Nightwing (character) 30

Nimoy, Leonard 371-380, **373**, 388, 550

Nite Owl (character) 218, 220, 221

Niven, David 12

Nolan, Christopher xii, 7, 10, 24, 28, 362, 499, 523, 524, 527, 539, 545

Norton, Edward 4, 230, 525

Nygma, Dr. Edward (character) 502

Obama, President Barack 3, 161, 288

Octopussy 17, 19, 395

O'Donnell, Chris 288, 501-502

Olsen, Jimmy (character) 21, 22, 31, 155, 211, 265, 266, 272-296, 547

O'Neil, Dennis 30-31

On Her Majesty's Secret Service 13, 14-16, 381-387, **382**, **384**, 447, 449, 449-450, 451, 550

O'Toole, Annette 23, 289

Palicki, Adrianne 359-368, **365**, 549

Parker, Aunt May (character) 1, 68, 457

Parker, Peter 1, 8, 30, 31, 65, 68-69, 71-72, 74, 76, 98, 102, 113, 118, 424, 426, 458, 462, 472, 509, 534, 535, 545

Penguin, The (character) 476, 486-487, 497-498, 545

Perlman, Ron 155, 511-512

Pfeiffer, Michelle 4, 28, 31, 302, 364, 494, 498-499, 534

Phantom, The (character) 502

Picoult, Jodi 217, 363-364, 366

Pratt, Chris 538

Prince, Diana (character) 359-368, 488, 549

Prince, Hal 49-57

Princess Leia (character) 75, 76

Professor Xavier (character) 166, 169, 174-175, 176, 255

Pryor, Richard 443

Punisher, The (character) 165, 513

Punisher, The 513

Purcell, Dick 100

Pyun, Albert 98-99, 100, 102-104

Quantum of Solace 10, 18, 393, 518
Quesada, Joe 457-466
Quill, Peter (character) 538
Quinn, Harley (character) 129, 156
Quinto, Zachary 372, 376

Raimi, Sam 509
Ratner, Brett 170
Reeve, Christopher xi-xii, 22-23, **22**, 23-24, 51, 56, 67, 84, 85, 86, 91, 99, 108, 109, 138-139, 144, 145, 157, 160-161, 177, 195, 203, 204, 209-210, 244, 269, 270, 289, 290-291, **291**, 294-295, 312, 315, 317, 383, **440**, 441-449, 482, 490-493, 517, 536, 547
Reeves, George 91, 127, 141, 144-145, 154, 262, **267**, 269, 270, 271, 272, **273**, 274, 275, 277, 280-287, **283**, 290, 491, 547
Reid, Britt (character) 487-488, 528
Return of the Swamp Thing, The 496
Return to the Batcave: Misadventures of Adam and Burt, The 39, 302, 484
Reynolds, Ryan 526-527
Richards, Reed (character) 336-358, 424
Riddler, The (character) 39, 476, 484, 485-486, 502
Rigg, Diana 14, 449-450
Robin (character) 27, 30, 42, 67, 129, 136-137, 185, 191, 192, 199, 219, 288, 309, 348, 484-485, 501-502, 503, 505, 545
Robinson, Jerry 496
Rockwell, Johnny 299
Rogen, Seth 488, 528
Rogers, Steve (character) 95-112, 417-421, 530-531
Romero, Cesar 486
Romijn, Rebecca 9-10
Rorschach (character) 525-526
Rosenbaum, Michael 312-324, **315**
Routh, Brandon 23-24, 146, 150, 152, 155, 280, 383, 517-518, 521
Ruffalo, Mark 327, 405, 525, 531-533

Salinger, Matt 95-112, **101**, 421
Saltzman, Harry 10, 383, 388, 441, 449
Sandrich, Mark 275, 547
Sassone, Oley 336, 342, 345, **347**, 347, 352, 355, 356
Schwartz, Julius 180, 543

Semple Jr., Lorenzo 13, 38
Shatner, William 92, 194, 372, 375, 379-380, 395
Shazam! 58-64, **60**
Sherry, Diane 298
Shipp, John Wesley 42, 76-77, 93, 113-127, **115**, **123**, **125**, 176, 197, 227
Siegel and Shuster viii, 24, 52, 90, 262, 272
Silk Spectre (character) 218-228
Simmons, Al (character) 502-503
Simon, Jim 417-421
Simon, Joe 95-112, 417-421, 544
Sinestro, Thaal (character) 527-528
Singer, Bryan 9, 10, 23, 24, 168, 170, 171, 174, 471, 507, 517
Six Million Dollar Man, The 428-429, 436-439, 550
Skyfall 5, 11, 17, 18-19, 518
Slater, Helen 200-210, **202**, **205**, 211, 289
Smallville 4, 21, 23, 84, 85, 154, 201, 211-215, **212**, **214**, 289, 312-324, **315**, 508
Smith, Michael Bailey 336-358
Smith, Rex 242-245
Snipes, Wesley 165, 505-506
Snyder, Zak 24, 219-220, 223, 322, 499, 525, 539
Solo, Han (character) 173, 538
Sorbo, Kevin 146
Space Ghost Coast to Coast 39
Spacey, Kevin 4, 312
Spader, James 107
Spawn (character) 502-503
Spawn 502-503
Spider-Man (character) ix, 3, 4, 5, 7, 30, 49, 65, 66, 71, 72, 73, 75, 76, 79, 113, 118, 146, 174, 177, 216, 232, 240-241, 247, 288, 339, 417, 423, 424, 427, 457, 458, 459, 460, 461, 462, 463, 468, 471, 472, 473, 480, 503, 505, 509, 510, 534, 535, 549
Spider-Man (movie) 1, 7-8, 31, 459, 460, 509, 535
Spider-Man: Turn Off the Dark 49, 50, 55
Spider-Man 3 1, 30, 509
Spider-Man 2 1, 30, 31, 472, 509
Spy Who Loved Me, The 16, 441, 455-456
Staab, Rebecca 336-358, **339**
Stamp Day for Superman 263
Stamp, Terence 23, 289, 493

Stark, Tony (character) 31-32, 216, 402, 405, 412, 414, 424, 458, 462-463, 467, 468, 469, 471, 472-473, 473, 474-475, 478, 521-522

Star-Lord (character) 538

Star Trek (TV) 25, 93, 143, 194, 196, 197, 198, 240, 323, 371, 372, 375-378, 395

Star Trek (2009) 372

Star Trek: Anniversary Enhanced 372

Star Trek V: The Final Frontier 372

Star Trek IV: The Voyage Home 372

Star Trek Into Darkness 372

Star Trek VI; The Undiscovered Country 372

Star Trek: Judgment Rites 372

Star Trek Prime 372

Star Trek: The Motion Picture 372

Star Trek: The Next Generation 25, 372

Star Trek: The Wrath of Kahn 372

Star Trek III: The Search for Spock 372

Star Wars 75, 173, 202, 246, 247, 248, 249, 250, 295, 323, 414, 477, 544, 562

Storm (character) 217, 507-508

Storm, Johnny (character) 96, 336-358

Storm, Sue (character) 336-358, 514

Story of Batman, The 39

Strong, Mark 527-528

Strouse, Charles 49-57

Summers, Jaime (character) 436-438, 439

Summers, Scott (character) 165-177

Superboy (character) 21, 67, 77, 80-94, 113, 124, 141, 196, 210, 297-300, 312

Superboy 21, 80-94, 82, 124, 196, 210, 297-300, 298, 547

Superfriends: The Legendary Super Powers Show 39, 128, 144, 298, 545

Supergirl (character) 5, 200-215, 216, 369

Supergirl 200-210, 202, 205, 211, 216, 289

Superman (character) vii, viii, xi, xii, 2, 5, 7, 8, 9, 22-23, 24-25, 29-30, 31, 50, 51-52, 53, 56, 58, 64, 65, 71, 81, 82, 83, 84, 86, 89, 90, 98, 110, 112, 116, 127, 139, 140, 141-142, 143, 144, 145-146, 147, 148, 150, 151, 154, 156, 157, 158-159, 160-161, 162, 163-164, 195, 200-201, 204, 206, 207, 208-209, 210, 211, 214-215, 216, 218, 224, 232, 239, 240, 241, 244, 259, 262, 264, 266, 267, 268, 269, 270-271, 272, 275, 276, 279, 285, 287, 289, 292, 298, 312, 313-314, 339, 347, 349, 359, 361, 417, 418, 419-420, 425, 441-443, 444-449, 460, 461, 462, 463, 465, 466, 470, 471, 480, 490, 491, 492-493, 517-518, 521, 536, 537, 545

Superman (cartoon) 545

Superman (video game) 155

Superman (serial) 21, 262, 263, 482

Superman (movie) xi, xii, 7, 8, 9, 15, 21, 23, 50, 80, 99, 108, 173, 202-203, 269, 270, 289-296, 291, 298, 312, 440, 440-449, 482, 490-493, 508, 517, 547

Superman/Aquaman Hour of Adventures 545

Superman/Batman: Apocalypse 128, 129-130, 155

Superman/Batman: Public Enemies 128, 155, 162

Superman: Birthright 25

Superman: Brainiac Attacks (movie) 155

Superman: Brainiac Attacks (video game) 155

Superman Classic 82

Superman Classic: Bizarro 82

Superman IV: The Quest for Peace 8, 90, 99, 289-296, 443, 444, 482, 490-493

Superman Lives 521

Superman Returns 3, 21-22, 23-24, 170, 264, 266, 280, 281, 289, 312, 468, 517-518

Superman: Secret Origin 25

Superman: Shadow of Apokolips 155

Superman's Pal Jimmy Olsen 272, 278, 286

Superman: The Animated Series 129, 155-164

Superman III 8, 23, 80, 289-296, 312, 443, 482, 490-493

Superman II 8, 15, 23, 80, 99, 289-296, 312, 482, 490-493, 517, 547

Super Powers Team, The: Galactic Guardians 39, 128

Swamp Thing 496

Swamp Thing, The (character) 496

Swamp Thing, The (TV) 496

Tales of Metropolis 129

Themyscira, Diana (character) 359-368

Thing, The (character) 336-358, 513-514

Thor (character) 32, 230, 240, 325-334, 403, 406, 423, 425, 523, 528-529, 549

Thor 32, 325-334, 402, 406, 414, 426, 467, 528-529

Thor: The Dark World 100, 325, 325-334, 407, 467, 528-529, 530

Thunderball 13, 17, 450, 483

Timm, Bruce 133, 155

Tracy, Dick (character) 497

Trial of the Incredible Hulk, The 230, 242-245, 489

Two-Face (character) 501

Ultimate Spider-Man, The (TV) 404

Underwood, Jay 336-358, **339**

Urban, Kal 534

Vandervoort, Laura 211-215, **212, 214**

View To A Kill, A 395

Wagner, Lindsay 429, 437-438, 438-439

Walker, Kit (character) 502

Ward, Burt 27, 187, 190, 192, 288, 484-485

Watchmen 113, 216-228, **218, 222**, 525-526

Waugh, Fred 65-79, **70, 73**

Wayne, Bruce (character) 7, 39, 41, 42, 43, 44, 98, 118, 131-132, 135, 302, 362, 461, 462, 475, 485, 494-495, 500, 503, 510, 514, 515, 516, 538

Welling, Tom 313, 508

West, Adam 26, 27, 37-48, **40, 43, 45**, 128, 138, 187, 190, 192, 194, 199, 216, 302, 304, 309, 484, 487, 488, 500, 534

Whedon, Joss xii, 230, 403, 406, 407-408, 409, 410, 413, 414, 526, 532, 533

White, Michael Jai 502-503, 524

Who Wants To Be A Superhero? 4

Widmark, Richard 486

Williams, John 23

Williams, Robin 138, 252

Williams, Van 38, 487-488, 544

Wilson, David 55

Wilson, Lewis 545

Wilson, Patrick 218, 220

Wolverine (character) 9, 165, 168, 169, 171, 177, 260, 461, 471, 506-507, 510, 545

Wonder Woman (character) 5, 65, 215, 216, 217, 224, 259, 359-368, 419, 420, 488-489

Wonder Woman (TV series) 259, 359, 361, 362, 363, 364, 366, 488-489, 549

Wonder Woman (TV movie) 359, 549

Wonder Woman (TV pilot) 359-368, **365**

World is Not Enough, The 16

X-Men (characters) 4, 9-10, 113, 165-177, 228, 241, 254-260, 470-471, 506-508

X-Men 2, 9-10, 23, 165-177, **167, 172**, 470-471, 505, 506-508

X-Men: Days of Future Past 2, 165-177, 506-508

X-Men: First Class 2, 165-177, 506-508, 545

X-Men Origins: Wolverine 2, 165-177, 506-508, 545

X-Men: The Last Stand 2, 165-177, 506-508

X2: X-Men United 2, 165-177, 254-260, **254**, 506-508

You Only Live Twice 14, 17, 483

Zane, Billy 502

Zappa, Frank 484

Zien, Chip 246-253

Zod, General (character) 23, 24, 493

Photo: Susan Shapiro

ABOUT THE AUTHOR

Mark Edlitz grew up on a steady diet of superhero movies and TV shows, and though his interests expanded considerably as he got older, his fascination with superhero stories and their lore has not diminished. After graduating from New York University's film school he interned for Batfilm Productions, the executive producers on every feature length Batman film since Tim Burton's *Batman*. He went on to work on a variety of films including *Batman Forever*, where his responsibilities included the crucial task of holding up a large sheet of cardboard, intended to prevent photographers from taking pictures of Val Kilmer in the Batsuit.

His writing has appeared in *The Huffington Post, Los Angeles Times' Hero Complex, Moviefone*, Sirius/XM Radio's *Slice of SciFi* and *Empire* magazine online. He has worked as a writer-producer for ABC News and National Geographic's *Brain Games*.

Edlitz wrote and directed the award-winning independent film *The Eden Myth*. He also directed and produced *Jedi Junkies*, a film about extreme Star Wars fans.

Edlitz lives in New York City with his wife, Suzie, and their two children.

CPSIA information can be obtained at www.ICGtesting.com
Printed in the USA
BVOW08s2341260615

405906BV00010B/246/P